FOUCAULT
AND
AUGUSTINE

FOUCAULT
AND
AUGUSTINE

Reconsidering Power and Love

J. Joyce Schuld

University of Notre Dame Press
Notre Dame, Indiana

Manufactured in the United States of America

Library of Congress Cataloging-in-Publication Data
Schuld, J. Joyce.
Foucault and Augustine : reconsidering power and love / J. Joyce Schuld.
p.   cm.
Includes bibliographical references and index.
ISBN 0-268-02868-0 (cloth : alk. paper)
ISBN 0-268-02869-9 (pbk. : alk. paper)
1. Foucault, Michel—Religion.   2. Augustine, Saint, Bishop of Hippo.
3. Religion and sociology.   4. Religion—Philosophy.   I. Title.
B2430.F724 S37   2003
194—dc21

                                        2003012645

FOR MY MOTHER & FATHER

*who have borne so gracefully the risks and costs of love
as well as its many joys*

Contents

Acknowledgments

I offer deep appreciation to my professors at Yale University. I am one of many who have benefited from their commitment to providing a rich education while devoting precious time and energy to their students' personal welfare. They set the highest examples of the socially engaged scholar and caring teacher. I would like to single out those who so readily welcomed my first attempts to compare Foucault and Augustine: Gene Outka and Cyril O'Regan, co-directors of my dissertation; and Margaret Farley, Rowan Greer, David Kelsey, and James Bernauer of Boston College, my perceptive readers. Their invaluable guidance during the writing of my dissertation and their intellectual and personal support emboldened me to undertake this new book. I express my gratitude too for the precision and discernment with which the reviewers, especially Margaret Miles and Jeremy Carrette, the editors, Rebecca DeBoer and Sheila Berg in particular, and the staff of the University of Notre Dame Press attended to my manuscript. Barbara Hanrahan has been generous beyond measure. I cannot imagine working with a more intellectually engaging, dedicated, and enthusiastic director.

I wish to extend a special word of thanks to all the friends, colleagues, and teachers who have given me balance during the last wild year, notably Jim Bailey, Leon Bloomfield, Jean Harum, Marcus and Marianne Borg, Lindsey Tucker, Zach Bowen, Jim and Olga Hutchingson, Margaret Farley, Gene Outka, James Bernauer, and Barbara Hanrahan, among others. I am particularly indebted to my dear friend, Shelley Thacher, for her wisdom and care, which over so many years have provided safe harbor. And, as in all things, I am grateful to my husband, Tom Dickens, not only for the delights of fifteen years of friendship but also for his counsel in every step of writing this book. He is my most trusted reader and critic as well as cherished companion. His tireless efforts in sustaining me personally and intellectually have made this project a shared adventure. Finally, I am thankful for the love and faith of parents. Odie Dickens, my mother-in-law and "third" parent, has patiently remained by my side throughout my writing, strengthening my resolve, and engaging me in stimulating discussion. This book is dedicated to my mother and father, Betty and Jim Schuld, to whom I can trace every achievement. Their selflessness and encouragement in the face of all obstacles, and good humor have filled my life with blessings I can never repay.

Introduction

In an unpublished interview from the last year of his life, Michel Foucault attempts to dispel some of the fog that had descended over his work. Pessimism, he argues, has never been the driving force of his research. Rather, he has been inspired by something that is both more promising and more dangerous—hope.

> I don't think that to be suspicious means that you don't have any hope. Despair and hopelessness are one thing; suspicion is another. And if you are suspicious, it is because, of course, you have a certain hope. The problem is to know which kind of hope you have and which kind of hope it is reasonable to have in order to avoid what I would call not the 'pessimistic circle' you speak of but the political circle which introduces in your hopes, and through your hopes, the things you want to avoid by these hopes.[1]

Robert Bellah, one of the interviewers, points out to Foucault that his response sounds remarkably Christian. Without bristling or apologizing, Foucault admits, "Yes, I have a very strong Christian, Catholic background, and I am not ashamed." Foucault, the atheist, acknowledges without embarrassment his Catholic heritage and indeed welcomes discussing how others have identified him as a "pseudo-Christian." Yet he does not understand why this particular description of hope is Christian. Bellah explains: "Because you don't absolutize that hope, in terms of some notion that you're going to control history and create the paradise on earth. You know that any gain can only be relative." Still baffled, Foucault asks with a note of surprise, "That's Christian?" "Yes," says Bellah, "being pessimistic without being hopeless."[2]

Bellah has exaggerated, of course, since this stark distinction between relative and absolute hope is not one that all Christians would find

1

illuminating and useful. Nevertheless, I believe it comports well with much of the Christian tradition. Moreover, it can help to answer a question that has dogged Foucault scholarship since its beginning: Is Foucault a radical relativist? From literary theory to philosophy and from history to political ethics, unresolved arguments abound concerning how best to evaluate his work. To those who identify Foucault as an extreme relativist, anarchist, or nihilist, his thought poses a deconstructive danger to humane modern discourses and practices. To others, however, his suspicion neither enervates nor prevents but vitalizes contemporary social criticism by providing it with new analytical outlooks, strategies, and tools. Foucault's relentless questioning, from the former perspective, assaults modernity as a whole and undercuts foundations necessary for maintaining a civilized order; from the latter, it simply makes us restive with specific aspects of modern thought and practice about which we should never be complacent or overly self-assured.

Due in part to the tone of Foucault's unsettling rhetoric and in part to the fact that, given his philosophical presuppositions, he is disinclined to put forward alternatives to the practices and social institutions he criticizes, one can make a case that Christian scholars should regard him from the less charitable point of view. One might argue that the best use a Christian theologian or ethicist can make of Foucault is to classify him on one end of a spectrum as a dangerous post-modern, one who leaves in his wake practical and theoretical hopelessness.[3] Even though such an interpretation may be useful in certain contexts, especially in light of its seeming conceptual tidiness, I am convinced that it misconstrues the scope and purpose of Foucault's historical analysis and fails to note the prophetic-like features of his discomforting rhetoric.[4] While some critics have depicted Foucault as dispassionately removed from a living world of relations, exhibiting in the words of one, an immovable "stoic gaze . . . frozen into an ice-berg,"[5] I will point to a strikingly different focus of attention that is empathetically drawn to stories of vulnerability and suffering. Other reviewers have dismissed his work as the mere high-pitched whine of an adolescent political philosopher whose primary aim is to flaunt rebelliously shocking and theatrical rhetoric.[6] However, I will argue that if readers are to appreciate the richness of Foucault's thought, they must remain attuned throughout the shifts in his writings to a lower and more somber tone that resonates with forgotten voices found in the midst of our workaday routines and places. Although Foucault unsettles, agitates, and provokes his readers, and although he advances toward and then hesitates along the borders of certain extremes, nevertheless, his descriptions of the ingeniously manipulative dangers of social power should neither be foreign to nor offend Christian sensibilities. Foucault's attentiveness to the outcast and the pariah, to the socially branded and the politically dispossessed, combined with his utter disdain for exploitative historical patterns, should, I will contend, be welcomed by the Christian community as an uncannily familiar stranger.

This book argues that Foucault's post-modern approach does not vitiate a theologically oriented cultural analysis. Indeed, his writings strengthen such efforts by making it possible to recover some of the critical leverage theology has lost as a result of a broad array of modern transformations that have altered, along with the culture at large, its methods and content. It is true that Foucault scrutinizes Humanist and Enlightenment assumptions, and to the extent that one's theology, ethics, or politics rests on such, his efforts will be deeply disturbing. I would wager, though, this uneasiness has more to do with philosophical than theological commitments. That is why I look to a theologian who is not ensnared in contemporary philosophical debates for assistance in slipping the grasp of those modern presuppositions that have hamstrung, for many Christian scholars, an understanding of Foucault's cultural analysis. Exploring the parallels between his perspectives and those at home in a pre-modern frame of reference makes it possible both to appreciate Foucault's work from a supportive theological position and to reconsider some neglected or discarded theological insights that are useful in a post-modern context.

The pre-modern thinker I believe offers the richest reserves for understanding and creatively applying Foucault's cultural criticisms is Saint Augustine. There are numerous reasons why Augustine is able to speak theologically and philosophically to many post-modern concerns. First among them, I would argue, is his remarkably similar sense of subversive hope. R. A. Markus helpfully describes this:

> The reference to the eschatological Kingdom, the fully human community of love promised by God, discloses injustice and inhumanity in the best of social structures. The Christian hope is of its nature a searchlight which, turned on its social *milieu*, seeks out the opportunities for protest. The Gospel can never be at home in the world, and cannot fail to bring a true believer into conflict with any existing order of things. It is in essential and permanent tension with the world. This tension should be a fruitful one, from which awkward questions are continually being put to the world. Hope is a permanently unsettling force, . . . one that is bound to be subversive in that it must subject the

existing social order—whatever it is—to a questioning more radical than that to which it may be exposed from any political party or
programme.[7]

At least later in his life, Augustine openly criticizes many of the reigning values and norms of his culture. His "deconstruction" of Roman and competing Christian assumptions of sociohistorical progress brings into focus the
potential risks and real costs of beneficent-seeming as well as clearly maleficent social plans and projects. In so doing, he throws into relief the dangerous privileging of certain cultural discourses and probes the rhetorical de-
vices that shield them from moral and political scrutiny. Augustine is also a
forceful rhetorician, making jarring political comparisons and blurring presumptuous moral and social distinctions. By leveling an often blistering critique, he shocks his audience into viewing their history, culture, and politics
from an unguarded perspective. Consequently, Augustine often generates
discomforting political, historical, and personal tensions as he brings to the
surface the moral ambiguities and performative weaknesses that attend all
human judgments and activities. Although many commentators have seen
in Augustine's thoroughgoing skepticism the lineaments of a familiar, "modern" sensibility, it is driven by presuppositions that are not at all modern. I
will be claiming that it is precisely his pre-modern assumptions that, when
coupled with his post-modern-sounding suspiciousness, make him such a
useful conversation partner for Foucault. Augustine thus opens new paths of
critical inquiry while also challenging those privileged modern presuppositions that have made it difficult to understand and appreciate Foucault theologically and philosophically.

Such themes provide broad possibilities for exploring, evaluating, and
applying Foucault's works to further the ends of Christian cultural analysis.
However, Augustine's suspiciousness is not confined to the arenas of history
and politics. He is keenly attuned to the perils of an arrogant lust for certitude and mastery in even the most unnoticed inter- and intrapersonal interactions. One cannot fully understand the complicated social problematics
he and Foucault identify without first comprehending these most basic relational dynamics. Therefore, while the overlapping targets of their historical
and political criticisms may seem to be the natural point of entry for examining their apprehensions about pervasive social dangers, I begin my comparison by analyzing how their fundamentally interactive notions of power
and love shed light in complementary ways on the very finest threads of our
relational fabric. Having established the underlying concepts and metaphors

that support their more extensive cultural critiques, I then turn to the wider-ranging personal, political, and historical consequences created by our relational frailties. This makes it possible to construct a much thicker redescription of Foucault's writings in theological terms that does justice to the complexity of his rhetoric, his analytical strategies and tools, and the particularity of his social observations. Such an approach also facilitates deeper discussions of the intertwining personal and political implications of pride, humility, original sin, social evil, communal commitments, and hope than would otherwise be possible if one were examining cultural problems solely from a macro perspective. I contend that holding all these topics together is Foucault's and Augustine's correspondingly dynamic understandings of how power and love configure individual persons and communities, making everyone simultaneously fragile in all of their relations and yet also capable of being caring and socially engaged in the face of radical ambiguities.

One other point concerning the usefulness of Augustine for theologically explicating Foucault's works bears mention. Augustine writes during a time that is of particular interest to Foucault and, indeed, one that he frequently turns to in depicting the modern transformations that took place between the seventeenth and nineteenth centuries. We are thus entering a conversation that Foucault himself has initiated. In his mid- to late career, early Christianity plays a pivotal role in casting light on how modernity has appropriated and transfigured pre-modern beliefs and practices to serve novel and entirely secular ends. Various commentators have complained about Foucault's sloppiness with the historical details of the ancient period and have concluded that this undermines the credibility of his insights. I agree that Foucault can be careless—in fact he concedes as much—but I disagree that this invalidates his social critique. Since Foucault is analyzing cultural trends that have become reconfigured in the modern period, our focus should be on whether he constructs a critically perceptive social contrast for understanding our own culture. If the cultural transfigurations he portrays are largely accurate, the fact that he has misinterpreted the specifics of certain beliefs and practices should not negate his analytical value. That being said, however, I believe a more accurate reading of early Christianity, and especially of Augustine, who breaks the mold of many Christian expectations of his time, can actually sharpen the cultural contrasts that Foucault is attempting to make. This conversation, then, which is already under way in Foucault's writings, can be considerably strengthened and used to further a Foucauldian analysis of contemporary social discourses and practices. The conversation into which I draw Foucault and Augustine also, not insignificantly, helps to dispel certain caricatures of Augustine and his work that have gained currency among some post-modern political theorists and liberation theologians. Since the secular transformations Foucault depicts have come at a significant price to theology, a more accurate reading of Augustine helps us to perceive much more clearly some of what has been theologically lost, subjugated, or colonized to serve nontheological aims in modern culture.

Finally and perhaps surprisingly, this book answers a summons Foucault himself issued. He called on others to experiment with his critical instruments for purposes and in reference to evaluative contexts that are different from his own. In an interview with researchers in an unrelated field, he says: "If one or two of these 'gadgets' of approach or method that I've tried . . . can be of service to you, then I shall be delighted. If you find the need to transform my tools or use others then show me what they are, because it may be of benefit to me."[8] In exploring the theological and ethical implications of Foucault's efforts, therefore, we should thoroughly investigate but not feel fenced in by the conversations that he initiates in his texts. Foucault invites us and others to employ whatever is analytically fruitful, and by refusing to tie his critical methods and tools to any foundationalist or meta-narrative frame of reference (including an atheistic one) that would exclude their use by social critics from different disciplines, he makes his writings available for creative analysis and appropriation.

This book relies principally on conceptual and literary analysis of primary texts. Although I frequently cite secondary sources so that readers may pursue particular issues, I concentrate on drawing out of Augustine's and Foucault's sprawling and unsystematic writings what I consider to be key, thematically related passages that best illuminate basic concepts and metaphors informing their cultural critiques. Accordingly, I do not feel bound to mimetically reproduce Augustine's and Foucault's arguments in a rigid expository sequence but often range over diverse texts so as to present a more synthetic theological and philosophical reading that remains, I am convinced, faithful to their respective concerns.

Dynamic Fragility

An Analysis of Power and Love

Many of Foucault's detractors target his alarming pessimism about our social condition as the primary weakness of his philosophy. That we live in
a world saturated with power relations, a world permeated with infinitesimal ruptures and unstable differentials, means that there is no externality to
power, and thus, no opportunity to act free of its constrictions. Like a di-
aphanous sheathing that enfolds every possible thought, encounter, and activity, power relations form an inescapable yet often imperceptible limit
within which we must make particular decisions and undertake defining
courses of action. To his critics, Foucault's vision darkens social reality un-
necessarily because it conscripts individuals into a long and tedious war in
which new battles constantly erupt, intensifying and extending the already
complex fields of conflict. Foucault's portrayal of this precarious relational
environment with its manifold divisions and instabilities and its continual
threat of subjugation appears to his opponents to vitiate the most hopeful aspects of human existence and unfairly sentence everyone to the drudgery of
unending warfare.

    Augustine's theological account of social reality at once corresponds to
and sharply contrasts with Foucault's pessimistic portrait. This is because
Augustine's basic insights about society are held in tension. They encapsu-
late the observations of an expectant eschatological optimist and an appre-
hensive moral realist, and each of these contrasting perspectives is indispen-
sable to his assessment of our present social condition.[1] I argue in this chapter
that Augustine's analysis of interdependently vulnerable relations provides
an instructive interpretive framework within which Christian theologians,
philosophers, and ethicists can appreciate the radicalness of Foucault's cultural
criticisms. At the same time, I claim that Augustine's intrinsically active and

generative understanding of love constructively broadens Foucault's concept of power and thereby helps to break it free from the stranglehold imposed on his work by Humanist and Enlightenment perspectives.

I am persuaded that Foucault's disturbing depictions of certain pervasive social dangers are not so much un-Christian or anti-Christian as they are colorful fragments of what for Christian cultural analysts forms a more intricate and extensive mosaic. As long as Foucault's intentionally partial social descriptions can be placed within this larger frame, his subversive (and, I would argue, frequently prophetic) questioning of contemporary assumptions poses no threat to Christian discourses and practices. Moreover, if we properly understand the bounds of Foucault's accounts, his distinctive insights about our social interactions not only can be appreciated from an Augustinian standpoint, they also can creatively criticize and enrich it, thereby making it better suited to detecting and responding to the shifting risks of a post-modern world. After briefly recounting the dialectical tensions that ground Augustine's view of sociality, we will examine Foucault's and Augustine's nonmodern presuppositions by comparing their surprisingly similar relational concepts of power and love along three lines: their omnipresence, their social mechanics or functioning, and their moral ambiguity.

Harmony and Rupture:
A Theology of Relational Dependence

For Augustine as well as for Foucault, the inescapable hazards of our social environment are rooted in the fragility of human relationships and the formative dynamism of relational desires. On Foucault's view, such inherently unstable and complex social patterns present the only critical problematic with historical or cultural significance. When this precarious social condition is looked at from Augustine's perspective, however, always in the background of his realistic appraisal lies his starkly contrasting understanding of what God ideally created human communities to be like and what they hopefully will become through the transformations of grace. Augustine's fundamental notion of relationality, therefore, acts as a hinge on which in one direction he swings remarkably close to Foucault's observations about inter- and intrapersonal social dynamics, while in the other direction he pivots completely away from his secular conceptions of community.

According to Augustine, the determining factor shaping the character of all human relations is the disposition toward the most primary relationship, namely, that with God. Augustine renders two diametrically opposed portraits of society depending upon its orientation and active constitution of human desires and habits.[2] The love enacted by the eschatological community that Augustine refers to as Holy Jerusalem represents the model community and the original created potential of all human relationships.[3] He speaks of this social reality as something to be experienced by grace intermittently in the life of the pilgrimaging church and anticipated in its fullness through hope. But it is also something to be mourned since it demonstrates all that fallen creatures are not and everything that they have lost in their present social condition. The defining feature of Holy Jerusalem is its unwavering focus on God as its Supreme Good (*bonum suum*) and its referencing of all lower relative goods to this ultimate divine reality.[4] In absolute dependence and obedience, Augustine writes, its citizens ceaselessly "cleave to God, so as to live for him, to gain wisdom from him, to rejoice in him, and to enjoy so great a Good without death, without distraction or hindrance."[5] Even though the community is composed of discrete individuals, its diverse members are able to participate in one single and unifying social vision because each continually orients his or her private objectives and particular cares to God. Bound together by mutual love of the Supreme Good, the community is never torn by conflicting purposes or competitive tensions, by sectional interests or factional discord. Their commonly shared subordination to God establishes "a perfectly ordered and perfectly harmonious fellowship."[6]

Whereas the ontologically optimistic vision of Holy Jerusalem represents the created and eschatologically fulfilled potential of human beings, the actual moral performances Augustine documents reveal a fragile social environment that stands in considerable tension with the social ideal.[7] In place of the seamless order of perfect proportionality and equilibrium, Augustine describes an asymmetrically unbalanced social world that is riven by relational disturbances.[8] Set off by a fundamental rupture in their original dependence on God, innumerable fractures spread into all human relationships. Like a pane of glass that develops one crack, tiny fissures form along the edges of the break and crawl across the plane until what was once rigidly stable and whole becomes fragile over the entire surface. Although these minuscule fractures gradually crisscross, crazing the surface in a seemingly random fashion, each one ultimately traces back to the first rupture. For Augustine, the confusingly intricate network of power relations must be understood in this manner.

When looked at individually, each division may appear random, but when seen as a whole, an unmistakable pattern emerges. The ever-changing and distorted ways in which human beings relate to one another all derive from a distorted relationship with God. The love of God (*amor dei*) characterizing Heavenly Jerusalem is supplanted by an exaggerated love of self (*amor sui*).[9] The lust such self-love generates (the *libido dominandi*) seeks to attain not simply an individual freedom from certain chafing restrictions, but an expansive and vanquishing freedom that puts the world and all other human beings under one's personal dominion. At the root, then, of even the most complex forms of social disorder is the longing (*appetitus*) to acquire as one's private possession the unlimited power of the divine Creator.[10] This inflated self-rule, or pride (*superbia*), lies at the heart of sin, profoundly disrupting all relations. As fallen creatures cease to recognize others as equal in their mutual adoration of and subordination to God, they develop an unnatural superior-inferior status among themselves.[11] United no longer by the shared love of a common good, human bonds increasingly become forged by an arrogant love of self, a love which has as its object not God but the perverse desire to secure and exploit the innately vulnerable dependence of persons and communities.[12] The very dependence that once made human obedience and eternal sustenance possible now, in this distorted social world, turns all individuals into targets for those attempting to position themselves in the place of God. The capacity to love, once it is directed away from God and toward the self, perpetually fuels the desire to control others.

In being shaped by arbitrary standards, agendas, and interests, this asymmetrical order of finite relations creates a radically unstable and insecure social environment. At any moment, seemingly submissive individuals or associations can undermine those who an instant before appeared invincible, thereby substantively altering the strategic field of play. Therefore, alliances of power, which in Holy Jerusalem are eternally balanced in a peaceable equilibrium, are in this fallen world constantly shifting as individuals preoccupy themselves with tipping conflicts between competing sectional interests in one direction or the other.[13] Having forsaken the changeless Good that they ought to have found satisfaction in, humans are now forced to contend with being endlessly "distracted and tossed about" by varying possibilities and purposes, by fluctuating desires and volatile motivations.[14] Torn this way and that, individuals aggressively struggle to put their own imprint on the present constellation of order, and in so doing, they perpetuate the latent restlessness that lurks within and around all established arrangements of power.[15]

Ironically, even though such self-assertive acts reveal an essentially divisive and antisocial disposition, they nevertheless knit human beings together, intimately binding them in community through the irresolvability of these temporal struggles. A strategic shadowboxing, an artful cunning and scheming tie even the most antisocial persons to one another in permanently conflictive relationships. Incessant tactics and countertactics weave a distorted social fabric that nevertheless holds competing participants together. Inevitably, in all that they do, human beings are caught up in the inescapable crosscurrents of being at once drawn together and pulled apart. For as Augustine put it, "The human race is, more than any other species, at once social by nature and quarrelsome by perversion."[16]

Augustine held that power relations are at work in creating both the satisfying harmony of Holy Jerusalem and the grating asymmetry and inequality of the present social order. Clearly, from his point of view, the problem leading to relational and social disturbances is not power per se but a disorienting selfishness that uses power without proper reference to God, wielding it in support of one's own interests and against those of others. "Pride is not something wrong in the one who loves power, or in the power itself; the fault is in the soul which perversely loves its own power [*perverse amantis potestatem suam*], and has no thought for the justice of the omnipotent."[17] Because of the immense sway of love, power imbues all relationships. There is no way to extract power from human encounters and activities because there is no way to extract the interactive potency of love from everything that we do and everything that we are. In this broadly defined sense, power is coterminous with relationality. Since relationality is fundamental to our existence and we can never step outside its sphere of influence, neither can we somehow slip free of the broadest reaches of love's formative forcefulness.

When properly ordered, the pervasiveness of such power is not a social problem but an asset. The fact that the influencing power in this dynamism of love is so widespread in Holy Jerusalem means that every fiber of desire can remain focused upon God and God's purposes and that this shared concentration of energy creatively sustains differentiated yet unitive bonds of community.[18] Unfortunately, however, given its pervasiveness, once power becomes distorted through misdirection and misuse, the ramifications permeate the most intimate parts of life and suffuse, through relationality, every form of human association. Just as the love of God affects all aspects of life for the citizens of Holy Jerusalem, the factious and inequitable effects of the inordinate love of self, with its lust for domination, give rise to unstable differentials in every quarter of the earthly city. Augustine warns that a complicated and confusing array of social dangers are generated by such distorted relations of power. They create turbulent pressures ranging from those over-whelming in force to those so slight as to be almost undetectable.

Augustine acknowledges that the social problems that are easiest to identify as being engendered by distorted power relations are those involv-ing the largest numbers of people. Just as an ocean is filled by tributaries, so the world draws into itself and magnifies on a grander scale the rela-tional dynamics of many smaller social bodies.[19] The inevitable tensions and conflicts that arise among a few individuals are dangerously compounded in a global social environment because of, first, the sheer number and com-plexity of the competing selfish interests involved, and second, the mani-fold resources available to large groups for settling any controversies that develop in favor of their own personal objectives. Although operating on a relatively smaller stage, the divisiveness and malice that prompts wars erupts within the precincts of the city as well. Such factional dynamics, Augustine asserts, whether they lead to noninjurious deception or a cutthroat insur-rection, help to produce a constantly unstable social atmosphere. Fomenting both mistrust and retribution, these unsteady relations cultivate a defensive-ness that, in conjunction with a desire for dominion over others, perpetually disposes civic communities to instability and disintegration.[20] Even within one's family and among one's closest confidants, Augustine warns, it may be difficult to tell an enemy from a friend. For hostility may dress itself in the sweetest pretense; deceit may persuade us to rely upon the compact of the vilest traitor. Soothing assurances, then, cannot always quell the sus-piciousness we carry forward from past encounters with the untrustwor-thy.[21] Moreover, he laments, even if we need not be concerned about per-sonal betrayal by friends and family, we must still be anxious about injury or illness befalling our loved ones. Rather than provide us with any abiding security, our dearest relations simply multiply the potential dangers we face, through wrongs done either to our own person or, by extension, to those whom we love.

Finally, distorted power relations, though less dramatically visible, can be the most deeply disruptive as they govern an individual's relation to his or her own existence and identity. Although a person does not constitute a community, he or she does engage in a dynamic process of self-relation. According to Augustine, this process, like any other relationship after the fall, is vulnerable to the destabilizing effects of disordered love. For him, of course, it is pivotal to an individual's self-identity what love (and thus what kind of power) governs his or her personal activities—the other-centered love of God or the self-centered love of domination. However, in light of the penetrating fragmentation that results from their fundamental breach with God, individuals are no longer constituted by a single unitive love but by many desires that draw the fractured self into divisive personal conflicts. The images of strife, struggle, and conquest help Augustine describe competing power relations that unfold not just among different persons and different groups of persons but also among different fragments of the individual self.[22] Such personal struggles are especially perplexing because they simultaneously involve the ever-changing energy and movement of fluctuating desires and the resistant inertia of habits that have gradually hardened over time. Both their changeability and their resistance to change make persons vulnerable to internal dissension. And the two together make the resulting battles that erupt self-propelling and extraordinarily complex.

In describing the intricate range and variety of power relations, Augustine portrays a deeply disturbed geography riddled with dynamic instabilities. In contrast to the natural harmony and integrity of Holy Jerusalem, the present social landscape is scarred by both massive chasms and minuscule rifts. This alarming depiction conveys Augustine's belief that there is no secure domain in our social world where persons are utterly free from the dangers of struggle and domination.[23] This radically unsteady environment is not simply outside, surrounding individuals in the world, the city, and the home; it is also internal, permeating the most intimate dimensions of the person's self. It thereby influences the great external struggles and calamities in the world that are so spectacularly visible in history, as well as the least considered desires, habits, thoughts, and activities of any single human being.

Augustine's portrayal of the constitutive dynamics and precariousness of human relationality opens a number of illuminating and as yet unexplored conceptual paths for evaluating the theological value of Foucault's writings. The most serious misinterpretations of Foucault arise, I would argue, when commentators try to make sense of his social analysis within the boundaries of a traditional description of political power.[24] Surveying Foucault's work through an Augustinian lens makes it easier to free his cultural insights from such distorting limitations and appreciate their broader social significance and application. To that end, the remainder of the chapter examines three aspects of power: its omnipresence as rooted in relationality, its modes of exercise, and its moral ambivalence.

Power's Social Omnipresence

Perhaps the most striking feature of Foucault's description of power is its omnipresence. In contrast to most progressive political models, and to the alarm of many contemporary theorists, Foucault describes social reality as being saturated with power.[25] Power is an inescapable component of human existence because it is an inescapable facet of being relational. Power and relationality are intrinsically bound together.[26] Power cannot exist separate from varying forms of relationships and relationships can never remove themselves entirely from power's dynamic sway. Power is omnipresent, contends Foucault, "not because it has the privilege of consolidating everything under its invincible unity, but because it is produced from one moment to the next, at every point, or rather in every relation. . . . Power is everywhere; not because it embraces everything, but because it comes from everywhere."[27] This is so, he argues, because human existence is characterized by a multiplicity of relations. Since power, when seen in this light, is necessarily "co-extensive with the social body," Foucault concludes that, though it be in ever-changing configurations, it "*is* 'always already there', that one is never 'outside' it, that there are no 'margins' to gambol in. . . . [T]here are no spaces of primal liberty between the meshes."[28] As social creatures, we are inevitably born into a relational world and are interactively constituted as relational persons. Since it is impossible to be human without being relational, we cannot but be immersed in a sea of power.

When we look at Augustine and Foucault from this broad social perspective, with power being linked to the influences of interactive relations and interactive relations being understood as basic to and indeed inextricable from human existence, their conceptual presuppositions, observations, and insights are compatible. This is confirmed not simply because they concur that power, when conceived relationally, is inevitably present in society but also by further parallels that emerge in the course of a threefold analysis of their shared claim about power's omnipresence. As will become clear, they agree that power relations intimately penetrate individuals, that power relations are extensively interconnected, and that power relations transgress traditional personal and public boundaries.

Explaining power's omnipresence in society should, first of all, not be confined to external conceptions, as though power were some kind of forceful energy that simply develops *in between* established objects and that simply *impinges* upon them by applying influence externally. For Augustine and Foucault, power's inherent relationality gives it both external and internal dimensions. All individuals, of course, participate in multiple relationships in the public sphere, but they are also—and always—simultaneously engaged in a web of interactive dynamics internal to themselves. Of particular interest to Augustine and Foucault are the roles that different and often divergent desires, dispositions, self-interpretations, and habits play in constituting the individual and shaping his or her relations with others. On their view, power continually rises out of and sinks into numerous overlapping and competing micro-relations within the self. Every individual is thus thoroughly laced with crisscrossing patterns of power. Of course, Augustine is famous for having plumbed the mysterious depths of intrapersonal relationships. But Foucault also dwells on dynamic desiring and habituation, on interactive power relations at the smallest levels of the human person that have become so familiar that they are effectively hidden from view.[29] He describes these as slowly permeating our daily lives, there to gain a firm yet frequently unnoticed hold over both our bodies and our self-interpretations.[30]

The omnipresence of power is due not only to its penetrating depth or density but also and more significantly to how this becomes interconnected with dispersed relationships that extend over the entire surface of the social body.[31] By linking, one by one, widely scattered interactive dynamics, power relations gradually reach into ever broader social fields. Although these expanding fields can be examined as larger wholes, it is essential to recognize that they are continually supported and nourished by all sorts of smaller domains of power without which they would ultimately dry up and disappear. Augustine's metaphor of an ocean being fed by many rivers that are themselves fed by myriad streams and rivulets illustrates this point well.[32] One can, of course, look out over and appreciate the great expanse of an ocean without first tracing each individual tributary, but if one wants to comprehend the vitality and organic functioning of the sea, it is necessary to understand its dependence upon smaller and smaller sources. What might appear at first glance to be a monolithic force in nature is really only a confluence of many interacting minuscule dynamics. For Augustine, alliances and counter-alliances of power enacted in the largest conceivable social domain, that of international relations, ultimately trace back through the busy goings-on in the city; through the daily intimacies, challenges, and responses of the family; through the established social roles and religious identity of the individual; to the minute movements of love that are continually defined by and expressed through a multitude of competing and/or conjoining desires, habits, and activities. All of these diverse circles of sociality intricately relate to

one another, and all are finally sustained by the smallest interactions and determinations of power.

Foucault, like Augustine, is keenly sensitive to the ultimate reliance
of socially far-reaching exercises of power on "power at its extremities . . .
where it becomes capillary, that is, in its more regional and local forms."[33]
Without a multitude of "infinitesimal" relations upon which to draw, such
expanding, colonizing, and "ever more general mechanisms" of power would
be unable to extend and maintain themselves.[34] For any global social environment to persist, Foucault contends, there must be constant sources of
nourishment available "at the lowest level[,] . . . at the effective level of the
family, of the immediate environment, of the cells and most basic units of
society."[35] In other words, if a particular social field is to flourish, there
must first exist and continue to be created a "concrete, changing soil" composed of fertile particulate matter.[36] The radical extension of power throughout society should never be thought of as a single, uniform, and unchang-
ing totality. Power is socially omnipresent not as a rigidly unifying force but
as a richly stratified and variegated composite, one that can only subsist in society dynamically. Just as complex compounds intermingle and spontaneously react with one another, creating conditions for interconnecting niches
to develop in the global environment, so do micro-power relations continually engender a prolific, diversified, and yet intricately interrelated world of
social power.

Foucault and Augustine, although using different metaphors, are making similar observations. Both hold that power is able to spread over every
surface and into every crevice of the social world because of the complex
linking of all relations, from those so microscopic they are difficult to perceive to those so monumental they are impossible to ignore. Power relationships interconnect one by one, spreading from locale to locale and from depth
to depth, gradually interlacing in so many places and on so many different levels that they form an uninterrupted mesh. Power endlessly draws from
both densely internal and broadly external sources. One reason it can seem
so boundless in society is that, in constantly intertwining at every point, its
interiority and exteriority are each able to intensify the expansiveness of the
other. They push into ever broader terrains while remaining tightly interwoven on the most basic and micro-level.

Given their particular visions of a minutely differentiated and yet
elaborately interwoven social environment, neither Augustine nor Foucault
hesitate to cross traditional boundaries separating the public and the private, the communal and the personal.[37] We cannot dissociate these when

discussing the omnipresence of power, not only because they are inevitably entangled in and supportive of one another, but also because many power relations simply refuse to obey such distinctions. They traverse indiscriminately any and all social interactions, be they remote and intensely political or intimately familiar. In Foucault's words, power relations produce manifold "cleavages in a society that shift about, fracturing unities and effecting regroupings, furrowing across individuals themselves, cutting them up and remolding them, marking off irreducible regions in them, in their bodies and minds."[38] The dynamic and defining influences of competing loves, anticipations, desires, and habits operate similarly for Augustine. They slice through personal, sociological, and historical planes, cutting across and carving out both individuals and diverse social groupings, and glide without notice over artificially conceived borders that sever communal and personal relations.[39] For both Augustine and Foucault, the empirical consequences of this are that the extensiveness of social power becomes both partially obscured and so elaborately complicated that it is often difficult to track down and grasp as a whole, let alone disentangle, delimit, and reorient.[40]

Although Augustine and Foucault provide a similarly complex account of the omnipresence of power as being rooted in and ultimately sustained by the omnipresence of intertwining relationships, each thinker is drawn to view these relational intricacies from a very different angle of vision. Again and again, Augustine's theological impulse is to step back from the many interlacing threads of power in order to discern the patterns that play across the broader social weave, all of which, of course, tie into a single generative relationship with God. Foucault, on the other hand, being utterly uninterested in all-encompassing interpretations of the origin and consequent meaning of our sociality, focuses his attention up close, anxious to see any small variations in the fine texture of power relations—the bulging and narrowing of its fibers, the fluctuating hues of intertwining filaments. Foucault has a consuming passion to describe the minute and the microscopic in detail. Augustine is equally passionate in his concern to tie the minute and the microscopic into larger designs of harmony and disharmony, into meaningful patterns of beauty and discord.

The fact that these two thinkers, in the end, choose to view power from separate and indeed distant interpretive perspectives does not make their empirical observations about its omnipresence in the social world incompatible. Since Foucault never argues for a different comprehensive vantage point, his specific insights about social interactions do not present a competing frame of reference and, therefore, do not contradict Augustine's wider analysis of interrelational dynamics.[41] I would argue that rather than create any difficult interpretive problems, Foucault's microscopic perspective is precisely what makes him so valuable to a theologically attentive social analysis. As a practiced observer of detail, Foucault is able to notice and describe in original ways features of power relations that others, caught up in surveying a much more expansive societal landscape, fail to see. His narrowly restricted vision does not prevent his empirical observations from being contemplated, interpreted, and put to practical use from a broader social perspective. But in doing so, one must learn to accept what he offers for what it is and not demand that he give more than he actually does. Christian cultural analysts should acknowledge that this piecemeal, unsystematic, and non-Christian perspective, though intentionally incomplete, can nevertheless enrich and deepen their understanding of the social world. Foucault ought to be read as providing a highly nuanced critique of distinct segments of the contemporary social environment that Christians can then examine with a different sort of attentiveness that is guided by a different set of presuppositions.

Power's Social Mechanics

Foucault's conceptual binding of power and relationality guides his understanding of not only why power is omnipresent in the social world but also what the concrete conditions and possibilities are for its effective functioning. "I hardly ever use the word 'power,'" Foucault explains to one interviewer,

> and if I do sometimes, it is always a short cut to the expression I always use: the relationships of power. . . . [W]hen one speaks of "power," people think immediately of a political structure, a government, a dominant social class, the master facing the slave, and so on. That is not at all what I think when I speak of "relationships of power." I mean that in human relations, whatever they are—whether it be a question of communicating verbally, as we are doing right now, or a question of a love relationship, an institutional or economic relationship—power is always present: I mean the relationships in which one wishes to direct the behavior of another. These are the relationships that one can find at different levels, under different forms: these relationships of power are changeable relations, i.e., they can modify themselves, they are not given once and for all.[42]

The mechanics of power, according to Augustine and Foucault, develop through a finely textured and diversified interactive environment—one that embraces, beyond just a world of politics and public governance, all of the casual and intimate encounters of everyday life where one desires to move and influence the thoughts, attitudes, gestures, and habits of oneself and others. Commentators are bound to misinterpret both figures if they fail to appreciate sufficiently their shared view that power's range and all its potential successes and failures are inextricably connected to the pervasive and dynamic patterns of particular relations. The following section teases out of the scattered and unsystematic reflections of Augustine and Foucault four features or strands of power that I argue must be firmly grasped in order to untangle the specific ways it operates socially. Once again, I maintain that all four accurately describe each author's convictions while allowing for a conversation that is at once mutually informative and critically enriching.

First of all, Foucault argues, in order to understand power's functioning accurately, cultural analysts must always examine its exercise as a dynamically shared and thus socially dispersed activity.[43] As an inherently relational force, it is continually being co-created by interdependent presences.[44] While power can be and often is intimately personal, Foucault adamantly rejects any notion that it can be privatized. Countering what he considers a serious modern misconception, Foucault asserts that, unlike a substantive object or commodity, power is not "something that one possesses, acquires, [or] cedes . . . , that one alienates or recovers. . . . Power is neither given, nor exchanged, nor recovered, but rather exercised, and . . . it only exists in action."[45] Power, then, on Foucault's view, differs significantly from the privileges granted to a few, elite members of society, like wealth or office or title. Even though these select advantages are rooted in and feed back into power relations, they should be distinguished from power itself.[46] For power, argues Foucault, is not something that any single individual or family or social class can hold.[47] No solitary entity can ever produce, reserve, administer, take over, or transfer power. As an inherently interactive engagement, it can only be generated through and sustained by participatory relationships and mutually supporting social alliances. Hence, because we are naturally social creatures, everyone in society partakes in constantly changing variations of distributed power and everyone partakes in these with and through others.[48]

Again, as in the previous section, the primacy of this relational linkage in Foucault's empirical accounts of the workings of modern power makes them relevant to and constructive for theologically oriented social analyses, especially those informed by Augustinian traditions. An Augustinian under-standing of love can, in important ways, strengthen our grasp of this initial feature of power's mechanisms since love is less burdened than power by delimiting political or material definitions. The western traditions Foucault challenges as primarily constricting our social imagination and thus our view of power are monarchical, contractual, and economic theories. All three, he believes, employ variations of a substantive understanding of power as a valuable but limited social commodity that can be given, bargained over, traded, or seized. From this perspective, power is deemed to be an individual possession granted to some and withheld from others. Given the conceptual constraints imposed by this heritage, it may be easier to comprehend and ap-preciate how love, as fundamentally relational, is a synergetic force that can never be located in the hands of any one entity. Love's pervasive energies and influences cannot be attained, hoarded, and "expended like money."[49] They cannot be haggled over and transferred in a commodified social trade or securely managed and withheld from the reach of all others in society. Love, like Foucault's notion of power, is not a private holding that can be clutched by an imperious person or community.[50] It is an inherently participatory activity that is continually exercised by all age groups, genders, economic classes, and societies. This means that love can never be safeguarded as an individual belonging, but also that it can never be ripped away and force-fully taken by an aggressor. As with power, love exists only in and through dynamic and interactive social desires, habits, and deeds. "For love [amor] is not loved unless as already loving something; for where nothing is loved, there is no love."[51] Since these relational activities are a part of everything that we do and everything that we are, love, whether it be constructive or de-structive, is at once a personally inalienable and a mutually shared potency. It is a collaborative inclination and movement that draws persons into fluid and, as such, malleable patterns of community. Even the most selfish and antisocial love is still a love in active relation. It may be motivated by private yearnings and expectations, but in the end, like power, it can never be priva-tized.[52] Ultimately, there is no retreat or hidden lair where love can be soli-tary. This Augustinian concept of love can thus shed light on Foucault's un-traditional view of power by helping us to stretch the boundaries of what power is and does.

A second feature of the social mechanics of power that Foucault iden-tifies arises from the first. Since power is an interdependent and therefore socially dispersed activity, it is never wholly at anyone's command. Power relations qua relations involve co-creators and co-participants. They connect heterogeneous and multidimensional actors. Particular persons can thus manage the employment and experience the consequences of power in part, but its processes inevitably go beyond their own individuality in complex ways that exceed their personal governance. Over against Humanist and Enlightenment perspectives, Foucault examines power as an intrinsically dependent, responsive, and thickly interwoven social activity, not as an autonomous attribute or strength that is occasionally relied on and rationally justified by an atomistic self.[53] Even if we were to consider a single relationship isolated from all others, we would have to acknowledge that one participant alone can never control its interactive dynamics and that even together, the two involved are often unable to guide and control the consequences of where their interactions lead. Once we broaden our outlook to view the linking of that single relation to other close relations and close relations to less intimate and more impersonal ones and distant relations to heavily knotted historical webs of relations, we begin to perceive the vast interactive potencies that elude the mastery of the single individual. And this wider scope of vision still does not account for all of the micro-relations within individuals that converge and conflict with each other as they perpetually influence and are influenced by such expansively intertwining sociohistorical patterns.

Being a responsively reciprocal process makes the administration of power far less certain and precisely manageable, but it also makes it more open to local and specific alterations. Since there are innumerable small joints and interstices that are mutually configured, power can never be centrally consolidated without the cooperation of a multitude of diversified capillary relations. As a consequence, tightly strung social and historical meshings may not be disentangled and transformed all at once, but their particular threads and interlacings can be reconfigured by individuals who join in concert with others. With sufficient collaboration and patient work among co-participants, such efforts can extensively alter even the most rigidly bound social and historical customs.

Although many philosophical and political criticisms of Foucault focus on this descriptive feature of power, a pre-modern figure like Augustine can help us to see beyond our Humanist and Enlightenment horizons to the rich religious terrain in which this idea has often taken root. The decentering of human power lay at the very heart of Augustine's understanding of rightly ordered and disordered loves. Genuine power, he argued, never rests in the autonomous human self. "[T]hrough the desire [*cupiditate*] of proving his own power [*potestatis*], man by his own will falls down into himself, as into a sort of center. . . . Along what road, then, could he pass so great a distance from the highest to the lowest, except along that which leads him to himself as the center?"[54] Only delusional power attempts to ground itself in and justify itself by means of its own narrow self-enclosure. To Augustine, this is nothing more than blinding self-grandeur.[55] Because of the fundamental inclination to love, human beings are inexorably drawn out of themselves and subjected to transcendent influences and forces. Every person at every moment acts under the shadow of someone or something else. Those in Holy Jerusalem do not struggle against this reality and are thus able to relax in and draw sustenance from their dependent status. Surrendering their solitary command and allowing themselves to be wholly interconnected with God and, through God, with the entire community does not threaten or diminish their personal effectiveness but rather increases their actual power. "When you are our strength," writes Augustine, "we are strong, but when our strength is our own, we are weak."[56] Paradoxically, Augustine argues, individuals are only able to gain control over their own desires, habits, and activities, and thus over their participation with others, when they give up the atomistic illusions of a detached self-mastery and direct their lives within the complex parameters of social dependencies.

Fallen creatures constantly fight against these constrictions. It may look as though some have attained an autonomously independent social power, but their mastery is inevitably fragile and fleeting as they "scramble for their lost dominions."[57] They are never fully under their own control.[58] On Augustine's view, by cutting themselves loose from the protective moorings of their relationship with God, they have become both more vulnerable and less free and are thus "reduced to [exercising] a poverty-stricken kind of power."[59] As such, they are subject to all sorts of temporally and socially fluctuating dependencies. What could have been a calm harbor of social reciprocities becomes a tempest of susceptibilities that perpetually "pitch and toss [them] like the waves of the sea."[60] Everyone, according to Augustine, is swayed by and subjected to some relation. If it is not to God, then it is to other-relating social and historical pressures.[61] The only centralized consolidation of power conceivable to Augustine has God at its hub. Once reliance on this unifying relationship is severed, the uncertain opportunities and dangers of power become disseminated and open to contestation everywhere.

A third feature of power that, according to Foucault, helps to illumine its social functioning is the manner in which it shapes and constantly reshapes participants as it brings them into active relation. Although power itself, as a perpetually dynamic exercise, possesses no lasting substance, it is nevertheless a formative force that leaves behind material imprints in a relatively solid world of beings and objects. One of the more curiously widespread misconceptions, Foucault declares, is to think of the individual "as a sort of elementary nucleus, a primitive atom, a multiple and inert material on which power comes to fasten or against which it happens to strike, and in so doing subdues or crushes."[62] Power does not simply act on inert targets or at the voluntary direction of decisive persons. It does not merely *accompany* a fully constituted entity as an *attached* restriction or extension. The two poles of coercive repression and voluntary acceptance both rely, according to Foucault, on a skeletal and impoverished conception of power as a heteronomous law to which the independent person merely says yes or no, a primarily constricting force that individuals either actively conform to or are violently compelled by. "Far from being essential forms of power," counters Foucault, such prohibitive modes of influence "are only its limits, power in its frustrated or extreme forms."[63] Such power "is poor in resources."[64] What strictly juridical notions of power fail to account for, he contends, are the multiple and complex ways in which relationships, and thus relations of power, are creative and radically transformative. While acknowledging that power can operate heavy-handedly through extrinsically persuasive measures, he argues that it functions most efficaciously when it materially penetrates co-presences, mutually investing and altering each actor. Much more significant than just controlling and being controlled by persons, power relations are central to the actual formation of persons. Foucault claims that only when we perceive how power functions socially in relation to "the bodies of individuals, to their attitudes and modes of everyday behavior," are we able to understand, first, the full depth and breadth of power's molding effects and, second, the many complicated ways in which different subjects come to be "gradually, progressively, really and materially constituted" by transformative human interactions.[65]

As with the previous two features of power, Augustine's notion of love here again can help to loosen the grip of restricting political interpretations of power. Augustine's work not only conveys a similar general observation that relations of power, which for him are fueled by rightly ordered or disordered loves, dynamically constitute and continually alter who we are and who we become as persons. It also parallels Foucault's description (although not his explanation) of individuals being materially saturated and actively formed by these interdependent processes. For Augustine, love is the most fundamental shaping force in life.[66] It is an animating power that flows through, permeates, and stirs every fiber of individual persons and every particular of their social acts and encounters.[67] It is a creative and generative energy that brings into being desires, attitudes, capabilities, habits, acts, and interpretations.[68] It is an alluring power that transfixes persons and entices them to enter into certain constitutive self and other relations.[69] Love actively shapes the body's flesh as it intermingles habituated appetites and activities, the mind's imaginative reach as it stretches beyond or retreats back into its insulated self-enclosure, and the heart's dispositions to engage and be engaged in specific ways with others.[70] All of us, according to Augustine, become what we love, and when what we love is multifold, then our identity, our very self is constantly shifting and being transformed.[71] As with Foucault's notion of power, the shaping forces of love are never externally affixed as an overlay to the individual but instead penetrate to the core of his or her ongoing co-creation.[72] Persons are constituted not all at once as an elementary nucleus or a primitive atom but along formative social and historical paths involving different active relations of love.[73] And it is only in light of these ongoing relations that they develop a perduring self-identity.

Since both Foucault's and Augustine's terminology is rooted in the familiar dynamics of everyday relations rather than the exceptional and occasional encounter with political figures and institutions, their descriptions of power's invasively molding influences mirror one another in interesting ways. "The exercise of power . . . ," Foucault claims, "can pile up the dead and shelter itself behind whatever threats it can imagine. In itself the exercise of power is not violence; nor is it a consent which, implicitly, is renewable. . . . [Power] incites, it induces, it seduces, it makes easier or more difficult."[74] Put another way: "If power were never anything but repressive, if it never did anything but to say no, do you think one would be brought to obey it? What makes power hold good, what makes it accepted, is simply the fact that it doesn't only weigh on us as a force that says no, but that it traverses . . . , it induces pleasure, forms knowledge, produces discourse."[75] Now listen to Augustine describe in his admittedly personal religious language the alluring powers of love that constructively shape his desires, attitudes, and habits: "Come, O Lord, and stir our hearts. Call us back to yourself. Kindle your fire in us and carry us away. Let us scent your fragrance and taste your sweetness. Let us love you [amemus] and hasten to your side."[76] "To whatever place I go I am drawn to it by love [amor]. By your Gift, the Holy Ghost, we are set aflame and borne aloft, and the fire within us carries us upward. . . ."[77] "I take refuge in this pleasure [voluptatem] . . . and . . . an inward sense of delight [dulcedinem]."[78]

For both Augustine and Foucault, truly effectual power draws persons in. It does not drag individuals along hollering and kicking in protest; it captivates and holds them. Functioning by enticement rather than blunt restriction or coercion, these forms of power do not so much intrude from without upon an independent self as subtly persuade and transform from within by engaging the self's own passions, customs, and modes of reasoning.[79] They thereby gain the advantage of effortlessly guiding rather than laboriously forcing. As Foucault put it: "Perhaps the equivocal nature of the term *conduct* is one of the best aids for coming to terms with the specificity of power relations. For to 'conduct' is at the same time to lead."[80] Augustine would agree at least with Foucault's empirical observations. As with power, love above all leads individuals by patterning their fluid yearnings, impulses, and activities. So effortless is this guidance that, according to Augustine, it comes to appear as completely natural, or what he calls "second nature."[81]

A final feature of Foucault's understanding of the overall functioning of power I would highlight is that although it inevitably shapes and defines persons and communities as it acts through their many relations, its molding influences are not thereby totalizing. Power, for Foucault, is without a doubt omnipresent throughout the social world, but it does not follow that it omnipotently defines every aspect of that social world.[82] "[T]here is indeed always something in the social body, in classes, groups and individuals themselves which in some sense escapes relations of power."[83] Foucault speaks enigmatically in this regard of "an inverse energy, . . . a diversity of forms, [and] irreducibilities."[84] His language is intentionally obscure because in being irreducible, such inverse energy or diversity of forms perpetually defies the limits of description. Any definition undermines the fact that this elusive dimension of persons cannot be further analyzed into purportedly more basic elements.[85] Foucault's point, however, if not his terminology, is clear. Something viable in human beings always evades the control of power relations. There invariably remains an active remnant or residue in persons and communities that cannot be overtaken completely. Although social relations are unavoidably and deeply influenced by power, they are also indescribably more complex than the mere function of power alone.

Foucault is most discursive and lucid when he turns from discussing ineffable definitions to that which dynamically cultivates and sustains such irreducibility. While this mysterious aspect of particular persons remains indefinable, it is nevertheless, according to Foucault, always protectable through the *intransitivity* of human freedom.[86]

> [A]t the heart of power relations and as a permanent condition of their existence there is an insubordination and a certain essential obstinacy on the part of the principles of freedom, ... there is no relationship of power without the means of escape or possible flight. Every power relationship implies, at least *in potentia*, a strategy of struggle, in which the two forces are not superimposed, do not lose their specific nature, or do not finally become confused. Each constitutes for the other a kind of permanent limit, a point of possible reversal. .... Accordingly, every intensification, every extension of power relations to make the insubordinate submit can only result in the limits of power.[87]

"Intransitivity" is a difficult term to comprehend. It conveys a certain *gravitas* so that persons are not necessarily flung about by the changing circumstances of daily life. Individuals possess a basic capacity to resist the pushes and pulls of passing forces. They are able to develop a weight unto themselves that keeps them from being attenuated in an infinite array of competing relations. This weightiness, however, is a function not of being firmly fixed, solidified, and stationary but of being engaged in unceasing activity. The intransitivity of freedom is like gravity in this respect. If the earth stood still, everything on it would fly into space. By the same token, it is only through the constant whirl of movement that individuals are able to position and balance themselves in society. The natural creative energies exercised by all persons make it possible for them to configure, transform, and sustain an aesthetic integrity that is neither dissipated in nor eclipsed by pressuring influences and attractions.[88] Foucault depicts this essential restlessness of freedom as akin to flight.[89] Because of its gravitational balance and facility for resistance, no force can permanently weigh down or bind the human person in place. Maneuvering, agility, and, ultimately, escape are always possible, no matter the seemingly hopeless constraints of the present situation. Characterized by continual motion and change, the countervailing weight of liberty can always pry itself free from controlling influences that attempt to congeal the natural dynamism and fluidity of power into artificially static relations.

Although Foucault fervently argues that practices of liberty can always slip loose from particular relations of power, he maintains that freedom should not be conceived along the lines of much contemporary thought as the antithesis of power. Freedom and power do not function as lethal enemies wherein the triumphant succeed only at the cost of the vanquished.

Indeed, freedom and power cannot even exist outside of and separated from one another.[90] The two operate symbiotically, mutually conditioning and being conditioned by the rich stimuli of the other. Freedom always engages relations of power and relations of power always engage freedom. "Liberation," Foucault maintains, inevitably "opens up new relationships of power, which have to be controlled by practices of liberty."[91] Together they configure the concrete potentialities and enabling limits that make it possible for individuals to pattern historical and social processes as well as be patterned by them. Thus conceptualized, freedom and power are not necessarily determinative of one another, but they inevitably interpenetrate as they open up and shape various fields of possibilities. Foucault describes this creatively tense relationship as an irresolvable *agonism*. "[T]here is no face to face confrontation of power and freedom which is mutually exclusive . . . , but a much more complicated interplay. . . . Rather than speaking of an essential freedom, it would be better to speak of an 'agonism'—of a relationship which is at the same time reciprocal incitation and struggle; . . . a permanent provocation."[92] The vitally creative energies of prompting and wrestling bring an empowered freedom to life. Practices of liberty, Foucault contends, are always provocatively configured and situated. A purely unconditioned freedom that is in essence untouched and unmoved by everyday power struggles is, on his view, an empty, lifeless abstraction. Such freedom is completely devitalized, stripped of its generating and sustaining capabilities. Without the enabling potentialities and consequent vulnerabilities of power, freedom is nothing more than a meaningless phantasm.

Foucault's discussion of freedom and power is central to understanding his work accurately because it rounds out and softens the other sharp features of power's social mechanics. Without his emphasis on practices of liberty, the individual would be easily overwhelmed by power's other traits: the fact that it is socially dispersed, not wholly under one's individual control, and subjectively constituting.[93] Foucault is adamant that he is not pointing readers down a path of fatalism or determinism: "A society without power relations can only be an abstraction. . . . [But] to say that there cannot be a society without power relations is not to say either that those which are established are necessary, or, in any case, that power constitutes a fatality at the heart of societies, such that it cannot be undermined."[94] On Foucault's view, we should never expect to be "liberated" or "freed" from power relations. That is a false hope, a naive, utopian wish that may actually undermine our capacity to appreciate—and modify—the microfibers of power's network. He urges his readers to have confidence in the human ability to exercise freedom potently within power's broad and pliable matrix. "We can never be ensnared by power: we can always modify its grip in determinate conditions and according to a precise strategy."[95]

No matter what the given circumstances may be, we always maintain a capacity to influence power's controlling mechanics and functions. We can alter relational processes by changing tactics, shifting the balance more or less favorably toward particular individuals, groups, and objectives. Like a game of chess, all of the participants involved have multiple moves before them. They can reposition pieces on the board and await with fresh anticipation a different configuration to respond to.[96] Although we can never completely withdraw from "games" of power, we nevertheless constantly possess an array of options and choices, each one of which can potentially make a material change and, over time, work to rearrange fundamentally the composition and rules of the "game."[97] Here, once again, we can see why Foucault preferred to speak of power *relations*. All parties to this relation exercise power in virtue of their freedom. They are all (in some measure) free participants choosing among a range of strategic and tactical options.

> [A] power relationship can only be articulated on the basis of two elements which are each indispensable if it is really to be a power relationship: that "the other" (the one over whom power is exercised) be thoroughly recognized and maintained to the very end as a person who acts; and that, faced with a relationship of power, a whole field of responses, reactions, results, and possible inventions may open up.[98]

Human freedom is both the precondition and the consequence of power relations; without the perseverance of practices of liberty, no power can enter into dynamic play.[99]

The terminology Foucault uses to describe the complex relation between practices of liberty and the shaping forces of power is haunted by a perplexing ambiguity that he never fully resolves. A certain conceptual tension, even discomfort, is evidenced in his dueling depictions of human liberty as *agonistic* and *intransitive*. On the one hand, agonism clearly highlights the boundaries of relations of power: such relations can be provocatively engaged by practices of liberty, but they cannot be escaped. Like generals embroiled in war, individuals have numerous options for choosing when, where, and how to fight, but they cannot flee from the exigencies and intensities of the campaign. They can innovatively take on and alter but never completely retreat from the power relations that entangle their lives. From this perspective, the most practices of freedom can hope for is to transform incrementally, negotiating a piecemeal and painstaking transition from one prevailing arrangement of power to another. On the other hand, in contrast to the inescapable relational confines of agonism, Foucault employs the word "intransitivity" to signify the endless possibilities for human flight and evasion. The term portrays not so much a freedom *in relation* as a freedom that can disentangle itself from any relation. It is a self-created and self-sustaining exercise of liberty that is able, through its own perpetual activity, to separate and insulate itself from the determining pressures and controls of sociohistorical communities and practices. In being *intransitive,* nothing outside of such freedom can ever complete the individual's meaning. This fundamentally restless human capacity always remains, to some degree, independent from and irreducible to particular social and historical conditions.

While relational constraints form the foreground of Foucault's discussions of power and freedom over most of his career, lingering in the background is the often unarticulated anticipation of breaking loose from such limits and personally fashioning a nonreductive aesthetic potentiality. Especially as he approached the end of his life, Foucault's more emancipatory concerns moved from the background to the foreground of his analysis. For someone who so many times claimed to shun lofty visions, he paradoxically seemed to long for a social world without confining borders where the conflictive tensions that tend to fabricate and then bind individuals to delimiting social identities could be creatively transfigured into a self-composed harmonious beauty. Although Foucault's competing descriptions of freedom are not necessarily contradictory, he never explicitly accounts for how they should be coherently related.[100] In his characteristically unsystematic manner, Foucault simply wanders back and forth in his work between these two depictions of human possibilities, leaving all discussions of their illogical opposition or dialectical correlation to his readers.

Augustine likewise wrestled with ambiguities in the complex relations of power and freedom, but his theological perspective gave him different conceptual resources for addressing potential contradictions. As we have seen, Foucault is pulled philosophically in two directions. He argues that individuals are shaped by relations of power and that this shaping percolates all the way down into the smallest micro-dynamics as they interactively formulate personal as well as sociohistorical desires, dispositions, and habits. Yet Foucault is loath to concede that individuals are inescapably indebted to and completely defined by interpersonal relations. He repeatedly tries to create space for a nonreductive potentiality—a kind of mysterious personal integrity—that can disengage itself from and, in the end, outdistance the indignity of being determined by other-relating dependencies and pressures. Foucault is anxious that particular persons not be explained away by simplistically pointing out the historical, social, psychological, and intellectual components that constitute specific relations of power. With respect to this philosophical conundrum, Augustine is much less embattled than Foucault with logical tensions because he depicts the personal integrity of individuals as being nonreducible in light of rather than in spite of power relations. The irreducibility of individuals intrinsically depends upon their relationality. The former flourishes only because it is firmly rooted in the latter. Consequently, Augustine is, in many ways, much more radically "post-modern" than Foucault because relationships do indeed shape individuals all the way down. This is especially so for the most mysterious and indefinable dimensions of human beings.[101] No personal "residue" needs to flee from power relations to protect the particularity and worth of individuals. Their unassailable value rests in and is sustained by the dynamic forces of properly oriented love; it is an integrity that utterly depends upon intersupporting alliances of power. This involves first and foremost, of course, the primary relationship with God, but it also entails manifold alliances that radiate into and connect the community of faith. What is most essentially and nonreductively personal, then, is the fact that individuals are fundamentally other-related. The less other-related they are, the more their integrity is pulled apart and threatened.[102] The more other-related they are, the easier it is to hold together as a coherent unity. It is only in attempting to disentangle themselves from and gain dominion over their natural interdependencies that human beings become susceptible to reductionistic dehumanization. Even when individuals are detrimentally shaped by sociohistorical manipulations of power, Augustine argues that there always remains a centering relation that safeguards their irreducible human dignity.

If the notion of gravity helps to explain Foucault's descriptions of freedom as a constant whirl of creativity and resistance, it is a freedom that maintains a personal balance by revolving on its own axis. The metaphor of gravity works for Augustine as well. Only here, the *gravitas* of freedom (*libertas*) functions solely in response to and moving under the influence of another attracting force. Without the pull of the most fundamental relation of power, human freedom loses control over its natural positioning and becomes radically disoriented. One can never completely sever that essential relation, but even if traces of it remain, one can still become utterly lost in confusion. Once the attracting weight of our relationality is disrupted, freedom becomes entangled in the alliances and counteralliances of lesser forces of power.[103] It is thus drawn this way and that, and is constantly absorbed in trying to reorient itself. Augustine would concur with Foucault that human freedom does not and indeed cannot function in opposition to relations of power.[104] He would challenge Foucault, however, by distinguishing between disparate potential paths of freedom based on the nature of the empowered love it cultivates.[105] A strongly attracted and well-balanced love and a gravitationally disrupted and unsettled love will provide human beings with radically different relations of power, and thus radically different opportunities for exercising freedom, change, and resistance.

Augustine and Foucault both depict the cultural functioning of power relations as intricately influencing all that we do and all that we become as social and historical persons. While Augustine speaks through the language of love and Foucault through the language of power, their fundamentally interactive concepts converge at a number of crucial points, helping not only to clarify and enrich each other's social descriptions but also to guard one another against damaging misinterpretations. With one examining social relations from a pre-modern and the other from a post-modern perspective, their observations and assessments challenge in different ways certain modern presuppositions that make it difficult to appreciate the full significance of their cultural analyses.

An Augustinian understanding of love, on the one hand, can divert criticism from and conceptually embolden Foucault's understanding of power by stirring readers to venture beyond the restrictions of orthodox political definitions. Love, for Augustine, saturates every single relationship, bringing the sway of power into all personal, interpersonal, and political dynamics. The suffusing energies of each individual and of the social body continuously function through the interactive formation of fluid desires, dispositions, preoccupations, habits, and flesh. Love has traditionally been given far greater latitude than power to be intimate as well as communal, nonpolitical as well as socially forceful, generative and transforming as well as destructive, materially penetrating as well as physically capturing. Moving away from the descriptive landmarks and familiar safety of autonomy to the uncertain terrain of interdependence has been taken as more natural and socially acceptable for human loves than for power. That we are drawn out of ourselves and influenced by something not wholly under our own control may be construed as less threatening in the context of love precisely because it has so often been portrayed in literature, philosophy, and theology as creating a personally expansive rather than simply constrictive sense of individual and social identity. Such decentering experiences, thus understood, can open individuals through reciprocal and responsive participation to ever deepening and enlarging worlds. However, as a densely interdependent process, human loves inevitably remain ambiguous—holding at once constructive and calamitous possibilities as they gain more and more access to remote recesses of embodiment and imagination.

What benefits Foucault most in Augustine's theology is the conceptual leeway love offers to power. It helps to break through the prohibitive and substantive limitations of juridical, institutional, sovereign, and economic notions of force, and breathes life into the everyday closeness of a world animated by the capillary intricacies of flowing desires and habituated flesh—or by what Foucault calls the "micro-physics" of power. As with love, human power is not merely a weapon wielded by certain individuals and social groups against one another at critical moments; it is the perpetual weaving of living relations that at once configures and circulates through daily existence.

Foucault's notion of power, on the other hand, equally serves an Augustinian cultural critique by pushing contemporary conceptions of love against the strong currents of reductive psychological interpretations. Modern expositions all too often leave Augustine stranded in the simple solitude of a conflicted mind. No reader can question that Augustine's *Confessions* intimately reveals to his audience a painfully torn self. But it is a self torn in layers of fragile relations that stretch simultaneously inward and outward, backward and forward. Searching the depths of the most personal love always leads back to a shared social and historical world, and probing this far-reaching complexity always leads back to the particularity of jockeying passions, preoccupations, and minutely patterned behaviors.[106] The commonplace portrayal of Augustine as the father of western introspection—the first psychological analyst—tends to bind our theological imagination, limiting the vastness and transcendent intricacies of human loves to a one-dimensional internal battle.[107] The contemporary reader can easily get lost in a maze of myopically private passions, failing to see beyond the immediacy of an internalized psychological drama to the looming social horizon.

Desires and habits, on Augustine's view, are all fundamentally rooted in other-relating histories. As we will see later, especially in the next two chapters, even the most intimate experiences of personal intellect, emotion, and embodiment have transcendent dimensions and should be understood as developing within and through formative relationships. Human loves, above all, draw persons beyond their individual boundaries and open them to countless possibilities of influencing and being influenced by something uncontrollably other. Every aspect of our internal and seemingly private self-relations thus bears sociohistorical traces of an interactive co-creation. They are dynamically and temporally shaped by the ways in which they work with or against their inevitable sociality—whether they function graciously as a synergetic part of an interdependent community or combatively strain to construct an atomistic potentiality.[108] One's theological focus, therefore, should not be one-sidedly internal or external, psychological or political; what it must invariably be, however, is relational.

Foucault's analysis is particularly useful in highlighting the social and historical elements of Augustine's thought that have all too often been displaced by a modern obsession with psychologizing and privatizing human loves. Foucault reminds us of something that Augustine knew well: any analysis of empowering love must make sense of specific patterns of desiring and acting not only in the context of intrapersonal and interpersonal relations but also in reference to longer ranging cultural preoccupations and habits. Foucault's culturally attuned grammar and analytical tools makes it possible to examine from a fresh perspective the social and historical interworkings of love that are far more complex than any insular motivational psychology can account for. Foucault's concept of power in this way stretches contemporary views of love as much as Augustine's concept of love stretches traditional views of power. Each alone is vulnerable to becoming petrified into opposite and yet equally limiting social configurations. Placing these concepts into conversation helps to break apart such rigid interpretive frames and pushes readers to acknowledge the immensity of both the intimate and the far-flung functionings of power and love.

Ambiguous Relations and Intransigent Dangers

As we have seen in the discussion of power's omnipresence and social functioning, Augustine and Foucault concur that power is not necessarily insidious. It is always ambivalent, but it is not intrinsically harmful. "Relations of power," writes Foucault, "are not something bad in themselves, from which one must free oneself. I don't believe there can be a society without relations of power, if you understand them as a means by which individuals try to conduct, to determine the behavior of others."[109] Augustine echoes Foucault's sentiment when he notes that there is nothing wrong "in the one who loves power, or in the power itself";[110] the problem lies in the self's privatizing orientation. "Let a man will to be prudent, brave, temperate, just, and that he may be able to have these things truly, let him certainly desire power and seek to be powerful in himself, and strange as it may seem, to be against himself for himself."[111] For Augustine, the guiding and molding influences of love permeate the interactive dynamics of the heavenly and earthly cities. It is a social force that can be generative and life affirming as well as life destroying; it can be other-serving as well as domineering. Foucault would agree that the same root of power, a yearning to influence and move oneself and others, can and often does shift imperceptibly back and forth between the salutary and the injurious. Each element in the functioning of power—the decentering effects of co-creation and a mutually dependent participation, the dispersal of social mastery and control, the varying allurements that lead as they pattern personal desires and habituation, and the endless wrestling of freedom—can be shaped to drastically different ends. The social mechanics of power are all neutral or formal. It is their fluctuating and arbitrary uses that open individuals to peril. For both Augustine and Foucault, therefore, although power in itself should not be considered a social evil, it must be regarded in light of its radical ambiguity as an inescapable social threat. What has always motivated his cultural analysis, Foucault reflects, is not that, because of power, "everything is bad, but that everything is dangerous."[112] Throughout their various writings, ambivalent relational hazards transfix Augustine and Foucault. It is the perplexities of a constantly shifting and precarious social environment that arrests their historical and political attention.[113]

When addressing our social vulnerability, both thinkers would agree that one should distinguish between processes of power and its uses. While Foucault shies away from offering what he would consider absolutist standards of evaluation, he sprinkles his accounts with stories and examples that coherently draw certain key social distinctions.[114] Two especially stand out for Foucault. One indicator of moral peril he often looks for is how the naturally moving currents of power circulate among participants.[115] In their patterning influences, do the dynamics of power remain fluid and unobstructed in all directions, or do they coagulate at particular points, choking off their own invigorating flow and slowly congealing, thereby trapping participants in a rigid and seemingly unchangeable asymmetry? For Foucault, it is not the asymmetry per se that is the problem here but the immovability and fixed inertia of such power differentials.[116] Foucault uses the two examples of lovers and teachers to clarify his argument.

To exercise power over another, in a sort of open strategic game, where things could be reversed, that is not evil. That is part of love, passion, of sexual pleasure. Let us also take something that has been the object of criticism, often justified: the pedagogical institution. I don't see where evil is in the practice of someone who, in a given game of truth, knowing more than another, tells him what he must do, teaches him, transmits knowledge to him, communicates skills to him.[117]

Foucault sharply contrasts interactions that he describes as "variable[,] . . . allowing different partners a strategy which alters them" to deleterious relations of power that tend to become "firmly set . . . , impassive and invariable."[118]

    The former manner of interrelating involves no less power than the latter.[119] Both evidence unstable social dynamics and the desire to shape or move another. But whereas in one, the persons involved temporarily situate themselves in uneven or unlike roles so as to acquire certain skills, attitudes, and relational experiences, in the other, they struggle to petrify and permanently exploit the unevenness of social power. What concerns Foucault is whether such imbalances remain transitory and whether they remain permeable to alteration, adjustment, and reversibility. As is the case in certain longer-lasting asymmetrical relations, such as parenting or teaching, a clear transposition may not take place for a long period, but even in these instances, there are constant small opportunities for power dynamics to flow both ways, and eventually a shift in status will be possible. Love, passion, friendship, child rearing, educating, and associating with colleagues all involve different degrees of being effective, and thus are capable of dramatically altering participants. Our perpetual challenge is, as Foucault sees it, "to know how you are to avoid in these practices—where power cannot not play and where it is not evil in itself—the effects of domination which will make a child subject to the arbitrary and useless authority of a teacher, or put a student under the power of an abusively authoritarian professor, and so forth."[120] In virtue of being human, we are always actively involved in unsettled situations wherein we can and do influence the conduct of others. The interminable problem is how to keep these transformative interactions from becoming knowingly and unknowingly manipulative. Or, in Foucault's words, we must continually concentrate our social attention on ensuring that "these games of power be played with a minimum of domination."[121]

    This brings us to the second and more basic moral distinction in Foucault's work. Do specific power relations generate and nourish personal desires, attitudes, and capacities so as to help individuals gain greater mastery over their own lives, or do they cultivate such dispositions and skills so as to make persons more serviceable to the instrumental needs and demands of others? One of the more intriguing examples Foucault reaches for in illustrating this point is monasticism. Socially exploitative disciplines of power, he explains, are "different from asceticism and from 'disciplines' of a monastic type, whose function was to obtain renunciations rather than increases of utility and which, although they involved obedience to others, had as their principal aim an increase of the mastery of each individual over his own body."[122] In contrast to this form of submission where the individual subjects private yearnings and behaviors to the guidance of another so as to transfigure the relations one is able to have with one's self and one's social world, the coercive dynamics that most worry Foucault are "directed not only at the growth of . . . skills, nor at the intensification of . . . subjection, but at the formation of a relation that in the mechanism itself makes [a person] more obedient as [he or she] becomes more useful, and conversely."[123] Foucault argues that in these instances, power relations gain a materially penetrating hold over the micro-physics of the bodies and minds of others "not only so that they may do what one wishes, but so that they may operate as one wishes. . . . [L]et us say that disciplinary coercion establishes . . . the constricting link between an increased aptitude and an increased domination."[124] Of course, this does not mean that ascetic practices are never or were never manipulative. Since, as I will discuss later, exploitation has often been effectively hidden in a so-called master's enticement of self-improvement or self-liberation and since exploitation often works, as does asceticism, by subtly altering the micro-dynamics of personal desires and habituation, monastic practices are more vulnerable than many other relations of power to the possibilities of manipulation.[125] What this example points out is that Foucault is not advocating a reductionistic mode of individualism that rejects all influencing forces external to the self. It is not individualism but instrumentalism that is at issue here. Foucault is not rebelliously questioning authority or obedience so much as the shaping and using of persons for purposes other than their own. Naturally, when authority and obedience become entangled in manipulating processes—which, in Foucault's opinion, they are always in jeopardy of—he targets them for a withering examination.[126]

At this broad level of analysis, Foucault's moral concerns about human exploitation are not so different from Augustine's. In the *City of God*, Augustine repeatedly scrutinizes the mistreatment of persons in subjugating relationships. One of the fundamental social distinctions he returns to throughout the text as he evaluates various communities is the irresolvable polarity of coercive subordination and benevolent service. Juxtaposing the "self-indulgence" of "the passion for domination" and the "pride in taking precedence over others" to the other-regarding tenderness of "loving concern" and "compassion in taking care of others," Augustine brings into relief the two sharply opposing potentials of all human interaction.[127]

On the one side, Augustine, like Foucault, sees in certain daily interactions promising traces or epiphanies of attentive care. Expressions of familial devotion and fidelity, above all, offer glimpses of a paradigmatic relationship.[128] If we were to consider all persons "as if they were [our] children, longing and praying"[129] for the preservation of their well-being and the flourishing of their interests, even at the cost of forgoing our own personal advantages, we would attain some sense of unblemished affection. The shared intimacies of friendship and the self-surrendering commitments of monastic community also throw light on this ideal human affinity.[130] These tightly knit alliances all disclose, if only momentarily, the possibility of treating social dependencies and vulnerabilities not as an opportunity for control but as an occasion for generosity and mercy. The pervasive fragility of individuals, when attended to with a proper attitude of loving service, cultivates and strengthens our created bonds of solidarity. Rather than weaken and fracture relational ties, frailties can melt away the isolating boundaries of self-sufficiency and move persons to become more deeply interwoven in naturally given or voluntarily constructed "families." Human frailties, in such instances, do not become a target of control but a motivator of care.

The grammar of kinship, however, also shows us the darker side of human relations. The very same language of family loyalties, being of service, and ministering to the personal frailties of others are regularly used for purposes that Augustine regards as morally ambivalent. When looked at in part as social fragments, such communal sentiments always appear to be commendable, but as a whole, these are as readily disrupted and disordered in relation to each other as any other dynamically finite desires. Benevolent justifications for forcefully shaping and directing weaker persons often sound as though they are based on other-regarding compassion when in reality they rest on nothing more than a warped paternalism that delights in taking precedence over others as it governs. As we saw in the discussion of the *City of God*, 19.5, family and friends offer no permanent refuge from the vagaries of our sinful existence. This is due not only to the difficulty we have determining the motives of others and discerning whether loving gestures are feigned or real. It is also because we are unable to know with certainty our own desires and impulses as we attempt to help others.

Augustine discusses two especially illuminating examples of how we can become entangled in self-glorification when we suppose we are humbly caring for others. The first concerns our desire to be kind to the needy. "For although a man who is sorry for the sufferings of others deserves praise for his charity, nevertheless, if his pity is genuine, he would prefer that there should be no cause for . . . sorrow. If . . . kindness were unkind, a man whose sense of pity were true and sincere might want others to suffer so that he could pity them."[131] Feelings of superiority, Augustine worries, easily creep in when we assume the lofty place of the "giver" and see our generosity as a confirmation of our self-sufficient exaltation and the lowly stature and dependence of the sufferer.[132] The second, more personal example Augustine puts in terms of the inevitable, if lamentable, temptations involved in being a moral and spiritual exemplar for his parish.

> Yet in what others say about us and in what they know of our deeds there is grave danger of temptation. For our love of praise [*amore laudis*] leads us to court the good opinion of others and hoard it for our personal glorification. And even when I reproach myself for it, the love of praise tempts me. There is temptation in the very process of self-reproach, for often, by priding himself on his contempt for vainglory, a man is guilty of even emptier pride; and for this reason his contempt for vainglory is an empty boast, because he cannot really hold it in contempt as long as he prides himself on doing so.[133]

For Augustine, our most virtuous aspirations and behavior present us with the danger of instrumentally using those whom we lead to inflate our own sense of strength and self-worth. Intriguingly, such social ideals, Augustine cautions, can be more harmful than blatantly aggressive ambitions since their distorted images can create a socially alluring mirage. Promising relational interactions, therefore, offer us not just a beautiful social vision of loving service by which to evaluate different communities; they also open a window onto our own moral confusion. Even Augustine's noblest moral models both clarify and muddy our view of our social situation.

Like Foucault, Augustine's best attempt to see through this moral haze is to focus his critical attention close in on varying shades of coercion and instrumentalism. Both would agree that authoritatively guiding others who are dependent and open to suasion does not necessarily indicate misuse, nor do asymmetrical variations in social capacities and positions.[134] Differentials and vulnerabilities can and do exist in human societies without entailing harm. For Augustine, these are naturally present in every community, whether it be prelapsarian, fallen, or redeemed. What starkly sets off fallen relations is the unnatural dynamic of servile inequities where other persons are put to the relative use of providing for one's private concerns and where events and encounters are always shaped to one's particular advantage.[135] Human nature, Augustine argues, was intended to be subjected solely to God's sovereign rule, never to the subjugating interests of one or another forceful individual. "He did not will the rational being, made in his own image to have dominion over any but irrational creatures. . . . Hence the first just men were set up as shepherds of flocks, rather than as kings of men."[136] Augustine's eschatological vision contrasts just as sharply with fallen relations in that its fulfillment is expected to annihilate every trace of human coerciveness and, in so doing, restore a finely balanced social harmony.[137] Thus, the moral ambiguity Augustine wrestles with does not lie in the eschatological standard by which we judge but in our performative frailties as we try to distinguish coercive from noncoercive interactions in this fallen world, with its "light that fails,"[138] where we cannot but influence one another.

For both Augustine and Foucault, the emphatic presence of beneficence is never sufficient for a power relation to be judged beneficent. There must be, in addition, a lack of any forceful subjugation. Beyond an other-regarding attitude, one must perpetually be aware of the social dangers of paternalistic instrumentalism and vigilantly eradicate, as much as possible, its subtly invasive effects.[139] Augustine and Foucault would agree that once any particle of human dominion enters into interpersonal relations, even the loftiest aims become subsumed under and transfigured by its contaminating effects. Human beneficence alone is too beset by the arbitrariness of a finite perspective to shield itself from the moral perils of exploitation. Both figures continuously struggle with the difficulties of finding a human place of judgment that is able to extricate itself enough from its own vested interests so as to be certain that it can perceive and lovingly respond to the "real" concerns and needs of others.

The instrumental use of persons is only one guide that Augustine and Foucault depend on in helping them to remain alert to the wide-ranging possibilities of social danger. The other significant indicator that helps each figure to stabilize finite human judgments about such relational hazards is, as we have already seen with Foucault, the patterning flow of power. Augustine and Foucault construe the movement of power through distinct interpretive frameworks and thus read into the evidence they see variant meanings, but they nevertheless share an important strategy about how to perceive relational dangers that reflects their compatible understandings of the social functioning of power. For Foucault, power dynamics are least threatening when they flow with unimpeded ease among all co-participants.[140] Widely dispersed participation inhibits the hardening of problematic social interactions and thereby clears the way for invigorating relational energies to pump from one part of the social network to another and vice versa. Conversely, the most obvious and readily detectable social hazards arise when interrelationships become so viscous they disrupt the fluid interchanges that take place at the capillary level, eventually clogging vital arteries of power.

One can likewise see in Augustine's work a concern with the ways in which power, or in his words, rightly ordered or disordered love, circulates. But he would place at the heart of such a vascular metaphor the moving grace of God without which all other life-sustaining movements would cease to function. One cannot participate in nourishing loves or powers by severing the social body into separately interacting parts, one cut off from the other. Even the most intimate and heartfelt affection between friends or lovers can remain viable only if it continually streams through and is swayed by the love of God and a correspondingly intricate love of self.[141] One can try to devote oneself solely to a beloved person, directing all of one's energies and yearnings to that individual as a good in and of herself. Inevitably, however, because human beings are expansively interactive creatures, this adoration ends up relating to other things. If it does not relate to God and one's self as moving through God to the other, then it will be related primarily to the pieces and parts of an isolated self that cannot help but seek an atomistic good even as it tries to focus on the good of another. The beloved's interests and one's own interests can come together in the shared process of flowing through something else, or they can become disconnected and weighed down by the natural sedimentation of self-referencing desires, preoccupations, and habits. To love something other than God for its own sake as a solitary entity does not allow a circular form of love but only a stagnated one that cannot move far from itself, caught up, as it always becomes, in the standing pools that collect around self-absorbing persons and ends. Ironically, Augustine argues, the only way that even the most personal love can be considered in any way one's own is by not holding it too close to oneself. "Everything which is not exhausted by being given away is not yet owned as it ought to be, so long as we hold on to it and do not give it away."[142] Paradoxically, in allowing love to course away from oneself—or from one's self and one's companion—there is no risk of either diluting it or losing control over its momentum and direction; rather, the energy of such love increases in both concentration and force as it interacts with a greater unifying power. "Whatever else comes to our attention to be loved is to be carried along to that place to which the whole torrent of our love rushes. . . . For, thus loving [another] as himself, he refers all the love of himself and the other to that love of God which suffers no trickle to be led off from Itself by those whose diversion Its own volume might lessen."[143]

Love of God, however, is only one part of the ever-circulating movement of power that interests Augustine. Persons cannot simply adore God and have this involve no other relationships.[144] Love of God participates with love of neighbor just as love of neighbor participates with love of God.[145] The power of love "by which we are carried along" can only be rightly oriented when it flows through the entire social body, including friends and enemies in the earthly city and even the inhabitants of the heavenly city.[146] We cannot ignore our neighbors. As Augustine admonishes his listeners, "You can say to me: I did not see God, but you can never say: I did not see the human being."[147] Of special concern is the incorporation of the farthest reaches of one's social network, bringing into the circulating movement of love outcasts and vulnerable strangers. Love must necessarily be performative, then, and not just contemplative. It cannot, on Augustine's view, remain merely mysterious and ethereal but must anchor itself as it moves from one locus to another in concrete deeds of mercy.

Even the tangible beauty of the created world presents specific occasions for experiencing and participating in God's love and mercy, as long as these natural delights draw us closer to their and our creator and redeemer and do not become objects that we try to possess, consume, and be fully satiated by. Augustine is inspired by the fact that "the psalm says, 'You have clothed yourself in praise and beauty.'"[148] Indeed, he finds his words falling short as he tries to capture the overflowing glory of the natural world all around us. "How could any description do justice to all these blessings? The manifold diversity of beauty in sky and earth and sea; . . . the dark shades of woods, the color and fragrance of flowers; . . . the sea itself, putting on its changing colors like different garments, now green, with all the many varied shades, now purple, now blue."[149] Augustine cautions that relating to God is fundamentally different from relating to created beauties through God, but the latter are nevertheless described by him as being taken up into and transformed even during the quietest meditative experiences:

My love of you, O Lord, is not some vague feeling: it is positive and certain. . . . [A]ll about me, heaven and earth and all that they contain proclaim that I should love you. . . . But what do I love when I love my God? . . . not the brilliance of earthly light, so welcome to our eyes; . . . not the fragrance of flowers . . . ; not manna or honey; not limbs such as the body delights to embrace. . . . And yet, when I love him, it is true that I love a light of a certain kind, a voice, a perfume, a food, an embrace . . . when my soul is bathed in light that is not bound by space; when it listens to sound that never dies away; when it breathes fragrance that is not borne away on the wind; when it tastes food that is never consumed by the eating; when it clings to an embrace from which it is not severed by fulfillment of desire. This is what I love when I love my God.[150]

All of our relationships, with God, with human beings, with the natural world, dynamically interact with one another as they move through both small social capillaries and major arteries of power under the force of rightly ordered loves. Relational hazards and already existing harms surface, therefore, not only in our encounters with other human beings—with friends, lovers, and family; with doctors and psychiatrists; with factory workers, prisoners, and those who are destitute—but also in our encounters with nonhuman creatures and the natural environment. In all of these relationships, one can detect through the circulation of power signs of social danger. Augustine would have us ask in every encounter whether power flows away from the self such that it comes to regard other created objects in a new light of respect or whether it becomes so encumbered by accumulated desires and habits that it cannot venture away from its own perspective. Does it prod one to seize, master, and devour living entities with a privatizing love or to delight in them through God with an other regarding love?

Given their different philosophical and theological orientations, some illuminating differences emerge when we compare Augustine's and Foucault's analyses of how social power engages and spreads among participants. The most obvious is that whereas Augustine envisions an ontological and evaluative center to networks of power, Foucault pictures an arbitrarily interwoven mesh of relations that has no centering axis. For Augustine, all rightly ordered loves must flow through the same transforming hub as they engage with various parts of the social body. They still interact with an elaborate web of living beings, but they do so through a common pattern of departure and return. For Foucault, power relations pulse through small capillaries that branch out in a variety of directions over the social body. These relations progressively engage larger and larger domains, but they do not move in any unalterable order. Consequently, new forms of circulation can develop without necessarily creating heightened social dangers.[151] The ability to change such circulatory patterns is in fact imperative to safeguarding participants from danger because the channels or vessels through which social energies flow tend themselves to ossify over time. They can only retain their vitality, therefore, if they take different courses and form fresh passages. From Foucault's standpoint, nothing transcends these various interconnected and yet contingent relations of power. For him, the central moral issue is whether and how they allow interactive fluidity and reversibility so that renewing social energies can transfigure historically established problems, especially those that encourage the instrumental use of persons.

A second but closely related difference is that Augustine, in contrast to Foucault, distinguishes between good and bad forms of instrumentalism. This is because for Augustine the referencing of one being to another, by definition, involves an instrumental process that does not simply tend to an object in and of itself but moves through that object to tend to someone of higher value. Of course, that ultimate relation comes back to and enables a noninstrumentalizing respect for particular human beings, but the route for getting to this inviolability is always a circuitous one. Augustine, therefore, maintains that humans cannot and do not need to repudiate all instrumental uses of love and power in order to protect themselves from instrumental abuses.[152] They must, however, take scrupulous care to refer these uses away from themselves and even away from the object they are focused on so as to safeguard the encounter from their own finite judgments and self-interests. Once again Augustine may seem in some ways to be more radically postmodern than Foucault in that he depicts interdependent relations as permeating persons entirely. There is no irreducibility or socially valid judgment separable from relational encounters and interactions. These reside not in the self but in the interaction of the self with something that is transformatively other. Foucault is just as interested in gaining new perspectives by stepping away from the self into strange and foreign points of view, but because, under Foucault's guidance, we can never be quite sure where to step or from what angle to peer, Augustine would suspect that our inexorable self-interests would subtly bamboozle us and eventually commandeer whatever new outlook we adopted. Of course, Foucault could counter that Augustine's defense of a good form of instrumentalism dangerously opens persons to being hoodwinked by established and yet historically developed interpretations of God and God's purposes. Although Augustine has tried to guard against harmful instrumentalism by rejecting coercion, Foucault would argue that instrumental relations can work so subtly that coercion does not appear to be coercive.

Both, in their criticisms of each other, would actually be working off the same concern and intuition: a profound suspicion of all temporal judgments and the socially and historically constituted desires and habits that inform them. And each, at different times in his career, seems to recognize to some degree his own vulnerabilities. Augustine, although he looks to an eschatological perspective for guidance in stabilizing noetic and moral activities, admits that we can only see ourselves and our world through a glass darkly and thus must remain vigilant about the possibility of misinterpretation and becoming puffed up with arrogant certainty. Foucault is also keenly aware of the ingenious ways that our self-interests can co-opt even the best effort to see things anew and so prods us to move around constantly, shifting about and peering from this view and that in an endless search for critical insights.

A final comparison regarding the movement of power and its consequent social dangers concerns how these relate to nonhuman entities and things. Foucault's analysis often goes beyond human beings to examine how individuals interact with architectural structures, with how different spaces are externally and internally divided, with their openings and their closures, with their illuminating capacities and their ability to throw things in shadow. Foucault is fascinated with the inventive possibilities of isolating and creatively engaging persons as well as monitoring, examining, and socially registering them through varied designs and the constructive use of materials.[153] "Power has its principle not so much in a person as in a certain concerted distribution of bodies, surfaces, lights, gazes; in an arrangement whose internal mechanisms produce the relation in which individuals are caught up."[154] Some of Foucault's early works go so far as to experiment with purging his analysis of all anthropocentric concentration, depicting an almost stylized world that is filled with discursive remnants but emptied of human faces and bodies and void of any painful signs or consequences of time.[155] Yet, in all of these efforts, Foucault finds himself immersed in and intrigued by human artifacts. His is a largely urban world with prisons and factories and imposing medical facilities. Although Augustine spent much of his life in cities, he is nevertheless much more attuned than Foucault to a natural as well as a human web of relations that can be harmfully disrupted by domineering desires and a self-absorbed consumption that refers all uses to its own pleasure. The natural world along with the human world will, on Augustine's view, share in the glories of the heavenly city, though it now suffers together with us under the weight of both intentional and unintentional evils.[156] Augustine's and Foucault's insights about nonhuman interrelationships can be useful in exposing important avenues of thought that neither thinker himself chose to pursue. Foucault's exploration of the "play of spaces, lines, beams, degrees" in spatial designs and elaborately interrelated material structures disclose a deeper complexity in human interactions in that various desires and habits are historically and socially constituted not merely through interpersonal relations but also in and through a frequently unexamined engagement with artificially constructed spaces.[157] Augustine's inclusion of the natural world in his analysis of rightly and wrongly oriented loves also opens the way to apply Foucault's detailed observations about the instrumental uses of power to a larger and more diverse circle of vulnerable creatures and socially threatened ecological communities.

CHAPTER TWO

Vertigo and Complicity

Unraveling the Complexities of Social Evil

> This indeed is the diabolical aspect. . . . One doesn't have here a power which is wholly in the hands of one person who can exercise it alone and totally over the others. It's a machine in which everyone is caught, those who exercise power just as much as those over whom it is exercised. . . . So much so that one has the vertiginous sense of being in the presence of an invention that even its inventor is incapable of controlling.[1]

Foucault, in this response to an interviewer about specific manifestations of disciplinary power, sounds as if he could be describing what Augustine views as the endlessly perplexing character of original sin. As we saw in chapter 1, Augustine and Foucault portray power relations as ambivalent, sometimes enabling and sustaining individuals and sometimes manipulating them for instrumental purposes; and in light of this, they offer indicators for discerning when particular uses of power are socially reinvigorating or morally dangerous. But both figures press themselves to think still more deeply about forceful relations. In doing so, they are drawn to the far edges of explanation as they try to digest the darkest and most baffling features of power. The daunting complexities of social evil do not in any way diminish or supersede the importance of the clarifications set forth earlier. Augustine and Foucault would argue that we must use as best we can whatever we can firmly grasp in order to sort through the interactions and encounters that fill our lives. However, while each believed that such elucidations were critical for making our way through difficult situations, the daily needs and demands for moral clarity did not stop either of them from adventuring beyond the safety of its borders. To different degrees, they remained restless in the comfortable territory where everything makes sense, where we can always count on discerning where the land ends and water begins, where the constant whirl of people and conversations and activities that unfold all around us can be captured and passed on by good storytelling and crisp aphorisms. The real boldness of Augustine and Foucault, I would argue, is that they were not afraid to straddle two very different worlds—one clear in its distinctions, where maleficent actions could be observed and carefully analyzed; the other murky and chilling, where the seemingly hard-edged lines of suffering and human responsibility confusingly run together. The commentators who seem most disappointed by Augustine or Foucault question the logic of working in such very different worlds, as though the existence of the former wipes out all possibility of the latter. For both figures, however, even if it cannot be communicated in clean logical grammar, the hard fact that we live out most of our lives in an untidy paradox cannot be evaded. Therefore, if we are to grapple with the full complexity of love and power, we must come to terms both with what can be clenched without much strain and what wiggles away from our grip, enticing and besmirching our comprehension in the process.

For the sake of clarity, in what follows I will be isolating and comparing a number of central images and concepts that the two authors often mix. The reason I am examining them separately when they did not is to probe with more specificity their views of certain human frailties that make individuals particularly susceptible to social harms. Since each metaphor connotes a different aspect of the functioning and possible effects of social evil, it is useful to analyze them one by one rather than as entangled. We should keep in mind, however, that Augustine and Foucault use them together without hesitation, jumping back and forth between them in various contexts or even tossing them all into the same sentence or paragraph. In taking up this task, I am not ignoring Augustine's and Foucault's ad hoc approach; I am trying to honor it. I believe that coming at social evil from a variety of angles allows us to investigate its personal, social, and historical implications in greater depth while recognizing that we can only grasp them in part. This protects us from the illusion that we can systematically comprehend from any one standpoint the multiple frailties of persons and the diverse opportunities for social evils to inflict harm. I will be comparing clusters of images and concepts from two distinct but overlapping perspectives, one that explores the impersonally overwhelming character of social evil and the other, its intimate functioning in the performative fallibility of individuals and communities.

The Namelessness of Social Evil

One of the more interesting perceptions Augustine and Foucault share that challenges our capacities to describe social evil is its often impersonal and anonymous character. Foucault frequently jolts his readers with striking impersonal images and descriptions as he tries to apprehend the "diabolical" or "dark side of these processes" of interacting forces that are concurrently "diffused, entrenched, and dangerous."[2] Perhaps the clearest way Foucault conveys the anonymity of such power is through the language of mechanization.[3] He refers in various contexts to machinery and industrial operations where individuals, being caught unaware, can get themselves enmeshed in the "wheels of power."[4] The danger here is not that the ill-fated nameless will be crushed under the weight of its churning wheels but that people will begin to operate namelessly as components in the machine itself, acting as part of a "complex system of cogs and gears."[5] Social evils can therefore begin to run automatically and anonymously as a vast depersonalized mechanism. "Power is no longer substantially identified with an individual who possesses or exercises it . . . ; it becomes a machine that no one owns. . . . If the machine were such that someone could stand outside it and assume sole responsibility for managing it, power would be identified with that one man."[6] But there is no single person to whom one could tie the activities of the machine since he or she alone is unable to work the apparatus. Because its mechanisms are operated by everyone, it is controlled by no one. Certainly, this unowned "machinery that assures dissymmetry, disequilibrium, difference" can only run automatically and smoothly reproduce its functions over time through the complicity of each individual component.[7] This particularized complicity, however, is by its very nature rarely noticed or examined since it works as a whole so routinely and regularly, so effortlessly, and so anonymously. Such automated machinery, concludes Foucault, "makes it possible to perfect the exercise of power . . . because it can reduce the number of those who exercise it, while increasing the number of those on whom it is exercised. . . . Because, in these conditions, its strength is that it never intervenes, it is exercised spontaneously and without noise."[8]

Other images that elucidate the seemingly detached and impersonal presence of social evil are among Foucault's favorites: networks, grids, matrices, meshes, and interconnecting systems.[9] Like machinery, these descriptions necessarily include specificity in that their immense extension can only be formed by a multitude of fine lines and planes intersecting at definite points. But if one were to look at the whole from the embedded perspective of a single nexus, one's vision would rapidly spin away in three dimensions with wires and circuitry and twisted cords crisscrossing in different directions, leading from one convoluted level to another and another. Overwhelming one's view would be nonhuman surfaces, nodes, conduits, and tiers. The image of an impersonal matrix or interactive system with pulsating energies communicates both the cold breadth and remove of certain forms of power as well as its complicated interdependence on innumerable individual forces. It portrays, similar to industrialized mechanization,

> a multiple, automatic, and anonymous power, for although [it] rests on individuals, its functioning is that of a network of relations from top to bottom, but also . . . from bottom to top and laterally; this network "holds" the whole together and traverses it in its entirety with effects of power. . . . This enables [it] to be both absolutely indiscreet, since it is everywhere and always alert[,] . . . and absolutely discreet for it functions permanently and largely in silence.[10]

In contrast to his use of the image of mechanical instruments, however, Foucault employs these images more interactively to depict the inventive possibilities of circulating influences where individuals operate not simply as the nodes that pass social energies and social evils endlessly on, but at the same time become the fluid material that circulates through these anonymous threads.[11] They find themselves simultaneously swept away by forceful currents and acting as the conveyers of such overpowering effects.[12] Fluidity, in this context, does not safeguard persons by keeping social interactions from becoming congealed; rather, it openly exposes them to the ravages of the flowing process itself, making individuals vulnerable to being broken down into heterogeneous elements that can be relentlessly explored and reconfigured as they are engaged and acted upon.[13] Circulation, warns Foucault, can be as overwhelming and engulfing as revitalizing; persons silently interact and are drawn along not by the renewing forces of a vigorous web but by an unfeeling network that retains its extensive circuitry by continuously yet subtly managing the particularity of all movement and change.

Foucault's modern imagery of industrial machinery and technologically elaborate systems and networks would, of course, be totally foreign to Augustine. But the mind-boggling complexity and the cold anonymity that these images portray are also what most perplex Augustine. He uses much plainer language to convey the impossibility of fully comprehending social evil. Simply put, he admits, it "is like trying to see darkness or to hear silence."[14] At times, Augustine sounds as though he might be willing to throw his hands in the air and merely leave it at this—in darkness and in silence. "No one therefore must try to get to know from me what I know that I do not know, unless, it may be, in order to learn not to know what must be known to be incapable of being known!"[15] He does, however, plunge ahead with apprehension. Having been immersed during his adult life in the orderly rules of rhetoric and logic, Augustine realizes that he is heading into a maelstrom where normal compasses will not work, where our sense of personal orientation and familiar human surroundings will be upended and, in the end, rendered nearly unrecognizable.[16] Driving the assault on our reasoning is the impersonal immensity of social evil. The impact of original sin (*peccatum originale*) overwhelms the individual agent.[17] If one were to trace the line of a single sinful act, it would lead through the particularities of a person's life, through personal desires and preoccupations and gradually accumulated habits,[18] and then it would finely branch out in a multiplicity of directions, shattering the defined boundaries of the individual. It would first of all lead backward through a blur of faces and activities and intentions to lives that had never been encountered and specific surroundings and temptations that had never been confronted, coming finally to the familiar face of Adam. But between the particular sinful act and the first activating sin would stretch an immeasurable line of nameless persons and circumstances. One could also trace this seemingly isolated act forward, leading through a similar haze to diverse progeny who will never be known and yet will unthinkingly pass on a tangibly distinct but ubiquitous proclivity to sin (*concupiscentia*).[19] In both its depth and breadth, then, an Augustinian view of original sin takes one beyond the individual's purview just as confusingly as Foucault's immense matrix spreads out before one when looked at from any single nexus. The impersonal and unfathomable dimensions are about as dizzying for both.

In many ways, Augustine's ancient view of inherited guilt and responsibility, with its extensiveness and intricate interconnections, resembles Foucault's modern concepts of industrial machinery and interactive networks. Inherited sin combines in a multitiered complex of relations specific points of contact and interlinking grids that pass on through very particular acts a comprehensively circulating force or momentum that propels social evils forward.[20] It is both composite in structure and dynamic in operation. Although human beings find themselves already enmeshed in the massive, imposing, and depersonalizing structure of inherited sin, it is not socially or historically monolithic. Its many different parts minutely link with one another to make the whole appear uniformly domineering. Diverse institutional practices and discourses governing social, legal, political, economic, pedagogical, and familial interactions form, for both Augustine and Foucault, the coarser framework of a social matrix within which repeating patterns of instrumental coercion and asymmetrical iniquities are received, reconfigured, and passed on. The finer and finer meshes are constituted and continually shaped by every particular human being and every specific human act, and each of these involves a multitude of structuring desires, dispositions, social preoccupations, and behavioral patterns.[21] An anterior bondage requires all of these intertwining cords and small knotted points to retain its imposing power to shape the present and motivate it to shape the future.

If the social and historical structure of inherited guilt is not monolithic, according to Augustine, neither is its operation self-sustaining. The machinery and general mechanics of original sin cannot live off past energies and simply run on an accumulated momentum of prior injustices. It is absolutely dependent on the continued participation of every active social component. Far from being able to function on its own, inherited guilt must be fueled by fresh acts that, although they may simply repeat long-held and deeply ingrained practices, are nevertheless new in their social particularity and historical circumstance. The whole can recharge itself only by way of innumerable tiny sparks that fire at very specific and immediate loci, perpetually activating the coarser and finer elements that keep the multiform structures of social injustice operating. Yet such activities by themselves cannot drive the mechanics of original sin. The entanglements that currently bind us and the motivations that inspire and move us are not created from scratch. We work off of a momentum of social desires and preoccupations that has slowly built up over time, adding our own temporally distinctive yearnings and allurements to this already stimulating force, and together these propel our acts forward.[22] Previously established social customs continue to shape our daily habits, but we weave into and around them reconfiguring threads that preserve and reinforce their strength while at the same time making them new and our own. Augustine envisions all individuals of every age as being enmeshed in an interactive mechanism that is not just inherited and not just their own. It is an uninterrupted network that operates through the dynamic comingling of desires, attitudes, and behaviors from the past, the present, and the future.[23] Because its functioning is so repetitive in reenacting former sins and smoothly perpetuating future ones, and because it works so quietly through the tiny particulars of desire and habit, it certainly appears in its entirety to be automatic and self-sustaining. Looking from the outside, one has difficulty detecting how finely articulated and co-dependent this anterior bondage is on all of its separate yet interconnecting nodes of social and historical contact.

Since each particular component of original sin is required to drive the mechanics of the whole system and since the whole system can only have force if these individual parts are interactively co-dependent in their transmission of anterior guilt, then no one person can be singled out as operating the mechanism. Using Foucault's description, although such a machine is run by everyone, it is controlled by no one. Moral responsibility, then, can only be laid hold of in terms that unite the entire working system and the singular component. It must be inextricably corporate and particular. The constant comingling of past, present, and future impetuses makes it impossible, from Augustine's perspective, to separate sharply either a self-constituted from an inherited identity or an individual from a common debt and responsibility. We live in a matrix of social and historical relations, in a mesh of shared longings, stimulated appetites, engrossing preoccupations, and unrecognized habits. This does not mean, however, that everyone is exonerated because no one can be found to be solely responsible. In fact, because each specific piece is needed to run the co-dependent mechanism in its entirety, an individual part, even if it only plays a slight and incomplete role, carries the energy and guilt of the whole. Original sin creates through its interlacing threads a social and historical solidarity that pervades each piece of the social network.[24]

In sum, the images of machinery, matrices, and infinitely branching genealogies focus light in similar ways on the social and historical expansiveness of relational sins or human evils and the dynamic multiform structures of injustice they sustain. They all make the individual appear as little more than a small transmitter in an immensely complex, intricate, and impersonally operating system. The specific agent carries through its narrow walls an intense social force that requires the agent's interdependent participation for continued effect, yet which far exceeds its own fragile particularity in magnitude and scope. This distinct perspective on social evil offers us an external view, one that is removed to the outer rim of human comprehension. Looking from the immensity of evil toward the smallness and insubstantiality of the individual, it reveals a stunning anonymity and impersonal detachment.

One last metaphor that Augustine and Foucault employ concerning the cold anonymity of social evils is warfare. Although martial metaphors, like the other images discussed thus far, highlight a tragic depersonalization in which individuals are relied on for perpetuating the forces of social evil while at the same time being swallowed up by its overwhelming energies and consequences, they also highlight very different features of power and possibilities for resistance. Machinery, networks, and propagation all emphasize the uninterrupted movement of a co-dependent process that operates so smoothly that it can reproduce itself over time without much notice. In direct contrast, war erupts with clashing "lines of force, tensions and points of collision."[25] With the former, individual components interact through a self-propelling current that makes the mechanism as a whole appear to run automatically. With the latter, they must continually maneuver around unstable "ruptural effects of conflict and struggle,"[26] joining together from moment to moment in precarious alliances that shift about in support of or in opposition to one another. Both are shaped by a historically and culturally accumulated heritage. For one, however, this creates a momentum that quietly hums along, entangling participants often unawares. The other reveals that history is filled with agitations, fracturing disturbances, and abrupt reversals. It is not at all smooth but ragged and uncertain. History has been irregularly shaped by conflicting global forces that have scarred its surface as well as by unseen fault lines that have gradually built up tension and threaten to break forth from beneath its seemingly uniform and solid plane. The present is thus endemically fragile, filled with "innumerable points of conflict [and] focuses of instability, each of which has its own risks."[27] The strain of these uneven but changeable distributions of power charge the space with adversarial energies and pressures. All is contested, open to confrontation and reversal. Certain advantageous arrangements have taken shape that clearly tilt the odds of victory in one direction or another, and yet these coordinated relations can be penetrated, broken apart, and pushed into new formations. Unlike a mechanism that fuels itself by passing on continuous sociohistorical patterns through the particular acts of nameless components, here, the only constant is conflict and struggle. The sole element being transferred from one point to another is the striving to gain mastery over at least part of the domain. If skirmishes surround persons everywhere, then what is perpetuated endlessly is indefiniteness and uncertainty. A permanent but always reconstellating disequilibrium cultivates and transmits a social climate of insecurity, aggressive posturing, and maneuvering defenses.

Such a conflictive social atmosphere, from Augustine's perspective, is evident in every twist and turn in the long story of the fall and the destabilizing effects of the *libido dominandi*. Its unfolding is one of discord and erratic disruption, not continuity and progress. History, which is driven by the passion to dominate, is eruptive, tense, irregular, and precarious. The only thing reliably punctuating its course is the senselessness of factionalism, carnage, and brutality.[28] This makes it not only difficult to predict and command but also to interpret with ultimate purpose and meaning. Although early in his career Augustine distinguished between sacred and profane history, by around 410 he begins to equate the former solely with the Bible's narrative and declined to identify any post-biblical events as unambiguously salvific. All history becomes for Augustine at this time radically indeterminate.[29] The *libido dominandi*, with its self-serving exaltation, cunning, and treachery is evident in the devil's rebellion against the Heavenly City and Cain's fratricide and establishment of the first human city.[30] All of the characters whom Augustine sees as shaping the multiform, complex story thus begun—fallen angels, biblical figures, kings, generals, civic judges, and the rest of us—display a more or less forceful unwillingness to live within the limits of a properly balanced mechanics of power: that it is inherently co-created, socially dispersed, personally decentered, dependent, and relationally constitutive. This arrogant refusal is filled with irony for Augustine. In struggling against the natural characteristics of power, we spin increasingly out of control. The more we seek to possess it, the more it slides through our fingers; the more we set out to conquer those who are dependent, the more we become targets of violence and subjugation; the more we try to make ourselves into something substantial and permanent, the more we become vulnerable to being obliterated and left as nothing. In trying to master what transcends us socially and historically, we find ourselves caught up in a world of radical insecurity. "For when the soul loves its own power, it slips from the common whole to its own particular part. . . . [I]n that apostacizing pride, which is called 'the beginning of sin,' it sought for something more than the whole and while it struggled to govern it by its own laws, it was thrust into caring for a part, since there is nothing more than the whole; and so by desiring [*concupiscendo*] something more, it becomes less."[31] If individuals had been satisfied with being a part, they would have fit into the whole as differentiated and yet harmoniously related components. Now in struggling to take over the whole, they become tossed about as so many bits and pieces in "the stormy life of human society."[32] Trying to grab hold of power, they lay themselves open to being destroyed and swallowed up by its forcefulness.

Foucault uses martial imagery to describe a similar sense of depersonalizing discord, insecurity, and historical uncertainty that engulfs the individual. He interprets such radical precariousness not through the rebellious language of the fall but through anonymizing descriptions of strategic mobility and conflict. "The history which bears and determines us has the form of a war. . . . [I]t is intelligible and should be susceptible of analysis down to the smallest detail—but this in accordance with the intelligibility of struggles, of strategies, and tactics."[33] Foucault analyzes the "namelessness" of such strife in two different but related ways. The first analytical perspective can be likened to the strategic viewpoint of a commanding general in his map room. Spread before him are models and charts depicting the variously aligned and counteraligned capabilities engaged—divisions, regiments, and battalions; supply lines and reinforcements. They show in their complex relations the rapidly changing susceptibilities and opportunities combatants are confronting on the field, how "power can retreat here, reorganize its forces, invest itself elsewhere."[34] At this strategic remove, one can identify a whole variety of tactical dynamics at work across the broader domain and thus more effectively assess and redirect a targeted "manipulation of relations of forces [by] developing them in a particular direction, blocking them, stabilizing them, utilizing them . . . in a play of power."[35] Such an analyst knows, of course, that nothing can be achieved without individuals making on-scene decisions. But the primary focus from a strategic point of view is not the struggling, tense, and fearful "who's" enmeshed in the immediacy of battle, but the intricate material potency of how mobile forces maneuver to control various parts of different conflicts. From this perspective, we do not need to know "why certain people want to dominate, [or] what they seek," in order to understand "how things work at the level of ongoing subjugation."[36] "What is needed is a study of power . . . where [we can see how] it installs itself and produces its real effects."[37] It is not unimportant that people are endangering themselves. This fact, however, is not vital for analyzing the interweaving lines of force and locating the specific areas of solidity and fragility that make tactical adjustments more successful and effective resistance possible. This strategic knowledge is of use down in the trenches, just as the knowledge from the battlefield is of strategic use to those trying to make sense of the minutely shifting complexities. Yet a strategic viewpoint alone is insufficient for understanding the multiplicity of power in its full-bodied exercise. It must be based on and sustained by a tactical outlook where the local losses and local fighting occur.

A second perspective on power's dynamics that the war imagery helps to illumine concerns the disorientation plaguing those caught up in the play of social evils as they try to combat them. Foucault is sensitive to the vulnerability of persons becoming part of a swirl of activity that they contribute to but do not fully govern. Being co-participants in battle, as in relations of power, means that one's actions are not completely under one's own control. They develop in conjunction with those of others and thus are dispersed throughout the group. Our intentions, though surely considered by us to be "private" and "our own," are nevertheless immediately severed from us as soon as we put them into action. They are socially up for grabs: anyone can react to them, misinterpret them, or turn them back on us. We tend to think that our intentions make us sole possessors of our activities and the power (and/or social evils) they instantiate. But as Foucault contends repeatedly, power cannot be hung on to; it can only be jointly exercised. Consequently, we can become ensnared as shared creators in power relations that we never planned to partake in, may not be cognizant of, and may strongly oppose. Our activities have innumerable unexpected ramifications, argues Foucault, that have "nothing to do with any kind of strategic ruse" carefully thought out on the part of a "willing" subject.[38] They can generate, in relation to other activities, a cultural force of their own that follows a "coherent strategy, but one for which it is no longer possible to identify a person who conceived it."[39]

As with the machine imagery that betrays no sign of an inventor, here again we hear distant echoes of the anonymity of original sin. The social and the individual tragically share responsibility as they share the debt and obligation to continue combating, as best they can, the problems that morally threaten to soil their hands. Even as noble persons fight against targeted evils, they can become implicated in instrumental injustices in ways that far exceed their comprehension. Anyone who has been in combat can tell us that power does not always operate according to our anticipations of its lines of development. Battles often take on lives of their own. Certainly they are influenced by plans and preparations, but as the soldiers realized on the Normandy beaches or in the jungles of Vietnam, they unfold unpredictably and amidst perils that are difficult to foresee and even more difficult to negotiate. This is part of the fog of war. So too is the fact that such disorienting confusion can develop within as well as around us. We often end up struggling against unknown internal factions and enemies while wrestling with those that are external. When asked who are the combatants in his strategic analysis of power, Foucault responds: "This is just a hypothesis, but I would say it's all against all. . . . Who fights against whom? We all fight each other. And there is always within each of us something that fights something else."[40]

This points to the inadequacy of any binary model for understanding social evil's manifestations. From the distance of the headquarters' map room, war may appear to have a certain tidiness about it. One sees clearly the two opposing forces, the blue and the gray arrayed against one another. But on the field of battle, this tidiness disappears into the hurly-burly of combat. Simple images of "us" versus "them" fail to communicate the blinding confusion of war, its sheer volatility, the shifting tides of force and sudden eruptions that catch us by surprise, the intra- as well as interpersonal challenges.[41] Contrary to what most might expect, however, Foucault maintains that the fact that alignments of power are not binary and that we are not in complete control of our participation in power (since it is co-created) opens up diverse possibilities for fighting social evils. Tactical resistance means that "each offensive from the one side serves as leverage for a counter-offensive from the other. The analysis of power-mechanisms has no built-in tendency to show power as being at once anonymous and always victorious. It is a matter of establishing the positions occupied and modes of actions used by each of the forces at work, the possibilities of resistance and counter-attack on either side."[42] If no one is in complete control, he argues, then everyone has some control. And if the forces at play are not lined up in massive binary opposition, then we do not need to battle against such overwhelming forces to make important changes. The lack of static opposition means that the field of forces can be modified in a great variety of ways. "[T]he always open and hazardous reality of conflict"[43] is socially ambiguous for Foucault. On the one hand, we can never relax. We are inevitably in danger. On the other hand, change is possible and achievable as long as we recognize that risk and opportunity perpetually remain intertwined.

Martial imagery may be what is most prominently associated with Foucault. But he makes it clear that this metaphor is only one among many that help us to analyze social evils and that it can only take us so far.[44] In his mid- to late career, he seems to grow weary of any abstract remove and turns more and more to examining the "who's" stuck down in the trenches. "[T]he affirmation, pure and simple, of a 'struggle' can't act as the beginning and end of all explanations in the analysis of power relations. This theme of struggle only really becomes operative if one establishes concretely—in each particular case—who is engaged in struggle, what the struggle is about, and how, where, by what means and according to what rationality it evolves."[45]

Anonymity, Authorship, and Responsibility

Numerous criticisms have been leveled against Augustine's and Foucault's descriptions of social evil as exhibiting anonymous and depersonalizing features. The primary objection is that lines of guilt and innocence are intolerably blurred, threatening our moral potency and our clear-cut responsibility. When binary distinctions dissolve in a world of pervasive insecurity and unknowing complicity, we find ourselves thrown into a battle that has no easily discernible opponent.[46] We can target no single enemy against which to direct our energies and to protect our own interests. There is no one class or sociological group or individual instigator that we can safely contrast to ourselves. Instead, we discover to our dismay that we are all, individually and together, both the instigators and the targets of such evil. Looking backward, we are separated from its original source but implicated in its transference and present configuration. Looking forward, our own intentions are incapable of reliably guiding our social contributions and what we help to create can veer perilously off course in ways we never imagined. In both instances, individual control escapes us while personal complicity draws us in and attaches us to the specific functioning and consequences of evil.

The arguments for why Augustine's anonymizing portrayal of original sin is morally flawed could be just as well directed against Foucault's socially complicated understanding of the "darker sides" of power relations. Augustine's critics maintain, writes Malcolm Aflatt, that an unwitting social and/or historical complicity necessarily undermines human agency, "cutting away the ground upon which the responsibility, implicit in the idea of sin, is placed upon the sinner."[47] William Babcock contends that we can only assess as praiseworthy or blameworthy an "action performed in such a way that the action genuinely counts as the person's own."[48] And to count as one's own, an act has to bear certain marks of personal authorship: first, various alternatives must be available to be freely chosen at the time of acting;[49] second, a person must determine autonomously which alternative to take to be held responsible as the identifiable "author" or creator of any act;[50] third, an individual must have conscious control over how she directs the activity, so that we can trace back from a clearly intelligible act a line of "continuity with the dispositions, inclinations, aims, and intentions of the person acting."[51] If one is not "in command" in this manner, Babcock argues, one's "actions are not determined by one's 'self,' and the actions do not properly count as one's own."[52] Given such individualistic conditions, his conclusions, of course, are entirely negative: "Augustine was unable to conceive the relation between the agent and the evil act . . . in such a way as to make the act the agent's own."[53]

James Wetzel also voices concerns about the vulnerability of the individual agent to depersonalizing sins. Augustine "slides the most troublesome external sources of evil—the sins of my community, my society, my friends, and my associates—into the category of sin's penalty. . . . If I should experience another's sin as the source of my own sin, the fragile distinction between what I do and what the world does to me would collapse."[54] For this reason, he claims, from the perspective of conventional moral wisdom, "original sin is a moral scandal."[55] If power is co-created and dispersed, then human agency is stretched thin over a vast social space and time. If we participate together in the generation and operation of social evils, then my own power and responsibility becomes diffuse. If my power and responsibility cannot be given its own due weight, not only does this "do violence to our sense of fairness,"[56] but it also cripples our ability to offer forgiveness to one another. "If each of us stands guilty before all and for all, then it would seem that we live in a world where everyone needs forgiveness, but no one is in a position to offer it. Justice in a world thus fallen conforms to the iron law of retribution, of pain returned for pain caused. . . . My guilt is mine; yours is yours. In guilt we stand apart, and when the time of judgment comes, we stand alone."[57]

Foucault's detractors would agree with such "conventional moral wisdom" that an anonymous and depersonalizing characterization of social evil is "a moral scandal." The alarms they sound against Foucault are not too different from those summoned against Augustine. Stephen Lukes, Charles Taylor, and Michael Walzer would all concur that impersonal descriptions of social evil that "cannot be attributed to anyone as their plan, as their conscious purpose,"[58] endanger necessary notions of individual authorship, judgment, and accountability.[59] It is thus imperative that the act not be severable from the actor or the purposeful execution from the intention.[60] Walzer argues that beyond the evaluative social dangers of Foucault's account, he simply cannot make sense of how any power relation could be depicted as being both intentional and nonsubjective.[61] Walzer seems unable or unwilling to find any moral space for human complicity wherein an individual, along with others, consciously and yet unwittingly participates in setting into motion certain responses or patterns of behavior that then take on a life or practical social functioning of their own, hence being paradoxically connected to and yet disconnected from the objectives and projects of various persons. He is especially disturbed by the failure of Foucault's historically descriptive approach to differentiate "between guilt and innocence," going so far as to charge that Foucault denies any distinction whatsoever.[62] Taylor likewise complains that while power, for Foucault, always involves victims, he makes it difficult to locate and render judgments about "a clearly demarcated perpetrator."[63] The social distribution of power combined with its lack of any identifiable center exacerbates the blurring of innocence and guilt, according to Walzer and Taylor, because it does not leave regulative capabilities in place that enable us to recognize potential abuses and effect remedies.[64]

Lukes, Taylor, and Walzer are much closer to Babcock than to Wetzel in their reactions to anonymous evil. Although I would argue that Wetzel, along with the others, would like to leave behind the "moral scandal" of original sin, he attempts to do so in a way that preserves the challenges of its paradoxical mysteries. By reshaping the doctrine into a different form of shared guilt, he hopes to heighten what he considers most important about "the dark wisdom"[65] of original sin—the tragic necessity to cultivate capacities for mercy and care in a community inevitably wounded by moral blind spots—while eliminating what is most offensive to the modern mind, namely, the unfairness of living as one accused and being made to suffer for the maliciousness, deception, and thoughtless harm of others. Wetzel's overriding concern is that if all are individually preoccupied with and weighed down by the heavy load of an inherited debt, they will be unable to share in and ease the burdens of those around them. "If original guilt is a debt," he concludes, "it is a unique kind of debt, interpersonal and vicarious in character. I cannot pay off my debt, only yours, and you cannot pay off your debt, only mine. For the purposes of satisfaction, then your debt is mine, and mine is yours."[66] Babcock, Lukes, Taylor, and Walzer are fighting to reinforce and morally fortify what Wetzel is struggling against as an inescapable consequence of inherited sin: having to live in a black-and-white world of "iron law and retribution" that drives persons apart rather than one of self-giving atonement where individuals enact solidarity by forgiving and freely adopting each other's faults, imperfections, and afflictions. Whereas Wetzel focuses on the moral alienation of the guilty and the possibilities of alleviating their isolating journey, the other critics concentrate on the need for the guilty and the innocent to be strictly segregated so that human justice can remain accurate, clean, and swift.

Wetzel's aim of cultivating social solidarity is commendable and compatible with Augustine's sensitivities to the mists that obscure innocence and guilt in the morally hazy world of original sin. However, this similarity throws into sharp relief how different Wetzel's philosophical assumptions about persons and community are from the radically nonmodern stances of Augustine and Foucault. Although Wetzel emphasizes solidarity, his individualistic underpinnings surface in his expectation that we must free ourselves from socially and historically entangling encumbrances in order to be of loving service to one another. His descriptions of the paradoxical social mysteries of original sin still rest on the notion that communities comprise monads who decide to join together in love and responsibility. The social power Augustine and Foucault analyze does not just end with but begins as inextricably enmeshed in and operating through a mutually constituted solidarity. Moreover, it is a solidarity that always remains morally complex. It may be healing through shared acts of forgiveness and self-sacrificing service, but it can just as easily be threatening. Most important, we can never be absolutely sure which of these our actions will contribute to because we lack complete control over and awareness of what we co-create and disperse with others.[67]

"The Pelagian man," writes Peter Brown in *Body and Society,* "was essentially a separate individual: the man of Augustine is always about to be engulfed in vast, mysterious solidarities."[68] I would argue that Foucault, in his own unsettling way, resembles Augustine in this regard. By contrast, Richard Rorty articulates an engaging contemporary form of Pelagianism, only through the use of post-modern descriptions.[69] Like Wetzel, Rorty's self-determining optimism is expressed in his full-throated assurance that we can create "moral progress and that this progress is indeed in the direction of greater solidarity."[70] This solidarity, which is "made rather than found,"[71] promises to overcome the frailties and misfortunes of human life by learning to listen to the sufferings of others, by choosing—on the basis of an expanding knowledge of various self-descriptions and a progressively enlightened social vision—to enlarge one's community and broaden where persons can place themselves and belong. I would counter that when looked at from a performative (rather than ideal or intellectual) perspective, social solidarities are for Foucault, as they are for Augustine, much more engulfing, thickly mysterious, and difficult to manage harmoniously. Such noble and compassionate aims are of course laudable. The problem is putting them into practice in a selfishly competitive and exploitative world filled with ever-shifting power differentials.[72] Gilbert Meilander writes, as he reflects on the seductive yet illusory temptations of self-healing and self-liberating human expectations, that he hears in Wetzel's hopeful reformulation of original sin echoes of "a pelagian call"[73] where "the already present burden of guilt . . . is a burden 'we have inherited . . . from no one.'"[74] Even though Wetzel's portrayal overflows with the language of communal sensitivities and the concrete need for building social bonds, "it remains chiefly an account of individual agency."[75] Rorty, it would seem, likewise endorses inherently beneficent impulses, dispositions, and capacities of individuals when he says: "In my utopia, human solidarity would be seen not as a fact to be recognized . . . but . . . rather as a goal to be achieved. . . . It is to be achieved not by inquiry but by imagination, the imaginative ability to see strange people as fellow sufferers. Solidarity . . . is created by increasing our sensitivity to the particular details of the pain and humiliation of other, unfamiliar sorts of people."[76]

Wetzel's and Rorty's moral anthropologies grasp something important about social evils that Augustine and Foucault would strongly affirm: the necessity to deepen our awareness of the vulnerabilities of marginalized persons and the perplexing challenges of personal and social care. However, Wetzel and Rorty dwell overconfidently on the possibilities of being generously welcomed into and soothed by these self-made communities of inclusive respect. They thereby tend to overlook and fail to monitor sufficiently the menacing sides of solidarity that can tangle around and harmfully constitute individuals through an enculturation one does not wittingly choose but is born into and that eventually becomes simultaneously other and one's own. Both want to get rid of the uncomfortable moral scandal while preserving a purified social solidarity. Augustine and Foucault, however, persuasively argue that this aspiration is a mirage and can be, as we will see in chapters 4 and 5, naively dangerous. They maintain that we cannot understand social solidarity without confronting the moral scandal of an inherited world. Foucault, in particular, helps us to resist the allure of an optimistic individualism that hides itself behind the veil of communities. He adds a post-modern warning that supplements Augustine's pre-modern ones. Together, their work stands as a stinging rebuke of the otherwise admirable (because compassionate) aims of Wetzel and Rorty. It does so not to destroy all social hope but to temper it with humility. The depersonalizing aspect of social evil rightly takes our breath away by showing how insubstantial we are as singular individuals.

Since power and love, for both Augustine and Foucault, are created by co-participants and thus socially dispersed, decentered, and dependent, why would it be a moral surprise or scandal for the instrumental exercise of power to follow similarly intersecting lines of a shared complicity? I would suggest that it is not actually Augustine's and Foucault's notions of the anonymity of evil that are at the root of their critics' objections but their notions of power and love, particularly their notions of human identity and sociality.[77] We fail to grasp the depth of the disagreement if we focus too exclusively on evil. This is in fact an argument over self-constitution and the complexity of human responsibility. Meilander captures the density and richness of our social constitution especially well with a quotation from Austin Farrer:

> Our humanity itself is a cultural heritage: the talking animal is talked into talk by those who talk at him; and how if they talk crooked? His mind is not at first his own, but the echo of his elders. The echo turns into a voice, the painted portrait steps down from the frame, and each of us becomes himself. Yet by the time we are aware of our independence, we are what others have made us. We can never unweave the web to the very bottom and weave it up again.[78]

I agree with Meilander's conclusion that such social configuration is not something that happens to us as if it were intruding from without and violating our personal identity; it is just the way we have come to be as we make our way through the world. "This is not simply our misfortune—as if we were one thing and our character another. It is our very being."[79]

Many of Augustine's and Foucault's critics argue as if social self-constitution is necessarily morally crippling. From this perspective, a seductive refrain might be, "It is not my act." If I participate with too many others and dilute my responsibility historically and culturally, then it is not my act. If social forces or patterns are too influential in shaping who I am and what I do, then it is not my act. If I cannot clearly trace my individual intentions and the effects of what those intentions create in a socially messy world, then it is not my act. If this is the case, then it is a very small world for which I am responsible. And it is a clean and tidy place with easy boundaries to protect. However, this is not the world we live in—at least not according to Augustine and Foucault. Co-creation, or perhaps we might say "co-authorship," does not entail an absence of moral responsibility but rather a complicated sense of communal and individual responsibility that are elaborately interwoven. Because it may be difficult to analyze and judge such culpability, that does not make it any less important to try to do so. The ease or difficulty of our analysis should not guide what we determine to be morally relevant. Augustine's and Foucault's critics have accurately charged that the anonymous and depersonalizing aspects of many of their descriptions of social evil keep us from finding comfort in a reliably predictable world. They leave us feeling agitated, nervous about our activities. But should safety and clarity determine what we deem morally acceptable discourse? Is that the best measurement when we are dealing with the breadth and depth of sin? To close one's eyes to the fog of war does not relieve one of the responsibility to scrutinize and evaluate the behavior of combatants, and it certainly does not make it any easier to do so. Augustine and Foucault would admit, as we saw in the last chapter, that we do at times operate with relative degrees of moral clarity. Yet we also often operate in confusing situations, in threatening environments where it is difficult to pinpoint the dangers, find the solutions, charge the perpetrators. It is difficult to take our revenge and rid our world of the threat. Nonetheless, this realization makes the complicated analysis of our entanglements no less pressing. Our convoluted sociality does not drain the world of moral power or moral significance. Only from the perspective of an exclusivist or even imperialist individualism will such solidarity—of sorrow, of pain, of remorse—seem so menacing and isolating. Only when one privileges autonomy to such an extreme degree does participation with others appear to strip persons of a "self" and mean that they are not the author of jointly crafted projects or participants in shared acts of mercy.

The Enigmatic Closeness of Social Evil

A very different stance Augustine and Foucault find helpful in illuminating social evil is to explore its complex functioning not by following it out to the farthest extensions of power but by following it in to the intricate susceptibilities of human particularity. In other words, they adopt in various contexts an individualizing rather than an anonymous perspective. What threats can we identify in that which is nearest at hand and most familiar in our everyday lives rather than that which is most removed and depersonalizing? Foucault could easily be speaking for Augustine when he stresses the importance of searching for social evils up close, "where power reaches into the very grain of individuals, touches their bodies and inserts itself into their actions and attitudes . . . and everyday lives."[80] Both figures look to the materiality and vulnerability of the body for the most personal traces of social evil. It is here that evil comes to be at once intimate and foreign. It is intimate in that it gains a hold on what we consider to be most ourselves. It is foreign in that it works instrumentally against our own interests by permeating the interactive fluidity of our desires and the patterning of our habits, making it possible for manipulative relations of power to function spontaneously in our own bodies and minds. Of all the traces of social evil, these are the hardest to perceive since their effects are not forced upon us from without but are quietly embraced from within.[81]

Foucault often turns to biological metaphors and medical and scientific technologies to describe how "the materiality of power" is able to maneuver "through progressively finer channels, gaining access to individuals themselves, to their bodies, their gestures and all their daily actions."[82] A primary reason why Foucault depends on these terms lies in the fact that many of our daily attitudes and behaviors are shaped by medical or scientific ideologies and practices. The ways we relate to the micro-dynamics and micro-powers operating in our own bodies and our own minds largely fall under this framework of meaning. But medical vocabulary also helps to reveal particular characteristics of human vulnerability. Broad opportunities for social evil are brought into sharp focus using a grammar of biological manipulation and its corresponding instrumental utility. Scientific methods, diagnostic examinations, explorative techniques, and invasive procedures all highlight the exposure of the body to objectifying and penetrating regimens of power. And they do so in a way that is at once personal and impersonal. Anyone who has watched her organ being traced on a sonographic screen or has held in her hands a printed graph of her heartbeats or brain waves knows the eerie sensation of something being so intimately oneself and yet so antiseptically foreign. Body parts and their functioning are related to instrumentally in terms of their efficacy, whether they are contributing to or hindering organic energies, whether they require any interventions or therapeutic adjustments. They are clearly treated as vital life processes, but not necessarily as personal and one's own. It is in such a "network or circuit of bio-power, or somato-power," Foucault writes, that "we seem at once to recognise and lose ourselves."[83]

Foucault also finds scientifico-medical metaphors and terminology useful because their technologies are by nature innovative and resourceful in developing procedures that can modify biological activities with the least visible trauma. They are always searching for more precise techniques for getting in, altering or fixing particular micro-relations, and getting out with a minimum of mess, risk, and medical expenditure. Biological instrumentalism and utility, on Foucault's view, can be intensified and broadened in direct relation to their ease of operation or material application, to their economic feasibility and organic productivity, and to their diminishment of unsightly or contaminating social dangers. Human ingenuity is key to perpetuating this pursuit of ever more useful, efficient, and unobjectionable ways to manipulate the human body and modify its biological and social utility.[84] Finally, of special interest to Foucault is that the alterations such methods make possible, even if they are life-transforming, often remain hidden from public view. This is because these technologies work through and on biological particulars. They operate in many ways like a medical procedure, lacing sutures around delicate layers of tissues to configure, rearrange, separate, or pull together targeted dynamic processes. What catches Foucault's attention in this metaphor is how such techniques act not on the surface of the body but within the body's materiality, within its vital interactive functioning. In what ways, he asks, can the body's operational performance be permeated in depth so that a major social transfiguration or reordering of its micro-dynamics can be accomplished with little notice or monitoring? Like his apprehension about seemingly benign and thus unobjectionable instrumental precision and antiseptic orderliness, Foucault is attuned here to the dangerous possibilities of coercive social evils going unobserved.

Foucault's choice of language says something important about his concerns with both the influencing forces in the most intimate experiences of social evil and the susceptibility of the body to the material functioning of power. The two cannot be separated since the body's vulnerability is its materiality and the body's materiality is its power. "Materiality" here indicates a certain pliability or plasticity that can be handled or worked in various ways so as to foster or diminish one's physical and social well-being. As with anything related to power, the body exhibits a fluidity that can be shaped and modified for certain purposes. But materiality is not mere plasticity. It is not simply receptive and open to impression.[85] Plasticity, by itself, is passive and nonrelational. The material grains of the body that can be permeated and patterned in depth are not inert but intrinsically interactive, influencing life processes as well as being influenced by them. The materiality of power, therefore, must also be dynamic and relational; once one loses touch with or destroys this responsive vitality, one loses all power over the body. On Foucault's view, fundamental to being interactive is a capacity to act upon the actions of others and an ongoing potential to resist power's effects.[86] "Where there is power," he contends, "there is resistance."[87] Always, he insists, there must remain the possibility of "a reciprocal appeal, a perpetual linking and a perpetual reversal."[88] Such material resistance should be conceived less as a heavy weight tugging against something massively other and more as a movement that energetically spins off as it engages with something dynamically other.

Two questions come to mind in this discussion of the vulnerability of the body to the material functioning of power and its possible uses for social evil. First, are there not other more forceful and thus materially extreme modes of power? To many, a massive show of force would seem to wield the greatest power over the body since it can completely distort and break down its material structure. Power can flagrantly and without reserve disfigure the fragility of the body, lacerating, marking, and branding it as a publicly legible object.[89] It can exert such unbearable pressure on the whole integrity of the body's physical form that it turns its heavy and resisting substance into a light insubstantial powder, leaving it, in Foucault's words, as nothing more than "a body effaced, reduced to dust and thrown to the wind."[90] If such force can so abuse and deform the materiality of the body, how can it not be absolute power?

Foucault's response would draw us back to relationality and the central role it plays in power. Without question, this would be a horrendous and sickening display of raw violence. But, from Foucault's point of view, in refusing to engage with the interactive materiality of the subject and working instead to remake it into inert nonrelational matter, whatever power there may have been has chosen to emasculate itself.

> A relationship of violence acts upon a body or upon things; it forces, it bends, it breaks on the wheel, it destroys, or it closes the door on all possibilities. Its opposite pole can only be passivity, and if it comes up against any resistance it has no other option but to try to minimize it. On the other hand a power relationship can [be] exercised only over free subjects, and only insofar as they are free. By this we mean individual or collective subjects who are faced with a field of possibilities in which several ways of behaving, several reactions and diverse comportments may be realized. Where the determining factors saturate the whole there is no relationship of power.[91]

In essence, by treating the body as nothing but material, or by trying to turn the body into mere material, by grinding it to dust, power loses its own efficacy. It has nothing to work on; it can alter no dynamics; it can have no transformative relations and effects. Such force is so extreme that it forfeits in its own fury its ability to be in a power relation.[92] In this sense, from Foucault's point of view, domination and violence lose the game. Power is brought to bear on the body, but it is left in the end without any power over the body. Power works on the surface of the body, but it cannot permeate the functioning of the body and transform the body's living relations to itself. In sum, because it has no leverage over the interactive materiality of the body, it is incapable of exercising the materiality of power. As Foucault maintained about all restrictive and negative modes of power, a purely constraining or obliterating form of evil is "poor in resources, sparing of its methods, monotonous in the tactics it utilizes, incapable of invention, and seemingly doomed always to repeat itself."[93] It is paradoxically, however, also very costly. It only can maintain absolute dominance by expending excessive amounts of energy; by employing bodily force personally and with great intensity; by frequently reapplying physical abuse; and by leaving behind visible signs of a gruesome struggle that can be observed and objected to by other powers.[94] Raw violence plainly overwhelms the body, but in spending itself so completely and so publicly, it reveals its own uncontrollable weakness. It cannot help but be socially inefficient, difficult to implement, messy, and open to constant review.

A second perplexing question that arises is, Why would such a terrifying experience of force not be considered the most intimate form of evil? Absolute violence is certainly as direct as one can get in its bodily pain, as personal and heartrending in its anguishing distress, as particular in its often slow and precisely administered horror. But this is not the personal, intimate, and particular experience of social evil that Foucault sought to highlight. Foucault would wholeheartedly agree that such evils injure to an extreme, harming fragile bodies and fragile persons. The tangible costs of different forms of suffering were never far from his mind. Even though he prided himself on being a purely descriptive and not an evaluative historian, his writings and interviews are filled with a sense of pathos. He focuses on the small human details of broken and discarded lives. With an eloquent turn of phrase, he relates the stinging specificity of loss. He holds the reader's attention up close and for an uncomfortable length of time to long-forgotten wounds from long-ignored torments. Indeed, his portraits of personal misfortune can be so evocative and vivid as to make one's skin crawl. Foucault is thus not insensitive to the ravages that can consume utterly exposed bodies and persons. He conveys again and again how easily damaged human lives can become.[95] But Foucault's attunement to the fragility of individuals and to the ever-present possibilities for unjust discrimination, injury, and pain are distinguishable from his perceptions about the intimacy of certain social evils. The closeness of evil is not a matter of the closeness of suffering. Suffering can be intimate and personally degrading in all varieties of evil. Neither is it a matter of whether, or to what degree of extremity, the body is treated instrumentally. A person who is tortured, disfigured, and then put on public display is indisputably used as a political tool that serves the purposes of a dominating power.

For Foucault, the distinguishing factor is how different social evils function. How do they operate so as to work against an individual's well-being? How do they manipulate the particular vulnerabilities of various persons? How do they generate and spread? Since power can only be exercised in and through relations and since it is always created in an interacting network of multiple energies and dynamics, then the "demonic" or "darker side" of power must also function this way. It has to gain a firm hold over or covertly infiltrate the interstices where various relations cross and mutually influence one another. The finest grains of power work themselves into the cracks and joints of the most penetrating interrelations, those that actively constitute the ever-changing configurations of individual persons. These intimate micro-dynamics are constantly weaving laceworks of power that govern all of our activities and encounters. They shape perceptions, attitudes, and the various ways we give meaning to significant and insignificant events. They become part of the rhythm and spacing of our lives. By structuring our movements through different times and environments that are filled with other people and things, they form spontaneous interactive patterns that carry and sometimes sweep us along through hours and days and years. These most personal meshes of power pervade all of our energies and preoccupations. They are there when we engage with family members in the privacy of our homes, when we care for a friend in a tightly regulated hospital room, when we contemplate in the beauty of an empty sanctuary. They govern our gestures and words as we formally present arguments in public and our strategies as we struggle to find our way clear of embattling situations.

Such micro-dynamics exert pressure at all points and across all levels of individual persons. They filter through unreflective activities by maneuvering within, shaping, and controlling what Foucault calls "that whole lower region, that region of irregular bodies, with their multiple movements, their heterogeneous forces, their spatial relations."[96] By way of practiced, though often unthinking, repetition and regimented routine, they are able to "materially penetrate the body in depth without depending even on the mediation of the subject's own representations."[97] But they also can come into play through our conscious hopes and aspirations. These personal webs of power dynamically shape our reflective activities as we struggle with who we think we are and who we believe we should become; with which visions of perfection we should strive after and with what social goods, values, and norms we should judge by; with what persons we wager we can trust with our vulnerabilities and which dreams and desires we hope they will fulfill or emancipate us from. Constantly interweaving micro-relations make possible both our rudimentary skills and our highly polished aptitudes, talents, and aims. They mutually configure what we feel to be our deepest longings and the pleasures and allurements to which we seem naturally drawn. In short, such microdynamics form the closest and most intimate power relations because they operate everywhere a person goes and in everything that a person does, knowingly and unknowingly.

It is here, then, that social evils have the best opportunities to infiltrate and function as though they were simply a natural part of the individual's identity and daily life. As they penetrate personally interlacing depths and extensions, suffusing "those continuous and uninterrupted processes which subject our bodies, govern our gestures, dictate our behaviors," they seem more and more to just be there, intrinsically embedded in "our bodies, our lives, [and] our day-to-day existence."[98] This is obviously the most efficient and least costly way that social evils can influence persons. Rather than having to confront dangerous human energies, they can operate with complete ease. They do not have to work against the determined resistance of an individual, physically laboring to control a heavy substance that can shove its weight around and strain to break free. They do not have to inflict injury or disfigure or shackle the person, leaving traces of force that anyone can see. Instrumental coercion can enter into the minutiae of everyday life, slipping into even the most insignificant activities, movements, and gestures. Such manipulating power can trickle down into the finest grains of the body's functioning, being present everywhere—in the particularities of spatiality, temporality, habituation, reflection—and yet go largely unnoticed and unchallenged. Such hidden coercion can become self-perpetuating. It can thus act with complete precision, without any mess or violence, with no signs of struggle or possibilities of social revolt. And beyond this, it can appear as though it is giving individuals an affirming sense of order and security, even a promise of liberation from all that ails them.

While these most intimate of power relations govern all our personal encounters and accompany us wherever we go and in whatever we do, they do not function seamlessly or solitarily. Every person, as well as every community, is constituted by loosely coordinated relations that find support in one another, forming certain alliances here and counteralliances there. Particular micro-desires, pleasures, habits, rhythms, movements, and energies would have little effect on a person's life as small isolated pieces or bits. But when they become woven together, forming thickened strands that can extend into and across the individual's activities, they make specific attitudes, social skills, and aspirations more or less attractive and more or less achievable. They structure the possibilities of distinct patterns of behavior and guide the course and flow of varying desires. Likewise, other micro-relations can coalesce in opposite ways, forming alliances that work contrary to these and pull the individual in very different directions. Individuals can therefore never be monolithically saturated by instrumental power relations. They can only be permeated through various technologies and techniques that address, first, the ways in which tiny relations come to be strung together and can be made to run with or against one another and, second, how these aligning and counteraligning relations that govern the self in its own activities can be brought to bear on that self's relations with others.[99] As Foucault argues: "Power relations are rooted in the system of social networks. This is not to say, however, that there is a primary and fundamental principle of power which dominates society down to the smallest detail." They must always work through a diversity of finely articulated relations,

> taking as [a] point of departure the possibility of action upon the action of others (which is coextensive with every social relationship), multiple forms of individual disparity, of objectives, of the given application of ourselves or others. . . . The forms and the specific situations of the government of men by one another in a given society are multiple; they are superimposed, they cross, impose their own limits, sometimes cancel one another out, sometimes reinforce one another. . . . It would not be possible for power relations to exist without points of insubordination which, by definition, are means of escape.[100]

The possibility of resistance at the most personal levels through the use of micro-powers in modifying our relations to ourselves and to others conveys some of the most hopeful and overlooked aspects of Foucault's thought. "The exercise of power is not a naked fact, an institutional right, nor is it a structure which holds out or is smashed: it is elaborated, transformed, organized."[101] An individual does not have to defeat a threatening force in its entirety but can resist it in parts, at various points and at different levels, by working patiently and locally on one's own activities and on mutual activities in shared communities. One can still offer resistance and make significant alterations, though it be more piecemeal and indirect than, say, an outright assault on an imposing mechanism of power. "[P]ower relations are formed deep in the social nexus, not reconstituted 'above' society as a supplementary structure whose radical effacement one could perhaps dream of. In any case, to live in society is to live in such a way that action upon other actions is possible—and in fact ongoing."[102] Resistance, in this instance, involves the complex task of becoming aware of the effects of enculturation, and fighting against the alien and contingent but cumulative "naturalness" of certain damaging relations of power in oneself, in one's closest communities, in institutional and governmental structures, and in one's cultural and historical heritage.[103]

One does not have to break the back of a given social evil to resist its instrumental effects; important changes can be brought about even among the most insignificant seeming human interactions by working to alter the micro-fibers of power. If the tiniest threads can be frayed, an individual can weaken the heavy and intricate fabric that undergirds more socially consolidated and elaborately entangling manifestations of power's "demonic" sides. Foucault is drawn late in his career to broadly construed ascetical themes. He expresses an interest in the possibility that one can work against the grains of the self, sanding away gradually constituted attitudes and behaviors to open fresh social planes, and use meticulous self-forming activities to replace the old with new definitions and patterns.[104] He defines asceticism loosely as "a training of oneself by oneself" in order to become more personally adept at transforming particular micro-relations, so as "to moderate our acts, or to decipher what we are, or to eradicate our desires, or to use our sexual desires in order to obtain certain aims. . . . I call [this] the self-forming activity (*pratique de soi*) or *l' ascétisme*—*asceticism* in a very broad sense."[105] His last writings dwell increasingly on what he terms technologies of the self where particular techniques of training and concentration can be honed in service of one's own life.[106] "Care" best describes what Foucault is after here. "It does not mean simply being interested in oneself, nor does it mean having a certain tendency to self-attachment or self-fascination . . . ; it describes a sort of work, an activity; it implies attention, knowledge, technique."[107]

Such practices of care refer to another often overlooked possibility of resistance that Foucault finds attractive near the end of his life, namely, that the micro-dynamics and micro-powers that constitute individual persons can be brought into relation in such a way as to be given an aesthetic form. "What strikes me is the fact that in our society, art has become something which is related only to objects and not to individuals, or to life. That art is something which is specialized or which is done by experts who are artists. But couldn't everyone's life become a work of art? Why should the lamp or the house be an art object, but not our life?"[108] When Foucault talks about "an *art of existence* or, rather, a *technique of life*," he indicates that individuals have at least the potential to manage their lives according to some conception or vision of personal flourishing.[109] A highly skilled and carefully crafted life, he writes, would "permit individuals to effect by their own means or with the help of others a certain number of operations on their own bodies and souls, thoughts, conduct, and way of being, so as to transform themselves in order to attain a certain state of happiness, purity, wisdom, perfection, or immortality."[110] We have the potential, at least, "to build our existence as a beautiful existence," according to our own sense of social goods, values, and purposes.[111] Of course, that also means that a person can shape through a lack of personal governance an aesthetic disharmony or cacophony. Perhaps this would point to a hackneyed or vandalized rather than a beautiful existence and to inept or debilitating rather than skilled techniques of life. For Foucault, the one or the other—the harmonious or discordant existence, the skilled or the unskilled life—is not a matter of becoming free from all control. It concerns what kind of control and governance shapes one's life and how this control and governance interacts with and shapes the lives of others, and vice versa.[112]

Whether one is examining micro-dynamics and micro-powers in relation to instrumental dangers or in relation to aesthetic possibilities of resistance and creative transformation, they should not be considered self-isolating. Even the most personal micro-relations are not simply individual. Alliances and counteralliances of power continually permeate the boundaries of the self. This is why, in the context of social evil, they are so difficult to analyze in terms of the vulnerabilities they expose and the opportunities they create for different forms of social evil. Such personal webs of power tie in with people at home and at work; with political relations in local, national, and international communities; with institutional practices; with economic productivity and advancing technologies; with general cultural and historical trends that individuals simply find themselves born into. They certainly form in our most familiar and everyday interactions "an especially dense transfer point for relations of power: between men and women, young people and old people, parents and offspring, teachers and students, priests and laity."[113] But they simultaneously provide such transfer points for complex modes of social governance where "technicians of behavior: engineers of conduct, orthopedists of individuality,"[114] can involve themselves in the self's daily activities and interpretations by intervening, studying, and modifying the most intimate life processes.

Thus it is not only when Foucault examines the more personal arenas of power where "children, parents, students, educators, patients, doctors"[115] engage in relatively intimate settings that he analyzes the functioning and the effects of such small dynamics of power. These also form the center of his investigations of the largest and least personal institutions and state apparatuses as he tries to comprehend the particular hold they are able to maintain over individual persons, how deeply and extensively their diverse powers can move throughout different levels of society, and in what ways they have been granted cultural protection from social scrutiny, challenge, and monitoring.

> I think one needs to look . . . at how the great strategies of power encrust themselves and depend for their conditions of exercise on the level of the micro-relations of power. But there are always also movements in the opposite direction, whereby strategies which co-ordinate relations of power produce new effects and advance into hitherto unaffected domains. . . . [I]n order for there to be a movement from above to below there has to be a capillarity from below to above at the same time.[116]

One must be careful, Foucault insists, not to pursue a reductively "descending" analysis of power where a central dominating force simply reproduces itself over and over as it monolithically penetrates and controls lower and lower spheres of a pyramid. Even when targeting highly consolidated modes of domination, it is crucial to include in one's social critique "an *ascending* analysis of power, starting, that is, from its infinitesimal elements, which each have their own history, their own trajectory, their own techniques and tactics."[117]

The body and its dynamic materiality is a constantly changing field of struggle. It is a field of struggle for the individual as she attempts to shape and govern her life in relation to others. It is a field of struggle between individuals and their closest relations as communities mutually configure and reconfigure particular identities, values, and aims. And it is a battlefield where cultural and historical struggles play themselves out across the surface and in the depths of what we take to be most personally ourselves. The struggle over the control of the materiality of the body goes far beyond the body itself: it goes to the control of life, the control of aptitudes and skills, the control of discipline and habits, the control of values and attitudes, the control of desires and hopes. The body is a battlefield, but it is one of enormous proportions and enormous consequences.

Metaphors of Permeation

The metaphors Augustine chooses to convey the intimacy of a power that can reach into and shape the finest grains of individual bodies and lives are very different from Foucault's. We cannot dismiss the differences. For they will finally separate the two thinkers and set them on divergent paths. But such dissimilarities, for the most part, concern where the two figures envision their work taking them. In the everyday and incomplete task of simply trying to move along, they depict similar performative frailties or weaknesses that expose individuals to continual personal failures and coercively infiltrating social evils. It is in this common domain of human vulnerability—in the operational functioning and governing of everyday activities—that their descriptions of personally permeating and individualizing relations of power can be constructively examined together.

The most vivid metaphor for Augustine as well as Foucault for depicting the exposure of persons to the intimacies of social evil is the penetration and saturation of the flesh.[118] But their accompanying images could not be farther apart. When Foucault questions through "what channels . . . power is able to gain access to the slightest, most individual forms of behaviour," his answers often borrow language from the physical sciences.[119] Relations of power become "implanted in bodies, slipped in beneath modes of conduct" through capillaries that minutely interweave as they suffuse the social body, linking "molecular elements"[120] and "the most incalcitrant [sic] fibers of society."[121] An ever-circulating dynamism simultaneously "invests" bodies and persons as it is "transmitted by and through them"[122] in a "highly complex system of relations"[123] that includes but also elaborately extends beyond them. Thus, Foucault writes, the inherently interactive particularity of individual persons can be analyzed as "an effect of power, and at the same time, or precisely to the extent to which it is that effect, it is the element of its articulation. The individual which power has constituted is at the same time its vehicle."[124] I believe one reason Foucault employs such metaphors is that they allow him to communicate in tone, as well as description, the permeating yet seemingly detached and socially protected modes of power that he sees operating in diverse modern institutions that have been influenced by and continue to influence scientific discourses and practices. His analysis always anchors itself in people who suffer every day in flesh and blood: vulnerable children, women, and families; individuals being doctored for various illnesses and socially defined abnormalities; regimented workers and soldiers; prisoners, misfits, and outcasts. But the pitch of his language can at times allow the reader to drift rather far from the full, personal impact of ongoing human struggles.[125] That is why his writings at the end of his life are so important to moderate this tendency in his early and mid-career. "Technologies" are broadened so that they not only invasively work on and through human beings; they can also be used constructively by individuals, involving them in engaging projects and labors that require the intensive sharpening of personal skills, attitudes, and aspirations. The individual is still constituted in an intrinsically dynamic and interactive environment. But in the midst of dense yet richly diverse cultural relations, he or she can refine and create social techniques either to resist harmful relations of power and/or to shape his or her own aesthetic discernment and ethical interpretation of a beautiful existence.[126]

Augustine's rendering of the intimacies of social evil draw on experiences that are a world apart from the complicated micro-physics of organic processes. His most revealing descriptions and insights are wrapped in a language of longing. Indeed, Augustine's *Confessions,* the book that best details and examines performative frailties and struggles, is filled with the images of a love letter: "I . . . sing you hymns of love, groaning with grief that I cannot express as I journey on my pilgrimage."[127] He agonizes with the pain of separation and the toil of a long journey home. "[D]ay after day I poured out my heart to you,"[128] he writes. "Let the ears of my heart move close to your lips, and let me listen to you. . . . You are steadfast . . . ; but we are tossed on a tide . . . , and if we could not sob our troubles in your ear, what hope should we have left to us? . . . My soul was a burden. . . . It was tired of the man who carried it, but I found no place to set it down to rest."[129] "Let us come home at last . . . for fear that we will be lost."[130] The slowness of his progress and his many confused wanderings down deserted paths leading nowhere only heighten Augustine's language of desire and the intensity of the anticipated reunion. His searing tone could not be more different from Foucault's air of cautious remove: "how I burned with longing to have wings to carry me back to you";[131] "O Love ever burning, never quenched . . . set me on fire with your love . . . [132] so that I may come to you, my Sweetness and my Light."[133]

Augustine's narrative is obviously much more personal than Foucault's. It is an account of tender constancy and betrayal, joy and yet also unbearable grief and loss. Emotions for Augustine run close to the surface in images that often come from the Psalms and Paul's letters. He sighs and openly weeps on the breast of his beloved, allowing his tears to be gently wiped away; he yearns for the warmth of sheltering wings and a taste of refreshing water; he staggers in weakness and lets himself be carried when he finds himself too weary to journey on.[134] Delight and sadness are rarely separate in Augustine's metaphors but wash together in what he interprets as an offering of loving devotion. Describing his *Confessions,* he writes: "Let hymns of thanksgiving and cries of sorrow rise together . . . as though they were vessels burning with incense before you."[135] Naturally, Augustine's understanding of performative weaknesses and failures inevitably fall under this framework of love. Our human susceptibility to manipulation and injury is simply the reverse side of being able to be transfigured by an ardently faithful relationship. The way social evils enter into our lives is through a deficient effort to return love for love. Our vulnerability is the shadow side of our immense yearning to love and be loved. That we are utterly exposed in a relational world is not the problem for Augustine. The problem is that we have so little trust in and patience for fervent adoration and devotion that we move to control our own dynamic powers of loving and end up merely selfishly exploiting the fragile exposure of others.

In light of their dramatically different styles and preoccupations— Foucault looking to kinetic actions and reactions in the micro-physics of patterning energies, Augustine looking to rejuvenating rest in the expectant embrace of a transformative love—how extensive a conversation could develop concerning the ways in which individuals become interactively "invested" or subjectively constituted as dynamics of power in general, or social evils in particular, are "transmitted by and through them?"[136] As has been the case throughout my analysis, it is in the finer working details of their conceptions of love and power and not in their broader interpretative or explanatory frameworks that the two have the most socially useful insights to offer each other. No metanarrative pressure has to be brought to bear at this operational or performative level. Any direct dialogue would have to honor the fact that Foucault has carefully focused on the often unnoticed particularities of human fragility so as to alert readers to contemporary opportunities for and dangers of a "political investment of the body."[137] The "micro-physics" of power that Foucault tries to fix in his lens allow in the mundane course of daily activities the infiltration and spread of what he describes in one context of institutional exploitation as "[s]mall acts of cunning endowed with great power of diffusion, subtle arrangements, apparently innocent, but profoundly suspicious, mechanisms that obeyed economies too shameful to be acknowledged, or pursued petty forms of coercion."[138] The penetration and transmission of such a hidden coerciveness, he argues, can only be described "in the inextricability of a functioning" and "with great attention to detail.... For the disciplined man, as for the true believer, no detail is unimportant, but not so much for the meaning that it conceals within it as for the hold it provides for the power that wishes to seize it."[139] His intent in describing these relational vulnerabilities in such extensive specificity and minuteness, he explains, is to "seek not a meaning, but a precaution."[140]

I would wager that Augustine and Foucault would both agree on the need for such precautions. And the very ordinariness of our performative strivings, frailties, and failings should make the sounding of any alarm appreciated by each. Moreover, Foucault does not deny that a more expansive analysis about meaning could have importance. So one would be justified, I would argue, in applying his analysis to sociological, ethical, or even theological questions that stretch beyond the limited scope of his research. "If, for the time being," he writes, "I grant a certain privileged position to the question of 'how' it is not because I would wish to eliminate the question of 'what' and 'why.' Rather it is that I wish to present these in a different way."[141] Because Foucault tends to emphasize the dangers of an extrinsic intrusion into and political manipulation of day-to-day life while Augustine is caught up in investigating both the constructive and coercive potential of internal self-relations of power, they can extend what one might call the geographic reach of the other. They can provide more detailed precautionary maps of complicated territories that each shows an interest in and, indeed, explores in his most mature works—as Foucault demonstrates in his writings on the technologies of the self and Augustine in his discussions of numerous historical and political exploitations in the *City of God*. Any conversation between Augustine and Foucault on performative vulnerabilities has certain definable limits, but these can be stretched in various directions that do not violate the other's work and may indeed enrich the possibilities of their social and historical explications.

The densest and richest area of overlap in Augustine's and Foucault's analysis of the intimate functioning of power relations is the shared conviction that the materiality of flesh and the particularity of subjective identities are both at the same time radically configurable and configuring. Augustine would agree with Foucault that this does not point to a plasticity that renders individuals passive and nonrelational; rather, it reveals the fundamentally dynamic and interactive character of human persons and activities. Although Augustine dwells frequently on the sweetness of rest, his own life and all human lives are indelibly marked by restlessness.[142] We remain, he says, perpetually "in suspense."[143] Human beings are always on the move, pressing forward with objectives, straining to reach and either embrace or consume various loves, being pulled here and there by alluring or coercive forces, and pushing others here and there, applying vigorous powers of persuasion and seduction. Even when Augustine is weighed down with exhaustion, he still characterizes his experience as one of unceasing movement: "I went on my way, farther and farther from you, proud in my distress and restless in my fatigue."[144] Sometimes Augustine depicts this intrinsic dynamism as a sheer burden.[145] At other times he portrays it as a necessary, stimulating tension that breathes life into an ever-moving adoration and devotion: "[P]erfection in this life is . . . to press forward with purpose . . . ," he writes, and "the safest purpose for him who seeks is to continue seeking. . . . Let us, therefore, so seek as if we were about to find, and find as if we were about to seek. For 'when a man has done, then he begins.'"[146] Love is a perpetual striving toward the unattainable, a yearning that cannot be fulfilled. It can be inflamed to strain more ardently, but it cannot be quenched or soothed into a quiescent immutability. Such love, he writes, never stops pursuing so that what it seeks "may be founder sweeter" and so that what it finds "may be sought more eagerly. For what is said in the book of Ecclesiasticus can be understood in this sense where Wisdom says: 'They that eat me shall yet hunger, and they that drink me, shall yet thirst.' For they eat and drink because they find; and because they eat and drink, they yet seek."[147] If there is rest at all, it is the rest of a circularly flowing love.[148] Whether Augustine describes dynamism positively or negatively, he is adamant about one thing: it goes to the core of being human. When he asks himself the all-embracing question, "What is my nature?" his reply is simple and to the point: "A life that is ever-varying, full of change, and of immense power."[149] Even Holy Jerusalem is essentially dynamic. Because it energetically cleaves in love without interruption, it becomes "free from all vicissitudes of time."[150] But it still remains engaged at every moment and is therefore interactively configurable. "[M]utability is inherent in it," Augustine writes, "and it would grow dark and cold unless, by clinging to you with all the strength of its love, it drew warmth and light from you like a noon that never wanes."[151]

There is a certain kinetic energy in striving continuously after temporal or divine loves that is reminiscent of the vitality that Foucault describes as characteristic of all power relations. Just as seeking is immediately ignited by a finding that can be participated in but never possessed, and finding is immediately ignited by a desiring that can be intensified but never sated by what it seeks, so too do the active and reactive energies in Foucault's understanding of power perpetually spark new engagements, reconfiguring relations but never coming to rest in them. The primary difference between the two conceptions of such ceaseless activity is that for Augustine all loves are purposive. They move toward a goal that shapes them directionally, even if that goal can only be anticipated and not reached in this life. This purposiveness, however, does not diminish the radically active foundation of human life. Instead, it increases it since, on Augustine's view, it involves foretastes that are simultaneously intimate and distant. It naturally produces a bittersweet savor that stimulates the intensity of yearning and thereby electrifies its dynamic drive. There is actually a greater tension in Augustine's temporally extended kinetic activities than in Foucault's more compressed notion of a present wherein actions and reactions constantly engage with each other. Of course, for Foucault, even if such activities shape instantaneously, their energies are structured by social and historical patterns that inevitably leave their mark on us as they are acted upon. What sets Foucault apart from Augustine is that they configure presently and historically, but not expectantly, which is the primary configuring mode Augustine looks to in his moral analysis.[152] The future is really the present for Foucault. His questions always probe how the present has been constituted and, given this, what can be made of the present now.[153] The future may offer a contrasting conception that helps to reconfigure the limits of the past in the present or one that helps to break out of the encrusted ruts that would otherwise make a determined future into one's present. But this is still solely oriented to clearing space for oneself and one's community so as to construct and reconstruct in the inspiration and creative power of the present. In Augustine's understanding of the term, this is not a real future that has any performative tension to it. For Foucault, the future does not demand things from us; only the present does. Augustine holds just the opposite view. The future calls to us, and our personal successes and failures are all measured by how far we are able to move toward its embrace, that is, to move out of a temporary and fractured present and into an enduring future.[154]

Obviously, the evaluative interpretations of the dynamic character of life and the moral challenges individuals and communities confront as they struggle to govern their activities accordingly are different for each figure.

Augustine will assess such performative demands and patterns by way of a purposive and transforming future whereas Foucault will look to a creatively centered and supple present. However, this distance in perspective quickly diminishes as they turn from the larger personal implications of being radically dynamic creatures to the configuring minutiae of individual lives. As they look closely not at performative objectives per se but at the potential problems with performance itself, their analyses of the intimate functioning of social evils begin to converge. Standing out clearly to both are the vulnerabilities of persons to finely adjusted alterations or radical permutations in a social world that is interactively constituted. For Augustine as well as Foucault, individuals are never configured and do not operate monolithically. Rather, they are laced by minuscule relations of empowering loves that, as they become tied in different ways, sometimes work together and sometimes work against each other, making certain courses of action more appealing and performable and others less so. Because intermingling and often competing desires and habits structure the possible field of personal activities, Augustine would generally agree with Foucault that shaping these smallest dynamic relations is the easiest way for social evil to disrupt a person's overall functioning. Augustine would further agree that working at such an intricate operational level makes it possible for an individual to be harmfully influenced not by violent force that transgresses one's personal will, but effortlessly and unreflectively as such transfigured self-relations become more and more a "natural" part of one's everyday routines and sense of identity. As we will examine in the next chapter, what Augustine gives us that Foucault does not is a personal account of how such "micro-dynamics" or "micro-powers" actually play themselves out in an individual's life. By inviting us to view his own performative struggles, we are able to examine more concretely how a person's ability or inability to govern his everyday activities can be minutely yet pervasively influenced in both visible and invisible ways. Augustine thereby offers thicker descriptions of a process that Foucault seemed interested in, first, because of its political implications for instrumentally controlling other persons, and, second, because of the opportunities that may be created for controlling one's own self.[155]

Desires, Habits, and Governance

A Case Study of Performative Vulnerabilities

To better understand our relational frailties and the invasive reach of social evils, we need to analyze how desiring and habituation constitute personal and communal identities and effectively structure everyday capacities. A range of more or less performable activities are continually being shaped through intra- and interpersonal configurations of specific pleasures, dispositions, aspirations, and aptitudes. Augustine's autobiography offers us a theologically nuanced and descriptively rich case study for examining the ambiguities that both he and Foucault identify as operating in these most vital of all micropower relations. By considering the ways that Foucault would make sense of Augustine's struggles in commanding his day-to-day aims and activities, we get an illuminating look at both the vulnerabilities involved in being desiring and habit-forming creatures and the theological applicability of Foucault's critical perspective, analytical tools, and social precautions.

In the *Confessions,* Augustine is very clear that he finds life in all its diversity and complexity a bundle of perplexing questions, the most baffling of which have to do with managing his own life. "O Lord," he laments, "I am working hard in this field, and the field of my labors is my own self. I have become a problem to myself, like land which a farmer works only with difficulty and at cost of much sweat."[1] His questioning takes him in a variety of directions—wondering about time and eternity, about the interactive functioning of the mind, and about wisdom, knowledge, and the philosophical search for an elusive certainty. However, for most of the *Confessions,* the problem Augustine wrestles with is not one of discerning the truth about himself or the universe or the right courses of action that he should follow but one of motivation and ability.[2] The majority of his labor is spent on simple governance, on trying to mold desires and construct habits such that he can move closer to what he envisions as a glorious or "beautiful existence." He often finds himself at a performative impasse that he interprets as expansively social and historical, not simply personal. When he says he is a problem to himself, that self has permeable barriers, just as Foucault's does. This is not a modern notion of an autonomous subject. It is a deeply interrelated self that cannot seem to get moving in directions conducive to its own best interests. Augustine's most personal problems do not even start with his own life; they are rooted in a shared performative history that entangles all of human society. "If Adam had not fallen from you," he writes, "the seed that flowed from him would not have been this bitter sea, the human race, forever chafing for knowledge in the profound depths of its ignorance, buffeted by storms of its pride and never at rest from its surge and swell."[3] There is an intimate solidarity in Augustine's confessions about his personal frailties and failures that points beyond the narrow boundaries of his own self. They speak, as he puts it, to "all who accompany me on this pilgrimage, whether they have gone before or are still to come or are with me as I make my way through life."[4]

Before we undertake a closer examination of desires and habits, one other point bears mentioning concerning Augustine's personal sense of social solidarity and the questioning of his performative abilities. It is not the case that Augustine thought of himself as a moral problem only prior to conversion. Given his great status in the church, Augustine's openness about the continuing inadequacies of his spiritual progress would have been shocking to his audience, especially when compared to the stylized accounts of heroic Christian figures that were circulating at the time.[5] Readers would have expected the *Confessions* to end after his conversion, when he seemed to be at a spiritual pinnacle. But instead Augustine continues, even in his role as bishop, to be profoundly humble about his abilities, saying such disquieting things as "The pleasures I find in the world, which should be cause for tears, are at strife with its sorrows, in which I should rejoice, and I cannot tell to which the victory will fall."[6] Or, in relation to understanding God's law in the universe: "I have long been burning . . . to confess to you both what I know of it and where my knowledge fails; how far the first gleams of your light have illumined me and how dense my darkness still remains and must remain, until my weakness is swallowed up in your strength."[7] The metaphor Augustine repeatedly relies on for describing his experience of persisting spiritual and moral weaknesses is infirmity and ongoing rehabilitation. The model of the Christian life Augustine exemplifies and commends, therefore, is not one of perfection that would set him apart from his congregation but one of shared wounds and ongoing suffering that demand the healing mercy of God and a constant attentive care for one another. Understanding this pervasive fragility and susceptibility demands that we explore the complex involvement of human desires and habits in our loftiest as well as our most mundane endeavors. Although desires and habits function together, in what follows I tease them apart for the sake of analysis before examining them in relation to one another.

The Power of Desiring and Social Configuration

Certainly what has been identified with Augustine's performative struggles more than anything else is his battle with the disrupting influences of sexual concupiscence. Most would probably think it not far off to say facetiously that while Foucault wrote a book entitled *The History of Sexuality,* Augustine wrote one that should have been entitled *The History of My Sexuality.* That is true enough to be misleading. There is much in the *Confessions* dealing directly with Augustine's struggles with sexual yearnings. However, his dramatic recounting of this, especially in the earlier parts of his life, can lead to hasty conclusions about his broader understanding of faithfulness, temptation, and sin, and about the extensive ways in which desires work in conjunction with habits to configure the materiality of the flesh and the subjective identity of the whole person. There is ample evidence in Augustine's narrative to demonstrate that sexual concupiscence is not the root cause of disorder. It is merely a symptom of a much more foundational problem with governing human life.

Examples of illicit sexual experiences are important for Augustine not only because they consumed so much of his energies in the past and make up so much of his present regret but also because they provide him with a metaphor for the complete abandonment of self-control. If desire is understood as a longing that moves one toward or away from the love of God, sexual cravings can be described, according to Augustine, as a torrent that carries the body away in a flood of self-referencing pleasure. Augustine often associates sexual lust with images of being overwhelmed by natural forces. In his youth, he says, it was like being pulled by a rip current into a roiling sea or swept along by a tide and plunged off a precipice into a whirlpool.[8] But even here, when he seems most focused on pure carnal passion, he tucks his description into the more significant surroundings of love. "I cared for nothing but to love and be loved [*amare et amari*]. But my love went beyond the affection of one mind for another, beyond the arc of the bright beam of friendship. Bodily desire [*concupiscentia carnis*], like a morass, and adolescent sex welling up within me exuded mists which clouded over and obscured my heart, so that I could not distinguish the clear light of true love [*serenitas dilectionis*] from the murk of lust [*libidinis*]."⁹ Just as Foucault does not regard the violation of the body as sheer body to be the most "intimate" use of power, neither does Augustine view evil as simply acting on the mere physicality of the person. It is the body in relation that concerns Augustine, and this takes one beyond the overpowering features of sexual lust to a more interactively engaging and meaningful distortion of desire. Carnal lust by itself is too bound to biology to convey the intimacy of betrayal. It focuses on organs and not on the adulterous spirit. What is more personally hurtful in an affair, an act of two lustful bodies coming together or an act of love that expresses devotion and loyalty to someone else? Especially in the context of Augustine's intense language of longing and love, I would argue that forms of betrayal other than sexual concupiscence better communicate the intimacy of sin. These are betrayals of the heart acting in unison with the body, betrayals of the whole person.¹⁰

Some of Augustine's other images more vividly portray the disrupting desires that undermine a relationship where one partner is defined as "*a lover of faithfulness.*"¹¹ Two especially stand out in his text. The first draws on the language of fornication without attaching it to sexual wanderings. One who has promised himself to another is led astray not by carnal lust but by the attraction of a competing love that turns the heart away from an ever-faithful and patient lover. Augustine describes himself in this way as he recounts his passionate pursuit of literature and philosophy. Rather than bring him nearer to God, his enchantment with learning drew him away to a scintillating world of illusory truths, certainties, and successes. "O God, you are the light of my heart . . . and the Power that weds my mind and the thoughts of my heart. But I did not love you. *I broke my troth with you* [*fornicabar abs te*] and embraced another while applause echoed about me."¹² In a different context, when Augustine describes some of his wayward students, he focuses on the purposeful desires that orient their lives and interprets their lusts not in the narrow terms of violating this or that rule but as instances that convey a sweeping spirit of infidelity to a steadfast lover. "*They break their troth with you* [*fornicantur abs te*] by setting their hearts on fleeting temporal delusions and tainted money which defiles the hands that grasp it, and by clinging to a world they can never hold. And all the while they turn their backs on you who are always present, calling them back, and ready to pardon man's adulterous soul [*meretrici humanae animae*] when it returns to you."[13] Augustine's reference to fornication and adultery is not associated at all here with sexual lust or sexual misdeeds. This is a much more profound and expansive form of betrayal. The body, intellect, and heart comingle in the desirous movement that spurns the constancy of love and chases after affections that hold out the hollow promise of a self-absorbed freedom and happiness.

The second image Augustine comes back to again and again is the tireless love of a parent who worries about and waits for a reckless child to return home. The prodigal son who has only taken but never given seems an especially apt description to Augustine when reciting his earlier achievements in life. He relates the misuse of his own intellectual gifts for instrumental ends and contrasts his self-consuming desires with the forgiving tenderness and forbearance of a God who does not desert, even when one runs adrift.[14] Rather than use the talents he had been given so abundantly for the common good, Augustine says he left with them in hand, and wandered off "*to a far country* to squander [God's] gifts on loves that sold themselves for money."[15] Similar to the adultery image, the disordering of desires in this metaphor go far beyond the body. The shallow one-dimensionality of carnal desire is incapable of capturing the depth of this kind of betrayal where one has been moved to take everything from another who has chosen to give everything. Nor can it convey the graciousness of a love that withstands the sufferings of betrayal and freely forgives when the ingrate finally decides to come home.[16]

As these examples indicate, concentrating too narrowly on sexual concupiscence directs attention to a single instance of desiring that cannot possibly communicate the full forcefulness of human desires in configuring individuals as a whole or their extensive exposure to being penetrated and altered in depth either through their own or through others' activities. Notwithstanding the fact that Foucault discusses at length the role that early Christianity plays in developing a western cultural preoccupation with sex as *the* defining desire in human life, I am persuaded that he would have concurred with much of Augustine's broader social analysis of desire—had he understood it better. Most important, I believe they would have been able to agree on some of the key disadvantages of focusing on sexual concupiscence as the all-illuminating category for analyzing human frailties and performative weaknesses. Before turning to habits, we need to examine four points of comparison, not only to clarify the limitations of a preoccupation with sexual concupiscence, but also to elucidate their more complex understandings of the desiring person and the vulnerabilities that such desiring opens them to in a dynamically constituted social world. If Augustine and Foucault had engaged each other on these issues, the main areas of compatibility hark back to the relational parallels I discussed in the first chapter between their conceptions of love and power.

First, targeting sexual concupiscence as the sole or even primary villain disrupting our daily activities entails at least an implicit dualism that both Augustine and Foucault would have found untenable. Not only does it locate desires in the body as a brute physical force that is at odds with the rest of the person, seducing the chaste mind to participate in the body's shameful urges. It also locates such desires in a very specific functioning of the body, thereby reducing all other bodily meaning to one physical component of the person. Augustine's images of sex often seem to support such a view. The language of being dragged out by a tide or pitched off a cliff does not leave much room for the mind or the body to be meaningfully engaged with one another—or with anything else, for that matter. Such arresting images have given credence to the arguments of those who identify the cause and vehicle of original sin as carnal, or more specifically, sexual.[17] Objecting in part to the hostile ramifications of sexual concupiscence for the body as a whole, other commentators have pointed to Augustine's repeated emphasis on Adam's pride as the originating motivation of sin[18] and have argued that concupiscence is primarily a spiritual rather than a sexual disorder. Performative failures exhibit a sickness in the ordering soul.[19] I am much more persuaded by the latter than the former reading of Augustine. But I believe that it too must be careful not to slide into dualism. The privileging of either one or the other carries risks because both can disrupt the sustaining dynamism of desire as it simultaneously works through the body and the spirit.[20] The configuring power of desire draws energy from and shapes both the interactive materiality of the body in all of its relational capacities and the relational ordering of the spirit in all of its receptive and creative sensual capacities. The body or the spirit would languish with any severing of its complex web of relations that allows for circularly flowing desires to operate throughout the entire person.[21]

Let us look at two examples from Augustine and one from Foucault that illustrate this more integrative view of desires and the challenges it presents for analyzing the performative vulnerabilities of desiring persons. The first, adultery, we have already touched on. However, here, rather than focus on its metaphorical implications for betrayal in general, I want to consider the symbiotic functioning of desire that shapes and is shaped by individuals as they participate in such a sexual relation. If we were trying to depict an adulterous affair of love, we would risk distorting the interaction if we artificially separated the desires associated with the body and those associated with the heart or mind. The forging of the relationship and of the individuals involved would include not just the desires of the body but those of the spirit as well. We would not say that one desires only with the mind or only with the body; nor would we say that the desires of the mind do not influence the desires of the body or vice versa. They mutually engage and configure one another. In the fullest sense of the word, passion is the act of having the customary barriers and structuring contours of the mind, the heart, and the flesh permeated in such a way that intellectual, emotional, and sensual desires freely flow together. As they intermingle and suffuse the person as a whole, these differentiated but interpenetrating desires are dynamically transfigured in relation to one another. Being saturated by other desires, the mind and the heart, along with the body, are imbued with and altered by sensual sensitivities, receptivities, and longings; and the body, along with the heart and the mind, is likewise imbued with and altered by emotional and cognitive orderings and interpretive meanings. In Augustine's earlier description of sexual lust, he speaks of his bodily desires being allured by a confused understanding of love and his emotions and heart being enveloped in a dense mist of fleshly desires as his body together with his mind and his heart thirsted insatiably for delight and pleasure.[22] The sway of love is always primary for Augustine, but it is inevitably shaped by intermingling physical, emotional, and cognitive strivings. If we overly scrutinize the body alone, we end up, ironically, with an anemic understanding of the hold that desiring flesh can have on the entire person. The same would also be true if we were to try to isolate emotional or intellectual desires as the driving operational force or problem in our lives. The desiring flesh, the desiring heart, and the desiring mind cannot be easily separated from one another since, in light of our being intrinsically interactive, their energies are constantly engaging, supporting or counteracting, and reconstituting one another.

Augustine's experiences of beauty illuminate these issues from a different perspective. Beauty, I would argue, presented a far more persistent and perplexing challenge for him than did sexual lust. As book 10 in the *Confessions* reveals, even as a bishop, he had an intensely ambiguous relationship with beauty.[23] Throughout his life, he was easily entranced by the loveliness of light and fragrances and tastes and colors and rich textures and shapes.[24] So much so that he finds it difficult to tear his attention away or becomes dispirited if he is deprived of them for too long.[25] These were not occasional difficulties that surfaced as he walked in the country or contemplated beautiful art. They were at the center of his daily life, which he makes clear by relating how he wrestled with devotional hymns that he would have sung many times a day. In becoming absorbed in the sounds, Augustine describes his mind being more vigorously stirred and inflamed by words that are sensually sung rather than plainly spoken and his emotions being mysteriously stimulated by inspiring variations of voice, rhythm, and melody.[26] His intellect and his heart, along with his body, are sensualized in this experience of ritual beauty. The sensualization, in and of itself, is not problematic for Augustine; it can either heighten or diminish his devotional capabilities. His spiritual struggle is not over whether his bodily, emotional, and intellectual desires intermingle in such a way that they mutually intensify and configure one another. It is whether he refers these desires as a whole to the love of God or simply surrenders himself to the sweetness of their immediate pleasure.[27]

Beauty, for Augustine, is always a blessing and a temptation. As he confesses the many ways in which he continues toiling with all of the glorious things around him, he thanks God for the goods of creation before admitting his own weakness in properly valuing them in relation to God.[28] Being carried away by the senses can be spiritually beneficial, not harmful, as long as they carry one toward God. "No part of your creation ever ceases to resound in praise of you," he writes, " . . . our soul leans for support on the things you have created, so that we may be lifted up to you from our weakness and use them to help us on our way to you who made them all so wonderfully."[29] The irony in Augustine's life is that he allows himself to be so caught up in the resplendence of the world that he becomes unable to enjoy through these created blessings God's glory. God is present in them and they respond, he believes, with admirable praise and rejoicing, but he ends up lost in his own self-consuming enthrallment. Augustine thus envisions God as having to break through a world of sensual beauty that God is already manifest in so as to beckon Augustine's desires to what they are actually thirsting for, a transfiguring sensuality.

> I fell upon the lovely things of your creation. You were with me, but I was not with you. The beautiful things of this world kept me far from you and yet, if they had not been in you, they would have had no being at all. You called me; you cried aloud to me; you broke my barrier of deafness. You shone upon me; your radiance enveloped me; you put my blindness to flight. You shed your fragrance about me; I drew

breath and now I gasp for your sweet odour. I tasted you and now I thirst for you. You touched me, and I am inflamed with love.[30]

Perhaps the most important interpretive lesson to draw from this in understanding Augustine's view of desires is that he does not devalue the body or the material world over against the spirit; nor does he see these as functioning in separate, incompatible domains. He is not afraid of sensuality per se because it does not necessarily thwart his movement to God. Indeed, it seems to be one of the primary means by which he enjoys and expresses, in his limited human terms, the foretastes of Holy Jerusalem. The vision Augustine offers is of a "passionate" intermingling of desires where mind, heart, and body can freely interpenetrate and empower one another to cleave to God more energetically. Augustine can only maintain briefly these anticipatory experiences of rapture, but even so, they offer him moments of spiritual and sensual refreshment, reinvigorating him for what he expects will be a long and tiring journey.

While Foucault would never think in spiritual terms, I believe he would nonetheless appreciate Augustine's description of desires as being inextricably interwoven in embodied persons. Foucault, like Augustine, would object to any view of desiring that regionally segregated the interactive vitality of the whole individual, setting various functions apart or against one another in rigidly bounded and impermeable domains. Augustine's more symbiotic understanding of passion or even of rapture where the structuring boundaries of the mind, heart, and body can be permeated and dynamically transfigured would have been interesting to Foucault in many ways. Especially intriguing, I think, would have been the sensualizing potentialities and vulnerabilities of such interlacing relations, not just for governing the body, but the entire person. Because these desires can penetrate and deeply alter one another, emotional and interpretive influences can be as seminal as physical influences in shaping experiences of the body, and sensual formation and reconfiguration can be fundamental to constituting experiences of intellect, emotion, and will. Both Augustine and Foucault would have viewed these possibilities as personally and socially ambiguous. Clearly, for Augustine, his anticipatory moments of feeling sensually transfigured seemed to refresh his whole person, invigorating him to move forward with a greater sense of ardor and purpose. However, he also found that the free intermingling of desires made it difficult to control his daily activities. These relations could be so complex and overwhelming that it was hard for him to know where to begin unraveling the convoluted threads of desiring. Or they could be so subtle in their effects that he was not aware of how they influenced his sinning or even that he was sinning.

For Foucault's part, with his later emphasis on the personal opportunities for creating an aesthetic harmony in life, one would expect him to be interested in pursuing how a sensualization of the person as a whole could cultivate a governing balance in that individual's life. However, for most of his career, he spent more time worrying about the ways in which such configuring desires increase the opportunities of a political investment of the body. An enduring concern was the possibility that certain desires and areas of life could be altered in a seemingly innocuous and even solicitous manner while in fact bringing about changes in all sorts of activities, reshaping substantially a person's overall sense of self-identity. One could thereby become politically rearranged at the deepest levels of the self by way of simply having his or her personal desires modified. Like Augustine, Foucault cautioned that this could happen without an individual knowing it because of the minute relations through which such desires constantly move and interact. Such imperceptibility, he worried, heightens the political opportunities for intruding into the desiring process and culturally manipulating the relational fluidity of desiring creatures.[31] For Foucault as well as Augustine, therefore, nondualistic and integrative views of comingling desires generated, on the one hand, a vigilant awareness of susceptibility and, on the other, a sense of promise for transfiguring change.

Seen against the background of this dynamic and formative understanding of desires, one can see why both Augustine and Foucault would be wary of trying to make a single function of the body answer to all of our performative problems. By focusing on sexual concupiscence to the exclusion of other meaningful desires, we give it enormous power over ourselves while, oddly enough, not being aware of the full power of the interactive materiality of the flesh. We look so hard for a firm impression at the core of the body, for a branding mark that can reveal all that ails us, that we miss the fluidness of sensual desires—their openness to configuration, their ability to saturate and be saturated by every other form of desiring. For Augustine, that meant not being sufficiently aware of betrayals of the heart and the mind, of the subtle ways that the intellect and emotions can lure the body away from a steadfast love. Augustine indicates in one of his later writings that he had believed "for some time" that sexual continence is best understood as a manifestation of the higher continence of the heart.[32] Because the heart motivates and nourishes the striving for love, individuals can remain faithful in their activities only if they remain faithfully shaped by their hearts.[33]

Continence and infidelity should be construed, therefore, in broader terms than sexual concupiscence alone. The real intimacy of betrayal arises from a failure to govern the heart's inclinations that make a person actively receptive to the passing titillation of unfaithful sensual impulses. Such transient fascination takes hold not just of the body but of the mind and the soul in relationship with the body. What one misses, Augustine maintains, when focusing too closely on sexual concupiscence is the shattered chastity of the whole desiring person.

While Foucault would share Augustine's concerns that being preoccupied with finding a clear identifying mark in the lustful body blinds us to the extensive configuring powers of human desiring, he would interpret the resulting social toll differently. Because Foucault gives no purposive description of desires in the context of love, what stands out to him when we attempt to trace all of our performative problems to the fragility of sexual desires is not a deficient recognition of the breadth of betrayal and personal failure but an inadequate alertness to social exposure. Augustine and Foucault are both mindful that such a myopic focus on human desiring is costly to relationships. Both acknowledge that it diminishes our capacity to be attentive to others in society. However, to whom and how we specifically fail to be attentive differs considerably. Foucault's analysis makes visible relational dangers where desiring individuals are subjected through their own and others' expectations to social manipulations without sufficient cultural questioning or vigilance. It thus illumines especially well performative problems that threaten socially vulnerable persons. It is limited, however, in how much light it can cast on the moral failings within truly committed relations of love. Foucault offers little direct insight into the personal struggles individuals confront as they try to requite selfless acts of loyalty, trust, and unconditional devotion.

Nevertheless, while Augustine's and Foucault's analyses target distinct areas of human life, they are not mutually exclusive, and indeed work well together. They examine different performative weaknesses and different ways in which we are socially engaged. But such weaknesses function simultaneously in the same persons, in the same relationships, and in the same communities. They may at times operate at separate levels of a person's life, although they may also become imperceptibly interwoven. When Foucault speaks of individuals who are vulnerable, he is not simply addressing the special situation of outcasts in our society, although that is one of his burning interests.[34] Vulnerability can point to persons who are unloved and uncared for, persons who are either socially unnoticed and forgotten or who are treated as socially dispensable. However, vulnerability also inevitably points back to us all. Various individuals are more or less fragile, more or less socially exposed. But no one is invulnerable. Foucault, therefore, in many ways shares Augustine's sense of solidarity concerning the performative frailties of human desiring. We are all vulnerable, even if we do not recognize it, and even if we are in loving relations where we manage to be devoted and faithful.

The reason Foucault gives for dwelling on social exposure rather than the more private concerns of fidelity and betrayal is because of a modern cultural transformation in which, he contends, sexual desires are "no longer accounted for simply by the notions of error or sin, excess or transgression, but [are] placed under the rule of the normal and the pathological."[35] Thus desires are increasingly given meaning and value in our society in terms of health and sickness, beauty and ugliness, normality and abnormality, rather than sin and salvation. This is true for believers and nonbelievers alike in that they all are influenced by similarly unexamined social trends. Foucault does not imply that because of this cultural transformation, personal disloyalties cease to matter to individuals or that infidelities no longer involve the intermingling desires of the whole person in relations of love. He leaves those questions aside and instead pushes us to realize that in addition to intimate interactions in daily life, layers of cultural influences extensively configure our sexual desires and thereby shape our personal activities and identities in ways that we are not fully aware of. Foucault wants us to perceive and be continually alert to the complicated manner in which we become constituted as sexual persons, not simply through sensualizing relationships and sensualizing acts, but through the saturation of a sensualizing culture.[36]

We do not have to stretch our imaginations to recognize that Foucault has a valid concern. Just standing at the checkout line in a grocery store provides evidence enough that he is on to something. Magazine after magazine offers us an inside look not only into who among the famous are being unfaithful to whom and what this reveals about their private relationships or naughty characters. They also promise us an inside look into our own personal activities and identities. Definitive tests are proffered that can determine whether you and your partner are sexually proficient and compatible, whether you are sexually deserving of one another and what to do if one fails to satisfy. Sexual, beauty, and health tips are dished out to help observe and gauge self-esteem, emotional well-being, personal pleasures and happiness, relational aims and the means for reaching them. And of course beyond all of the "expert" advice on how to evaluate and modify yourself as a sexual person and how to alter your partner to better meet your needs, there are the endless messages about bodies themselves—thin bodies, tanned bodies, young bodies smoking as they wear provocative clothing and thrill in their seeming rebellion.[37] All these run along the lines Foucault suggested of a twin cultural obsession with pathology and normalcy. Am I sexually healthy and meriting of love? Does my partner measure up to my sensual expectations, my emotional needs, my relational fantasies and dreams? How do we both stack up against others in how we behave, how we look, what we find desirable, what we fail to find desirable? This self-absorbing emphasis on pathology and normalcy becomes strangely intertwined in that, on the one hand, such magazines and advertisements lure people in fascination toward the abnormal while, on the other, rigidly binding them in what they accept in themselves and their partners as relationally normal or worthy.[38]

Such cultural influences are difficult to evade. If one stays away from magazines, one still sees billboards, hears the radio, watches television, goes to the movies, tries to squeeze into clothes according to changing fashions, socializes by following the rules of one's peers. None of these cultural influences, Foucault would argue, form a part of a sinister master plan of sensualization. However, in practice, they connect loosely related power relations in our lives and communities, creating "'erotic zones' in the social body" and a cultural mesh of sensuality that saturates personal identities and behaviors as much or more than our intimate relationships.[39] Without being aware of it, Foucault argues, we partake in a "sensualization of power" wherein personal interpretations about one's body and self-identity are deeply configured by diverse cultural discourses and practices, and personal experiences of the body in daily life tangibly establish and sustain the "reality" and force of those cultural influences.[40] An unmonitored process can thereby become self-propelling so that pleasure spreads "to the power that harried it" and power is "anchored" in "the pleasure it uncovered."[41] Because of the symbiotic dynamics of human desires, these "perpetual spirals of power and pleasure" are able to sensualize, along with one's body and one's sense of sexuality, one's intellect, emotions, and will.[42] All of these shape and are shaped by one another; and all shape and are shaped by the practices of a specific culture.

The performative frailties that emerge in Augustine's and Foucault's analyses of human desiring do not contradict one another. In fact, when viewed together, we see a much larger and multilayered picture of relational dangers. Augustine offers a richer description of the personal vulnerabilities of friendship and love while Foucault gives a much thicker account of the social vulnerabilities involved in being culturally constituted creatures. Either one alone, I would argue, risks leaving us with a diminished notion of our performative weaknesses. If we just look to Augustine for guidance, it may appear that human desires are formed one-dimensionally through more or less easily monitored personal relations and acts. If we look to Foucault alone, it may appear that individuals cannot maintain a loving intimacy because their privacy is constantly intruded upon by the culture at large. When taken together, Augustine and Foucault give a more accurate portrayal of the constructive opportunities and the perils of desiring than either one alone. Since they operate with a similar understanding of desires as being fundamentally dynamic, nondualistic, and integrative in their functioning throughout the whole person, we can combine the best of their insights without violating the integrity of each one's thought. They can thereby extend the range of what we must attend to in human relations.

A second main point of comparison concerning the drawbacks of relying too exclusively on sexual concupiscence as providing clear-cut answers to the difficulties of daily governance pertains to Augustine's and Foucault's understanding of how desires operate and are optimally managed in relation to power. If sexual concupiscence is targeted too narrowly as the primary weakness in our lives, it may entice us into thinking that if we can just impose this or that rule on our bodies we can successfully rein in desiring. As such, it assumes that the chief functioning of power is repressive, its task being to chase down runaway desires and fence in their rebellious impulses and energies. This holds out the illusion that if we can crush or muscularly restrain desiring, governance will freely return. Implied here is the notion of desire and power as operating separately, coming together as mortal enemies so that one or the other, but not both, will be left standing at the end of their battle for dominance.

Augustine and Foucault both advance an opposing conception of desires in relation to power. In his treatise "On the Spirit and the Letter," Augustine asserts that the negative coercive force of law "which forbids sin fails to give man life, but rather 'killeth,' by increasing concupiscence, and aggravating sinfulness by transgression."[43] Imposing restrictive rules not only fails to control and abolish unruly desiring, it may actually kindle the flame and fan its spread. That is because the inherently dynamic energies of desiring cannot be pulverized or intimidated into passivity. Nor would we want to demolish the force of desiring since it is the motivating and sustaining drive in our lives. We must live with the difficult practical reality, Augustine argues, that human desires can only be redirected by stronger desires. The one sure way to reconfigure desires is through the interactive process of desiring itself. Rather than have the life squeezed out of them, therefore, disorienting desires must be drawn to a new and reinvigorated life. They must be persuasively allured and transfigured by the appealing power of delight, not by the threatening power of destruction. Only through this more constructive functioning of power can desires be redirected through love to their proper end and spontaneously fulfill the law they pursue. "For no fruit is good," he writes, "which does not grow from the root of love."[44] Spontaneous love, however, cannot be generated in our own self-enclosed circle of desiring. It must be given as we participate in and are transformed by God's transcending dynamics of love.

While Foucault has no use for the religious language of grace, he comes to a similar conclusion about the inadequacies of restrictive notions of law. "Repression" is the weakest rather than the strongest use of force in power relations.[45] Indeed, he would agree with Augustine that it often paradoxically stimulates and spreads the very desires and pleasures it sets out to control. His discussion of the "repressive hypothesis" in *The History of Sexuality* provides a case in point. Although, Foucault argues, we have tended to think of the seventeenth century as having established a rigid censorship of sex, the forbidden secrecy such tactics cultivated did not dampen but rather aroused interest in the fascinating dangers of lust. The concupiscence that was supposedly shut behind locked doors and whispered about in hallways ended up being inflamed, not extinguished. Instead of eliminating public discussion, Foucault asserts that this prohibitive exercise of power ironically resulted in "a veritable discursive explosion" aimed at uncovering, monitoring, and mastering the hazardous mysteries of sex.[46] "Repression" turned out to be not static at all in its constraining force but formative and transfiguring. It shaped cultural attitudes in unexpected ways as it captivated people's imaginations about the social dangers it forbade and as it opened access to threatened personal "sites" in the social body for therapeutic examination and intervention. This is just one example showing that desires, for Foucault as well as Augustine, are so inherently active that sheer coercive repression does not bring about passivity but simply a different form of responsive activity. The most efficacious and transformative power relations are therefore those that configure desires by alluring and enthralling, those that work with rather than against the inherent activity of human desiring. A narrow reliance on prohibitive rules for restraining and governing the body will always be frustrated unless they somehow are able to enter into the desiring process itself and transform the interactive dynamics of the desiring person as a whole and his or her relation to a desiring culture.[47]

A third point of comparison addressing the limitations of an exaggerated focus on sexual lust has to do with the language of creating and transmitting sin. By concentrating too intensely on sexual concupiscence, we can blind ourselves to the full generative power of human desiring. This may sound implausible at first since rooting sin and evil in the biology of sex would seem literally to explain its begetting and spreading. However, this very literalism that accounts for the universality of sin so straightforwardly hinders our appreciating Augustine's metaphorical use of images of propagation for understanding the wider productivity and spreading forcefulness of desiring. Augustine is drawn to the concepts of begetting and conceiving to illustrate the interactive and creative powers of love. Desiring, because of its intrinsic dynamism and relational "coupling,"[48] is always involved in producing and reproducing, bringing forth and passing on. His positive and negative use brings to light the ambiguity of desiring and the ways it can enhance or disrupt the governance of our activities.

Consider what Augustine says about knowledge. He describes desire (*appetitus*) as the generative energy "by which knowledge is conceived."[49] The mingling dynamics of human desires engender a "birth in the mind, and by means of it, by our seeking and finding what we wish to know, an offspring, namely, knowledge itself is born."[50] Knowledge can be pursued contemplatively as one selflessly strives to embrace the love of God. Here, desire gives birth to the other-referencing activities of *caritas*. But knowledge can also be used instrumentally, as, for example, when we engage in investigations in an attempt to control and manipulate the object of inquiry. According to Augustine, this selfish craving for dominion "masquerades under the name of science and learning."[51] It does not love the unknown, he writes, but actually hates it. It is a goad in the side, spurring one on to acquire and intellectually master objects "merely for the sake of knowing."[52] Such attempts Augustine describes as a prideful but, in the end, futile grasping after certitude. As it "lusts after the knowledge which is derived from experience with changeable things, [it] is puffed up, but does not edify."[53] Because of the intrinsic futility of its quest, it develops an insatiable hunger to chase after and consume the unknown. The sexual overtones are obvious, but his point concerns the misuse of a wider range of appetites.

The same pattern of employing the metaphor of procreation to illuminate the ambiguity of desiring more broadly understood is evident when we turn to Augustine's view of sensual desiring. As we saw in the earlier discussion of beauty, he relishes sensual experiences, he delights in them, and it is possible for them to carry him closer to God.[54] More often than not, however, he finds himself so fascinated by them that his imagination becomes absorbed in them. He enjoys them for their own sake or for his own pleasure, instead of loving them in and through God. He tries to prolong what is fleeting, to possess what can never be owned, to embrace what cannot be held. A rightly oriented will, Augustine writes, seeks only that which can be

> possessed in a chaste embrace, not privately but commonly, without any narrowness or envy by all who love such things. . . . But when it does anything in order to obtain those things which are perceived through the body, because of its lust [*cupiditatem*] for experiencing them, excelling in them, or handling them, so that it places the end of its own good in those things, then whatever it does, it does shamefully; it commits fornication, sinning against its own body . . . ; covetous of its own selfish possession it becomes prolific in errors.[55]

Once again, sexual imagery is being used to represent the consuming and domineering desires of other behaviors. Sexual fornication exemplifies but does not exhaust the ways we act to master and devour.[56] In the case of self-centered acquisitiveness, Augustine declares, what is relationally "conceived by desiring [*cupiendo concipitur*] is born by attaining."[57] Since such attainment is always transitory and ultimately unfulfilling, it excites but never satisfies the yearning. This sets off a pattern of grasping engagement with no lasting gratification. What can only be embraced momentarily conceives fresh longings to possess and consume that, in turn, beget still more disappointments and renewed yearnings for control, ensnaring one in an endless cycle of illegitimate reproduction.

When used metaphorically, such procreative images convey the much broader disseminating powers of human desire than can the body alone. In any activity of a given day, when one is out running errands or working closely with colleagues or picking up children from school, the dynamic and life-giving force of relational desires can issue in new acquisitive impulses and acts that then engage with other selfish and consumptive desires, thereby spreading "fornicating" evils through even the most insignificant and innocent-seeming encounters.[58] The spreading of sinful desires is certainly rooted in and depends on the body in its daily round of activities, but it is also embedded in social and historical attitudes to attainment that culturally influence a community's longings and aims.[59] Since all of these together constitute who we are as desiring persons and form our specific aspirations, they all participate in the productive processes of conceiving and begetting.

As we have seen, one of Foucault's most important contributions to cultural criticism is his perception of power relations as being fundamentally creative rather than just oppressive and prohibitive. Our modern social preoccupations and our individual patterns of desiring, Foucault argues, are culturally, historically, and biologically shaped by "a power bent on generating forces, making them grow, and ordering them, rather than one dedicated to impeding them, . . . a power that exerts a positive influence on life, that endeavors to administer, optimize, and multiply it, subjecting it to precise controls."[60] Foucault's detailed historical descriptions of varying creative and dispersing capabilities of power can be related in constructive ways to Augustine's metaphorical discussion of human desires and social evils as "procreating."

Such productivity is first of all for Foucault as well as Augustine socially ambivalent. It is the most promising and the most hazardous aspect of power. It is what gives us the greatest hope that we will finally not be trapped by social evils, that we have the constructive ability as potent creatures to transfigure our lives and significant portions of our culture that we will pass on to later generations.[61] However, the power to generate and influence life also exposes us to dangerously subtle and difficult to monitor techniques of exploitation. That is because, to repeat a point from chapter 2, this creative productivity can enter into our desires, and through our desires, sink into our bodies and biological functioning. It thus can modify material traces and interactive capacities that we are unaware of in our daily lives and that we can unconsciously transmit in our life-affirming or life-fostering engagements with others. Such productivity can also seep into the social body more broadly understood, generating and directing the life forces and energies of whole populations.[62] In a context of power's (pro)creativity—whether it be dealing with individuals, local communities, or large populations—Foucault would find especially interesting Augustine's metaphorical use of propagation to elucidate the dynamic activity and social ambiguity of knowledge. Augustine's description of an arrogant and instrumental acquisitiveness trying to take cover under the name of "science" is, as we will see in the next two chapters, Foucault's central concern with modern instrumental uses of life-administering discourses and practices. Finally, for those Augustinian scholars who would like to jettison biology completely from an analysis of original sin and focus essentially on pride, Foucault provides an interesting rationale for why that may be unwise. He alerts us to the potential biological dimension in pride's exercise and transmission. We are materially (and not just psychologically or spiritually) invested by social, historical, and personal prideful patterns of behavior, and the biological functions that become thus interactively configured in turn actively fashion new prideful modes of activity that spread through social, historical, and personal relations. Biology, in this sense, along with culture and history, does have a significant role to play in the conception, birth, and spread of social evil.

The final problem with overemphasizing sexual concupiscence is that it does not sufficiently convey either the magnitude or the emotional richness and complexity of competing loves. Of all the ways that desires can disrupt or cripple performative capacities, conflicting goods, loyalties, and devotions that entice the desiring self to move in opposing directions are, on Augustine's view, the most chronic and painful. While Augustine is adamant, at least in his mature writings, that persons should be understood in nondualistic terms, he is equally certain that this nondualistic self is fractured through and through.[63] Sexual lusts account for many of the splintering desires that tug against one another, but they do not prove to be the most powerful. As we have seen from earlier examples, Augustine attaches deeper significance to struggles of the heart. Considering his life as a whole, his love for learning, his absorption in writing and teaching, and his enjoyment of beauty presented stronger or at least longer-lasting conflicts than did sexual yearnings. Perhaps the most bittersweet tension for him was his proclivity to love friends and family too much.[64] He describes friendship as "sweeter . . . than all the joys of life"[65] and says, "I had poured out my soul upon them like water upon sand."[66] Bouts with grief paralyze him, leaving him incapable of carrying out even the most basic activities. As "life becomes a living death,"[67] he experiences the full force of his divided loyalties between earthly and divine attachments. Sexual desires, in their shallow flatness, cannot show the full complexity of how competing goods or competing loves dissipate energies, making one less able to focus ardently on God.

Foucault offers a more politically attuned and nonreligious grammar for describing a finely fractured self. Recall that for Foucault, the materiality of the flesh that at once empowers and makes persons socially vulnerable is intrinsically dynamic and interconnecting but not monolithic. "Microdynamics" and "micro-powers" run through the entire person, forming diverse, shifting alliances that can support and strengthen one another or work at cross-purposes. The added political sensitivity is evident in his assertion that any micro-power can be targeted and permeated in its own domain, without overtly contending with the whole person. It may eventually suffuse the individual's functioning through its relations with other micro-powers, but even when this occurs, the individual may or may not be aware that he is being rendered thereby of political service. Whereas Augustine tends to interpret—of course, in his own terms—the divisive internal complexity of desiring as a primarily moral or theological threat that may have political consequences down the road, Foucault is inclined, at least in the bulk of his writings, to look at it the other way around. What would first catch his attention are the innumerable surfaces of social vulnerability that can be manipulated politically and eventually influence the most personal dimensions and relations of one's life.

By dramatically shifting his perspective late in his career, Foucault looks from the new angle of a subject who patiently labors against political technologies in order to fashion her own personal aesthetic discernment and ethical skills. But strange as it may seem, given his preoccupation with political vulnerabilities of which we are often unaware, he is very optimistic at the end of his life about freedom's ability to struggle effectively against such hazards. From his outlook, the fact that one is fragile and fractured actually creates opportunities to mold the self according to one's own aims and techniques. It makes one more pliable to change. Foucault's significantly greater confidence in the capacity of human freedom to use the divisiveness of desiring to its own advantage in shaping the life that it envisions will depend largely on his view of habits as being more readily open to revision than Augustine believes. For Augustine, desiring must be transfigured by a stronger desiring, and this can only be infused in one by God. No matter how hard an individual strives to restructure habits, she will ultimately fail unless her desiring itself is transformed by grace. Such transformation, however, only begins a process of healing. Similar to physical therapy for a chronic injury, one must continue a painstaking rehabilitation of habits in relation to desires (and desires in relation to habits) for the rest of one's life. Foucault, on the other hand, believes that through careful personal exercises, one can bit by bit not only alter habits and routines, but can deeply penetrate and reconfigure the self as a whole, including one's own desiring.

The Power of Habituation and Social Configuration

Whereas the performative fallibility associated with desires concerns their dynamic fluidity—the fact that they are radically configuring and configurable; that they freely intermingle throughout the whole person and thus can influence all aspects of functioning; and that they actively push and pull against one another, producing fissures that can disrupt or sap motivation— the vulnerability habits pose is their capacity to solidify and so harden patterns of desire that they become difficult or impossible to change. If we were to consider, from Augustine's point of view, desiring alone without the complicating entanglements of habits, it might appear that our problems with self-governance would be solved if we could only get past our indecision about conflicting goods and loves. We could then rid ourselves of internal divisions and take charge of the shaping aims and influences in our lives. However, because we can never strip habits from desires or desires from habits, the fallibility of the one inevitably contributes to the fallibility of the other. Thus, simply reorienting present desires does not enable us to control our lives the way that we would like. We may ardently desire to progress toward a given end, yet fail because we simply do not have the constitutive power or ability to act on that desire. Although we may intensely wish to move, we may not be able to move. Artificially separating desires and habits can be useful to certain analytical aims. In life, though, the vulnerability of day-to-day activities comes from both habits that have been gradually formed by desiring and desiring that cannot seem to shake established habits.

This is the performative impasse Augustine faces at the beginning of book 8 of the *Confessions*. He draws a picture of a man suspended in dynamic tension. Although he is unable to move in one direction or another, there is nothing motionless in Augustine's equipoise. Indeed, he is spilling over with energy and agitation. He is about to clasp his most beloved desire for which he has long been sighing as he has caught whiffs of sweet fragrances and tastes from a distance.[68] "[W]hile I stood trembling at the barrier," Augustine writes, " . . . I could see the chaste beauty of continence in all her serene, unsullied joy, as she modestly beckoned me to cross over and hesitate no more. She stretched out loving hands to welcome and embrace me."[69] However, as Augustine strains forward to reach her enfolding arms and finally savor her sweetness, he is incapable of acting on his strongest desire.[70] "I did not do that one thing which I would have been far, far better pleased to do than all the rest."[71] It is not that Augustine does not know what he loves and wishes to embrace but that knowing this, he is still unable to do so. "I was on the point of making it, but I did not succeed. . . . I stood on the brink of resolution, waiting to take fresh breath. I tried again and came a little nearer to my goal, and then a little nearer still, so that I could almost reach out and grasp it. But I did not reach it. I could not reach out to it or grasp it."[72] His failure to act was all the more frustrating since, he concedes, he was being driven not by the compelling attraction of a rival devotion but by small inconsequential habits. The only thing preventing him from reaching his goal were "mere trifles, the most paltry inanities, all [his] old attachments."[73] He was not inflamed by alluring loves he had difficulty choosing between. He simply could not extricate himself from the mundane patterns of everyday life, from the clutch of past desires and behaviors that he had become accustomed to and yet now had grown weary of. The new "which had come to life in me . . . was not yet strong enough to overcome the old."[74] Like a man nearing the end of an affair, his heart's attention had turned elsewhere, but his body was still caught in the grooved routines and expectations that had become "hardened . . . by the passage of time" and as such were difficult to break.[75] "[I]t was only a small thing that held me now. All the same it held me."[76]

As Augustine tries to make sense of his performative weakness, he turns to the language of war, but in so doing, he refrains from blaming an alien power for overtaking his desires against his will. The battle he joins does not involve two natures or combative selves. It does not play out between a dueling evil substance on one side and a good substance on the other.[77] Rather than view his role in the conflict as a victim of some intruding force, Augustine shoulders responsibility for leading both sides of the fight. This was a struggle "in which I was my own contestant," he freely admits.[78] "[I]t was I who willed to take this course of action and again it was I who willed not to take it. It was I and I alone."[79] The same nondualistic yet nonmonolithic self was acting and resisting, pressing forward and drawing back, leaving him incapable of decisive movement. Augustine also describes his inability to act as a self-induced constraint. "I was held fast not by fetters clamped upon me by another but by my own will."[80] Being self-induced, however, does not make these coercive bonds any less confining than if they had been secured from without. The "shackles" he speaks of do not encircle or manipulate his body externally, but they nevertheless coil around his individual habits and desires so tightly that they have the effect of physical captivity. The image of a chain captures for Augustine his condition, since it is formed through connecting "links" that one by one can bind together into a constraining whole. Alone, each ring of distorted desire and habit might be easily broken apart, but joined one to the other they acquire "the strength of iron."[81] "[M]y will was perverse and lust [*libido*] had grown from it, and when I gave in to lust habit [*consuetudo*] was born, and when I did not resist the habit it became a necessity. These were the links which together have formed what I call my chain, and it held me fast in the duress of servitude."[82]

The restraints that burden Augustine as he battles to gain power over his activities should not be thought of reductively as the body fastened onto the spirit or habit onto desire. These all necessarily intermingle as they establish the individual's embodied potentiality. Severing any one would not empower but devitalize the person. Augustine's struggle is better understood as past interactive patterns of desires having formed and become formed in relation to habits and together having configured his proclivities in the present. In changing his present desiring, then, Augustine has merely redistributed the forces on one side of the battlefield. New desires must combat by themselves an alignment of old desires and old habits that have gradually constituted and materially structured his current capacities. Augustine's possible future decisions and acts have to face down a history of prior decisions and acts. His present freedom is thus waging war on the freedom of his past. And since Augustine holds a permeable view of the self and its performative history, he includes in his own intimate life story of what has brought him to this critical moment of debilitation the "sin freely committed by Adam, [his] first father."[83] Augustine's radically expansive view of history leads him to interpret even the most individual moral opportunities, responsibilities, and repercussions from God's perspective rather than from what he would consider a narrowly human outlook. "The countless days of our lives and of our forefathers' lives have passed by within your 'today,'" he writes. "And so it will be with all the other days which are to come."[84] Any "battle" Augustine sees himself as engaging therefore stretches far beyond himself and his own vision to social and historical influences that fade into the distance.[85]

How would Foucault understand Augustine's struggles with governing his day-to-day habits? In many ways they parallel one another fairly closely in their understanding of the forcefulness of habits in configuring the individual's capacities, sense of identity, and relations with others. Augustine, however, as always, will be watching more for internal dangers while Foucault will be scanning broader horizons for potential social vulnerabilities and threats. With that proviso in mind, a number of points would likely strike Foucault as having not only inter- and intrapersonal but also sociopolitical significance. As in our discussion of desires, Foucault would be much more intrigued with the performative difficulties in Augustine's ordinary functioning than with the specific performative goals he aspires to attain. Augustine's use of the images of chains and self-captivity when describing how habits can be formed and effectively structure one's everyday activities opens a productive space for commerce between the two thinkers.

Both the performative opportunities and the dangers of habituation are conveyed by two features of the chain imagery: first, chains are forged minutely link by link; and second, the links interconnect so extensively that they support and reinforce one another beyond their own individual strength. Augustine was exasperated with the disproportionate power of small habits that held captive his current desires and aims. How did such trivial patterns of behavior gain such a fierce hold over his overall capacities and attitudes? How could it come to be that they now structured his life in such a way that he could not act on his most precious desire? Foucault would concur that even the most minuscule habits can pack a forcible punch. And, in fact, he would maintain that much of the reason for this power is precisely their particularity, their ability to shape and influence seemingly insignificant details. Habituation can be aptly described as an "art of constructing" the "smallest fragment of life and of the body."[86] The very smallness of this formation makes it difficult to be aware of what habits are being solidified in relation to which desires and how such hardened patterns of desiring behavior will influence current and future freedoms. Habits are the accumulation of often trivial and apparently harmless desires, attitudes, decisions, and actions. As Augustine put it: "For as a snake creeps along not with open steps, but by the most minute movements of its scales, so the slippery movement of falling away . . . takes possession of the careless little by little."[87] We give habits life through our own acts, yet this happens much of the time without our being aware of it. Since most of us do not feel threatened by the infinitesimal and the mundane, we are not inclined to monitor the barely perceptible habits that organize our minutes, hours, and days. This leaves us susceptible to being carried along willingly but unwittingly in their stream. Because we have set up the straits through which we find ourselves vigorously swept, Augustine argues that we are endlessly maneuvering against an adversity of our own making. "[T]he rule of sin," he writes, "is the force of habit [consuetudinis], by which the mind is swept along and held fast even against its will, yet deservedly, because it fell into the habit of its own accord."[88]

Foucault is quick to note several political dangers in this aspect of habits. A political investment of the body, first of all, is least observed and most effective when it uses "the minutest of operations" to alter "the small temporal continuum of individuality" that configures over time "the minimal gestures, the elementary stages of actions, the fragments of spaces occupied or traversed."[89] From a political angle, this feature of habituation means that it can be manipulated by others without our noticing or objecting. Because these political mechanisms do not draw attention to themselves, they do not raise personal or social suspicions.[90] They can thus easily cultivate and master without moral questioning or protest "a political awareness of these small things, for the control and use of men."[91] Second, since habits are themselves linked with other habits in broad crisscrossing patterns, alterations in one habit can reverberate throughout the person. Again, politically this allows a hidden coerciveness to gain tremendous extension without social exposure or scrutiny. Instead of having to obtain "wholesale" control, it is possible, Foucault argues, to work the body "retail" through a meticulous exercise of "a subtle coercion, of obtaining holds upon it at the level of the mechanism itself—movements, gestures, attitudes, rapidity: an infinitesimal power over the active body."[92]

Third, even though the image of a chain suggests an obvious encumbrance, it can nevertheless be difficult to discern how, in connecting with others, it marks out and delimits specific areas of activity. Unreflective acts thus wind up as time passes fashioning links in the chains that bind us within certain modes of behaviors and prevent us from moving beyond their boundaries as surely as a dog being snapped back when reaching the length of its tether. Augustine spoke of this problem, which he conceived of (in the *Confessions*) as having primarily personal rather than sociopolitical impact, in terms of the inertia of habits, or their sheer dead weight dragging behind us. Foucault tended to think of it as our historical, social, and personal practices of freedom having structured a present field of possible action. Our individual and cultural habits do not determine what we will do at any given moment, but by establishing certain social preoccupations and dispositions, they demarcate what would strike us as viable alternatives and make some actions more easily accomplished than others. We tend to follow the ruts of established practices. What makes this politically problematic is our perception that such encrusted ruts cannot be broken or ruptured. Habits accumulate such weight that they come to have an apparent inevitability. If we should want to change our habits, they confront us as gigantic, seemingly fixed structures that cannot be modified. In their distinct ways, Foucault and Augustine both challenge this. Each is drawn to the possibilities of developing and honing ascetical techniques that can reconfigure the particularity of habits. Plainly, Augustine thinks that at bottom any such restructuring requires an infusion of grace and Foucault does not. But they are alike in the conviction that what appears monolithic and unalterable is neither. Habits are to be undone the way they were created, link by link.

Foucault notes that a "certain fragility has been discovered in the very bedrock of existence—even, and perhaps above all, in those aspects of it that are most familiar, most solid, and most intimately related to our bodies and to our everyday behavior."[93] Such fragility is ambiguous. As we saw in chapter 1, it points to our relational vulnerability. But if it lies at the "bedrock" of our existence, nothing about our "bodies and . . . our everyday behavior" is inevitable. What has been done can be undone. Herein lies Foucault's hope.[94]

Finally, both thinkers contend that since we acted freely when forging each link of the chain wrapped around us, we are in some measure at least responsible for it. We are not purely victims. This means that we may free ourselves (of course, for Augustine, only with divine assistance) from the binding necessity of particular chains. But it also has a more sobering political consequence, namely, that we act in our self-induced captivity not just as one who is judged and jailed but as our own judges and jailers. We become our own internal supervisors and correction officers, a fact that can be put to political use by those wishing to make individuals socially pliant and productive with the least political expenditure. What could be more efficient than shaping the unreflective personal habits that govern our daily routines into a politicized self-monitoring and self-disciplining presence? Foucault would emphatically agree with Augustine that we often languish in self-captivity. He writes that if one has been complicit in configuring such habits, one allows and even stimulates constraints of power "[to] play spontaneously upon himself; he inscribes in himself the power relation in which he simultaneously plays both roles; it becomes the principle of his own subjection."[95]

While the imagery of politicizing yet personally maintained chains depicts many of Foucault's concerns with how habits can form, structure, and limit everyday life, such captivity tends to emphasize a single dimension of our performative fragility as relationally configured creatures. To recall a point regarding the interactive materiality or vital functioning of the body, biological metaphors do a better job, according to Foucault, of portraying the infiltrating and life-fostering possibilities of habituation. They convey the dynamic power of habits that are less petrified in their present constraint and more energetically guiding and sustaining. Rather than merely hold persons back, they can also propel them forward. Augustine has some inkling of this when he recognizes that habits involve movement as well as resistance, that they can sweep us along as well as bind us. But he focuses for the most part on the ponderousness of habits: how they drag him down and fasten him in place, constraining his every effort. He more often than not struggles against habits as hindrances blocking his way. An advantage of the more dynamic biological metaphors is their ability to render the inertial solidity of habits without risking the dualist interpretations that, say, manacles being fastened about one might elicit. They help to make clear that habits are not merely an ossification of old desires. These images vividly illustrate the present, bodily impact of old habits. Past desires become habituated as they participate in the active processes that, for Foucault, constitute our bodies. They do not just motivate the flesh, they get embedded in it, thus giving it relational depth and an inertial bulk. Augustine seems to glimpse this same feature when he describes himself in book 8 in the *Confessions* as unable and unwilling fully to shake off the twilight of sleep. His mind, when he tried to direct it to thoughts of God, remained shrouded with grogginess. He declined to resist the "leaden . . . inertia" and was "glad to settle down once more" in slumber.[96] Here body and mind, habits and desires, intermingle in a sagging torpor. Foucault would read such remarks as confirming his sense that habits, by sinking into our bodies' functions, shape our motivating desires, our wants, our hopes, and our needs. Like desires, then, they have more of an interactive and constitutive power than the notions of restraint or inhibition can convey. Habits are settled desires that construct certain aptitudes, dispositions, evaluative frameworks, and conceptions of personal and communal identities.

Foucault's principal concern with habits so understood lies in the fact that their being molded by and then molding desires gives them great power in configuring not only the flesh but also a larger sense of who one is and why one exists. Because of this, they allow for maximum coercive control with minimal physical effort. As we change our routines in response to socially constituted standards of normalcy, we are doing much more than restructuring certain patterns of behavior that order our days. The most minute transformations of habits can create new, politically useful and efficient "souls."[97] Such politically expedient reconfigurations of persons deeply troubles Foucault. He sees in habits potential inroads by which disciplinary technologies can slip within and imperceptibly alter the micro-relations governing "problematic" individuals in order to fit them neatly within a normalizing, political scheme. These technologies serve less to penalize than to discretely transform "worthless," "dispensable," or "disorderly" individuals into "productive" members of society. They can be used to "neutralize . . . dangerous state[s] of mind" in order to influence "what they do, but also . . . what they are, will be, may be."[98] The sociopolitical examinations, judgments, and recommendations of those whom Foucault labels moral orthopedists are employed, he argues, not to punish or remove "abnormal" persons from social circulation; rather, "they are intended to correct, reclaim, 'cure'" so as to reintroduce them as "contributing" to the "social good."[99] The thrust is to "heal" troublesome individuals through the restorative reordering of habits and desires, to bring them into the mainstream of normalcy and health, to refashion them into persons with more socially acceptable attitudes, capabilities, and activities. From Foucault's perspective, habits can serve such purposes because they are intimately tied to our sense of self. Habits seem, after all, so natural that it is difficult to discern which ones work for and which against our own interests. In Foucault's more pessimistic moments, he worries that habits can be used to produce well-adapted, cooperative citizens not altogether different from those of Huxley's *Brave New World*. For Foucault, social outcasts are not the only ones who face such vulnerabilities. They are, of course, particularly exposed, especially when institutionalized and regimented into supervised programs. But, as with desires, Foucault wants us to recognize that we are all vulnerable to sociopolitical influences that subtly mold us into efficient and docile subjects.[100] Although, as we will see in detail in chapter 5, he concentrates intensely on institutional abuses, he also follows the insidious threads out to the edges of the social fabric. He would contend that while such personal and social manipulations may be most apparent in the macro-structures of society, they work even more effectively, because stealthily, in the micro-structures that organize our everyday lives.

CHAPTER FOUR

Fragile Relations and the Price of Perfection

The Lust for Certitude

This chapter and the next explore the personal and communal risks of human arrogance and the critical strategies that Augustine and Foucault adopt to question certain prideful trends in their respective cultures. As we look back, it is evident that a privatizing arrogance lies at the root of the problems we have thus far examined. It can be seen as driving the distorted functioning of power's interactive mechanics and as fueling original sin and social evils in their various manifestations. Such self-grandeur also stands out when we look through the lenses Augustine and Foucault use to detect indicators of exploitation. Rather than share in a co-created, dispersed, and circulating network of power relations, pride instrumentally manipulates others so as to shift and harden differentials of power to its own advantage.

Given that Augustine and Foucault portray precarious social dynamics as an inescapable part of human existence, these last chapters turn to a new question about how prideful tendencies influence cultural patterns. What relations of power, domineering desires, and practices of control develop when we try to transform a morally ambiguous world into one of certainty and perfection? Augustine and Foucault agree that this dimension of pride's outworking is especially dangerous because it so easily becomes hidden within our most noble-sounding endeavors as we seek to improve ourselves and others. Believing that power that aims at bettering the world can be more reliably possessed and meticulously managed than devious forms of power entices individuals into absolutizing their own finite perspectives and standards. Inflaming these hopeful acts of arrogance, assert Augustine and Foucault, is an unrealistic optimism in the self-determining capabilities of persons to judge rightly and act wisely, unhindered by contingency, error, and selfishness.

Both Augustine and Foucault thoroughly examined aspirations to acquire indubitable certitude and the distinct social costs of trying to procure perfection through eradicating the fragility intrinsic to all human relations. The present chapter analyzes the personal vulnerabilities such illusory expectations create; the next investigates the corresponding political consequences. Being on either side of the modern divide, together they bring into sharp focus specific transformations that continue to shape our present discourses, desires, and habits and that structure our future social expectations and possibilities. The core of each chapter compares Augustine's and Foucault's works in order to understand their own cultural concerns and clarify how specific modern trends gradually took shape—how they adopted, transfigured, expunged, and passed on fragments of various social heritages.

Moral Ambiguity and the Search for Social Perfection

As Augustine aged, he grew increasingly suspicious of cultural discourses that lured individuals into presuming they could extirpate moral fallibility by simply acquiring an emancipating self-knowledge. This yearning to seize individual clarity and control endangers the hopeful, Augustine maintains, not because of their aspirations for virtue and happiness, which are empowering social goods, but because such aspirations entail a distorted vision of what virtue and happiness are and an unrealistic assessment of the remedial powers of all temporal efforts. Genuine wisdom, Augustine would counter, can only be approached paradoxically—by surrendering commonsensical expectations and strategies for securing personal certitude. This unavoidably launches one on a confusing journey of self-revelation that hermeneutically highlights rather than erases all traces of interpersonal frailties. Virtue, from this perspective, can only be shaped receptively as one humbly acknowledges the enabling and constraining limits of finitude, contingency, ambiguity, and relational dependence.

Augustine offers a complex analysis of the varying personal and social dangers cultivated by presumptuous overconfidence. All his targets of critique, however, mirror in one way or another the first rupturing interactions of sin. Openly rebelling angels illustrate the most basic and conspicuous feature of pride: it is always interpersonal. Although an arrogant deed may look like an individual act of power, it can be exercised only in relation to others.

Augustine focuses, as he gives shape to the angels' defiance, not on any one object of temporal desire but on the simple relational act of turning away.[1] Delighting in their power, writes Augustine, "as though they themselves were their own Good[,] . . . they have fallen away from that Supreme Good which is common to all . . . and they have devoted themselves to their own ends."[2] The offense of these angels, he avers, "consists solely in falling away from God and deserting him."[3] Ironically, however, by trying to acquire this illusive autonomy, they bartered the very ends they were striving after: glory, truth, certitude, control, and stability. "They have chosen pride in their own elevation in exchange for the true exaltation of eternity; empty cleverness in exchange for the certainty of truth; the spirit of faction instead of unity in love"; becoming, in the end, nothing but "arrogant, deceitful, and envious."[4]

Acts of human arrogation cultivate similarly disordered social patterns. As the autonomous individual comes to regard himself "as his own light," he "turns away" from the shared animating power of the Good to the tantalizing possibilities of his own self-defining and self-interpreting activities.[5] Believing himself to constitute his "own ground," he determines "to be self-sufficient and defects from the one who is really sufficient for him."[6] Truth, meaning, value, and utility are hence construed and assessed by all that the proud have at hand: "the standard of their human intellect, with its mutability and narrow finitude."[7] One must therefore be vigilant, cautions Augustine, when putting stock in finite orderings of knowledge and normative customs. It is difficult to be sure, because of the sheer delight in ordering itself, when one is discovering and when one is imposing, when one is measuring up in commitments and conduct, and when one is luxuriating in the complacency of self-congratulation. Without common ground, a multitude of interpretations circulate through every culture, each vying for attention, each soliciting itself as the final arbiter. "The poverty of our human intellect generally produces an abundance of words, for more talk is sent in search than in discovery."[8] The seductive appeal of such quests preoccupies Augustine during much of his *Confessions*, where he describes the haggling of those "who traffic in literature" and those "who buy their wares."[9] The skilled, presenting themselves as "masters of words" and the "art of persuasion," peddle their rhetoric, as he learned to hawk his own, "like choice and costly glasses."[10]

Augustine's insights into knowledge as contending in an unstable world of truth and power began to develop when he was a student. Over time, this allowed him to gain critical distance from teachers and helped him to make his way as he explored one discourse after another in his search for illumination and liberation. "I had learnt," he writes, "that wisdom and folly are different kinds of food. Some are wholesome and others are not, but both can be served equally well on the finest china or the meanest earthenware."[11] With this lesson in mind to strengthen his own discernment, Augustine's lively engagement in tournaments and debates reveals the sense of gaming he associated with competing cultural discourses. In this, he gestures toward a strategic understanding of knowledge as tactical play and maneuvering in a jostling field of power, a notion, as we will see, more explicit in Foucault. With contestants bumping up against the boundaries of finitude and the passions of persuasion, Augustine depicts rhetoric as an instrument or a weapon that individuals wield for social advantage. In this context, the ways knowledge, truth, and power relate to one another and to those in positions of authority are central to their ambiguous practical utility and cultural forcefulness. Although, of course, Augustine recounts experiences of graced knowledge, they provide but anticipatory glimpses of an eschatological triune vision. "[K]nowledge will only be perfected after this life when we shall see face to face. Let us then be of this mind: so as to know that the inclination to seek the truth is safer than the presumption which regards unknown things as known."[12] Even as momentary and incomplete, however, the persuasive social power of such knowledge gives him confidence that discursive tools are not merely arbitrary and mundane and that the game, even as a game, is one of grave seriousness.

The rivaling cultural discourses Augustine finds fascinating and dangerous can be usefully examined in light of the interactive dynamics they foster among wisdom, truth, virtue, and power. In the *Confessions* and the *City of God,* Augustine takes as one of his principal tasks a public accounting and assessment of his religious and philosophical competitors. To grasp his appraisals, we can use the same metaphors he borrowed from the din and commotion of urban marketplaces. What wares do his rivals offer? What goods do they promote? What claims do they advance for their restorative properties and powers? What hopes do such promises inflame, and with what coin are these promises purchased? Like Foucault, Augustine is keenly aware that rhetorics with their cajoling vendors, trinkets of certitude, and pledges of deliverance and contentment operate amidst the tumult of a conflictual social world. Consequently, he was unusually perceptive about something Foucault stresses again and again: there are prices to the truths we endorse, follow, and seek to enact. They have practical costs as well as practical benefits. What we long to embrace and escape in our pursuits of wisdom and virtue tangibly shape how we construe and apply values and meanings to ourselves, others, and the natural environment, and thus condition the interactions by which we live. They structure personal and interpersonal activities. They open and close possibilities for experiencing ourselves and others. They legitimate and discourage specific desires, attitudes, habits, justifications, and authorities. In sum, they carve out distinct social spaces that empower and disempower particular modes of life, individuals, and communities.

Augustine's analysis of the main contenders of his day makes it clear that even though he does not use the words, he perceives, in his own fashion, that their exhortations about virtue relate power, wisdom, and truth in importantly different ways. Manichees and Stoics decisively separate wisdom and power. Each promises individuals an escape from the vagaries of the latter through the invulnerability of the former. Wisdom, when acquired rightly and strengthened through self-disciplines of detachment, becomes a refuge from the changes and distresses of worldly existence. The Manichees in the process cleave the self, construing any lightness of spirit as akin to the undiminished brilliance of truth and any heaviness of embodied desire, habit, and power as akin to the dark material forces of life. The Stoics' wisdom and virtues promote a more rigorously whole yet no less impenetrable sanctuary within the self. Their vision of complete intellectual control over affections and passions promise the autonomous person the opportunity to master every movement—within and without—and to direct all objectives, motives, interactions, and encounters.

Although the allure of both philosophies is obvious, the costs, given the limits of the human condition, are high. For the Manichees, Augustine charges, self-grandeur goes hand in hand with an abdication of human responsibility. Having severed from themselves the presumed darker, destructive, and tragic aspects of their identities, "they think themselves as high and bright as the stars" and so "their conceit soars like a bird."[13] What should therefore function socially as uncomfortable self-criticism becomes the effortless hatred of an externalized and objectified enemy. For the Stoics, the price of certitude and self-perfection is indifference. The need to defend reason against the dynamic and unexpected influences of power leads them to so thicken the walls of the self that over time they cease choosing to be unaffected and become simply incapable of being moved. In deadening the affections, they simultaneously deaden what Augustine asserts is life's fundamental power, namely, love. The ensuing social consequences are widespread. For along with eradicating the ambiguous fragility of love, they extirpate the unpredictable sacrifices of charity. Commenting on an anecdote about a sinking ship, Augustine charges, "The Stoics, to be sure, are in the habit of extending their condemnation to compassion; but how much more honourable would it have been . . . to have been 'disturbed' by compassion so as to rescue someone, rather than by the fear of being shipwrecked! What is compassion but a kind of fellow-feeling in our hearts for another's misery, which compels us to come to his help by every means of our power."[14] Stoicism, he argues, in fearing too intensely the unruliness of power, fails to be aware of how power relations unjustly harm the less socially secure and fails to risk its own power by becoming involved in the fray. Finally, Augustine argues, even though their wisdom may be tantalizing, such naive optimism is not supported by the evidence of daily experiences. First, life is filled with suffering, as he makes clear by documenting, page after page, all of our common distresses.[15] Human character, from his perspective, is not a matter of how well one escapes these miseries but how well one bears them and reorients them to the service of community. Second, virtues will always have to engage vices within the constrictions and entanglements of finitude so that "though command be exercised over the vices it is assuredly not by any means without conflict."[16] In light of the inevitable tensions between different embodied desires and habits, "even when a man fights well . . . ," he admonishes, "the battle is fraught with peril."[17] Unable to grasp this basic reality about embodied existence, these intellectually arrogant philosophers deny their own creaturely limits and "fabricate for themselves an utterly delusive happiness" that can never be achieved "for all our wishing."[18]

Many of Augustine's most critical assessments target Roman assurances about wisdom, virtue, and self-perfection. This cultural discourse harnesses wisdom and power together in order to actualize a transcendent glory. The promises of self-improvement and self-completion work in tandem with the appeal of immediately realizing an all-embracing order of social meaning. For his Roman opponents, individual freedom and self-reliance are the driving forces of social perfection. The good life is the autonomous life, one voluntarily constructed by dint of meritorious and praiseworthy personal efforts. The Romans' confidence, in this regard, is not accompanied by the same suspiciousness as found in the Manichees and Stoics. Whereas the latter promote human optimism only by disempowering or denigrating certain dimensions of the self, either corporeal or emotional, the former relies on the created capacities of the entire person to attain excellence in the pursuit of glory. The Romans creatively synthesize individualizing capacities of autonomy with the transpersonal participation in glory so that for exemplary persons, social honor continues to circulate and often excels "after death on the lips of those who praised them."[19]

The single-minded dedication and willingness to sacrifice themselves for a larger social purpose is commendable in and of itself since it can moderate self-centered tendencies. "They were passionately devoted to glory; it was for this that they desired to live, for this they did not hesitate to die. This unbounded passion for glory checked their other appetites."[20] Many pursuing this social ideal, Augustine acknowledges,

> took no account of their own material interests compared to the common good . . . ; they resisted the temptations of avarice; they acted for their country's well-being with disinterested concern; they were guilty of no offense against the law; they succumbed to no sensual indulgence. By such immaculate conduct they laboured towards honours, power and glory, by what they took to be the true way.[21]

Not only did their striving for a transcendent glory help to involve individuals in shared efforts for a common goal, it inspired the imagining of admirable endeavors so that "today [their initiatives] enjoy renown in the history and literature of nearly all races."[22] From every conventional measurement of worldly success, therefore, the wisdom and heroic virtues of Roman society elicited from both individual persons and the community as a whole "marvelous achievements, which were, no doubt, praiseworthy and glorious in men's estimation."[23]

What is the cost, then, of such social elevation? Why would Augustine quarrel with this transforming vision of glory? Naturally, his primary concern is that it competes with the highest glory and, as such, can confuse individuals about to what they owe their ultimate allegiances and how that allegiance should be demonstrated. As with any passion, the desire for praise easily distracts the faithful or devolves into the simple greed of hoarding.[24] Being transient, however—utterly dependent on the judgments and opinions of human beings—such honor can never have lasting value, for as Augustine describes it, "smoke has no weight."[25] In light of this, he reminds readers of a very different way, "the royal road, which alone leads to that kingdom whose glory is not the tottering grandeur of the temporal, but the secure eternity of the eternal."[26]

Augustine finds more than the transience of earthly glory troubling. Since it is built on the basis of and evaluated by the standards of fallible creatures it is a purely human construct and not a gift of divine grace. As such, it affords no critical leverage with which to judge the workings of pride and it is not receptive to being shaped by unexpected and uncontrolled influences that question and/or challenge its so highly esteemed powers. Even one who excels in rigorous exercises of self-discipline so that his appetites appear harmoniously ordered is still unable to determine whether, in pursuing glory, he is sacralizing his own finite perspective or fulfilling that which is ultimate. Is he simply conforming others to his relative discernment of how things ought to be with the seemingly beneficent justification of a glorifying perfection? When backed with military might, this becomes especially hazardous, as Augustine demonstrates at length in his scathing remarks about Roman expansionist aggression. He brings this out eloquently in describing Rome's efforts to unite its subjects in language and custom. By forcing its knowledge, truth, and norms on others through the use of power, Rome believes itself to be building a unified people who will forthwith live peaceably together under a single comprehensive ideal of glory. Those being overrun, however, unavoidably harbor animosity against this despotic coercion. They remember only the muscle, not the glory.[27] Augustine is careful to nuance the degrees of harm in pursuing human glory. "There is a clear difference between the desire for glory before men and the desire for domination."[28] However, even that which is most inspired by aspirations for honor, dignity, freedom, and fellowship can slide, he maintains, with little notice to the darker sides of ordering control. "There is, to be sure, a slippery slope from excessive delight in the praise of men to the burning passion for domination."[29]

The last misgiving Augustine raises about combining human power and truth in the pursuit of earthly glory is its implicit trust in the efficacy of human virtue, strength, and merit. Self-reliance is detrimental, he asserts, not because reason or virtue or freedom is socially problematic but because of what relying on these too extensively does to relationships. Augustine adamantly emphasizes this point about self-sufficiency and relational dependency by comparing the mutually exclusive forms of glory emanating from the earthly and heavenly cities. "[T]he earthly city glories in itself, the Heavenly City glories in the Lord. The former looks for glory in men, the latter finds its highest glory in God. . . . The earthly lifts up its head in its own glory, the Heavenly City says to its God: 'My Glory; you lift up my head.' . . . The one city loves its own strength shown in its powerful leaders; the other says to its God, 'I will love you, my Lord, my strength.'"[30]

Of the diverse cultural discourses competing during his lifetime, those that deserve to "be raised above the rest," declares Augustine, are the Platonists.[31] Because they "have conceived of God, the supreme and true God, as the author of all created things, the light of all knowledge, the Final Good of all activity, and . . . have recognized him as being for us the origin of existence, the truth of doctrine and the blessedness of life . . . we rank such thinkers above all others and acknowledge them as representing the closest approximation to our Christian position."[32] Setting them apart from the philosophies discussed above is their profound appreciation for relationality and dependence and their corresponding recognition that human creatures are utterly indebted in both being and action to a transcendent glory not of their own making. They "even use the word 'grace' itself quite openly," Augustine notes, "[asserting] without hesitation that man cannot by any means reach the perfection of wisdom in this life, but that, after this life, all those who live the life of the intellect receive all that is needed for their fulfillment from the providence and grace of God."[33]

Augustine plainly admires the Platonists for seeing these truths "through the obscurities of a subtle imagination."[34] In the *City of God,* however, he does not linger on talk of shared sensibilities. Instead, he uses their congruencies to place into higher relief his alternative discourse. Only in dialogue with those Augustine considers to be so near, who see "with clouded vision, the country in which we must find our home" but who "do not keep to the road along which we must travel,"[35] does he most clearly pinpoint his objections to classical pride. Here he gets to the core of the problem. For Augustine, the whole weight of his critique comes to rest on "the shame of the cross"—its confounding wisdom, truths, virtues, and power.[36] The proud are unable to walk in its shadow, even if through such darkness, glory is revealed. The very closeness of the Platonists, from Augustine's perspective, simultaneously shows their great distance. For they cannot go down this path of "dishonor." In describing the demanding humility of the cross, Augustine castigates Porphyry, saying: "[Y]ou are of course, the kind of thinker to reject such lowliness with disdain, and to cull your exalted wisdom on the heights."[37]

Augustine knows that for classical thinkers the narrative of Christ's passion and the symbolism of the cross upends their cultural traditions about wisdom, truth, and virtue: shame within a society of honor; humility in a community that seeks praise; lowliness for the spiritual who expect ascent; bodily sufferings that disrupt intellectual control and happiness; extremes of martyrdom in contrast to the proportionality of a well-balanced life. In the competition of this culture's discursive marketplace, it would seem that all one is receiving from Augustine's strange rhetoric is the price. Augustine's chore is to convey how such unseemly paradoxes bestow dignity and power. What transforming wisdom do the incarnation and the cross promise? The answer turns on his contrast between mere optimism and hopefulness. "My purpose is to make clear the great difference between their hollow realities and our hope, the hope given us by God."[38]

The Wisdom of Sorrow and the Ethic of Humility

Since pride is the underlying problem in life, Augustine describes its "cure"—God's selfless act of humility[39]—both to reveal the profound divide between classical and Christian expectations and to offer a way to move from the "hollowness" of the one to the "hope" of the other.[40] The spectacle of the cross, according to Augustine, especially disturbs the shallow optimism of "the wise."[41] It is not only where "God . . . became of no account in the eyes of the proud," but a symbol of human contingency, suffering, and death.[42] The cross on this side of transfiguration shows the afflictions of everyday life. Like Augustine's eloquent portrayal of our common miseries in book 19 of the *City of God*, it reminds individuals that they cannot delude themselves about life's hardships and fabricate a world of invulnerable happiness. In this sense, the cross reflects their own humanity back to the faithful. They are brought low in witnessing Christ's sacrifice and ritually participating in it through baptism and the Eucharist.[43] On Augustine's view, coming face-to-face with the harshness, the stark corporeality of the crucifixion is imperative for grasping the relational significance of Christ as mediator. As Christ is pierced with the implacable realities of finitude, the faithful have pressed upon them their own limits as creatures who are at once entangled in the flux of time and the inevitability of their own end.[44] No matter the worldly wisdom one attains, he argues, one cannot ascend, or overcome through honor and praise, or indifferently ignore this fundamental helplessness. Therefore, Christ must reach to the faithful in their weakness; they cannot reach to him. "This was the mediation, the stretching out of a hand to those who lie fallen."[45] As finite, the faithful cannot span the chasm between creature and creator, between finitude and eternity. Christ must become the bridge.[46]

The way he reaches out to the fallen, Augustine acknowledges, troubles the classical mind.[47] For Christ fully enters life's griminess—not simply in dying a brutal death but also through the ordinariness of birth and the messy demands of caring for the sick. This humble incarnation, which Augustine renders, borrowing the words of Exodus, as "the back parts of Christ," enables followers to "recognize . . . how much Christ has first loved us."[48] He does not minister to and transform the lowliness of suffering from the heights of heaven; he fully descends into it. He participates in humanity's lowliness by becoming lowly himself. Divine transcendence alone is insufficient, insists Augustine, for "we need a mediator linked with us in our lowliness."[49] As mediator, however, Christ, in his kenotic descent, offers "divine assistance for our purification."[50] This involves more than just being present—like a parent lovingly attending to a sick child. Christ takes on the affliction, the sickness, and glorifies it as such by bringing it into the divine life. Citing Philippians 3.21, Augustine explains: " 'He transfigured the body of our lowliness, conforming it to the body of his glory.' . . . His body in both things, that is to say, in the death and the Resurrection was served to us as a kind of medical remedy."[51]

Being a perpetual "remedy," this glorification, in contrast to earthly glorification, does not eliminate humility and lowliness but raises them to new purposes. The "shame of the cross" is not left behind or negated. It is "re-formed," along with the sinful, so as to structure their service back to the world. As an imitative self-emptying, self-giving, and self-forgetting love, *caritas,* Augustine declares, can only be "perfected in the weakness of humility."[52] This unreservedly vulnerable love does not triumph over human knowledge but transforms it into a wisdom of sorrow: "[F]or him who so acts and laments, knowledge does not puff up because charity edifies. He has preferred the one knowledge to the other; he has preferred to know his own weakness more than to know the walls of the world, the foundations of the earth, and the heights of the heavens; and by acquiring this knowledge, he has acquired sorrow."[53] In being transfigured by love, argues Augustine, such knowledge, which "knows itself as seeking and not knowing," helps to keep love continually humble.[54] The wisdom and virtues that are re-formed in light of the cross are, he admits, from the standpoint of a successful world, tragic virtues: they are shaped and moved by the painful awareness of human frailties, shortfalls, dependencies, and finitude. From the standpoint of a broken world, however, these virtues inspire persons to reach out in love from a shared sense of hardship to "those who lie fallen."[55] Rather than encourage one to know so as to better possess the self, he claims, humility prods one to dispossess the self out of compassion for another. The wisdom of sorrow, then, whose source is the glory of the cross does not elevate the social elite with immortalizing praise; rather, it tends to the forgotten, the abandoned, the sentenced—those who have no earthly honor and prestige.[56]

The "cure" Augustine offers for moving individuals from the "hollowness" of naive optimism to the hope of sacrificial love fundamentally changes their relationship with God, and through God, to other persons. This involves two distinguishable but related beliefs: (i) God loves without reserve; (ii) this boundless love is founded on sheer mercy rather than natural human merit. Together, Augustine asserts, these guard the faithful from the twin perils of hopelessness and arrogance, either of which render persons incapable of loving relations. "[F]irst of all, we must be persuaded how much God has loved us, lest through despair we should not dare to be lifted up to Him. But [in addition to this] we needed to be shown what kind of men we were whom He loved, lest being proud of our merits, we should draw away the more from Him, and fail the more in our own strength."[57]

The solidarity of the community, Augustine reminds his followers, depends on individual and collective remembrances of these relational insights and on their reenactment in concrete deeds of mercy. The constant interweaving of sacrifice and compassion knits the entire community together.

> [T]rue sacrifices are acts of compassion, whether towards ourselves or towards neighbours, when they are directed to God. . . . This being so, it immediately follows that the whole redeemed community, that is to say, the congregation and fellowship of the saints, is offered to God as a universal sacrifice, through the great Priest who offered himself in his suffering for us. . . . [I]t is under this form [of the servant] that he is the Mediator, in this form he is the Priest, in this form he is the sacrifice. Thus the Apostle first exhorts us to offer our bodies as a living sacrifice . . . and not to be 'con-formed' to this age, but to be 're-formed' in newness of mind . . . because we ourselves are the whole sacrifice. . . . This is the sacrifice which the Church continually celebrates in the sacrament of the altar . . . where it is shown to the Church that she herself is offered in the offering which she presents to God.[58]

Because "sacrifice" creates these bonds of unity, Augustine declares, the solidarity it shapes through imitative acts of self-emptying love always interacts with another solidarity that binds all persons together, inside and outside of the church—the solidarity of Adam. The community should thus form (and continually "re-form") itself through sacrificial acts of compassion as an outwardly and not just inwardly looking body. This is especially true since from a sociological perspective, no person can be certain who stands on which side of the redeeming boundary. That will be settled, on his view, only at the eschaton. "Right now both [the earthly and heavenly] cities are mixed up together, at the end they will be sorted out and separated."[59] Augustine's sociological perceptions here again attest to the centrality of a chastised knowledge and humbled love working together in all relations, even those within the church, to keep them open to unexpected transformations. The participation in an awaiting hope is essentially different from the grasping of certitude. Hope must remain uncongealed, receptive to the unknown, for it to be properly oriented: "But as yet we are light *with faith* only, not *with a clear view. For our salvation is founded upon the hope of something. Hope would not be hope at all if its object were in view.*"[60]

As a bishop in this community, Augustine would have seen himself as playing a pivotal role in the sustenance of such solidarity through "sacrificial," that is, self-emptying, enactments of love and knowledge. This would naturally pertain to priestly and pastoral duties. But it would likewise pertain to his own efforts as an author to make sense of his desires, attitudes, habits, and activities. If we are to discern the richer meaning of Augustine's self-interpretations as he searches for wisdom and virtue, we must consider his reflections as, at least from his perspective, a form of "sacrifice" or participatory offering that is meant to nourish, in the self-emptying exercise of confession, bonds of social solidarity. Confession, when interpreted in a "self-emptying" light, fulfills two functions for the community. First, it offers a way of personal decentering that keeps individuals mindful of their utter dependence on God's mercy and sustenance, thereby helping them to navigate between the dangers of despair and arrogance. In this "deconstructive" capacity, it acts at once as a petition of lamentation and a remembrance of thanksgiving. Second, as a public activity, it disturbs the pride of others.

Augustine exemplifies both functions in his *Confessions,* but because of his stature in the community, he is unusually effective in fulfilling the latter. As noted in the previous chapter, conventions of religious autobiography in antiquity dictated that they climax in a renunciation of past iniquities and the full embrace of a radically new form of life. The effect of "conversion was often thought of as being as dramatic and as simple as the 'sobering up' of an alcoholic."[61] Given these literary customs, Augustine's audience would have expected from a celebrated leader of the church a story about sustained spiritual ascent that would have clearly set him apart as an ideal of human sanctity. What they got instead was a shockingly honest look at personal struggles even after conversion—of moral and spiritual feebleness, hermeneutical uncertainties, and noetic conundrums. His portrayal of religious confession thus reminds his readers that the self-identity they so desperately seek to secure is incomplete, finite, and, most important, relationally dependent. In his endless journey of self-discovery, he studied with esteemed philosophers, experimented with diverse religious practices, and rose to great heights in the church. And yet he emphasizes again and again the praiseworthiness of humility rather than attainment, what he does not know rather than what he has mastered. Augustine's life, therefore, can also serve as an antiheroic model. In its nonglorification, it critically punctures the pretensions of his fellow Christians.

How successful Augustine was at following his own ethic of humility or in encouraging others to pursue the same is debatable. But it is important for interpreters to attempt to comprehend the way his work may have functioned against the background of his broader theological and ecclesiological interests. For modern readers, this thick communal weave is often difficult to see, much less grasp. This is due partly to the fact that many have no appreciation for the ethic of humility or self-sacrificial *kenosis* he was concerned to demonstrate. It is also due partly to the fact that many have grown comfortable with the interpretive ease afforded by either simplistic psychological renditions of Augustine's internal drama or post-modern political assessments of it as a poorly disguised will to power. It may seem that all Foucault would have to offer in conversation with Augustine on this range of issues would resemble the criticisms of other post-moderns. Indeed, a number of comparisons of Augustine and Foucault have pursued this line of inquiry.[62] Although these studies raise certain legitimate concerns, which I discuss in the epilogue, they often do so by flattening Augustine through caricature and emaciating his critical thought. My assessment takes me in the opposite direction. I am persuaded that only by considering seriously Augustine's complex ethic of humility are we able to understand Foucault's full critical value. Ironically, on my view, when scholars reduce Augustine to a kind of cartoon representation in comparison to Foucault, Foucault likewise suffers. One ought not conclude that I am advocating an uncritical acceptance of either figure. Neither is immune from critique. However, I believe one of the best means we have for measuring their successes and failures, as well as for evaluating cultural trends, can be elicited from their own critical reflections.

The remainder of this chapter considers some of the ways Foucault can be constructively used to broaden Augustine's analysis of the desires for an illusory human perfection. By examining contemporary aspirations and practices to master a redeeming or liberating self-knowledge, Foucault can perceptively extend Augustine's critique of prideful social patterns into our current sociohistorical situation. Further, because Augustine and Foucault are situated on either side of the modern divide, comparing their critiques brings into view specific cultural transformations, and thereby reveals how various social heritages concerning knowledge, truth, and power have been fragmented, co-opted, transfigured, or expunged. Before turning to these historical and cultural comparisons, let us pause to reflect on other, perhaps more suggestive possibilities of constructive influence. Apart from a specifically modern analysis of cultural transformations, can Foucault add deeper coloration to Augustine's ethic of humility? Does he have only historical import, or are there ways to put his work to more general theological use?

Foucault first of all excels at bringing out the hues and textures of finitude. Whether speaking of the vulnerabilities of the body or the constraining rhythms of time or the structuring rituals of self-interpretation, he heightens his readers' awareness of the ever-shifting ground of contingencies on which they build expectations of certitude and perfection. Along with these precarious notions, the myth of personhood as self-originating being is shattered by his intense concentration on the ineluctability of historical and social fragility. The extent to which Foucault's attunement to finitude struck a modern nerve is revealed by the uproar that arose when he wagered that recent conceptions of "man" constructed in the social sciences would gradually "be erased, like a face drawn in sand at the edge of the sea."[63] This seemingly solid human image being washed away particle by particle was more than his critics could bear. A cascade of criticism fell on Foucault. For being slowly eroded was not simply a familiar human form, but the accompanying promises of security and certitude the knowledge derived from this form guaranteed. But would Foucault's provocative image have rankled Augustine, who describes himself, in all his pride, as *"no better than a breath of wind that passes by and never returns"*?[64] Here is a man who recalls again and again that he is but "dust and ashes,"[65] mercilessly buffeted by winds that shift "hither and thither,"[66] distended and scattered by fugitive spans of time.[67] Although his images act as mournful petitions, they also serve as admonitions of his own insignificance. One must recognize one's ontological dependence on God, the senselessness that surrounds any assertion of self-originating being, for Augustine's theology of the cross and ethics of humility to have meaning. One must confront one's finitude. One must feel the washing of the tide over all that has been so meticulously etched by hand. This unsettling attunement to contingency may produce a philosophical dilemma for the modern mind. But it should not raise religious problems. As long as relationality forms the centerpiece of faith, as it does for Augustine, the washing away of a human image of our own making can be experienced as a confirmation of creatureliness and the need to depend on God's sustaining love.

Related to Foucault's sensitivity to finitude, his ascetical interests and deconstructive aims to detach himself from the unnoticed hardening of culturally configured identities also can be correlated to an Augustinian process of kenotic humility. The *Confessions*, in large part, tells a story of the presumed naturalness of accumulated cultural norms and attitudes. Augustine is captivated as he surveys his life by the pervasive grip normalization has on his capacities, interpretations, and relationships. As he peels away thin layers of identity, we learn how difficult it is to comprehend, let alone tear away and replace, culturally imbued aspirations, habits, values, and judgments. Augustine points us to such cultural subtleties early on. Even as an infant, when he discovers that "crying out and making various sounds and movements" do not convey his meaning, he learns the shared yet unstated rules of gesture and language by means of which he can direct others to fulfill his needs.[68] Schooling continues to build and shape these capacities but adds a normative glaze of social expectations: what merits praise or ridicule, what creates happiness or regretted hardship, what elicits compassion or insensitivity and disregard. In short, Augustine absorbs the social mores governing what will be considered of value as he makes his way into the future. He recounts such normative lessons with irony: "I was already being prepared for [life's] tournaments by a training which taught me to have a horror of faulty grammar instead of teaching me, when I committed these faults, not to envy others who avoided them."[69] These small lessons pave the way for more and more callous behavior. To make his point, he uses the example of a lawyer who takes the greatest pains to avoid humiliating slips of tongue, "and yet the thought that the frenzy in his own mind may condemn a human being to death disturbs him not at all."[70]

What Augustine understands himself and his classmates to have acquired in this "naturalizing" process is the practical know-how of "the way to gain respect of others and win for [himself] what passes for wealth in this world."[71] He describes this normalization as participating in so many "games" as one moves from one social role to another. And though, he observes, such games change in the seriousness with which they are regarded by society, there is a monotonous sameness to their play. "For commanders and kings may take the place of tutors and schoolmasters, nuts and balls and pet birds may give way to money and estates and servants, but these same passions remain with us while one stage of life follows upon another, just as more severe punishments follow upon the schoolmaster's cane."[72] The social and historical momentum of the disciplinary tactics and norms that accumulate in cultures is captured by Augustine this way: "Countless boys long since forgotten had built up this stony path for us to tread and we were made to pass along it, adding to the toil and sorrow of the sons of Adam."[73] The "empty dreams" of these blinding endeavors of honor and praise led him to pursue numerous religious philosophers, but there too he was left disappointed, realizing again he had been socially "misled and deluded by promises of certainty."[74] As one can detect from the bitterness of Augustine's invective, loosening the grip of such normative aspirations and values is an arduous, painful, and lengthy process. It is against this background that self-*kenosis* must take place so as to "re-form" the heart and mind.

Foucault's own ascetic detachment also involves a blunt challenging of cultural norms and values: unquestioned social rules governing failure and success, disgrace and prestige, repression and liberation, infirmity and health, flaws and perfection. Like Augustine, much of his own self-emptying involves taking the "natural" and making it seem strange. What passes unnoticed by their peers stands out to both figures in virtue of the burdens imposed on themselves and others. All of his works, Foucault admits, are to some extent autobiographical. "Whenever I have tried to carry out a piece of theoretical work," he writes,

> it has been on the basis of my own experience, always in relation to processes I saw taking place around me. It is because I thought I could recognize in the things I saw, in the institutions with which I dealt, in my relations with others, cracks, silent shocks, malfunctionings . . . that I undertook a particular piece of work, a few fragments of autobiography.[75]

They function as cultural critiques as well as exercises of self-detachment from expected cultural identities and practices.[76] Augustine's aims, in many of his writings, could be described in the same way. Both men see themselves as out of step with prevailing cultural norms. They feel "homeless" in that they are detached from customs and comforts others take for granted. But this does not undercut their critical power or commitment. In fact, it makes both more rather than less critically engaged because being detached from the world and the self—and therewith the need to preserve either—allows them more critical leverage.

However, even though Augustine and Foucault may be drawn together by their "self-emptying" aspirations, an absolute difference emerges between the two thinkers in their sharply contrasting hopes for what this will accomplish. For Foucault, decentering the self opens unexplored terrain for artistic self-creation. Being worldless or homeless is a joy to him, an opportunity to re-create his identity continually. Augustine could not see the end result more differently. "Can it be that any man has skill to fabricate himself?" he asks. " . . . Surely we can only derive them from our Maker."[77] Deconstruction is always in preparation for a relational self-identity that is given, not made. He understands himself as participating in a co-creation, but this is a graced process:

> [T]hey were all gifts from God, for I did not give them to myself. His gifts are good and the sum of them all is my own self. . . . My God, in whom is my delight, my glory, and my trust, I thank you for your gifts and beg you to preserve and keep them for me. Keep me, too, and so your gifts will grow and reach perfection and I shall be with you myself, for I should not even exist if it were not for your gift.[78]

Thus, through a *kenosis* that strips away cultural values and norms as well as minuscule desires and habits, Augustine prays: "Let me not be my own life, for . . . I was death unto myself. But in you I live again."[79] "Let God possess [my soul], he who made [all things] very good."[80]

One of the most fruitful applications for Foucault's deconstructive insights is to reinforce Augustine's efforts to chasten human knowledge and transform it from an arrogant exercise of self-assertive control into a self-humbling "wisdom of sorrow." Whereas the former aspires to its goals by presuming it can defy creaturely limits, the latter works hesitantly, attentive to the social and historical complexities that influence every human striving. Although Foucault does not use such evaluative terms, he clearly distinguishes between prideful and unpretentious forms of knowledge. Since knowledge is not something that we merely have but something we do, it can manifest itself arrogantly or humbly.

On Foucault's view, modern arrogant modes of knowledge secure their own refuge of power by defining themselves with certitude as "purely" neutral and disinterested. Seeing themselves thus removed from the skirmishes of power plays, they presume not to require, and indeed proclaim their humanitarian pursuits to be threatened by, deconstructive moral scrutiny. By covertly linking their own "naturalized" power to their ability to protect truth from the disorderly effects of power, they adopt the ultimate defensive advantage. Anyone assaulting their shielding tactics is thereby attacking a consecrated sanctuary. They are assaulting not the unstable dynamics of power that unfold in a complex performative world but the hallowed trappings of Sovereign Truth. To question, then, how particular truths socially and historically function becomes an act of blasphemy.

For Foucault, the discourses in our society with the cultural power to shield themselves from moral and political scrutiny are those that associate themselves with scientific or pseudo-scientific language and practices. Of gravest concern to him is when such presumptuous modes of knowledge take as their task examining, classifying, and eradicating the frailties and imperfections of human lives. Ironically, such discourses have only been able to gain this power through the desires of fallible persons who yearn to be liberated from "blemishes" and "defects." In an attempt to flee their fragility, however, they have made themselves more vulnerable. Augustine's distrust of religiophilosophical wisdoms of his time that sorted and evaluated persons by way of socially constructed mores of honor and shame clears an area of common concern with Foucault. Augustine articulates an alternative Christocentric discourse, one that encourages humbly participating in the experiences of the lowly and the imperfect, in order to undercut the truths glorified by Greco-Roman culture. On his view, no strivings for certainty, security, or perfection can escape the critical scrutiny of humility. He argues that no one will be wholly perfected in this life. If one comes to be changed, it is only by being attentive in and to one another's sufferings, not by trying to force oneself and others to fit a model of heroic self-achievement.

Humbled modes of knowledge, in contrast, are for Foucault those that make room for knowledges that have been judged inadequate and dismissed as of no account. A chastened perspective recognizes its own contingency and consequent inability to proclaim with full assurance normative assessments and judgments for all persons and times. Unlike what Foucault calls the universal intellectual, one adopting this frame of mind realizes the limits of its reach, surveys social and historical influences, remains attuned to local problems and failures, and stays open to the possibility that it may be justifiably challenged by others advocating rivaling truths. As with Augustine, from the standpoint of a successful and advantaged world, such chastened knowledge may seem to promote only tragic virtues, ones that cannot extend intellectual claims far enough to protect the inviolability of justice and accord. But in an ambiguous and fragile world (where powers of suasion, whether they be for the good or the bad, are always at work), such virtues are better able to attend to the dispossessed. Although hesitant to presume to speak in place of the silent or the suffering, those with influence should try to find domains where the marginalized can raise their own voices and address their own contexts and concerns. Corresponding to the prideful side of knowledge, Foucault's primary focus lies with "naive" and "low-ranking" knowledges that have been devalued by the expertise of social scientific discourses. The psychiatric patient, the infirm, the criminal, the deviant or defective—these are the stories that he is most interested in trying to give voice.[81] And the institutional settings in which such fragile persons are subjected to unmonitored and asymmetrical exercises of power are those he is most concerned to scrutinize.

Any tools that address the needs of the dispossessed are of obvious benefit to the church understood in Augustine's terms as a "sacrificial" or self-emptying community. Foucault's humbling of the grandiose presumptions of certain modern forms of knowledge can help to focus attention more narrowly and directly on local problems that are easily overlooked when surveying where and how to offer effective care. His insights remind those who wield ecclesial power to be cautious about paternalistic presumptions that can inform being "charitable." In attempting to rectify the domination of "naive" and "inexpert" persons through "professional" solutions, they may unintentionally be contributing to rather than relieving their silencing. If it were to follow Foucault's warnings, the church would not simply intervene and reorder from above, but always open itself to the advice and labors that arise from the "untrained" in specific locales. Clearing spaces where "disqualified" voices can be heard requires that the church risk itself. This means that its authority, discourses, and practices may be challenged from all quarters, from within and without. Being called, however, as Augustine believes it is, to shape itself by reenacting sacrificial love demands that such risk be part of the community's continually "re-forming" identity. Solidarity is not thereby lost but understood differently as one that allows diverse and sometimes clashing threads to make up a less monochromatic and therefore, it is hoped, richer and more dynamic ecclesiological weave. Foucault's thoughts concerning cultural dynamics can thus push Augustine's conception of the church, sacrifice, and solidarity farther than he was willing to take them and correct his more unfortunate positions on enforcing unity.

Finally, an appreciation for subjugated knowledges that must compete with culturally privileged discourses in order to be heard and seriously considered offers the socially engaged in the church renewed opportunities to speak. In a society, such as ours, profoundly influenced by the norms and values of scientific materialism, social Darwinism, and consumerism, religious voices are often devalued and disqualified as either hopelessly "naive" or lacking the "objective" credentials to contribute to the shaping of the public domain. Foucault can help to embolden a Christian social critique of the sinful social consequences of these very discourses and the practices they sanction.

Modern Transformations of Sin and Salvation

> Whence a metamorphosis in literature: we have passed from a pleasure to be recounted and heard, centering on the heroic or marvelous narration of "trials" of bravery or sainthood, to a literature ordered according to the infinite task of extracting from the depths of oneself, in between the words, a truth which the very form of the confession holds out like a shimmering mirage.[82]

> It was a time when the most singular pleasures were called upon to pronounce a discourse of truth concerning themselves, a discourse that had to model itself after that which it spoke, not of sin and salvation, but of bodies and life processes—the discourse of science.[83]

Foucault, like Augustine, understands that the search for knowledge, truth, and ultimate fulfillment orients all of one's relations. Under their everyday logic, personal and communal values are shaped, desires interpreted, and habits consciously and unconsciously configured. In light of this, individuals are empowered to influence and guide others and are open to falling under their sway. Dynamics of power, being fundamentally relational, suffuse all of our efforts to discover who we are and should be; what frailties, vulnerabilities, and ailments threaten our "true" reality; and the most efficacious paths to perfect ourselves and others. Foucault also discerns, as does Augustine, that the truths we pursue and the perfection and happiness we anticipate always exact tolls. Some of the cost involves sacrifices we make in service of our loves and aims. What are we willing to give up and what are we willing to endure in dedicating ourselves to these ennobling promises? Others relate to what we must control to make the world we live in one where such hopes can be realized. As we attempt to rid a fragile world of its disorder and sorrow, its uncertainty and risk, its finitude and ambiguities, how do we end up commanding ourselves and others? At what price do we order human reality to our conceptions of the true and the perfect? At what price do we direct and remake ourselves and others? As we have seen, Augustine aims such questions at himself as he struggles with his own spiritual progression and at influential religious philosophies that he believes are either overly optimistic about or oblivious to the dual social dangers of arrogance and despair. Foucault similarly challenges a naive presumptuousness in his own culture, but he places in his sights a radically altered understanding of human wisdom, values, and persons. Given the general cultural shift from a God- or cosmic-centered to a human-centered world, his questioning about the personal and communal costs of our peculiarly modern appetites for knowledge, truth, emancipation, and perfection refers to how these have come to be grounded exclusively in the human subject. "[T]he question I asked myself was this: how is it that the human subject took itself as the object of possible knowledge? Through what forms of rationality and historical conditions? And finally at what price? This is my question: at what price can subjects speak the truth about themselves?"[84] Foucault observes that the basic desire to know who we truly are, what risks we must be attentive to and how best to attain fulfillment, still has the same breadth and power it did in antiquity to define all of life's relations and values. What has changed is where we look for that essential truth and how we bring others into our search. "Whenever it is a question of knowing who we are, it is this logic that henceforth serves as our master key."[85] Holding that comprehensive power in mind, Foucault probes the social prestige and authority we give to those who proffer themselves as experts at locating and disclosing the meaning of this precious jewel. The problem for the modern self, he writes, is in discovering "what marvelous ring confers a similar power on us, and on which master's finger it has been placed."[86] Through cultural analysis, we must scrutinize the often unnoticed influences of that "privileged place where our deepest 'truth' is read and expressed."[87] In this final section, I analyze from Foucault's perspective the cultural transformations involved in modern aspirations for a "redeeming" self-knowledge and truth. What social risks do our hermeneutics of the self share with ancient cultures, and what dangers are uniquely our own? How do these relate to our broader social values and to the formation of interpersonal bonds and commitments?

As we reflect on our changing attitudes, expectations, and powers, three theological and sociohistorical themes provide a basic structure: (i) interpretations of "confession" in shaping personal and communal identity; (ii) interpretations of "infirmity" in sanctioning cultural responses to human differences, deviations, and imperfections; and (iii) interpretations of "healing" as a process of convalescence or transfiguring cure requiring critical intervention by specialists. Foucault maintains that all of these, in different ways, have been appropriated from early Christian practices and tailored for secular purposes so that the social desires attending each have shifted significantly from a paradigm of sin and salvation to one of "pseudo-scientific" pathology and well-being.

Up to this point, I have been relying primarily on Foucault for conceptual analysis. Before using his research as a historical resource, however, it is important to consider how he conducted and viewed himself as a "historian." With good reason, Foucault is often criticized for being substantively sketchy and careless in his accumulation and construal of particular facts and events. Sometimes when reading Foucault, I am reminded of a scene from *Schindler's List* in which Schindler tells his manager, who will be stuck with the workaday demands of running his business, that he himself can't get lost in balancing all the minutiae of accounts and ledgers. When asked what exactly he will be contributing to the business, Schindler replies theatrically: "Not the work, not the work—the presentation!" Of course, this caricature only captures Foucault in moments. But such moments are nevertheless revealing—not by showing what an inept scholar he is (although he does at times deserve stern rebuke for historical sloppiness), but by showing how strikingly different his thinking can be. Foucault is a wanderer, who dislikes being hemmed in by any discipline, be it historiography, philosophy, social science, or political theory. When he writes as a historian, then, he simultaneously acts in many other capacities. Foremost, I would say, he works as a cultural critic, using tools from various disciplines to serve his creative critical purposes. Although Foucault gets absorbed in "the work" of history—indeed, some of his most perceptive analysis excavates details so obscure no one else has thought them worth noticing—his genius for seeing the ways historical and social threads interweave often leads him away from a rigorous analysis as he follows out and then "presents" their cultural implications. He has the advantages and limitations of a novelist who attempts to render something that rings true about important but often overlooked experiences in modern culture, or who forces readers to see their everyday familiar surroundings in an unexpected light. All this he brings to life through a situated and historically investigated yet also imaginative medium. In one of his more interesting interviews on *The History of*

Sexuality, Foucault gives us a glimpse into his unusually creative attitude to history and cultural criticism:

> This book does not have the function of a proof. It exists as a sort of prelude, to explore the keyboard, sketch out the themes. . . . I am well aware that I have never written anything but fictions. I do not mean to say, however, that truth is therefore absent. It seems to me that the possibility exists for fiction to function in truth, for a fictional discourse to induce effects of truth, and for bringing it about that a true discourse engenders or "manufactures" something that does not as yet exist, that is, "fictions" it. One "fictions" history on the basis of a political reality that makes it true, one "fictions" a politics not yet in existence on the basis of a historical truth.[88]

Guiding Foucault most frequently in his research is an attentiveness to the forgotten and undervalued. For example, in *Discipline and Punish,* when he seeks a date for the completion of the carceral system, he mentions the opening of the reformatory, Mettray, but then immediately throws this well-documented public event in the shadow of a historical marker that was "better still:" a day that went "unremarked and unrecorded, when a child in Mettray remarked as he lay dying: 'What a pity I left the colony so soon.' "[89] The narrative of the introductory volume of *The History of Sexuality* is also punctuated with small, seemingly insignificant vignettes, especially when compared to the extensive reach of his historical investigation. Foucault is moved along in his telling of this history by accounts of suffering that he has pulled from archival obscurity. Whether such overlooked stories give voice to persons who have been hounded, cast out and abandoned, or turned by their contemporaries into freakish case studies, their unremembered lives mark for him the movement of time. Foucault traces out complex historical lines and vast political, economic, and institutional influences. But as we saw with his attitude to the opening of Mettray, it is not imposing forces and public events so much as unnoticed, brief reports—often told in only a few lines—that provide the most revealing historical milestones. In a telling description of his research for an anthology on infamous lives, Foucault eloquently expresses his empathy for and attention to the marginalized: "they exist now only through the few terrible words which were destined to render them unworthy."[90] "And I confess that these 'nouvellas,' suddenly rising up through two and a half centuries of silence, stirred more fibre in me than what one usually calls literature."[91] Seeing their stories buried in history as in "the darkness of night," Foucault is moved to awaken his readers not just to remember but fervently feel, "under words polished like stone, the relentlessness and the ruin."[92] In doing so, he allows the voiceless to speak while also reinvigorating history by bringing it back to its animating roots. Given such sensitivities, it is perplexing that Foucault spoke almost whimsically at times about the ancient Greek desire to leave behind "beautiful memories." His own work was unquestionably committed to the opposite aim: unearthing in place of the culturally praiseworthy and glorious, the unsightly, socially "imperfect," and neglected.

Foucault's sympathies for the dispossessed and his unorthodox wandering can be a rich asset as long as we keep in mind what he is up to, remain cognizant of his limitations as a historian, and not force him to provide us with what he admits his work lacks. For our purposes, it is perhaps most constructive to look for his broader strokes that give shape to a central modern transformation that has great import for theology, rather than allow ourselves to get bogged down in punctilios. We could spend the rest of the chapter investigating where and how Foucault misses the mark in his descriptions of pre-modern Christian practices. I will only dwell on those historical problems that have import for my analytical purposes. Interestingly enough, challenging Foucault's historical misunderstandings of Christian practices as well as his theological omissions does not undercut his critique. It actually strengthens the cultural contrast he makes between pre-modern and modern social patterns, thereby sharpening rather than blunting his criticisms of current practices.

Foucault's investigation of early Christian culture is fairly limited. Both his angle of vision and his scope of analysis leave him with a lopsided picture. What stood out to Foucault as socially important were elements that would later be transformed by modern culture. He often explores particular practices strategically, less for how they actually shaped persons than for how they prefigure the shaping of persons now. Nevertheless, Foucault is usually careful, at least in his books and lectures, in contrast to his interviews, not to collapse the cultural patterns together.[93] The two eras are kept distinct, in that they live under the logic of different conceptions of the self, knowledge, fulfillment, and perfection. Foucault's view of Christian practices, however, is difficult to pin down because it changes as his research interests change. He tended to be most negative in his descriptions when he had strategic purposes in mind, especially as he readied himself to criticize specific modern discourses and practices. His most sympathetic portrayals come from the end of his life when he immersed himself in studying monastic texts, especially the works of John Cassian. I will depend on his later writings first and then turn to what he sees as their underside, which is both appropriated and significantly changed in the modern era.

Foucault uncovers in his historical research the bare cultural beams that will become co-opted, built on and around, and used to serve entirely new purposes and demands as the culture shifts from its privileging of truth in theology and philosophy to science. This social superstructure, when looked at in hindsight, appears to Foucault to be grounded in what were understood as four religious dangers: the endlessly desiring person who cannot control his intentions, thoughts, whims, fantasies, and dreams; the hidden and ingenious nature of concupiscence that can only be seized and eradicated through painstaking coercion; the ease with which evil can be made to appear good so that one can never know the real root of desire or trust even the most fleeting and innocuous-seeming images and sensations; and the inability of individuals to decipher adequately the spiritual temptations and struggles taking place within them so that for salvation they have to seek the aid of a human intermediary.[94]

Foucault describes the emergence of monastic practices of self-examination and spiritual direction in early Christianity as power technologies that enabled persons to navigate themselves and others through these common perils.[95] Although adherents lived under unquestioned beliefs about what constituted the true and false, the licit and illicit, they nevertheless were suspended in an uncertain moral world, one replete with furtive enigmas and shadows. In seeking out clarity and control, privileged social patterns arose to stabilize the moral and spiritual order and empower individuals in their pursuit of self-knowledge, truth, and perfection. These relational dynamics and differentials ritually established a "grid of intelligibility." With this, individuals could place themselves as desiring persons, gauge where they stood and should head in light of the mobility of both thoughts and activities, identify failures hindering progress, and adopt strategies of renunciation to gain control over all mental and physical movements.[96] Meditation, dependency, obedience, and self-sacrifice were the main transformative tools at their disposal.[97] Using these mechanisms of power, Foucault writes, Christians placed themselves "under the same sign of concern with the self" as did ancient Greek philosophy, only they used them to different ends and effects.[98] Whereas Greek ethics aimed at building "a beautiful existence" through technologies of self that make the individual sovereign and "dependent on nothing," Christians sought salvation by reminding anyone who thinks himself sovereign "that he is nothing" except in being utterly dependent on God.[99]

A number of structuring relational rules governed the self-examining and renunciating practices that developed in early Christian culture. As Foucault explores them, he always has one eye on particular historical experiences and the other on future cultural developments and consequences. Overall, however, he is interested in tracing how these patterns of interaction will later become colonized and put to use for foreign secular purposes. These stabilizing hermeneutical exercises were framed around the effective application of examination, disclosure, and decipherment. Although distinguishable technologies of power, each one required of the participant a "ceaseless watch over his thoughts and bodily movements" and aimed at transforming all human experiences—actions, intentions, memories, anticipations, imaginations—into a confessional discourse.[100] "[W]e have to examine any thought which presents itself to consciousness to see the relation between act and thought, truth and reality, to see if there is anything in this thought which will move our spirit, provoke our desire, turn our spirit away from God."[101] This was done not only through verbalization but also through self-reflective literature, as Foucault points out in reference to Augustine: "Attention was paid to nuances of life, mood, and reading, and the experience of oneself was intensified and widened by virtue of this writing."[102] Whether through the medium of speaking or writing, the power of confession was never simply an act of expression; it was an act of making or constructing. Working with and on the dynamic relations that constitute the self, even the most expressive speech and writing reconfigure minute interactions, and by reordering the particularities of the self's relations, remake the individual. To reinforce the notion of confession as labor rather than mere disclosure, Foucault highlights Cassian's images of plying a trade on the self. The monastic was able to perform "[t]he work of the miller sorting out his grain, the centurion picking his troops, the money changer who weighs coins before accepting or refusing them. . . . Such an effort will allow him to sort out his thoughts according to their origin, to distinguish them by their quality and to separate the objects they represent from the pleasure they can evoke."[103]

The critical and constructive mechanisms that confession affords do not flatten the self by hammering on it with a static set of rules; rather, they "deepen" it as one endlessly pursues varied human experiences and labors among their enigmas. As Foucault explains:

This has nothing to do with an internalisation of a whole list of forbidden things. . . . It is rather an opening up of an area . . . operating erratically and spontaneously, with its images, memories and perceptions, with movements and impressions transmitted from the body to the mind and the mind to the body. This has nothing to do with a code of permitted or forbidden actions, but is a whole technique for analysing and diagnosing thought, its origins, its qualities, its dangers, its potential for temptation and all the dark forces that can lurk behind the mask it may assume.[104]

Here is a densely animated world of self-relations, with multiple folds of intrigue, elusive images that dart here and there, and unexplored mysterious corners. Making and constructing should thus not be thought of as akin to work carried out in a factory. A better description is the creative exertions of participating in and interpreting a never-ending drama. It is with ambiguous and suspenseful stories that the hermeneutical self is called to labor. Augustine captures the tension of such drama better than Cassian when writing about his own uncertain journey in the *Confessions*: "There is, indeed, *some light in men:* but let them walk fast, walk fast, *lest the shadows come.*"[105] Peter Brown elucidates further, saying that for Augustine,

[t]he conscious mind was ringed with shadows. Augustine felt he moved in 'a limitless forest, full of unexpected dangers.' . . . 'For there is in me a lamentable darkness in which my latent possibilities are hidden from myself, so that my mind, questioning itself upon its own powers, feels that it cannot rightly trust its own report.' . . . [Augustine] still felt himself on a slippery slope: he speaks with the harshness and the fear of someone for whom the boundaries between a measured appetite and a shadow of greed were still not safely fixed.[106]

Foucault, reading such descriptions about dangerously twisting plots and suspicious actors, concludes: "In the Christian technologies of the self, the problem is to discover what is hidden inside the self; the self is like a text or a book that we have to decipher."[107]

Internal to the dynamics of the drama itself, and thus to the critical and constructive techniques of confession, is a complex web of interdependent relations. The hermeneutical depth of this storied self entails the inherent interplay of self and other. Given the apprehension of being encircled by shadows, the denouement of the self's deciphering narrative is that one finally will not be abandoned and forgotten in darkness. Rather, the lost will be retrieved by one who has "run the risk of losing himself for others."[108] The biblical images of the good shepherd establish the basic social expectations in early Christian monastic culture and shape, according to Foucault, a complex field of social power within which persons search for self-knowledge, truth, and perfection.

> [T]he shepherd's role is to ensure the salvation of his flock. . . . It's not only a matter of saving them all, all together, when danger comes nigh. It's a matter of constant, individualised and final kindness. Constant kindness, for the shepherd ensures his flock's food; every day he attends to their thirst and hunger. . . . And individualized kindness, too, for the shepherd sees that all the sheep, each and every one of them, is fed and saved. . . . Everything the shepherd does is geared to the good of his flock. That's his constant concern. When they sleep, *he* keeps watch. The theme of keeping watch is important. It brings out two aspects of the shepherd's devotedness. First, he acts, he works, he puts himself out, for those he nourishes and who are asleep. Second, he watches over them. He pays attention to them all and scans each one of them. Not only must he know where good pastures are, the seasons' laws and order of things; he must also know each one's particular needs.[109]

Structuring the social relations of this narrative, argues Foucault, are, on one side, a selfless kindness whose only concern is the welfare of those who need tending; a constant kindness that watches for unseen dangers that neither the awake nor the asleep can protect themselves from; and an intimate kindness that remains attentive to every particular desire, thought, habit, and need when caring for the vulnerable. On the other side, being looked after in such a way calls for and exemplifies a social response that is grateful, humble, and obedient. Ever-present care can only be assured by renouncing the self in "a kind of everyday death" and thereby becoming utterly trusting of and reliant on the devoted other.[110] If the four dangers mentioned earlier concerning the desiring person set the main cultural beams for later modern practices, then the loving protective knowledge and guidance of shepherding care provides the flooring on which this ancient superstructure stands.

Foucault describes the asymmetrical dynamics intrinsic to this interpretive matrix as laying the ground rules for "a strange game whose elements are life, death, truth, obedience, self-identity," and whose success can only be achieved by a "detachment with respect to oneself and the establishing of a relationship with oneself which tends towards a destruction of the form of the self."[111] Even though Foucault sees it as a strange game with strange rules, he indicates at least in some of his later writings that such "rules of life" nevertheless provided monastics with instruments of power to seek their vision of "the beautiful life." Essential to their efforts was acquiring the personal skills to shape a harmoniously centered self, revolving around the responsively asymmetrical aims of obedience, purification, and self-sacrificing humility. As Foucault warms to the idea of monastic technologies of the self, his understanding of their search for self-knowledge and perfection changes from his early writings, when he defined such pursuits as obsessively and narrowly focused on sexual lust (Augustine being one of his prime targets in this regard). He begins to turn ever so slightly to a new aesthetic possibility: an internally flowing, balancing, and constantly reforming chastity. "In this chastity-oriented asceticism," writes Foucault, "one can see a process of 'subjectivisation' which has nothing to do with a sexual ethic or physical self-control."[112] Renunciation works on the self as a whole. With its complex aesthetic relations, it weaves an interconnected yet richly dynamic web involving "movements of the body and the mind, images, feelings, memories, faces in dreams, the spontaneous movements of thoughts, the consenting (or refusing) will, waking and sleeping."[113] This is an ethic of purified unity, creating equipoise among the varying "internal play of thoughts" and "bodily and physical reflexes."[114] Truth of self is still the aim. The self-identity connected to such truth, however, is a much more relationally complex reality.

Foucault's deeper appreciation for the variegation and harmony of the monastic self rests on Cassian's perception that vices and virtues "do not exist in isolation."[115] They continually are moved by one another. Physical lust then never acts alone; it is inevitably rooted in and accompanied by other self-defining vices of greed, avarice, covetousness, and pride.[116] All are bound to one another and cannot be easily pried apart. To reform one, they must be reformed together.[117] Purity, therefore, is always a labor involving the whole, even though it works on particulars as it strives for a harmonious self-identity. Nonetheless, although the individual comes to possess a complex self-knowledge, he is unable to reach such truths by himself. As with the asymmetrical narrative through which he deciphers himself and his asymmetrical responses of gratitude, humiliation, and purity, so too must he labor on his own aesthetic identity by way of submission to the wise mediation of another. Here is where the overlapping powers of the self-sacrificing story, self-sacrificing renunciation, and self-sacrificing obedience coalesce. And it is here, of course, where Foucault becomes most concerned about such a battle with chastity. The monastic's search for self-knowledge and "quest for the truth . . . functions through complex relations with others. . . . [C]onfession to others, submission to their advice and permanent obedience to one's superiors are essential to this battle."[118]

To understand Foucault's assessment of the potential relational dangers here, we must recall that asymmetry, on his view, is not a social evil in and of itself. As we saw earlier, he even uses examples of monastic guidance and teacher-student relationships to make his point that it does not necessarily entail social harm. The problems with asymmetry are twofold. First, it inhibits a fluid and reversible flow of power among participants, which leads to the second. It increases the opportunities to manipulate and exploit others without their being sufficiently aware or sufficiently empowered to resist.

Foucault's wariness about uneven power relationships evidenced in early monastic communities increases substantially as these evolve and become reformulated in an institutional setting and for institutional purposes. The social risks he highlights in ancient monastic compared to late medieval and Tridentine practices are illuminating. They show both how certain ritual and cultural changes occurred through institutionalization and how these reconfigured relational patterns paved the way for modern secular transformations. Knowledge, truth, self-identity, and a concern with sexual decipherment and comportment relate to one another in all these social contexts. However, they interact in significantly different ways, creating different interpretive aims, capacities, and instruments. Distinct openings for social power are thereby cleared through the varied uses of changing human aptitudes and tools. With this, Foucault argues, specific cultural opportunities and dangers emerge as these become exercised in hopeful pursuits of knowledge, self-transformation, and social perfection.

By examining fractures and shifts that surface as ancient monastic practices of confession become institutionalized for medieval and Tridentine purposes, we begin to see the lay of geography that modernity builds itself on and adapts to its own secular ends.[119] Foucault, in asides tucked here and there, signals that something important has occurred, changing how these cultures comprehend and respond to the dangers of the desiring person. About Cassian's ethic of chastity, he writes: "Not one of the categories that in the Middle Ages were to be built up into a great code of sins is to be found here."[120] And commenting on how "unjuridical" his aims and methods of purification were, he concludes: "Cassian's specifications obviously have a different meaning."[121] If one were to read only *The History of Sexuality, Volume 1,* it would seem that, on the face of it at least, nothing significant had changed since like ancient monasticism, later popular and institutionalized practices encouraged participants to be ever watchful and to confess transgressions in great detail. When one listens to the words from a seventeenth-century penitential manual, it is difficult to distinguish them from ancient counsels:

> Examine, diligently, therefore, all the faculties of your soul: memory, understanding, and will. Examine with precision all your senses as well. . . . Examine, more over, all your thoughts, every word you speak, and all your actions. Examine even unto your dreams, to know if, once awakened, you did not give them your consent. And finally, do not think that in so sensitive and perilous a matter as this, there is anything trivial or insignificant.[122]

So why, in Foucault's later research, does he begin to perceive something different here? How could such watchfulness and care for detail be passed on in a way that preserves the ancient advice and yet alters it? How could such similar words involve a shift in understanding human desiring, sex in particular, and self-knowledge or self-identity? In looking for an answer, it is helpful to recall some of the insights Foucault gleaned in his last writings on monasticism. Because his views change, we have to ferret out clues from his latest research and then make our way back to the introductory volume of *The History of Sexuality.*

There are two distinguishable contrasts that can be drawn, one relating to medieval codification and the other to Tridentine. Both are important for understanding why modern practices and secular institutions eventually usurp confessional technologies of power as being particularly useful for medical and scientific ends. Foucault clearly sets the early monastic technologies of the self over against the amassing of specific human desires into "the catalogue of sins that are to be found when the medieval church organises the sacrament of penance on the lines of a penal code."[123] The effects of such regulatory ambitions in both the Middle Ages and early modernity are what one would expect from extensive codification. Compilations of rules, acts, and satisfactions could be classified in unambiguous categories of kind and degree, making it easier for persons to sort, identify, evaluate, and effectively make reparations for explicitly detailed transgressions. Shadows and enigmas, uncertainties and apprehensions finally could be controlled with precision. Through scrupulously regulated, universally explained, and neatly divided definitions, persons could disentangle themselves from the frightening risks of the early monastic world. The price of such certitude and safety, however, comes in rigidly trying to command the fluidity of desire. Rather than shape the desiring self as a dynamic aesthetic unity, one that is constantly balancing diverse interactive movements, desires become sliced up into manageable pieces and analyzed in isolation. By separating specific acts, attitudes, and gestures, and placing each in its own spotlight, desires can be interrogated as a multiplicity of discrete offenders and, with the aid of classifications and codes, be quickly judged and sentenced or discharged as if they had been brought into a courtroom. Verdict pronounced, case closed, next sin please.

Foucault could not portray the early monastic attitude more differently. It "has nothing to do with an internalisation of a whole list of forbidden things"; it "has nothing to do with a code of permitted or forbidden actions."[124] At least according to Cassian's ethic of chastity, adjustments must be made to a moving whole, not to isolated fragments. Rather than the rigid slotting of systematic codification and regulation, Foucault speaks of such practices as "opening up an area" where "impressions transmitted from the body to the mind and the mind to the body" freely flow here and there.[125] When cultivated through technologies of the self, they create a certain harmony; when not, they often produce a jarring discordance. Furthermore and importantly, in the strikingly different mind-set of early monasticism, no universal precision or regulatory clarity could throw light into all the mysterious corners or dispel all the shadowy images. This was a dramatic place alien to the atmosphere of the courtroom. In the world of the early monastic, the latter's systematized tactics would not have been able to supplant the intense technologies of the self by which the ascetic waged battles and underwent trials in pursuit of harmonious purity.

The other thread worth teasing out and considering is the subjectivizing influences of institutional codes and popular manuals that simultaneously expand and narrow their self-examining concentration on sexual lusts and acts.[126] In describing Tridentine practices, Foucault writes, they "attributed more and more importance to . . . all the insinuations of the flesh. . . . According to the new pastoral, sex must not be named imprudently, but its aspects, its correlations, and its effects must be pursued down to their slenderest ramifications."[127] By tending "to make the flesh into the root of all evil," the focus of such "meticulous rules of self-examination" came "at the expense of some other sins."[128] According to Foucault's understanding of the technologies of self, the impact would be widespread on the subject who, through such practices, attempts to shape and cultivate her religious character and identity. The deconstructing of the self piece by piece through classifications and codes rather than those ascetical techniques that attend to the self as an interwoven unity; the examining and interpretation of isolated pieces of the sexual life to the exclusion of pride, avarice, greed, envy, and covetousness; and the analytical identification of spiritual struggles with the ever-narrowing and yet ever-expanding terrain of sex rather than the comprehensive domain of purity or chastity all would have shaped how individuals could define themselves as religiously devoted individuals. Through self-examination, confession, and spiritual direction, the individual uses mechanisms of power both to dismantle and to reconstruct the self. As not merely expressive, but creative and constructive, confessional techniques have enormous power to form the religious subject, as a whole and in various parts.

One could argue that Cassian offered in his ethic of chastity techniques that enabled individuals, through their larger purifying aims, to work toward spiritualizing the embodied self. The danger of later codified approaches to the self that segregated, categorized, and defined various aspects of it would have been twofold. First, rather than desexualize the self, Foucault would argue that this intense concentration on specific details would have actually sexualized one's religious identity. Having no appreciation for a larger interactive framework within which to interpret and relate the isolated dynamics of desire, the frailties of sex that one would be constantly watching for, talking about, and battling against would become the defining features of the religious subject. Not just because one would be expressing what one actually is, but because, in and through confession, one would be establishing and solidifying certain experiences by attaching them to one's self-identity.

Second, in analytically breaking down the subject into fragments and privileging sexual vices and virtues over other formative desires, there is a dual danger of neglecting valuable aspects of the self while marginalizing and hounding others. Hints of the vulnerability of the overly and narrowly analyzed self can be detected in Foucault's description of Tridentine aims and influences:

> Discourse, therefore, had to trace the meeting line of the body and soul, following all its meanderings: beneath the surface, it would lay bare the unbroken nervure of the flesh. Under the authority of a language that had been carefully expurgated so that it was no longer directly named, sex was taken charge of, tracked down as it were, by a discourse that aimed to allow it no obscurity, no respite.[129]

Interpreted as inherently fragile and evasive, sexual desire is approached as something that "always hides" itself, "that speaks in a voice so muted and often disguised"[130] that the only way to force it out into the open is by removing all of the shadows from the self that offer elusive mysteries refuge. Only then can the "most tenuous [and] scarcely perceivable forms of desire"[131] be apprehended in a flood of light and analytically interrogated. According to Foucault, it is through both the meticulously descriptive and the broadly defining powers of confessional discourse that individuals and communities are assured, with proper assistance, of being able to flush out, catch hold of, and expel any such "disquieting enigma."[132] In contrast to ancient rituals of penance involving physical acts of repentance, persons are hereby challenged with a different duty and task, one of laboriously "passing everything . . . through the endless mill of speech."[133] To be secure, no aspect of desiring can be allowed to remain in nondiscursive mystification.[134] Everything must be exposed and compelled to account for itself discursively by way of an imperious classifying knowledge.

As Foucault begins to shift his attention away from religious practices to the secular adaptations of confessional techniques, his suggestive warnings about a tenuous fragility and vulnerability to coercion become more ominous. Widening his perspective from the hazy dimensions of the desiring self to hazy figures that wander along the fringes of society, he increasingly reveals the underside of "interrogation" and "inquisition" where confession operates as "a many-sided extortion" of confidences.[135] In its ever-expanding aim to extract every perceived ambivalence or "fragment of darkness," confession has socially developed, he argues, into "an entire machinery" that is fueled by a complicated network of asymmetrical discursive relations.[136] As such, it has slowly become not only institutionally centralized but also extensively dispersed and entrenched in the most unnoticed aspects of daily habits and relations. Foucault sees its morally ambiguous traces everywhere. We have become, he writes, "a singularly confessing society."

> The confession has spread its effects far and wide. It plays a part in justice, medicine, education, family relationships, and love relations, in the most ordinary affairs of everyday life, and in the most solemn rites; one confesses one's crimes, one's sins, one's thoughts and desires, one's illnesses and troubles, one goes about telling, with the greatest precision whatever is most difficult to tell. . . . The most defenseless tenderness and the bloodiest of powers have a similar need of confession. Western man has become a confessing animal.[137]

Fugitive human frailties combined with the search for a liberating certitude that leaves no place for obscurity have created effective handholds for some of the most historically forceful personal and impersonal relations of power.

With this, we come to our own drama. Of course, Foucault has always been heading here. Along the way, he has been reminding us that our tale is built on many older ones. As a storied people, we share a long history with others. In important ways, our drama is not so different from those played out in the past. Like the ancient ascetics before us, we exercise powerful practices on our desiring selves and submit ourselves to the wise counsel of others as we pursue promises of truth and perfection. Even in the most secular corners of the world, the story of the good shepherd still generally governs our expectations. As we conduct our affairs at home, in the workplace and schools, in clinics and hospitals, we set our hopes on living under some protective knowledge that is shielded from error. We long for a secure orientation and confidence in life's meaningfulness. To that end, we search for trustworthy guidance to help detect otherwise unseen dangers and lead us to safer and more nourishing pastures.

In other ways, our modern drama is quite unlike those of the past. What most marks ours as different is a refusal to acknowledge that we in fact live storied lives. Integral to our being a storied people, therefore, is that we believe that we are not embedded in and bound by any story. We desire a security that drama, with its contingency, plot twists, and unpredictability, cannot yield. We do not want to be surprised by the unexpected or the unexplained—by anything that lurks in dim corners. Foucault highlights an alteration in cultural sensitivities and preoccupations by comparing the imaginative ethos of the gothic novel, with its "fantasy-world of stone walls, darkness, hideouts and dungeons which harbor, in significant complicity, brigands and aristocrats, monks and traitors,"[138] with the social anxieties that gripped the late eighteenth century:

> the fear of darkened spaces, of the pall of gloom that prevents the full visibility of things, men and truths. It sought to break up the patches of darkness that blocked the light, eliminate the shadowy areas of society, demolish the unlit chambers where arbitrary political acts, monarchical caprice, religious superstitions, tyrannical and priestly plots, epidemics and the illusions of ignorance were fomented.[139]

For Foucault, this change in sentiment is the principal reason that our particular story has proven so compelling. It is a story that promises to alleviate all such fears and clean out all dangerous spaces, and it claims to have the power to do that precisely because it is no longer a story.

Now, in comparison to the old tales of the past, searching for the purity of truth and the safety of certitude becomes scientifically validated. The modern version of confession consists in using a variety of techniques that purport to provide an unclouded knowledge of ourselves and others through "the rarefied and neutral viewpoint of science."[140] We submit ourselves to a whole battery of tests, observations, categorizations, specifications, quantifications, analyses, questionnaires, transcriptions, recordings, and chart notes. Because these techniques arise from and are applied in the natural and social sciences, the examination of ourselves and others receives the imprimatur of scientific certainty. The worries of the eighteenth century are thereby alleviated with "[a] blanket guarantee under cover of which moral obstacles, economic or political options, and traditional fears [are] recast in a scientific-sounding vocabulary."[141]

This whole set of presuppositions and procedures, despite its own best efforts to withdraw itself from the messiness of drama and traditions and rituals, nevertheless, on Foucault's view, manifests elements of them all. Consider his description of the "carefully staged" regimens of a hospital: "its interplay of dialogues, palpations, laying on of hands, postures which doctors elicited or obliterated with a gesture or word, its hierarchy of personnel who kept watch, organized, provoked, monitored, reported, and who accumulated an immense pyramid of observations and dossiers."[142] Although Foucault was speaking about a specific psychiatric facility, his portrayal fits a wider array of institutional settings. This modern drama, when compared with premodern ones, clearly has different lines, different costumes, different props, and different sets, and it is acted on very different stages. But it still has privileged players and spaces and ritualized patterns of interaction with coded contents.[143] Its objectivity, precision, and cool disinterest, which appear to lack all trace of the theatrical, are integral to the acclaim this show receives. It bolsters our confidence that finally we have managed to leave behind fallibility, contingency, uncertainty, and disorder. In this well-lit and meticulously organized world, safe in its sterility, we can identify dangers and eliminate them. Through the careful application of dispassionate procedures, we can cleanly set our psychic and social houses in order. Now our desires can be efficiently managed, "inserted into systems of utility, regulated for the greater good of all [and] made to function according to an optimum."[144]

It is Foucault's genius to be able to see "this everyday bit of theater" overlaid with the "solemn discourse" of scientific and medical institutions of knowledge and power.[145] He identifies the intersection between human desiring and these "objective" technologies as the most recent act in a play whose beginnings he traces to antiquity. To draw on terms I have used in this chapter, we have moved from Cassian's harmonious spiritualized self to the highly systematized sexualized self of late medieval and Tridentine institutions to the scientized self of our own day. They all involve examination, they all involve direction, they all involve practices on the self, and they all involve sex. As we have seen, Foucault recognizes these lines of connection but is careful to enunciate the peculiar configuration they assume in relation to different conceptions of the hazards and aims of desiring. We can see in their development, he argues, "[a] visible continuity, therefore, but one that did not prevent a major transformation."[146] Though "it had its beginnings in the technologies of the 'flesh' in classical Christianity . . . today it fills a reverse function."[147]

The cultural change Foucault describes can be conceived as a shift from one governing metaphor to another. Transformations of the self are no longer interpreted in terms of the movement from sin to salvation, but from pathology to well-being. From the end of the eighteenth century, he asserts, "the technology of sex was ordered in relation to the medical institution, the exigency of normality, and—instead of the question of death and everlasting punishment—the problem of life and illness. The flesh was brought down to the level of the organism."[148] The purity Cassian was striving for in his ethic of chastity is now replaced with physical vigor and mental health. Today we strive to be autonomously well-adjusted, high-functioning, productive members of society. That is the vision of a redeemed life under this paradigm. "[I]t was no longer a question of leading people to their salvation in the next world, but rather ensuring it in this world. And in this context, the word *salvation* takes on different meanings: health, well-being (that is, sufficient wealth, standard of living), security, protection against accidents. A series of worldly aims took the place of the religious aims of the traditional pastorate."[149]

It is not just a traditional spiritual or religious quest that is being transformed in this cultural reorientation. Morality gets displaced as well. Foucault holds that the modern scientific-medicalized paradigms of knowing and perfecting presume to stand at a safe remove from traditional disputes over what constitutes the good. We are engaged in a pursuit of the true, the natural, the given—about which, once it is discovered, there can be no questioning or doubt. Such discourses tend to ignore the moral and social biases of those who decipher information and the moral and social consequences of their determinations. Because knowledge is always put to use by fallible human beings in a practical world of competing interests and visions, we are deluding ourselves, he insists, if we believe that questions of truth can be disentangled from questions of normative worth and value. Even what appears to be most self-evidently natural is inevitably situated in a cultural context, and thus, shot through with social meanings and moral ambiguities.

We must not misunderstand Foucault's point here, however. He is alerting us to potential problematic applications of scientifically derived knowledge. But we should take care not to confuse the matter, he argues, by reversing this process of problematization and begin measuring all fruits of scientific research in terms of its function in society. "It is not in the name of a political practice that one can judge the scientific quality of a science (unless the latter claims to be, in one way or another, a theory of politics). But in the name of a political practice, one can question the mode of existence and the functioning of a science."[150] Foucault does not want to undermine scientific research as a whole, but to get individuals to reflect soberly on their social ramifications. The social sciences are particularly problematic in this regard, from his perspective, because they attempt to ground their "objectivity" on themselves. As a pair of perceptive readers have put it: "[I]f the human sciences claim to study human activities, then the human sciences, unlike the natural sciences, must take account of those human activities which make possible their own disciplines."[151]

Once moral and religious discourses are transposed into a scientific key, a whole range of human frailties and fallibilities (of which Foucault highlights those from the "sexual domain") are "no longer accounted for simply by the notions of error or sin, excess or transgression, but [are] placed under the rule of the normal and the pathological."[152] With this, two separate human registries are created. Among that "numberless family" of the impure, abnormal, peculiar, and dangerous, Foucault is acutely attentive to specific groups: children, women, homosexuals, the mentally ill, and the condemned.[153] To get a feel for the exploitation to which such outcasts were and are exposed by confession and examination in their scientized forms, consider his following portrayal:

> It was a time for all these figures . . . to step forward and speak, to make the difficult confession of what they were. . . . From the end of the eighteenth century to our own, they circulated through the pores of society; they were always hounded, but not always by laws; were often locked up, but not always in prisons; were sick, perhaps, but scandalous,

dangerous victims, prey to a strange evil. . . . [T]hey haunted the houses of correction, the penal colonies, the tribunals, and the asylums; they carried their infamy to the doctors and their sickness to the judges.[154]

Foucault illustrates the fervor of the desire to scientifically define and manage such "infirmities" through the case of a simple farmhand who, arrested for "inconsequential bucolic pleasures," undergoes a medical examination that includes the measurement of his brainpan, an analysis of his facial structure, a thorough search for signs of anatomical degeneration, and a probing of his thoughts, his desires, his habits, his fantasies, and his opinions. Though acquitted of any crime, he is shut into a mental hospital where he becomes until death the subject of an exhaustive medical study.[155] In this example, Foucault wants us to see the extreme lengths our culture was and in many ways remains willing to go in its relentless attempts to eliminate disorder and clean up social messes. This was for them an undying dream. Just as they could not cease pursuing it, they could not let a simple man slip through their hands. The mystery must be solved even if it meant incarcerating someone guilty of no crime for the rest of his life. Here we find a new form of power exercised not in adherence to a law but to a natural norm; not by the invocation of rights but by the application of clinical techniques.[156] He was shut away because he was an unexplainable abnormality.

"Whence the setting apart of the 'unnatural,'" Foucault observes, "as a specific dimension in the field of sexuality."[157] The desiring self had always been an ethical and spiritual challenge—one with which ancient ascetics had struggled through temptations, epic trials, and battles; one that both medieval and Tridentine penitential guides scrupulously parsed and clarified through juridical codes and judged by illicit taboos and denouncements. Distinctive in this new way of being set apart by society is that rather than being excluded and reprimanded for forbidden acts in order to be later brought back into what Augustine depicts as a sorrow-sharing and convalescing community, the "defective" are inspected for certain scientific markers, carefully compared to others, and "naturally" sorted and placed on a differentiating continuum of normalcy.[158] Not exclusion, but specification, Foucault claims, relates these "abnormal" individuals to society.[159]

Such individualizing and differentiating techniques also function altogether differently from Roman distinctions of honor and shame. This non-heroic branding of persons Foucault describes as lacking all nobility and notions of communal identification,[160] "as the fixing, at once ritual and scientific, of individual differences, as the pinning down of each individual in his own particularity (in contrast with the ceremony in which status, birth, privilege, function are manifested with all the spectacle of their marks)."[161] On the ritual side, one is christened with "strange baptismal names" as oddities and aberrations are drawn out and disturbing moments are dramatized into peculiar characterizing features.[162] On the scientific and medical side, these experiences and traits are simultaneously "extracted" from and "implanted" in those who have been socially set apart and then symptomatically scrutinized in relation to "a natural order of disorder."[163] In contrast to "commemorative accounts" in which one's character becomes known through vicious or virtuous acts or "vouched for" by reference to others through "genealogies giving ancestors as points of reference," one becomes known by scientifically defined variances and anomalies, by isolating "'gaps' rather than deeds."[164] Whereas legends could capture the spirit of saints and the remarkable bravery of heroes, now individuals are captured by the amassing of medical documents.[165] Foucault argues that with the emergence of our distinctively modern epic genres—the psychological autobiography and the carefully monitored and charted case study—"[t]he turning of real lives into writing is no longer a procedure of heroization; it functions as a procedure of objectification and subjectification. The carefully collated life of mental patients or delinquents belongs, as did the chronicle of kings, or the adventures of the great popular bandits, to a certain political function of writing. . . . [By] substituting for the individuality of the memorable man that of the calculable man . . . a new technology of power and a new political anatomy of the body were implemented."[166] No longer moral transgression and guilt, no longer honor and shame, no longer action and social consequence, but nature and defect analyzed through rational quantitative study govern the relations of power to those falling outside expected norms, values, and behaviors.

Many of these persons and groups have long been regarded as among the most socially vulnerable. However, Foucault wants us to see that an unyielding passion for clarity about and control over our frailties and infirmities suffuses our culture. It makes its presence felt in even the most innocuous places: at cosmetic counters with their white lab-coated "clinicians," in the self-help section of bookstores, in gymnasiums with their personal trainers and videos, and the well-intended advice of family, friends, and counselors. Remembering that practices of confession are not simply expressive, but are technologies of power that deconstruct and reconstruct selves, we can see why Foucault would contend that, even in these moments, we too are vulnerable to becoming scientifically normalized subjects and scientifically normalizing judges. We map ourselves and others within "a modern matrix of individualization," according to both our pathologies and our aspirations.[167] Just as the ancient and medieval confessional practices focused on certain parts of the desiring self, intensifying some aspects over others, we also in novel ways highlight particular frailties or illnesses and accentuate certain longings and hopes. By drawing out and dwelling on selected personal experiences and by applying socially constructed interpretations to them, we establish and solidify individualized identities.

In the process, Foucault asserts, we have culturally created as modern "confessing animals" a new field of pleasure, the pleasure of analysis, and an unexamined devotion to the self-knowledge and bliss that it promises.

> We have at least invented a different kind of pleasure: pleasure in the truth of pleasure, the pleasure of knowing that truth, of discovering and exposing it, the fascination of seeing it and telling it, of captivating and capturing others by it, of confiding it in secret, of luring it out in the open—the specific pleasure of the true discourse of pleasure. . . . The learned volumes, written and read; the consultations and examinations; the anguish of answering questions and the delights of having one's words interpreted; all the stories told to oneself and others, so much curiosity, so many confidences offered in the face of scandal, sustained—but not without trembling a little—by the obligation of truth; the profusion of secret fantasies and the dearly paid right to whisper them to whoever is able to hear them. . . . [A]ll this constitutes something like the errant fragments of an erotic art that is secretly transmitted by confession and the science of sex.[168]

Compared to the "unstable pathological field" of the abnormal and defective, this new pleasure of self-analysis simultaneously plays on our fears and our hopes.[169] Employing the language of redemption, Foucault describes a social obsession both with discovering how we have "sinned" against ourselves, our nature, and, in this case, our supposedly basic sexual being, and with having to redeem ourselves through a newly reconstructed and unbounded freedom. This modern myth holds that not only those who are obviously vulnerable or infirm, those whom we regard as an "alien strain,"[170] but also the seemingly normal are haunted by dark yearnings that must be brought into the light and liberated. "[W]hen you want to individualize the healthy, normal and law-abiding adult," Foucault contends, "it is always by asking him how much of the child he has in him, what secret madness lies within him, what fundamental crime he has dreamt of committing."[171] In some ways, this mirrors Augustine's conception of the universality of sin and the need for continual confession. But here, "fragments of darkness" are countered not through confessing our fallibility and need for mercy and sanctifying grace but through bold exercises of autonomy. Not self-forgetting love and self-surrender but self-assertion frees one from all such dangerous impulses. Even though these modern practices are focused on controlling menacing dangers, they still are best described as a new experience of pleasure. Such analyses "function as mechanisms with a double impetus: pleasure and power. The pleasure that comes of exercising a power that questions . . . ; and on the other hand, the pleasure that kindles at having to evade this power, flee from it, fool it, or travesty it. The power that lets itself be invaded by the pleasure it is pursuing; and opposite it, power asserting itself in the pleasure of showing off, scandalizing, or resisting. . . . These attractions, these evasions, these circular incitements have traced around bodies and sexes, not boundaries not to be crossed, but *perpetual spirals of power and pleasure.*"[172]

Such paradoxical cravings have created, Foucault argues, a sparkling mirage of spontaneity and defiance. Before us lies the illusion that by simply rebelling against perceived power in society, by flouting stodgy mores and provocatively living in a manner that "smacks of revolt," we can abolish the limits of finitude that have historically burdened us and breathe life into a new "garden of earthly delights."[173] On his view, however, these dreams and expectations open us not only to new pleasures but also to fresh possibilities of manipulative seduction: "[I]t uses what people say, feel, and hope for. It exploits their temptation to believe that to be happy, it is enough to cross the threshold of discourse and to remove a few prohibitions."[174] The problem, Foucault maintains, is that what we are yearning to liberate "always eludes us,"[175] and so we find ourselves forever chasing after specters. Rather than the lightness of spontaneous freedom, Foucault dwells on all of the weight of our anticipations as we try "to draw from that little piece of ourselves not only pleasure but [redeeming] knowledge," vainly attempting to elicit "the truest confession from a shadow."[176] Ruminating on our arrogance, he writes, "people will wonder what could have made us so presumptuous" to believe that we could accomplish this ever-purifying and healing task and, in view of the vulnerabilities such desires create, will note the irony of it all since this particular deployment of manipulative power ultimately depends on "having us believe that our 'liberation' is in the balance."[177]

From Foucault's standpoint, the potential danger of these dynamics of normalization—those that feed off of our fears of pathology as well as those that entice us with visions of self-affirming health—is that the seeming naturalness of this "matrix of individualization" is warranted by a host of expensively trained and licensed experts. Consequently, many of the normalizing power relations operating within our scientifically charged culture are asymmetrical and nonreciprocal. These "canonical bits of knowledge" are the privileged possession of an elite few who are authorized "to store and distribute [them]."[178] As such, they are beyond the grasp of those for and on whom they are applied. Although self-knowledge supposedly resides within persons who are confessing, it nevertheless lies beyond their grasp. Thus, those who are pursuing the truth do not control this relationship. Sometimes they are asked to talk, sometimes they are talked to, and sometimes they are talked about.[179] The asymmetry and irreversibility of such relationships is readily apparent in the context of psychiatry. However, it also operates in other scientific and medical venues. Foucault compares this to past uses of confession. In modern and contemporary practices,

> [i]f one had to confess, this was not merely because the person to whom one confessed had the power to forgive, console, and direct, but because the work of producing the truth was obliged to pass through this relationship if it was to be scientifically validated. The truth did not reside solely in the subject who, by confessing, would reveal it wholly formed; . . . it could only reach completion in the one who assimilated and recorded it. It was the latter's function to verify this obscure truth: the revelation of confession had to be coupled with the decipherment of what it said. The one who listened was not simply the forgiving master, the judge who condemned or acquitted; he was the master of truth. His was a hermeneutic function.[180]

The emancipation we long for hence requires that we pass through a scientific gauntlet whose legitimacy is guaranteed by an innumerable set of presuppositions, apparatuses, and institutions.

While it is certainly true that such expertise is retained by a small cadre of specialists who are legally authorized to intervene on our behalf, even in an overtly coercive manner, they have not cornered the market on fostering our health and security. Due to the vigor of our desires for this-worldly well-being, in its manifold forms, the number of "experts" to whom we can turn for advice and analysis has mushroomed. Although their power may not be as hierarchical or potentially coercive, the fact that they have their own "canonical bits of knowledge" leaves their clients or customers vulnerable.

In both cases, the costliness of normalizing knowledge is that it often prom-ises more than it can deliver. We trust that by seeking the assistance of so many we can fulfill our desires for a scientifically mediated self-perfecting knowl-edge and all the security it purports to guarantee.

Throughout this discussion, I have been drawing out the implications, which Foucault usually leaves unstated, for a wider range of normalizing expectations than those from a more strictly defined sexual domain. I have been focusing on a broader array of our culture's desires. Foucault develops some of these in his earlier book, *Discipline and Punish,* which I turn to in the next chapter. On Foucault's analysis in the introductory volume of *The History of Sexuality,* after Freud, sex becomes the hermeneutical key, which science holds in its hand, to unlocking our identity. But the real significance of his study lies less in his contention about the centrality of sex than in our conviction that we can find some final answer to questions about our iden-tity that will yield without risk a variety of social goods. We believe as we come to know who we and others *really* are that we will be able to manage our lives and those of others; free ourselves from frailties and imperfections; eliminate the disorderly, the defective, and the degenerate; and optimize our social usefulness and productivity.

There are indications that biotechnologies and the science of genetics on which they depend are slowly replacing sex and its psychological funda-mentals as the hermeneutical key. If I am right in that judgment, then we are in the midst of another transformation in the way we use technologies of power to shape our personal and social desires, our relationships to and understandings of our bodies, what we deem to have social value and dig-nity, the definition of and paths for attaining perfection, and the meaning of our experiences and purposes of our lives. A genetically focused paradigm parallels the preoccupation with the science of sex in that it combines at-tention to the social dangers of pathologies with a Pelagian confidence in the capacities of the "healthy" and "normal" to take control of their lives and, through the power of knowledge wielded by experts, rescue them from the contingencies and ambiguities of finitude. What is different is the belief, at least at the popular level, that we can rid ourselves of the need for protec-tion and guidance because we can abolish what Augustine describes as the darkness of encircling shadows once and for all. This is not a trial to be fought generation after generation but a final cataclysmic conflict against the resistance of living tissues. By manipulating our malleable bodies down to their tiniest micro-dynamics of power, some seem to expect that we will finally be liberated from imperfection and fallibility, and along with this, the myth of the good shepherd that has governed our relations in various ways for so long.

Of course, this is illusory in two senses. The first, as Ted Peters notes, is that "we assume the DNA acts like a puppeteer and we dance on genetic strings like a puppet. If the DNA determines our hair color and what diseases we will have, then perhaps the DNA determines how we will behave and may even control our virtues and vices."[181] The second is the Pelagian or Promethean assumption "wherein we assume that once our scientists have learned how DNA works, we can take charge—that is, we can get into the DNA with our wrenches and screwdrivers and modify it so as to guide our evolutionary future."[182] Even though illusory, such hopes create social realities. For, I would argue, hand in hand with this desire to be free of imperfections and guidance is the desire to be free of the obligations, burdens, and risks of caring for others. Augustine and Foucault make clear that we are always at some peril when we care for others and allow ourselves to be cared for. Trying to insulate ourselves from the exposure of being influenced by others does not, however, necessarily increase our safety; it inevitably opens us to new and potentially more pernicious (because less examined) vulnerabilities. Thus they both argue for an ethic of care, even though it must be always offered in an uncertain world and always involve us in personal and social hazards. The illusion of genetics is simply a much more technologically sophisticated form of self-constitution, which seeks to overcome what they maintain are inevitable features of power: that it is socially dispersed, co-created, generative, and morally ambiguous. Regardless of whether I am right or wrong about a new cultural transformation, Foucault and Augustine would insist that whatever form our desires to liberate ourselves from life's vicissitudes may take, we need to be fully cognizant of the price they exact, both on ourselves and on others.

As we have seen, in the modern era, an Augustinian notion of the solidarity of sin where everyone is fallible, vulnerable, and sojourning is supplanted by a dramatically different conception of "community." Individuated persons now can be located in relation to one another within a matrix of normalcy where the gaps separating them are carefully measured and socially calculated. Foucault contends that our chasing after certitude has led us to search, on the one hand, for a scientifically definable fragility that can categorize and brand the defective few and, on the other, for a self-affirming wholeness that can be hermeneutically discovered and identified as "healthy," "happy," "free," and "true." By placing so much hope, he argues, in an illusionary promise that we can liberate ourselves from relational fragility, ambiguity, and finitude, we have culturally invested, through the fervency of our faith, scientific discourses with hallowed power and given them sanctuary from historical and political critiques. Ironically, in so doing, we have made ourselves more rather than less susceptible to the uncertainties we sought to escape. Our modern reliance on such secure "objective" knowledge, Foucault warns, has become so laden with human desires that any crack in its fortification risks the collapse of all sense of personal worth under the sheer weight of our frustrated hopes. By giving ourselves over uncritically to an invasive power of our own making, we have intimately exposed ourselves not only to socially exploitable technologies of personal formation and control but also to devastating disappointments when we realize it is not liberating and redemptive. On my reading, Augustine would agree with Foucault that such efforts are fueled by arrogance, a deluded sense of self-importance, and a refusal to acknowledge the limitations of finitude. Augustine's wisdom of sorrow and its associated virtues would require of us not the rejection of contemporary science or the denial of its manifest contributions to personal and social well-being but a clear-eyed vigilance concerning the ways in which it is applied, especially with regard to those who are most vulnerable.

Deconstructing Privileged Discourses

The Ambiguity of Social Achievements

As Augustine and Foucault widen their analyses of the dangers of seeking to perfect fragile human relations to the moral risks involved in trying to control disorderly social groups, two of their most fertile areas of political dialogue surface—first, in the range of social concerns they become preoccupied with in their respective cultural critiques, and second, in the rhetorical and historiographical tactics they employ to goad individuals into probing unexamined social assumptions that mask various forms of violence and domination. Both Augustine and Foucault scrutinize the posturing of sacrosanct discourses that were competing during their lifetimes to seize or retain cultural dominance. Although each challenges different governing authorities and social rituals, these function politically in similar ways by consolidating institutional power through the use of discourses that seem "naturally" self-evident, and thus beyond the bounds of cultural criticism. Even when coercive means are relied on to achieve exploitative objectives, these self-legitimating rhetorics are able to inoculate themselves from political inquiries that would otherwise monitor and censure morally questionable activities. For Augustine, this is most evident in the triumphalist rhetoric of glory at work in Roman republican and imperial attempts to solidify and expand political order. For Foucault, such political privilege, which was once reserved only for "majestic" power, now thrives behind the protective shield of scientifico-medical "objectivity," "neutrality," and "disinterested" progress that quietly works to insulate social institutions—here, those that are politically coercive—from moral review and protest.

Augustine's and Foucault's often blunt critiques of privileged discourses and the social practices they sanction are inspired by a shared sensitivity to the contingency and moral ambivalence of all institutional orderings of power as well as by the sufferings these inherently forceful relations create for the politically disadvantaged. Each time we try to impose order amidst disorder, new and complicated hazards emerge because the solutions expose us to unanticipated exercises of power. Every effort we undertake to respond to personal and social evils is threatened by similar sorts of insecurities and vulnerabilities that characterized the evils themselves. Augustine and Foucault maintain that all human achievements, no matter how lofty their intentions, are shot through with shifting differentials of power and thus must be approached with political suspicion and humility. No rhetorical legerdemain that obscures this fact can be tolerated.

Significantly, however, given their wariness, neither thinker takes pessimistic political convictions as a warrant for social inaction. Neither wants his audience to respond to injustices with complacency. They both agree that an active, engaged commitment to alleviate personal and social evils is essential to living in community. And they acknowledge that many attempts to ameliorate injustices have enjoyed some measure of success. Therefore, while they remain alert to even the most noble-seeming historical developments, as they assert that every success in this battle creates innovative and sometimes more insidious asymmetries of power, they urge their respective audiences to remain committed to the cultivation of more caring and socially attentive relations. The humility required of us by sinfulness or finitude must be coupled with an activism inspired by hope. Recognizing that the victories in such pursuits are always provisional, piecemeal, and temporary does not relieve one, so they both argued, of the responsibility to struggle on.

The Rhetoric of Glory: Ancient Dangers of Ordering Disorder

Recall that Augustine painted two vividly contrasting pictures of human society. On the one hand, he believed that individuals are created to live in loving fellowship such that each would order his or her own interests and objectives to the one Supreme Good. Had personal desires remained rightly ordered, a "natural" equality would have obtained within human organizations, each member being mutually and reciprocally related to one another by and through their shared loving relationship with God. On the other hand, and in tragic opposition to the original potential of created "social" nature,

Augustine believed that because of the rupturing consequences of the fall, all persons are more or less self-absorbed and aggressive, and thus to one degree or another disoriented from their proper end. Rather than interact with one another in light of a mutual love of God, they tend to regard their private purposes and needs as more important than those of their neighbors, and so form continually changing alliances in an effort to shape events to their advantage.

A distinctively "political" set of relations thereby develops in which inequities and conflict are commonplace and, indeed, inescapable.[1] Unlike his description of *social* relations, Augustine never portrays *political* ones as a natural part of the created order or as a redeemed component of the Heavenly City.[2] Absent the fall, there would be no need for a political safeguarding of communal order since all members of society would have the same fundamental love, namely, God. Under the dominion of original sin, however, Augustine forcefully argues that one must take protective measures to defend oneself and one's community against the dangers of social disintegration. But on what basis might persons with competing ultimate loves agree to such measures? If fallen human beings are prone to be self-absorbed and pugnacious, what kind of stabilizing political alliances could possibly be forged? On Augustine's view, though we may hope for more, we can only reliably count on a lowly compact, a compromise. Despite all their differences and disagreements, every person longs for some manner of earthly peace.[3] "In fact," Augustine observes, "even when men wish a present state of peace to be disturbed, they do so not because they hate peace, but because they desire the present peace to be exchanged for one that suits their wishes. . . . [E]ven robbers, to ensure greater efficiency and security in their assaults on the peace of the rest of mankind, desire to preserve peace with their associates."[4] Be their ends base or noble, he concludes, to accomplish the most limited objective, they must maintain a secure and reliable living arrangement so that others do not interfere with their activities. A provisional peace is thus an everyday material concern that more or less selfish people can agree on. If a band of robbers can be united through self-interested aspirations, Augustine asserts, effective political alliances can similarly establish a workable concord, cohesiveness, and sustainable social order.

Naturally, these mundane desires for peace tend not to transform people morally or spiritually, but, he would argue, because such security is fundamental to all persons, they remain our best prospect for fostering widespread political commitment. This may make possible nothing more than a minimal consensus, but it is one that self-absorbed and contentious creatures who have significantly different convictions and value systems can enter into together. Hence, even though these modest political bonds and compromises may not extensively reconstruct or greatly improve social existence, they can help to balance sectional interests that can tear apart diverse and often conflicting communities. Jean Bethke Elshtain aptly summarizes Augustine's views: "He offers in this regard a *via negativa*, the negative of ideology—not a political theory proper but a canny and scrupulous attunement to the here and now with its very real limits."[5]

Since it is pursued for moral and immoral reasons, this minimalist vision of peace is socially ambiguous. So too is its preservation. All political stability simultaneously enables and imperils social goods, from Augustine's perspective, in that it necessarily relies on coercion to enforce order. Perhaps more poignantly than anything else in life, the human desire to order captures for Augustine our bittersweet frailties and dependencies. For the redeemed, "ordering" promises loving relations free from contingencies, vulnerabilities, and harm. And yet it is also in this fallen world a fierce power susceptible to all of the distortions and dangers of finitude. Although he believes that the maintenance of earthly peace requires the deployment of certain forceful exercises of power, Augustine cautions that some variation of the *libido dominandi* operates in them all. Such ordering measures are continually exposed to the selfsame pressures that endanger communal security. He therefore exhorts those in authority to use coercive mechanisms and institutions with open eyes. They must take extreme care to avoid being swept up in prideful assumptions that they can resolve political difficulties without at the same time disrupting, in a different and often unintended way, some prevailing patterns of social stability. It is imperative to Augustine that human beings learn to live under the shadow of moral indeterminacy. The more the powerful refuse to acknowledge the risks of their desires for ordering, the more destruction they will, in the end, unknowingly bring about and perpetuate.

The failure of many of his contemporaries to recognize sufficiently the ambiguities of political power rests in large part on the success with which a triumphalist rhetoric of glory celebrating individual and collective human achievements blinds them to its darker dimensions.[6] To reveal the pretensions of this political discourse whose prestige eclipses critical scrutiny, Augustine uses two tactics, one rhetorical and the other historiographical. We will see him apply both in the three examples that follow. In all of them, Augustine aims to alert his readers to the unsettling precariousness of sociohistorical accomplishments, which is obscured by a self-serving rhetoric that provides seemingly indisputable justifications for intra- and intercultural conflicts and subjugation.

On Augustine's view, the most striking example of the indeterminacy of human accomplishments is the attempt to establish peace through warfare.[7] Much of the *City of God* is taken up with descriptions of tragic conflicts, from intimate betrayals of friends and family to the brutal rape and slaughtering of longtime enemies. This topic Augustine recounts and agonizes over, as though he were watching atrocities unfold in his own courtyard. "Who could find the words," he writes, "to match the gravity of the events—words adequate to express the horrors . . . ?"[8] Although he admits that no eloquence could convey the "misery of these evils,"[9] he tries to bring them to life in a variety of ways—through graphic details of butchery; stunning images of the slain strewn across fields or overflowing civic buildings, temples, and theaters; crowded and chaotic ventings of grief for the desecration of whole regions; small scenes of tearfulness among family members for a lost loved one. Both the overwhelming violence and the intimacy of sorrow grip Augustine, and he hopes to grip his audience with the same intensity. His emotions run the gamut of outrage at the brutality of perpetrators to the hesitant and loathsome realization that some new and imperiling aggression must at times be used to protect the suffering. Such injustices, he declares, demand from us a moral response. "[It] is the injustice of the opposing side that lays on the wise man the duty of waging wars."[10] Principled individuals cannot simply stand by passively and allow such horror to devour the innocent. They must at least try to confine the devastation and restore some working social order.

However, while Augustine feels passionately about the crimes being committed, he also feels passionately about the dangerousness of such responses. They thus should not be understood in seductively simplistic terms as a matter of right opposing wrong. We can identify three reasons for his caution and reluctance in this regard. First, even though the moral obligation placed on the wise person is perfectly clear ("to the good, it is a stern necessity"),[11] the required human act is inevitably haunted by moral uncertainties. For such aggressive actions, precisely because they are aggressive, can never be completely free of the moral transgressions that they are supposed to eliminate. The *libido dominandi* is too universally present for human beings to remain innocent in these pursuits.[12] Its power can subtly induce participants to act coercively and exploitatively, in ways they are either unaware of or choose to overlook. The presence of such mixed motives blemishes, to different degrees, every individual and social achievement. Of course, these are all the more dangerous when trying to control people and events to one's military advantage. Rome, according to Augustine, illustrates the dangers of a slippery slope where she entered battle "by the necessity to defend . . . life and liberty," yet along the way became enamored with triumphs and glory, so much so that she cultivated and refined a whole art of domination, the "arts of ruling, commanding, and subjecting other nations."[13]

In addition, Augustine claims that even if war is waged for a just cause (for instance, in defense of one's homeland in the face of "unprovoked attacks")[14] and with proper discipline, it still would generate widespread devastation and suffering, which all human beings, no matter how just they have been, should fervently regret. "And so," he admonishes, "everyone who reflects with sorrow on such grievous evils, in all their horror and cruelty, must acknowledge the misery of them."[15] Rather than exhilarate in the defeat of one's enemies, the wise person should be overcome "with heartfelt grief" at having had to participate in the agonies of war.[16] Unintended consequences, from the terrifying to the ridiculous, are unwelcome but inevitable companions of even the most clearly justified attempts to alleviate suffering.

Finally, Augustine warns us about the limits of how much war can realistically achieve. On his account, just wars defend against and punish wrongdoing.[17] As such, they function analogously to backfires set to stop the spread of a forest fire. They quell an intensifying disaster by using a destructive counterforce. But whatever is accomplished through this sanctioned violence, Augustine suggests, is essentially negative in character, merely guarding against something more destructive taking place. It keeps society from slipping backward into turmoil. However, by itself, it cannot constructively move it forward to a more just order. Social peace is indeed protected by using "just" violence to suppress "unjust" violence, but for all of the reasons above, it always remains an insecure peace, ever on the verge of disintegration. "The only joy to be attained" from such coercion, Augustine concludes, has "the fragile brilliance of glass, a joy outweighed by the fear that it may be shattered in a moment."[18]

In light of the moral indeterminacy of war, even those fought for a just cause, Augustine urges us to realize how ingenious human beings can be when peddling moral justifications for what are actually immoral activities. As part of his apologetic strategy in the *City of God* to refute the charge that the Empire's conversion to Christianity led to the sack of Rome, he sought to demonstrate that Roman history is filled with attempts to make moral crimes look as though they are heroic endeavors, ennobling not only military commanders but also the entire nation. Augustine reproaches Roman leaders and historians for seeing Rome's many triumphs over foreign nations as evidence of divine support and protection, the superiority of its civilization, and the justice of its aggression. Using morally "deceptive veils" and "screens of . . . senseless notions" such as honor, duty, unity, and glory, Rome tried to cover up bare violence with the dazzling splendor of victory.[19] For example, those wars that attempted to force Latin on the conquered people in order to establish sympathetic "bonds of peace and fellowship" simply ended up using political coercion to hide the scorched ground they created.[20] Augustine anxiously reminds readers that the anguish and bitterness generated by such misfortunes cannot be palliated. "[T]hink of the costs of this achievement! Consider the scale of those wars, with all that slaughter of human beings, all the human blood that was shed!"[21] Over and over, he describes conflicts that had been settled long ago, yet continue to live in resentment. By trading on the rhetoric of glory, Rome repeatedly tried to justify its appalling behavior. However, "the making of one people out of two by the remnants that survived," Augustine argues, demonstrates nothing but "the pitiable coagulation of all the blood which had already been poured out by both sides."[22]

To break the hypnotic spell of these warrants, Augustine develops various techniques. Perhaps the most arresting of these is his blurring of distinctions that his audience would have thought obvious, even incontrovertible. In a widely cited passage, Augustine compares unjust kingdoms to gangs of thugs, for both are groups of men bound together by a shared lust for power and plunder that they divide among themselves by common agreement. To seal the point, he cites Cicero's account of a pirate's retort when Alexander the Great demands he explain why he is infesting the sea. "And the pirate answered, with uninhibited insolence, 'The same as yours, in infesting the earth! But because I do it with a tiny craft, I'm called a pirate: because you have a mighty navy, you're called an emperor.'"[23] Augustine uses the anecdote to show how a discourse of glory exaggerates the normative differences that separate what we uncritically think of as the esteemed ruler and the contemptible outlaw, thereby ensuring that there will always be preserved a safe moral distance between the sovereign's accountability and the expected standards used to evaluate the rest of human behavior. "Remove justice," Augustine quips, "and what are kingdoms but gangs of criminals on a large scale? What are criminal gangs but petty kingdoms?"[24] If we pierce through the self-legitimating oratory of conquering monarchs, we realize that their "honorable" acts of aggression differ little from the "shameful" acts of pirates. In a culture of praise, such ridicule targets not just the military leader but also all who seek to be remembered and venerated with him through epic battles and victories.

Augustine's minimalist portrayal of earthly peace risks similarly offending his audience's sensibilities and yearnings for honor and glory. Such a peace is not socially exalting. Indeed, it is one that robbers and noblemen may share. Nor does it offer stable opportunities for immortalizing praise since it is always in danger of collapse. It is a simple provisional security aimed at the everyday needs of maintaining health; clothing, feeding, and housing family; earning a living; and so forth.[25] Stripped to its bare bones, this unpretentious peace shatters the romantic allure of "the splendid titles" and "deceptive veils" Augustine spoke of that can be used either to sanctify or disguise the horror of violence.[26] Its very barrenness can help us to form a more scrutinizing judgment so that we are not "fooled by empty bombast" in which "the edge of our critical faculties" becomes "blunted by high-sounding words like 'peoples,' 'realms,' 'provinces.'"[27]

In seeking to establish a seemingly ultimate and lasting peace, military aggression (whether it be just or unjust) can easily get transfigured into a radiant display of majestic power.[28] Augustine wants to keep our eyes firmly fixed on the carnage, on the physical losses, so that we do not allow the mirage of a glorifying end to draw our attention away from the tragic means used in trying to reach it. Even in those wars that are most just and those deeds that are truly heroic, he will not allow simple beautiful memories to circulate: grief must remain part of the story. Accordingly, he counsels those who would seek gratification, comfort, or refuge in the "honor" and "justice" of their aggression that they must never use moral probity to protect themselves from the anguish they have created. Even just wars have terrible costs. If we are to keep from losing "all human feeling," we must contemplate every act of violence, even those with just cause, with intense remorse and trepidation.[29]

A second technique by which Augustine punctures the inflating rhetoric of glory is to submit Roman history to an unyielding moral examination. To discredit the pretensions of Roman historians and orators, with their facile declamations about the magnificence of their nation's military achievements, Augustine urges readers to "remove the whitewash of illusion and subject the facts to a strict inspection."[30] This entails unraveling the myth of Roman superiority that has been so elaborately and painstakingly woven by public orators, historians, poets, and teachers. The crux of his complaint is with the notion that the destiny and progress of civilization can be traced through military victories. "Let those who have read their history," Augustine asserts, "remember how long were the wars waged by Rome in times past, and with what diverse fortunes and grievous disasters they were attended; for the world is liable to be tempest-tossed by such misfortunes, like a storm-swept sea. Let them acknowledge the facts, even if it goes against the grain."[31] Augustine does this in two ways: he deconstructs Rome's triumphalist history, and he presents a counterhistory that transposes honor, victory, crowns, and glory into a new key, thus radically altering their meaning.

The wars of Rome's past, from his standpoint, are not just horrifying, they are also frequently pointless. He sees no progress in them, just oscillation. As he says, they are characterized more like a stormy sea, simply rolling back and forth, in the end, doing nothing more than to "vex and exhaust"[32] the population. "Time after time," peace agreements settle conflicts "after colossal slaughter" only to have them start up "again and again."[33] "On and on" this goes between competing nations, he writes, "alternately in succession, now this way now that, ding dong, snatching the supremacy to themselves."[34] The pattern Roman historians, orators, and poets impose on this senseless back and forth, argues Augustine, is simply determined by might. The victor decides history's direction and meaning. To him belongs the spoils of war, the best and certainly most powerful of which is the writing of history. In this political drama, "grandeur of empire"[35] is defined by military conquest. Without bloodshed, there can be no heroics, no honor, no crowning victory. Augustine contends that often peaceful compacts "would have had better success; but then there would have been no glory for the conquerors."[36] They would have come home as ordinary men rather than soldiers who have been tested in combat; measured by the intensity of their battles and the magnitude of their plunder; and consecrated as winners by ceremoniously riding through streets in chariots, receiving laurels and applause. The spectacle of acclaim comes only with the spectacle of violence and triumph. You do not need to have "the vanquished" to secure peace. But you do to obtain glory.

Augustine breaks the presumed linkages among winning, historical progress, and praiseworthiness. "Let no one tell me, 'A, or B, is a great man: he fought C, or D, and beat him.'"[37] He sharply questions whether the accounts of historians, orators, and poets extol anything other than overpowering force. In his mind, it certainly is not progress that they record. It is just competition: one person wins, then another, and another. More to the point, the good and the just do not necessarily prevail. On Augustine's view, the differentiation between winner and loser is logically independent from that between good and bad or just and unjust.[38] "As far as I can see, the distinction between victors and vanquished has not the slightest importance for security, for moral standards, or even for human dignity. It is merely a matter of the arrogance of human glory."[39] These conquests get dressed up as something nobler by pomp and pageantry. They take on polish through the retelling of epic poems and historical narratives. But for him they remain at best "an empty show"[40] and at worst "crimes" that must be "seen, weighed, judged in all their nakedness."[41]

Against this triumphalist backdrop, Augustine relates an opposing history. The absolute contrast stands out when we examine how the lives of the martyrs would appear from the outlook he rejects. They carried with them a story that had no luster, being out of favor with the cultures they were working in. They labored under obscurity and amidst curses, slander, and hostility.[42] They did not know whether their movement would last or whether any of their efforts would be remembered and praised. Often they met with persecution, torture, and humiliating deaths.[43] At the time, they looked like they might be "the ruin of the Church."[44] In a society of honor and shame, there was no question that these people were the losers, the vanquished. And as such, the only lasting value of their losses would be in elevating the victors.

Augustine's theology of the cross and wisdom of sorrow turns this account on its head. "Our 'heroes' (if usage would allow this title)" conquer in humility, overcoming those who hate them through unanticipated acts of generosity.[45] They "help everyone when possible" and "do no harm to anyone."[46] Sufferings are inflicted on them, and yet, being "filled with charity," they never injure themselves or others.[47] They requite brutality with patience and forgiveness; they win over the hard-hearted through tenderness; they gain victory in being vanquished and losing themselves for others.[48] Though their efforts "brought them immense glory," they are most honorable when they remember that they are nothing without God.[49] They "were given crowns of indescribable beauty" and glorified by all in the church through Christ who defeats and transforms their afflictions.[50] However, they do not allow themselves to rest in exaltation and communal praise "as if they had attained the goal of their own virtue."[51] They ascribe everything that is beautiful and valiant "to the glory of God, whose grace had made them what they were."[52] Thus, "far from being the ruin of the Church," their sacrifices were "turned to its own advantage," inspiring persons inside and out through their self-emptying acts of mercy, and thereby "filling up" and unifying the community with more devoted followers.[53]

Augustine's counterhistory gives to the faithful "heroic" models that cut across the grain of not only classical pagan expectations but also those of many of his fellow Christians. By contrast to the muscular heroism typical of early martyrological literature, Augustine's mature writings humanize the martyrs. They struggle with fallibility and faithfulness in ways parishioners understand and can take comfort and encouragement in. "It wasn't . . . against the man persecuting them that they wrestled, but against the devil laying traps for them, and—if you want the whole truth—against their own weakness. It's within oneself, when all is said and done, that the great contest takes place."[54] What makes them praiseworthy is not so much their heroic nerve and personal strength as their overwhelming love in the face of such temptations and their humble patience in enduring sufferings they neither deserved nor sought out.[55] This helps to draw these stories deeper into the everyday life of the church, placing the martyrs well within the imaginative reach of the ordinary Christian.

As Augustine does this, he also and increasingly asks parishioners to interpret their daily temptations and trials in light of these heroic stories and face every adversity with the spirit of love and patience they exemplify.[56] One of the more common misfortunes of his day was becoming gravely ill. In a world where few lived past their third decade,[57] where the dread of disease was widespread, Augustine is at pains to urge his flock to avoid seeking cures in "spells and charms [that] are unlawful, diabolical."[58] Fighting a fever without succumbing to such temptations makes one every bit as much of a martyr as being torn apart by beasts or crushed to death. "Your feast day is not indeed in the calendar, but your crown is ready waiting for you. It is customary to celebrate the solemn feast days of those who fought in the public arena. How many martyrs have left this world from their beds, and as conquerors over that infirmity have passed to the realms above!"[59] He believed, moreover, that one need not actually die in defense of the faith, or "endure what they endured,"[60] to live like a martyr. This shows how much he wanted to draw the model of the martyr's life into the workaday world of the church. "What's required is the spirit of the martyr, because God after all does not delight in the shedding of blood."[61]

When describing the martyrs, Augustine highlights their love of God and their charity, patience, endurance, and compassion. On his view, to imitate the martyrs, "[w]e must love eternal life and count our present life as nothing. We must live well and hope for what is good."[62] Augustine is not advocating otherworldly spiritualism, but a deeper engagement with community. Although battles may take place within the self, the evidence of victory is manifested socially. "Mercy is, in fact, the true sacrifice."[63] Compassion involves a daily dying to the world, a perpetual self-mortification enabling one, by grace, to be of spontaneous service to others. Roman heroics, on Augustine's view, communally enshrine individual acts of bravery or cunning that distinguish individuals, setting them apart in glory. Christian "heroism," by contrast, participates in glory by weaving cords of unity. Even though martyrs may act individually in facing their afflictions, what they create through their self-sacrifice are examples of and demands for a self-emptying and self-forgetting solidarity.

By transposing the terms of honor and glory, Augustine asks his audience to listen in a new way to commonsensical questions about winning and losing in an insecure world. What does it mean to respond "successfully" to uncertainties, dangers, and enemies; to be "heroic" and live with dignity in community; to "triumph" over adversities? And what does it mean to be "vanquished"? What does it mean to be on the losing side of fragility, to have one's "heart bruised and humbled in the sorrow" of personal limitations and failings?[64] And most important, how are we required to act in light of human vulnerabilities and imperfections? Augustine's counterhistory tells his followers that even in the lives of those they most admire, ambiguities and insecurities are an inevitable feature of human existence. Attempts to control and eradicate them through violence have tragically fueled their growth, increasing the misery they create. Those who gain temporary mastery may believe themselves happy, but they simply pass "their lives amid the horrors of war, amid the shedding of men's blood," and thus, in everything that they do and in all that they hope for, they live "under the shadow of fear and amid the terror of ruthless ambition."[65]

The martyrs provide a different epic, one that seems nonsensical from the perspective of an optimistic and progressivist view of history. It looked as though life's vicissitudes and defeats would extinguish their vitality. However, out of compassion for their enemies, friends, and even themselves, they remained dedicated against all odds to a lifelong battle for peace. The indeterminacy of social accomplishments did not leave them with an excuse to withdraw or give up on perplexing difficulties in the world; indeed, it presented them with more opportunities to act with attentive care, to forgive, and to be merciful. Though followers may not live up to such an example, Augustine argues, the martyrs offer a new promise of peace on which to set their sights. With this pledge to orient their lives, he hopes they will be able to look beyond their fears and see, through their own remaining "vestiges" of peace,[66] how one may sojourn in a "foreign land"[67] filled with harms while remaining engaged in its everyday demands and committed to alleviating suffering.

From Augustine's perspective, attempts to secure peace in a conflictual world is but one instance of the ambiguity of human achievements and of the prideful risks involved in controlling disorderly social groups, especially when that ordering is rooted in a vainglorious cultural rhetoric. Another can be found within the jurisdiction of the city. While just war aims at enforcing peace abroad, governmental, legal, and penal institutions attempt to cultivate discipline and security locally. There is no question for Augustine that these institutions serve an essential purpose in a fallen world. They are morally necessary in order to preserve civic order. But this is a limited, indeed largely negative role. To highlight one example, the criminal and civil penalties imposed by legal authorities are a means of requital for the wrong committed. In themselves, they do not aim for the improvement of the one punished, though they may indirectly contribute to the common good by deterring others.[68] As with just war, such penalties restrain society from self-destructing. They are hindered, however, in their ability to advance society's causes in constructive ways since they are endlessly entangled in the dynamics of the *libido dominandi*. Although civic organizations and institutions may aim at the good of preserving domestic peace, they unavoidably involve imbalances of power, competing social interests and purposes, and potentially abusive hierarchies of authority that enforce subjugation of the many at the hands of the few.[69] In working to our benefit, they often do little more than shield us from the harms of social unrest. Accordingly, the mature Augustine understands the purposes of political life to be relatively mundane and provisional, contending with the lesser requirements of preserving domestic order rather than with the more exalted demands of securing ultimate personal happiness.

Augustine did not deny that Christian civil rulers may help their subjects to enjoy more loving and therefore more just relations. This is consistent with my analysis of the formative dynamics of love. Being ambiguous, it is not always tyrannical, but can be used for the good of the community. Augustine hoped that such rulers would be raised up among the people in order to extend the worship of God and the love of neighbor that he believed was "the perfection of justice."[70] "As for those who are endowed with true piety and who lead a good life, if they are skilled in the art of government, then there is no happier situation for mankind than that they, by God's mercy, should wield power."[71] But such remarks are misconstrued if read as part of a positive rationale for the role of political authority, particularly in its institutional forms. We find here, rather, a comment about how such leaders should use power if they happen to receive it.[72] I interpret Augustine's controversial paean to Christian emperors in book 5 of the *City of God* in this light. In the exercise of their office they must remain humble, he believes, in imitation of Christ who alone is holy and just.[73] They should therefore recognize that "they are but men, . . . put their power at the service of God's majesty," and "not fail to offer to their true God, as a sacrifice for their sins, the oblation of humility, compassion, and prayer."[74]

To the consternation of many contemporary readers, Augustine singles out Emperor Theodosius I as one such ruler.[75] Predictably, Theodosius is lauded for his tireless efforts on behalf of the church and his "just and compassionate legislation."[76] But what makes Theodosius especially deserving of praise, according to Augustine, is the "religious humility he showed" before Ambrose as public penance for the massacre on his orders of thousands in Thessalonica. Recalling a point made in chapter 4, the arrogant self-confidence that is reinforced by a rhetoric of glory is to be deconstructed by the practice of confession. The open avowal of shortcomings and the public, ritualized reintegration into the penitent ecclesial community are intended to cultivate a recognition of dependence on God and should yield, again hopefully, a self-forgetting love of God and neighbor. This would stand in sharpest contrast, for Augustine, to the ideal of leadership that Alexander the Great represents. Whereas Alexander is morally shielded by and distanced from his people in his exalted glory, the Christian ruler, in humbling himself through confession, acknowledges his lowliness and solidarity in sin. To be a good ruler, he must recognize his frailties, his fallibilities, and his creatureliness and not pretend to divine majesty. This "religious humility" is of paramount importance in coming to understand Augustine's view of the role of civil authorities. Even the very best Christian rulers, he maintains, must be extremely cautious as they attempt to guide citizens to a deeper love for God not to forget that whatever successes they may obtain are gifts of divine mercy. And they must be unflagging in their efforts not to let the government officials and institutional mechanisms they employ cause society to become less just and stable than it was before. Their only certainty can be that as they do so, they must contend with the impulses and effects of the *libido dominandi* not only in others but also in themselves.

Augustine's refusal to endorse the idea that political leaders and institutions can yield human self-fulfillment, happiness, and perfect justice rests in part on this conviction about the universality of our desire to force others into submission. Yes, he says, some Christian leaders may serve God's ends as they exemplify "true piety" in their conduct. But once he repudiates the idea that the Christianized Empire is a clearly discernible victory in God's war against paganism, he can just as easily say that Christian leaders may not be furthering God's plan, however pious they may wish to be.[77] By the middle of the fifth century's second decade, he is convinced that the so-called Christian era (*tempora christiana*) is a spectacle of duplicity. In a letter to Bishop Hesychius of Dalmatia, written in 418, Augustine sarcastically dismisses those who still hold that the Christianization of the Empire was an unequivocal turning point in the history of salvation. "The very same people who fill the churches on the festivals of Jerusalem fill the theatres for the festivities of Babylon."[78] There are two distinguishable points to be identified. The first and more familiar is Augustine's relentless questioning of how successfully we can do the good we will. Second, Augustine is also dubious about our ability to discern God's ways in the world. Not that Augustine doubts that God has a plan or that God is actively engaged in bringing it to consummation. This belief remains secure. Rather, in his later years he grows increasingly intolerant of those who claim to know with absolute certainty how God is putting that plan into effect.[79] Although he affirms that the faithful are vouchsafed glimpses of Heavenly Jerusalem as they make their pilgrimage in this world, all they can say for sure is that they know what their hoped for destination is. They do not know exactly how they may get there or what they may encounter on their way.

In light of our thoroughgoing performative fallibility, Augustine maintains, we must largely limit the scope of the politically possible to the preservation of a peace in which the inhabitants of either the earthly or the divine city can pursue their sometimes converging, more often diverging aims. That is no mean thing, of course, since both groups must daily contend with the same sorts of conflict, precariousness, and ambiguity. However different their ultimate loves from the residents of the earthly city, the residents of the City of God on pilgrimage cannot withdraw from them to form a segregated and pure Christianized community. No; the Christian life, Augustine maintains, must be faithfully lived out in the midst of a civil society populated with believers and nonbelievers alike. This leads him both to an acceptance of diversity and pluralism and to a recognition of the importance of the church in this mixed sociological community.

[S]ince this mortal condition is shared by both cities, a harmony may be preserved between them in things that are relative to that condition. . . . Thus even the Heavenly City in her pilgrimage here on earth makes use of the earthly peace and defends and seeks the compromise between human wills in respect of the provisions relevant to the mortal nature of man, so far as may be permitted without detriment to true religion and piety.[80]

The visible, institutional church can and should, therefore, play an active, indeed constructive role in the life of the *polis*. That is one of the implications of Augustine's advice to Christian rulers. His correspondence with Christian members of the Empire, such as his friend Marcellinus, could also be noted, as could his dispute with the sectarian Donatists.[81] Being so engaged in the political life will lead some to develop, in Elshtain's felicitous phrase, "a chastened form of civic virtue."[82]

In keeping with his concern to avoid the twin dangers of despair and pride, Augustine treads back and forth between acknowledging the potential achievements of political society and warning us of its certain risks. He leavens his sober pessimism about the political realm with a measure of hope for piecemeal and provisional advances in the pursuit of justice. Our humility, therefore, must work in concert with our hope. But if we let that hope slide imperceptibly toward expectation and thence to affirmation, we can imperil the very aims we seek to secure. To insist on more than this from either civil authorities or institutions, Augustine warns, jeopardizes the public. For idealized expectations can create a self-perpetuating motive and warrant for violence, subjugation, and exploitation. As long as political goals can be construed in terms of the victim's or society's ultimate ends, then virtually any means can be justified.[83] Because, as we saw in the discussion of war, it is so easy to use ennobling language to justify immoral actions, we must be wary of coercion that is legitimated with talk of ultimate political commitments.

The burdens borne by those who wrestle with this paradox of hope and humility are most eloquently evoked in Augustine's description of the reluctant judge. With a tone of weariness and regret, Augustine acknowledges that "judgements passed by men on their fellow-men . . . cannot be dispensed with in cities, however much peace they enjoy."[84] Taking on such authority subjects all to grave risks. The human costs are obvious to Augustine not only for potential victims but also for those who are forced to pronounce guilt or innocence. He especially wrestles with the unfortunate reality that the act for which a suspect is condemned is often "a doubtful crime," so dubious in fact that its circumstances will never be known with certainty, and yet the prisoner suffers for this "a punishment about which there is no shadow of doubt."[85]

This is most horrifying when a judge, in trying to discover the facts of a crime, forces a false confession that leads to the prisoner's execution. "And there is something yet more intolerable, something to be bewailed and, if it were possible, washed away by floods of tears."[86] As Augustine tries to express the poignant absurdity of such losses, he brings to light a tangle of tragic contradictions:

> [T]he judge tortures the accused for the sole purpose of avoiding the execution, in ignorance, of an innocent man; while his pitiable lack of knowledge leads him to put to death, tortured and innocent, the very person whom he had tortured to avoid putting the innocent to death. . . . Then after his condemnation and execution the judge still does not know whether it was a guilty or an innocent person he has executed, after torturing him to avoid executing the innocent in ignorance. Consequently, he has tortured an innocent man to get to the truth and has killed him while still in ignorance.[87]

Augustine is overwhelmed by the dark uncertainties that shroud the judge's actions. The judge is forced by his political office to appraise a situation without reliable access to the truth, and ironically, in the name of truth, he ends up endangering the very person whom it is the judge's role to protect. Rather than rectify a social evil, the judge finds himself complicit, even if unintentionally, in an iniquity perpetrated against a defenseless human being. In performing his required duties, he becomes paradoxically "a calamity for the innocent."[88] Although the judge hopes to avoid uncertainty by excavating a truth through torture, the only incontrovertible fact the judge ascertains is that another human life has been taken. His only certainty is that he will never know with confidence whether that death was fairly deserved.

There is nothing glorious, triumphant, or exalted in the picture Augustine paints. Rather, our eye is drawn to the sorrowful tragedy of the scene. "[T]he wise judge does not act in this way through a will to do harm, but because ignorance is unavoidable—and yet, the exigencies of human society make judgment also unavoidable. Here we have what I call the wretchedness of man's situation."[89] The necessity of pronouncing sentences and the extent to which the judge will never know how far he misses the mark should forever tax his conscience. His, therefore, is a "pitiable" and a "lamentable" burden.[90] Instead of feeling empowered by this position of authority, the judge, Augustine believes, should feel sickened and repelled. Nor should he shield himself from the stark reality of the ambiguities he daily faces by hiding behind the pompous ceremony and rhetoric that serves to legitimate the legal system of which he is a part. For the lofty aim of preserving civic peace does not wash innocent blood from his hands. And so, Augustine writes, knowing that the duty will not be lifted from his shoulders, he should pray to be delivered from having to render his judgments: "How much more mature reflection it shows, how much more worthy of a human being it is when a man acknowledges this necessity as a mark of human wretchedness, when he hates that necessity in his own actions and when, if he has the wisdom of devotion, he cries out to God, 'Deliver me from my necessities!'"[91]

The difficulties the judge confronts he shares with anyone exercising political authority. Not only do the problems of rendering uncertain empirical and moral judgments plague them, their personal fallibilities also constantly threaten to soil their hands. Augustine proclaims: "Kings, leaders, rulers, judges, they [who] judge the earth. . . . If the Lord's verdict *If any of you is without sin; let him be the first to cast a stone at her* [Jn 8.7] were to step forward surely everyone who is judging the earth would feel the earth quake!"[92] As he himself anguishes over the great consequences and complexities of such judgments, he admits: "These are indeed deep and obscure matters. . . . In all this I confess my sins and my ignorance everyday."[93] To exercise authority responsibly, Augustine concludes, "judges" must discern and acknowledge their own fallenness, always regarding themselves with suspicion and acting toward others as mercifully as possible. "God's judgement is there to inspire fear in them so that they remember that they stand in need of God's mercy for their own sins, and do not think that they have failed in their duty if they act at all mercifully towards those over whom they lawfully exercise the power of life and death."[94]

This does not mean that earthly justice can never be applied effectively or fairly. However, as with just war, applying judgments, especially when they are coercive, inevitably entails social risks that are hard to anticipate and fully control. As we have seen, Augustine's apprehension about the concrete responsibilities of "judging" shows how seriously he takes its tasks. Even if leaders cannot dispense a perfect justice, they must still seek some form of it. Part of the courage demanded of those who make decisions is that, though they are always working with provisional understandings and determinations, they do the best they can. This requires that they be aware of their own limits in implementing an unequivocal and impartial justice. Justice can be seen in a similar light as peace. The eternal peace that the martyrs struggled to instantiate in the world makes all earthly efforts at security look mundane and compromised. However, as pilgrims, they must simultaneously work in the realm of earthly peace and keep their sights on the promised end. No more than the martyrs could establish and count on perfect peace, judges cannot rely on achieving more than a rough approximation of the heavenly ideal. But that fact, so Augustine contends, should not dampen their dedication to alleviating injustices.

One of Augustine's enduring contributions to political thought is his linking of a vivid suspicion to the assertion that human frailties in no way release us from the demands of living together in society. Notwithstanding our troubling lack of moral certitude and comfort, everyone must engage in the political realm as concerned participants. We do not have the option of lifting ourselves above the fray simply because we find the moral and political messiness of the world distressing.[95] "In view of this darkness that attends human society, will our wise man take his seat on the judge's bench, or will he not have the heart to do so?" Augustine asks. "Obviously, he will sit: for the claims of human society constrain him and draw him to this duty; and it is unthinkable that he should shirk it."[96]

In his reflections on civic institutions and the role of magistrates, Augustine once again parts company with his contemporaries as he deconstructs the self-serving facade of Greek political philosophy and Roman historical and political oratory. He mounts a frontal assault against the classical Greco-Roman overconfidence about the origins and aims of our common life in the city (*polis, civitas*). The forcefulness of his attack may well have been prompted in part by a sense of shame at having once endorsed the very ideas he later rejects. Until the mid-390s, Augustine's writings indicate that he accepted the classical commonplace that men can enjoy happiness, fulfillment, and perfection in this life if they are sufficiently self-disciplined. A well-ordered society with its familial and political hierarchies, he believed, reflects and is grounded in the hierarchical ordering of the cosmos itself, whose transcendent divine source pervades it from top to bottom. On this view, human fulfillment consists in the soul's ascending this cosmic hierarchy to be reunited with its source and end. The wise ruler, whose reason enables him to control his passions, serves as both model for such self-perfection and as a more or less strict schoolmaster in the education of others into civic virtues.[97]

The Neoplatonic underpinnings of Augustine's conception of our common political life begin to come unstuck as he reads Paul. Under his tutelage, Augustine comes to believe that the classical ethical traditions rest on two fundamental and correlative mistakes. They ignore both our will's inability to do the good our reason recommends and our consequent need for divine assistance. John Milbank puts the first failing well: "For antique thought, on the whole, desire was split between an inherently 'proper' desire under control of right reason, and the excessive desires of disordered passions. But Augustine introduces the novel thought that reason itself can be perversely subordinate to a willful desire for a less than truly desirable object."[98] Accordingly, no matter how hard one might strive, no matter how severe the disciplines one endures or undertakes, without God's help no one can attain the good life he or she desires. Here we can let Augustine himself make the point: "[I]t is not in our power to live rightly, unless while we believe and pray we receive help from him who has given us the faith to believe that we must be helped by him."[99] Augustine therefore sees the claims of concern for nourishing the commonweal of the people uttered by classical political theorists as incoherent.

This is manifested most clearly in their lust for glory, which is corrosive of communal bonds. It celebrates individual achievement and the conquest of others. In the nature of the case, military or political supremacy is limited to very few. As Rowan Williams observes, "[T]he majority of the population, politically inactive, are kept united only by the fear of external enemies."[100] Augustine's critique of such glory, however, does not replace the "public" virtue of the classical, *polis*-centered life, with a "private" one. Rather, "Augustine's condemnation of 'public' life in the classical world is, consistently, that it is not public enough, that it is incapable of grounding a stable sense of commonalty because of its pervasive implicit élitism, its divisiveness, its lack of a common human *project*."[101] Theirs is a political ethic not of self-emptying, loving regard for others in relation to God but of heroic self-reliance—as their historiography, political oratory, ceremonies, and statuary bear testimony.

To unmask this incoherence, Augustine blurs the distinctions between relative degrees of earthly justice on which classical thought based its political confidence and certitude. We saw this same rhetorical technique at work in the discussion of war and peace. Here, he argues that when compared to the "true justice" of the Heavenly City, human justice blanches into sameness. True justice is a matter of being rightly related to God, and then only in and through this right relation, being properly related to oneself and one's neighbor. It is for Augustine the fruit of grace, giving practical expression to the theological virtues of faith, hope, and love, rather than, as it is for Cicero, a natural virtue that, by means of an intrinsic human reason and habitual disposition, is accessible to each individual and to organized political communities. Without assured access to this, Augustine deromanticizes political life, throwing into question attempts to perfect individuals through what he considers an inherently coercive political order. Making judgments is an essential part of political life, but earthly justice itself is too unreliable to warrant imposing finite standards as absolutes on those being governed. Fallen creatures must develop, on his view, political alliances and strategies not in light of what they can by nature rely on but with respect to what they cannot. Political theory should thus correspondingly base itself not on prideful presumptions of justice but on humbly recognizing the potential failures of justice; not on a confidence in the dominion of reason but on a suspiciousness about our human obsession with glorification. Augustine drives this point home with his unsettling portrayals of earthly peace, of justice, of leaders and judges who constantly question and prostrate themselves before the community and in the face of their uncertain duties. He creates a similarly disquieting effect in his discussion of slavery, where he easily slides over, and thus seems to ignore, the differences between it and the institutions of political authority.[102] Both are the result of the unnatural lust for domination that was unleashed by the fall, and both rely on coercion to the point of brutality to maintain their control. By disturbing established social sensibilities, Augustine removes the comfort and complacency his readers rely on and forces them to begin navigating in more dangerous political waters between the very real threats of arrogance and despair.

Central to Augustine's deconstructive questioning of glorified civic institutions is his critique of the social authority of educators and rhetoricians, whom he accuses of being instrumental in the perpetuation of the classical ethic of self-determination and in glossing over political and institutional problems. Relying on a sort of ridicule similar to that which he used with Alexander the Great, Augustine challenges certain prestigious positions of power that citizens would have counted on in positively assessing the empire. As I have noted, Augustine was sharply critical of teachers for using their social authority to cultivate a range of vices under the guise of public virtue. In the *Confessions* he brazenly likens the games they play with words to the taunts, rivalries, and competition of the schoolyard. And his teachers are the worse for the comparison since, he tells us, if any "were worsted by a colleague in some petty argument, he would be convulsed with anger and envy, much more so than I was when a playmate beat me at a game of ball."[103] Moreover, he sees the whole educational system, with all its dramatic props— its sober begowned masters and the heavy curtains hung like symbols of honor over school entrances—as nothing more than an imperial business.[104] Recalling a point made in chapter 4, it is a trafficking in literature that trains young boys to speak with "well-ordered and nicely balanced phrases" in order to satisfy "man's insatiable desire for the poverty he calls wealth and the infamy he calls fame."[105]

Augustine's uneasiness with the seductiveness of words and the unchecked political influences of those who have mastered the arts of persuasion does not just come from watching others exercise such power. He himself participated in all sorts of institutional activities as a rhetorician—a public debater, an educator, a preacher, and, most interesting of all, what we would call now a political spin doctor.[106] He had seen how easily one could cover rough blemishes with the sheen of beautiful turns of phrase and captivating yet empty accolades. He knew the transforming force of rhetoric. Augustine thus understood firsthand and remained attuned his entire life to the beneficial and dangerous possibilities of such institutional employments of power.

Together these deconstructive techniques help Augustine to mount an argument against the seeming inevitability and fittingness of the Greco-Roman conception of political association. By refusing to glorify existing or potential structures of political power, he desacralizes political society, both in its origin and in its justification. Since its institutions and mechanisms are not divinely grounded but a consequence of the fall, they should be used only as a last resort and with a profound sense of regret. Although he concedes that various forms of political coercion make possible a peaceful existence in the city, Augustine tends to dwell less on their social merits than on the unfortunate hazards that arise from such efforts to maintain civic order and control. Human societies, no matter how valiantly they try, cannot free themselves from the perils attendant to fallen existence. Therefore, all who use and benefit from political institutions, especially those in positions of authority, must never let a privileged rhetoric blind them to the fact that political activities are entangled in the morally treacherous territory of shifting and inequitable dynamics of power.

The Rhetoric of Progress: Modern Dangers of Ordering Disorder

On Foucault's view, the social dangers threatening modern persons and communities are far more convoluted than they were for Augustine. For one thing, Foucault never explained such relational risks as resulting from a common human rejection of God's offer of loving communion. What is more important for our purposes, however, is his contention that as available technologies for coercing individuals have multiplied, they have also become more socially subtle, diffuse, and intricately interwoven. Although he certainly would not have denied the dangers present in the practices and institutions Augustine examined, Foucault would argue both that they are actually more difficult to perceive and unravel than Augustine realized and that the attempts that have been made in the intervening centuries to address the dangers Augustine did note have actually spawned new and even more insidious forms of unbalanced power relations.

One of the principal reasons for the greater difficulty of discerning such dangers rests in the transformation of the privileged discourse behind which they now operate from one that celebrates the glories of personal and national conquest to one that trumpets the securities of scientific progress and therapeutic amelioration.[107] In ways not unlike the targets of Augustine's complaints, the discourses Foucault objects to base their privileges and protection on unchallengeable overarching convictions and agendas. Only in this case, ironically, they are shielded by their purported lack of any biasing conviction or agenda, their "scientized" canon of norms, and their pseudo-medical technologies and regimens. Foucault battles institutional power relations that deflect social criticism by meticulously depoliticizing rather than pompously politicizing their purposes, ideologies, and rituals. Instead of cloaking themselves with the mantle of divinely ordained majestic power, they secure terrain and the obedience of subjects by making themselves appear as though they are divested of all political objectives and activities. This alleged neutrality, argues Foucault, makes them especially dangerous because they exercise their coerciveness unobtrusively, thereby readily evading critique and accountability.

As we turn to examine Foucault's contribution to this conversation in more detail, three examples from his historical research in *Discipline and Punish* provide focal points: a response to natural evil, to moral evil, and the authority figures and judgments central to each. They serve to highlight areas of compatibility between Foucault and Augustine. But they also exhibit some of the ways in which Foucault's work enriches an Augustinian perspective, helping us to apply it to our different cultural context. Foucault's vivid depictions of the social hazards lurking within these modern attempts to minimize certain forms of communal disorder add an illuminating post-modern perspective that measurably extends and nuances Augustine's pre-modern insights.

Foucault, as we know, shares Augustine's general concerns about the ambivalence and indeterminacy of human achievements. He presses the point much further than does Augustine, however, especially in reference to poli-cies and institutions whose aim is to preserve and safeguard public order. While it is true, given Augustine's deep suspicions about all human projects, that it would not have been inconsistent for him to be more critical of the procedures for maintaining public order, his fear of social destabilization led him many times to protect them from the severest criticism. Foucault, by contrast, will cast an intensely critical eye on these organizing patterns of power distribution. He is therefore an interesting dialogue partner for Augustine on this point. Although some aspects of his work bear strong affinities to the sort of restless criticism advocated by Augustine, other parts offer a constructive critique of and warning against Augustine's preoccupa-tions with political stability and order.

Foucault's description of the ways in which a plague-ridden French city in the late seventeenth century was cordoned off and monitored in order to control the spread of disease illustrates both some of the commonalities with Augustine and some of the disagreements. The medical preparations began, reports Foucault, with posting guards at each of the city gates to pre-vent any from entering or leaving.[108] Sentinels were dispatched to the town hall and to every street corner "to ensure the prompt obedience of the people and the most absolute authority of the magistrates."[109] Freedom of passage within the city was strictly curtailed. With rare exceptions, only those re-sponsible for maintaining the quarantine were allowed to move about. Fami-lies were locked in their homes from the outside by the syndic assigned to their street, who, on daily rounds, spoke to each member of the families in his charge and inquired as to their health. The inhabitants were obliged to answer his questions truthfully—on pain of death—and to appear at a win-dow in order to prevent the concealment of the sick or dead. Those who fell ill were cared for only by physicians appointed by the magistrates, who re-tained complete control over the treatment. No other practitioners were allowed to attend to those infected and no independent apothecaries could prepare medicines. The magistrates also regulated the care of souls, limiting visits to the sick by priests and preventing the gathering of congregations to worship. This system of observation and inspection was based on a "perma-nent registration," the name, age, and gender of every resident having been supplied to the town hall. Further, regular and detailed written reports about "deaths, illnesses, complaints, [and] irregularities" were provided in duplicate by the syndics to their supervisors, who kept one copy and sent the other along to the magistrates.[110]

This system of monitoring and controlling the city's inhabitants, when weighed against the calamitous alternative of dying of the plague, may not seem politically excessive. Knowing that it was instituted not simply to protect those fortunate enough to live outside the infection's immediate locus but also to control the spread of the disease within the city itself, most persons would raise no complaints about a medically determined confinement, restriction of liberty, and invasion of privacy. Suspicions of coercion, given their desperate situation, would not be their principal concern. From Foucault's perspective, however, all is not well in this plague-ridden town. Although it certainly met the grave challenge of preserving the life of its citizens, the mechanisms it resorted to in maintaining the public's safety bore a distinctive human price. Foucault continuously intersperses his account of the preparations and procedures for dealing with the plague's outbreak with caustic images and evaluative descriptions that alert us to the social dangers he sees. Of the daily rounds he says: "Everyone locked up in his cage, everyone at his window, answering to his name and showing himself when asked—it is the great review of the living and the dead."[111] The confinement of the residents strikes him this way: "It is a segmented, immobile, frozen space. Each individual is fixed in his place. And, if he moves, he does so at the risk of his life, contagion or punishment."[112] And the hierarchizing of authority elicits this response: "The registration of the pathological must be constantly centralized. The relation of each individual to his disease and to his death passes through the representatives of power, the registration they make of it, the decisions they take on it."[113]

Each remark illustrates how morally ambivalent Foucault felt about such methods of registering, surveying, and controlling a given population. It is not merely the loss of privacy and personal freedoms, or even the artificial disruption to one's self and communal relations that worries Foucault, although he finds all of these problematic. And he does not dispute the relative social success of this program to fight the plague. He wishes us to notice that more happened in this well-intended medical response than the control of a natural evil, the stemming of the loss of life. Not only was a biological catastrophe averted, but also unintentionally, an enticing "political dream" of a "disciplined society" free of "rebellions, crimes, vagabondage, desertions, people who appear and disappear, live and die in disorder" was realized, if only fleetingly.[114] A perfectly ordered mirage shimmered momentarily on the horizon, eliciting sociopolitical as well as medical longings and hopes. "The plague-stricken town, traversed throughout with hierarchy, surveillance, observation, writing; the town immobilized by the functioning of an extensive power that bears in a distinct way over all individual bodies—this is the utopia of the perfectly governed city."[115]

Even when focusing his attention narrowly on this singular historical account, Foucault is keenly attuned to the coercive and potentially harmful consequences that the population may not have been aware of or else may not have been concerned to monitor or resist, given the obvious good such rules were instituted to protect. Remembering that for Foucault power is not merely negative, the social risk he detects involves more than restriction, limitation, and constraint. It actively creates, cultivates, shapes, and transforms persons. Meticulously governing measures like these do not just set up prohibitive boundaries, rigidly forbidding and thus determining what individuals cannot do, where they cannot go, and who they cannot see. It also sets up a complex and interactive social grid by which citizens come to account for and understand each of their particular interrelations and by which they administer each of their activities and anticipated goals:

> [I]ndividuals are inserted in a fixed place, in which the slightest movements are supervised, in which all events are recorded[,] . . . in which power is exercised without division, according to a continuous hierarchical figure, in which each individual is constantly located, examined and distributed among the living beings, the sick and the dead.[116]

Caught up in a mandated rhythm of their daily requirements and an enforced segmentation of their common living space, citizens would come to see themselves and relate to others in their community in light of a pathological dread of social disorder and the constant threat of infectious insecurity. Even if only temporarily, the plague-ridden town had the unrestrained power to engrave on people's lives and bodies a kind of road map of relational order and mastery that, through repeated exercise and habituation, could gradually become internalized and invisibly guide social attitudes and activities.

What alarms Foucault in translating this particular historical event into a more expansive "political dream" is the ease with which power relations can regulate and monitor a diverse multiplicity of people. By managing the details of each individual's existence, such a capillary form of power can create with little resistance a wide-reaching and intimately suffusing network of social control, and it can do so as a perfectly justified protection from danger. At least in modern times, Foucault believes, personal and communal identities, patterns of private and public interaction, value systems, ways of thinking and behaving—all, to some degree or another, have been influenced by various implementations of precisely laid out and minutely functioning disciplinary practices.

The success of such mechanisms for ordering large numbers of people can be traced, in part at least, to the ways in which who we become and how we learn to direct our lives are affected and, in many ways, controlled by how we as embodied creatures interact on a day-to-day level with a highly organized and stabilizing environment. Because our bodies are at once so dynamic and so malleable, the "meticulous tactical partitioning" of space and time can extensively shape our habits, dispositions, and self-understandings.[117] When coupled with a mode of thought that fixates on "binary division and branding (mad/sane; dangerous/harmless; normal/abnormal)," the sort of "coercive assignment" that identifies persons according to their location in an elaborately subdivided social, geographical, and temporal grid can, Foucault argues, leave a harmful and enduring mark on individuals. Indeed, he will go on to argue that the disciplinary mechanisms that we see here prefigured do not simply imprint themselves on persons, but actually create certain kinds of socially worthwhile subjects.[118] Thus it is not simply the limitations endured by the residents of that late-seventeenth-century French town that filled Foucault with a sense of foreboding. It is the political impulses and strategies there instantiated. It is the enforced ideological and behavioral conformity of the town that stirs his passions. In this seemingly benign plan to confront a natural evil, he sees the lineaments of what would later become a far-flung, inconspicuously governing, and potentially dehumanizing web of cultural expectations and practices.

Foucault's apprehensions about the plague-ridden town call to mind Augustine's hand-wringing over the manipulative hazards of justified war. In both situations, a political response is required so as to protect citizens from being physically obliterated. Something has to be done to safeguard the population. But the strategies and consequences of restoring social order are nevertheless, according to both thinkers, always and often imperceptibly ensnared in coercive relations of power. As such, they remain vulnerable to asymmetrical hardening and to self-serving aims and methods. In trying to ward off an impending danger and control a disorderly mass of people, authorities are given license to implement what would otherwise be morally objectionable measures. Given that these are deployed in the context of hierarchical and irreversible power relations and that they involve practices of aggressive ordering, they are disposed to an instrumentalism that cannot be adequately monitored, challenged, or changed. Moreover, such coercion inevitably spawns unintended yet harmful consequences that both the planners and the individual participants do not fully control and may not be aware of. They obviously take shape in fighting an indisputable enemy, but because they also can function and fulfill the purposes of other social desires and needs, such commanding tactics can become diverted from their original aims and take on a life of their own.

In addition to this parallel between justified war and justified medical intervention, Foucault's fears about the illusion of a perfectly governed community also echo Augustine's insights into the risks of the classical conception of the city as an arena for perfecting the social body and thereby realizing ultimate human ends. Especially in light of Augustine's warnings about the ease with which the morally despicable can be dressed in the cloak of moral necessity or social progress, Foucault's confined town can appear as a precedent that serves to justify a reconfigured and dangerously distorted political ideal. He observes: "Underlying disciplinary projects the image of the plague stands for all forms of confusion and disorder; just as the image of the leper, cut off from all human contact, underlies projects of exclusion. . . . All the mechanisms of power which, even today, are disposed around the abnormal individual, to brand him and to alter him, are composed of those two forms from which they distantly derive."[119] Once perfection becomes the goal, then not just medical but moral or ethnic differences can be construed as infectious "pathologies" that require extreme measures to contain and control. The Jewish ghetto in Nazi-occupied Krakow offers a particularly sickening case in point. The SS ruthlessly applied the same mechanisms of registration, surveillance, and containment that the French had put to such a different use in protecting their population from contamination.

Because Foucault was more keenly aware than Augustine of the potential dangers in our desire for order and in the mechanisms and procedures we use to fashion and maintain it, his work can shed light on one of the limitations of Augustine's political thought. Augustine was simply too resigned about the uses of coercion to maintain order. So concerned was he to secure and keep temporal peace, he often tolerated what he admitted was repellent. It seems likely that the disintegration of the Empire's social fabric after the sack of Rome had a great deal to do with his preoccupation with preserving social stability. Foucault, having witnessed (at least secondhand) the highly mechanized, calculated, and, indeed, rational manifestation of evil at the hands of the Nazis, saw better than Augustine that evil has its own logic and that order in and of itself does not necessarily act as a bulwark against disorder and its accompanying chaos and misery. It can be the actual cause of human suffering. We have been for too long, Foucault argues, laboring under the delusion "that reason can only produce the Good and that Evil can only flow from a refusal of reason. This would have little sense. The rationality of the abominable is a fact of contemporary history."[120]

The enticing ideal of social stability that was realized, if only momentarily, in the plague-ridden town, can be traced, Foucault contends, through the gradual transformations of Europe's penal reform system. He is particularly interested in the sociopolitical effects of this reform through the broad application of disciplinary techniques well outside the gates of any prison. The dream slowly perfected is one of social control by means of a disciplinary mode of power that appears uncoercive and that is shielded from observation and critique through the redefinition of political practices in terms of scientific and medical assessments, rehabilitation, neutrality, efficiency, and progress. As we saw in the previous chapter, such code words, to use Sissela Bok's term, along with their associated spaces, activities, and rituals, circumvent critical reflection because they receive, through their mutual interaction and support, culturewide sanction.[121] Owing to this apparently self-evident naturalness, it comes to seem that this disciplinary network is not simply the way things are, it is the way things must be. By means of his genealogical investigations of such modes of power, Foucault is saying, in effect: Do not assume that this is the way of the world; it is this way because we have made it thus. His research therefore provides another illustration of his suspiciousness of seemingly progressive achievements and his consequent concern to subject both inhumane- and humane-seeming social practices, as well as the privileged discourses that provide them cover, to critical scrutiny. To understand both the enduring problems surrounding coercive power relations and the ways in which these problems metamorphose over time, Foucault examines in *Discipline and Punish* how specific configurations of power shift and spread within circumscribed histories. To that end, he contrasts two strikingly different methods of combating crime, one from the eighteenth, the other from the nineteenth century. If our seventeenth-century town was subdivided, monitored, and controlled in an effort to manage a natural evil, then the following can be seen as attempts to confront the dangers of moral evil.

Discipline and Punish begins with a vivid and indeed horrifying account of an eighteenth-century public execution. First, we read the criminal's sentence:

On 2 March 1757 Damiens the regicide was condemned 'to make the *amende honorable* before the main door of the Church of Paris', where he was to be 'taken and conveyed in a cart, wearing nothing but a shirt, holding a torch of burning wax weighing two pounds'; then, 'in the said cart, to the Place de Grève, where, on a scaffold that will be erected there, the flesh will be torn from his breasts, arms, thighs and calves with red-hot pincers, his right hand, holding the knife with which he committed the said parricide, burnt with sulphur, and, on those places where the flesh will be torn away, poured molten lead, boiling oil, burning resin, wax and sulphur melted together and then his body drawn and quartered by four horses and his limbs and body consumed by fire, reduced to ashes and his ashes thrown to the winds'.[122]

Foucault then presents various observers' detailed descriptions, rendering first-hand the overpowering particulars of suffering: a precise tearing of flesh; the searing of bleeding wounds; straining sinews, muscles, and joints; horses starting and stopping as angles are inspected, recalculated, and changed; and finally, an executioner carefully cutting apart a brutalized body and throwing it piece by piece into flames. Through its excruciating movements, Foucault makes us spectators to the slow drama of violence and the refined art of directed pain, to the astonishing and uncontestable power unfurling itself in the public square.

Sadly, Augustine would not find this "monarchical" form of punishment, to use Foucault's term, all that unfamiliar. Although the mechanics of torture and execution may have varied, the imposition of raw force upon the body of another for the glorification of an individual or empire was a feature of his age's political operations.[123] In trying to bring the suffering to life, Augustine and Foucault focus on the physical ravages endured by victims. Both understand that these mangled bodies are essential elements in a social and political ritual that needs the vanquished to instantiate visibly the overwhelming power and majesty of the victor. They therefore share an analytical agenda, namely, illuminating the political function of violence. Like Augustine, Foucault sees in this mode of power that "[t]he very excess of violence employed is one of the elements of its glory."[124] On his view, extravagant brutality and unrestrained fury were not a matter of momentary irrationality or loss of self-control but integral to the logic of political intimidation and retribution. "[I]t was a spectacular expression of potency, an 'expenditure,' exaggerated and coded, in which power renewed its vigour. It was always more or less related to the triumph. The solemn appearance of

the sovereign brought with it something of the consecration, the corona-
tion, the return from victory."[125] The indisputable and personally experienced disparity of power was essential to the political success of such rituals.
They had to create "a spectacle not of measure, but of imbalance and excess;
in this liturgy of punishment, there must be an emphatic affirmation of
power and of its intrinsic superiority."[126] One party must be marked by and
through the ceremony as triumphant, the other as defeated. The body of the
condemned provided the anchoring point for this violent show of armed
might that reaffirmed the "physical, material, and awesome force of the sovereign."[127] Destroying the body of the "enemy" vividly demonstrated the
unchallengeable mastery of the sovereign over his subjects. The body fur-
nished the stage on which a massive play of power could be dramatized in
order to flaunt "before all eyes an invincible force."[128] This "theater of terror"[129] consequently had to be conducted in public with all the pomp and
ceremony we saw in Rome's hailing of triumphant battlefield heroes. "Its
ruthlessness, its spectacle, its physical violence, its unbalanced play of forces,
its meticulous ceremonial, its entire apparatus were inscribed in the political
functioning of the penal system."[130]

Augustine interprets this political functioning of power primarily in
terms of the *libido dominandi*. By setting it in a discussion of sin, his purpose is to desecrate such public liturgies with the spectacle of broken bodies.
His intent is to shatter glory and throw light on sorrow; to disrupt a perfectly orchestrated ceremonial with the remembrance of the slain; to bring
down the majestic by lifting up the crushed. He questions the presumed
successes and happiness of the politically powerful, but he never doubts the
efficacy of their power to subjugate. It represents for him the *libido dominandi* in its full earthly flower. Foucault, however, regards the monarchical
form of power as paradoxically vulnerable in its strength and inefficient in
its intensity. Force must present itself physically with great energy and flare.
It has to remain personally visible to subjects. It must lead them in pageantry
and rituals to retain its radiant image. It is thus incessantly expending itself
in displays of self-glorification. Such a dramatic power is also provocative,
inviting challenge. It must thus not only attend to the public tasks of en-
chanting its own citizens, it must stay on guard, ready to fight any who take
up the gauntlet. In doing so, it ends up destroying not just the expendable
bodies it requires for its triumphant ceremonials but also, in the case of war,
many of its own subjects it relies on and desires to enthrall.

Having been cultivated as a penal style in the late eighteenth and nineteenth century, a "disciplinary" mode of punishment would have seemed

much stranger to Augustine. Energized by the growing sentiment that "punishing power should not soil its hands with a crime greater than the one it wished to punish,"[131] a series of seemingly humanizing reforms largely brought to a close in Europe the judicial and political spectacle of public torture and execution. In its place, experimentations and prison projects began with the objective of rehabilitating, training, correcting, and curing the offender. Over time, a nonviolent mechanism for controlling and shaping human behavior developed that reassured the public that the infliction of pain and the exhibition of the prisoner's mutilated body are not ultimate ends of the penal process. Rather than present a triumphant display of judicial and political force, punishment was reconfigured into a technology that seeks to transform the criminal. "Now the scandal and the light are to be distributed differently,"[132] writes Foucault. "If it is still necessary for the law to reach and manipulate the body of the convict, it will be at a distance in the proper way, according to strict rules, and with a much 'higher' aim."[133] Instead of being the most visible and intense dramatic moment in the juridical process, "punishment" will become the most hidden and pedestrian.

Foucault maintains that one finds in Jeremy Bentham's Panopticon the clearest example of an ideal model that carries out disciplinary punishment's twin mission of controlling and transforming the criminal without soiling its hands. The key to its success lies in its simple ingenious design. A guard tower stands at the center of an encircling ring of prison cells. Each cell has windows lining its outer and inner walls, allowing light to suffuse the enclosure and fully illuminate the occupant. "By the effect of backlighting, one can observe from the tower, standing out precisely against the light, the small captive shadows in the cells of the periphery. They are like so many cages, so many small theatres, in which each actor is alone, perfectly individualized and constantly visible."[134] Bentham's design is founded on the two correlative principles of uninterrupted *visibility* and *unverifiability*.[135] With respect to the former, the referent of "the visible" is actually twofold. Not only is the condemned perpetually visible, the cell offering no nook or cranny in which to hide, but from the vantage point of the prisoner, the tower itself looms as a constant and massive reminder of his transparency. Whether the inmate is in fact being observed, however, is unverifiable. Because no light passes through the guard tower, it is impossible for the prisoner to determine whether and when he is being monitored. It is only natural for him to live as though surveillance is continual even if in actuality it operates discontinuously. This new mode and functioning of power "had its own type of ceremony. It was not triumph, but the review, the 'parade,' an ostentatious form of examination. In it the 'subjects' were presented as 'objects' to the observation of a power that was manifested only by a gaze. . . . The scarcely sustainable visibility of the monarch is turned into the unavoidable visibility of the subjects. And it was this inversion of visibility . . . that was to assure the exercise of power even in its lowest manifestations."[136]

In the Panopticon, then, in stark contrast to the monarchy, power is able to operate as an efficiently impersonal mechanism. The perceived permanency of surveillance assures its automatic functioning. "Power has its principle not so much in a person as in . . . a machinery that assures dissymmetry. . . . Consequently, it does not matter who exercises power."[137] Any manager, no matter how timid he may be, can step in and maintain precise control. Integral to the efficacy of this technology of power is the prisoner himself. Ironically, he becomes part of the mechanism inasmuch as he internalizes the monitoring function. As Foucault's image of a theater so aptly portrays, in this particular drama the condemned will, in time, take on the role of both the actor and the director. As such, he becomes complicit in this remarkably economical operation of power.[138]

By bringing the inmate into the surveillance process, Foucault argues that the Panopticon is able to dispense with the ponderous masonry walls, iron gates, and bars of an earlier era's prisons. "Bentham was surprised that panoptic institutions could be so light: there were no more bars, no more chains, no more heavy locks; all that was needed was that the separations should be clear and the openings well-arranged. The heaviness of the old 'houses of security,' with their fortress-like architecture, could be replaced by the simple economic geometry of a 'house of certainty.' "[139] But, Foucault interjects, it does not thereby surrender or diminish its degree of control. The structure fashions an exact mechanism of power that is unprecedented in its intimacy while simultaneously and paradoxically remaining antiseptically distant, depersonalized, and withdrawn. The panoptic model is truly inventive in this regard. On the one hand, it is a restrictive architecture designed to regulate and confine dangerous masses through the isolation of potential conspirators. On the other hand, it is a "creative" and "productive" space, allowing the disciplinary power not only to restrain but also to generate certain kinds of "worthwhile," that is, manageable, individuals.

So effective and flexible is this model of surveillance, Foucault claims, that it will be implemented not only in the prison so as to control and alter the condemned but also, with variations, in less omni-disciplinary and obviously oppressive institutional settings.

It is polyvalent in its applications; it serves to reform prisoners, but also to treat patients, to instruct schoolchildren, to supervise workers, to put beggars and idlers to work. It is a type of location of bodies in space, of distribution of individuals in relation to one another, of hierarchical organization, of disposition of centres and channels of power, of definition of the instruments and modes of intervention of power, which can be implemented in hospitals, workshops, schools, prisons.[140]

In time, he contends, panopticism will spread and strengthen, breaking out of institutional settings in bits and pieces, finally creating enough circulating nodes of power relations to become distributed throughout the social body.[141] As we began to see in chapter 4, a growing cultural obsession with individualization, normalization, and objectification; with scientific "health" and "progress"; and with psychological and physiological analysis would pave the way for a complex micro-physics of power to gain a material hold over increasingly large and diverse populations.

This innovative disciplinary technology and its recognizable utility for certain relations of power did not burst on the modern scene all at once, according to Foucault, nor did it derive from the expansionist designs of a single, unified and centralized retainer of power. The unbalanced interchanges that generated asymmetries and excluded reciprocities unfolded slowly and somewhat unconsciously. A primarily operational disparity of power developed according to the functional needs and reactions of localized sites that then spread through minimal points of contact that served as conduits to reinforce and support each other. Gradually, through the profusion of their social interactions, they formed a loosely coherent logic in a generalizable yet adaptable functioning of power.

Even though this apparatus evolves haphazardly in numerous places and in response to different problems, it addresses, on Foucault's view, one common need: the ordering and management of large numbers of people. Disciplinary techniques ensure the subjection and restraint of expansive segments of the population while simultaneously making it possible to extract from individual persons activities that are both profitable and efficient. At one and the same time, therefore, such mechanisms minimize the dangers involved in supervising human collectivities and maximize the potential serviceability of each individual member. "In a word, the disciplines are the ensemble of minute technical inventions that made it possible to increase the useful size of multiplicities by decreasing the inconveniences of the power which, in order to make them useful, must control them."[142]

The implementation of discipline as a penal mechanism would have fallen outside Augustine's own experiences. Nevertheless, the basic elements that Foucault believes constitute it as a broader mode of power and give it its material leverage over diverse individuals and groups would have been immediately familiar. A preoccupation with minor acts and thoughts, a use of partitioned space, a division of the day, and a honing of capacities through habit all formed a part of the monastic traditions of Augustine's day. These are clearly "an old inheritance."[143] What Foucault targets as new and historically significant are not these simple and everyday instruments of discipline but how such small and often taken for granted techniques have been deployed to achieve particular political objectives. Ascetical traditions certainly relied on similar practices of discipline, yet, as we have seen, he asserts that they often had as their aim, if not always their result, "the mastery of each individual over his own body."[144] For instance, in Cassian's ethic of chastity, examination, deconstruction, and confessional reconstruction are used to cultivate an increasingly harmonized unity and heightened self-control for the service of others and oneself. Foucault analyzes formally similar disciplinary exercises, only now they are put to the use of subjecting and manipulating specific individuals and groups. Ironically, the intimacy and perfusion of ordered power relations that make Cassian's ethic so personally forceful and efficacious here leave persons politically vulnerable.

> The historical moment of the disciplines was the moment when an art of the human body was born, which was directed not only at the growth of its skills, nor at the intensification of its subjection, but at the formation of *a relation* that in the mechanism itself makes it more obedient as it becomes more useful, and conversely. What was being formed was a policy of coercions that act upon the body, a calculated manipulation of its elements, its gestures, its behaviour. The human body was entering a machinery of power that explores it, breaks it down and rearranges it. A 'political anatomy', which was also a 'mechanics of power', was being born; it defined how one may have a hold over others' bodies, not only so that they may do what one wishes, but so that they may operate as one wishes, with the techniques, the speed and the efficiency that one determines. Thus discipline produces subjected and practised bodies, 'docile' bodies.[145]

Foucault understands his task in *Discipline and Punish* to be analyzing asymmetrical relations of power that target the political usefulness, the efficiency, the economy of the human body.[146]

The main instruments for distributing and mastering great numbers of people, Foucault argues, evolve around a concentration on "detail." This can be seen first of all in technologies of rhythm and precision that allow disciplinary power to manage one's movement through time, determining the when, what, and how of one's daily activities. "For centuries," he writes, "the religious orders . . . were the specialists of time, the great technicians of rhythm and regular activities."[147] They divided the day into cycles of prayers and scriptural reading, establishing times for work and for study, for examination and for confession, for eating and for sleeping. "But the disciplines altered these methods of temporal regulation from which they derived."[148] Refining them to a hyper-extreme, they meticulously broke down the day into hours with set activities, then into quarter hours, next into minutes, on down even to the regulation of seconds. The hospital, the factory, and the school all present examples of hyper-division: observing, assessing, noting the individual's condition and progress moment by moment. This metronic rhythm becomes attached to a quality of operation, to the continual vigilance over the sick patient, to the increasing productivity of the factory worker, to the evolving capacities of the student. It is a question of utilitarian purity "extracting, from time," writes Foucault, "ever more available moments and, from each moment, ever more useful forces."[149]

Central to capitalizing on both the accumulation and the passage of time is the resourcefulness of "exercise." By applying techniques of repetition, on the one hand, and calculated variations and gradations, on the other, exercise is able to get into the details of tasks—into the movements, the gestures, the potency of an act—in order to deconstruct them into separable and fundamental components, assess their relative proficiencies, and qualitatively reconstruct them. What is the best relation of a gesture to the position of the body, the position of the body to overall movement, overall movement to speed and efficiency; speed and efficiency to a desired and planned progression? "The act is broken down into its elements; . . . to each movement are assigned a direction, an aptitude, a duration; their order of succession is prescribed. Time penetrates the body and with it all the meticulous controls of power."[150] Again, in contrast to the monastic aim of increasing skills and capacities in relation to one's purposes, disciplinary institutions utilize time with the goal of domesticating others, controlling the dangerous forces of a given multitude, and simultaneously developing from all individuals an efficient and profitable application of their energies. "Time measured and paid for," Foucault concludes, "must also be a time without impurities or defects; a time of good quality, throughout which the body is constantly applied to its exercise. Precision and application are, with regularity, the fundamental virtues of disciplinary time."[151] Consequently, the developing "virtues" of disciplinary modes of power rely on a linear time that is purged of the frailties and mysteries of finitude as well as a hierarchized social time that transforms, corrects, and produces collectively "useful" individuals.

Hand in hand with governing the details of temporal divisibility and regulation, disciplinary modes of power also rely on the segmentation of institutional spaces. As was apparent in both the plague-ridden city and the Panopticon, the divisibility of space makes possible the art of distributing bodies within it. Building on the principle of partitioning, disciplinary mechanisms organize and administer large groups of people by establishing a specified place for each individual. Position and locality regulate relational dynamics: its proper management can prevent the formation of communal dispositions, dissipate the energies of "diffuse circulation" and "dangerous coagulation," and control the disorderly confusion associated with unaccounted for movements.[152]

> Its aim was to establish presences and absences, to know where and how to locate individuals, to set up useful communications, to interrupt others, to be able at each moment to supervise the conduct of each individual, to assess it, to judge it, to calculate its qualities and merits. It was a procedure, therefore, aimed at knowing, mastering, and using. Discipline organizes an analytical space.[153]

Such segmented spaces would gradually become "coded" for profitable use. They would become functionally oriented "therapeutic" spaces or "industrious" spaces or "learning" spaces focused on negotiating specific medical, industrial, or educational problems and needs. They not only provided "a hold over this whole mobile, swarming mass,"[154] and therein neutralized the potential dangers of multitudes, but in so doing, they also cultivated a qualitatively expedient mode and site of operation. Relying on varying daily, weekly, monthly, and yearly tasks and examinations, individuals could be placed in relation to one another, evaluated in reference to a fixed standard, but also moved—altered, modulated, trained, transformed—through a circulating network of differentiated and graduated interrelationships. "In organizing 'cells,' 'places' and 'ranks,'" Foucault argues, the disciplines create complex spaces that are at once architectural, functional, and hierarchical. [They are] spaces that provide fixed positions and permit circulation; they carve out individual segments and establish operational links; they mark places and indicate values; they guarantee the obedience of individuals, but also a better economy of time and gesture. They are mixed spaces: real because they govern the disposition of buildings, rooms, furniture, but also ideal, because they are projected over this arrangement of characterizations, assessments, hierarchies.[155]

Foucault argues forcefully that space has been consistently devalued in the modern era by both philosophers and political theorists. We profoundly misunderstand it, he writes, if we regard it as "the dead, the fixed, the inert."[156] A deeper understanding of rituals supports Foucault's notion that space is not without relational impact. It is dynamic, shaping the lives, self-identities, behaviors, attitudes, expectations, and hopes of those who interact within and with it. Plainly this has important religious implications for, say, designing shared worship and ministering spaces. But it is important politically as well for the planning of communal spaces—residences, workplaces, public commons. If, as is increasingly true in North America, public spaces develop in response to pressures brought to bear by commercial interests, that will have, according to Foucault, a profound impact on the sorts of relations—not only external but also internal—we can develop.

On Foucault's view, of all the modern institutions, one sees in the prison the manipulation of time and space in its most concentrated form, where elements from the other major disciplinary regimens are gathered together and refined. The isolating segmentation of the hospital finds its correlate in the prison cell, the observable grid of the factory is utilized in the productive labor process, and the school's hierarchical training is applied to the personal development of the criminal. The prison, writes Foucault, weaves together these different disciplinary strands, but it also exceeds them all in the intensity of their application.

In several respects, the prison must be an exhaustive disciplinary apparatus: it must assume responsibility for all aspects of the individual, his physical training, his aptitude to work, his everyday conduct, his moral attitude, his state of mind; the prison, much more than the school, the workshop, or the army, which always involved a certain specialization, is "omni-disciplinary."[157]

The combined use of disciplinary technologies for the supervision and transformation of the condemned is ratcheted up by the fact that there is no outside to prison life; it functions as a seamless web of coercion. Both because of the intensity and because of the ceaselessness of this mode of discipline, Foucault is persuaded that the dynamics of power exerted over prisoners is the most strikingly asymmetrical of all the institutional examples.[158] Not only is the application of discipline the most concentrated, their object, the complete rehabilitation or reformation of the individual, is by far the most sweeping. Beyond simply separating individuals from one another, imparting to them certain capacities and knowledge, and utilizing their energies as a labor force, the prison aims at completely reshaping the delinquent individual. Punishment is clearly not a matter of redressing isolated behavior or acts, as Foucault believes it was in the monarchical model, but of observing, controlling, and reconfiguring the person's entire existence.

Whether it be in the prison, hospital, workshop, school, or society at large, Foucault describes (and cautions us about) patterns of human relations that are asymmetrical and nonreciprocal and that have as their target the utilization of others. In distinct contrast to the open displays of force employed in Augustine's day, the peculiarly modern relations of power that interest Foucault lack drama and spectacle. They manifest no slowly simmering theatrics of political glorification—no excessive show of armed might, no exaggerated coding of the victor and the vanquished, no emblematic destruction of the enemy's body. In fact, argues Foucault, these modern apparatuses of power operate less *upon* than *within* the body being disciplined. Because of this hidden coerciveness, the intensity of the power exercised and the suffering apportioned may seem small in comparison to what was so extravagantly heralded by the sovereign's exhibition of force.

> Discipline . . . is not a triumphant power, which because of its own excess can pride itself on its omnipotence; it is a modest, suspicious power, which functions as a calculated, but permanent economy. These are humble modalities, minor procedures, as compared with the majestic rituals of sovereignty or the great apparatuses of the state.[159]

Instead of being visibly concentrated and publicly displayed, the effects of a disciplinary mode of power are subtle and diffuse; they operate through often imperceptible details.[160] If we examine disciplinary mechanisms piece by piece, Foucault concludes, the minuscule tools they apply will certainly seem innocuous; however, when we consider their interlocking and cumulative effects, we begin to see the outlines of a more alarming technology. Working loosely together, disciplinary mechanisms as a whole have great transforming power and pervasive physical consequences. They may employ no visible and external violence of the sort manifested by the monarchical mode of power, but they still apply a material force that deeply alters the individual. By segmenting spaces and times, manipulating activities, and normatively ranking improvements, the disciplines are able to inscribe a docility and obedience into the finest particulars of individuals' lives.

Ironically, according to Foucault, the penal reform movement of the eighteenth and nineteenth centuries issues in not so much a humanistic advancement as a reconfigured and inventive mode of subjection.

> This subjection is not only maintained by the instruments of violence or ideology; it can also be direct, physical, pitting force against force, bearing on material elements, and yet without involving violence; it may be calculated, organized, technically thought out; it may be subtle, make use neither of weapons nor of terror and yet remain of a physical order.[161]

That is to say, the reform movement established a more effectively targeted application of power at a minimum of economic and political costs. Once again, we see the dream of a well-ordered and submissive populace making its presence felt. Indeed, argues Foucault, it is the visible and pronounced "restraint" of such power that gives it its potency. The use of force can thereby be freed of those elements that make it grotesquely objectionable while increasing those that make it useful. "[T]he elegance of the discipline lay in the fact that it could dispense with this costly and violent relation by obtaining effects of utility at least as great."[162] No more harm seems to be inflicted than the mere intrusion of carefully tending to and balancing records, the simple numbering and ordering of scattered gestures, attitudes, and activities. It is in this distinct precision and seeming inoffensiveness, however, that Foucault pinpoints the social danger. "They are the acts of cunning," he notes, "not so much of the greater reason that works even in its sleep and gives meaning to the insignificant, as of the attentive 'malevolence' that turns everything to account."[163] That the consequences of disciplinary leverage can be at one and the same time so subtle and so thoroughly widespread gives them, Foucault solemnly warns, a nearly unrestricted domain of social power.

As we turn to a final example of Foucault's historical investigations, that of the transformed role of judges in the jurisprudential system, it would be well to bear in mind one preliminary point. Foucault's description of the anonymity of the disciplinary network should not lead us to forget that the institutions through which it has spread are administered by living, breathing human beings. Though highly depersonalized, these mechanisms nevertheless create environments where people interact with others as they earn their livings. That is why he believes we are all to one degree or another complicit in their ongoing operation. It is also why he urges us to join the fight against injustices at the local level, where we actually live and work.[164] Otherwise the carceral network is just a vague idea. By focusing our attention on the changing role of judges, be they magistrates or jurors, we can acknowledge the personal dimensions of the panoptic system while not ignoring that judges and their associates are entangled in a web of deeply enculturated disciplinary patterns of thought, speech, and conduct. Both aspects should be kept in view when examining Foucault's description of the following modern transformation.

During the Middle Ages, according to Foucault, judges addressed themselves to answering three relatively straightforward questions: Has a crime in fact occurred, who is responsible for it, and what is the appropriate legal sanction?[165] As we saw with Augustine's reluctant judge, this narrowly bounded concern still leaves plenty of room for confusion, doubt, and grave moral error. Circumstances may be unclear and eyewitnesses unavailable. Coercion may force an innocent person to confess, or it may lead to false accusations that entangle other innocent victims. Such moral and epistemic turbidity cannot be avoided, but neither can the necessity of rendering legal judgments. For without them, on Augustine's view, society's stability would crumble. They are lamentable and utterly repugnant political necessities.

Foucault reports that the indignity of having to make such morally indeterminate decisions, together with the eventual public outrage at the political spectacle of excessive violence, led to a slow transformation in the medieval mode of jurisprudential inquiry. Whereas the earlier approach had placed its emphasis primarily on the factual issues of act, responsibility, and punishment, now legal language and processes, although not ignoring the crime itself, tend rather to circulate around the criminal. More specifically, the questions with which a judge wrestles are inclined to devolve into an examination of the intentions, inclinations, habits, thoughts, and psychological profile of the suspect (or, in the case of sentencing, the condemned). "Under cover of the relative stability of the law," writes Foucault, "a mass of subtle changes occurred. Certainly, the 'crimes' and 'offences' on which judgement is passed are juridical objects defined by the code, but judgement is also passed on the passions, instincts, anomalies, infirmities, maladjustments. . . . For it is the shadows lurking behind the case itself that are judged and punished. . . . They provide the mechanisms of legal punishment with a justifiable hold not only on offenses, but on individuals, not only on what they do, but also on what they are, will be, may be."[166] Criminality gradually becomes, he argues, the greater focus of penal intervention.[167]

Consequently, judges in the modern era must consider and determine far more than ever before. In the hope of gaining a firmer grasp on the issues confronting them and to secure an objective foundation on which to rest their decisions, judges have taken on an additional and far more involved task. Ironically, however, as a result of this aspiration to attain more certitude, another layer of problematic questions and possible uncertainties gets injected into the penal process.[168] A whole set of decisions must now be made about kinds and degrees of deviance; about the nature and character of a criminal's past, present, and future; and, in relation to all of this, about the probable and quantifiable success of different forms of rehabilitation for him.

Since these determinations require expertise and training that is nonjuridical, Foucault asserts, judges are no longer able to render judgments by themselves. They "have begun to do something other than pass judgement. Or, to be more precise, other types of judgement have slipped in, profoundly altering its rules."[169] In turning to a "whole set of assessing, diagnostic, prognostic, normative judgements concerning the criminal,"[170] they have become dependent on an ever-growing army of "subsidiary authorities"[171]—experts claiming to have scientifically grounded opinions on the relevant questions at hand. The hope, of course, is that the elusive intangibilities of the offender's normalcy, motives, dispositions, sanity, state of mind, prospects for rehabilitation, and so on, can be mastered by the social sciences and thereby rendered sufficiently substantive to allow them to bear the full weight of judicial decisions. On Foucault's view, that hope is an illusion. The judicial reliance on the modern dissection of the human subject has not, he argues, created more determinate, less subjective legal judgments. If anything, speculation has gone on virtually unrestrained. For example, we no longer restrict the examinations to those accused. Now the victims of crimes, particularly rape and sexual harassment, are subjected to intense personal scrutiny and objectifying analysis. Judges and their experts appear to have taken on a task that involves an infinite regress. "The additional factor of the offender's [or the victim's, or a witness's] soul, which the legal system has laid hold of, is only apparently explanatory and limitative, and is in fact expansionist."[172] The continual deflection to others of the onus of judging has helped to establish economic incentives for the proliferation of experts in delinquency and its remedies so that now "minor civil servants of moral orthopaedics proliferate on the [social] wound" of judging and punishing.[173] Hence the responsibilities once shouldered by the judge alone have become decentralized and diffused throughout countless layers of ancillary nonlegal authorities. "Warders, doctors, chaplains, psychiatrists, psychologists, educationalists: by their very presence near the prisoner, they sing the praises that the law needs; they reassure it that the body and pain are not the ultimate objects of its punitive action."[174]

This points to a second of Foucault's concerns. The illusion of scientifically grounded objectivity in legal judgments is dangerous because of the scientific cover it provides the jurisprudence system. As a consequence of the judicial reliance on such experts, the decisions of judges and the operations of the penal system generally are shrouded with the aura of science's credibility and stature. Their work is taken to be above reproach, indisputably grounded on the foundation of rigorously scientific research and analysis. So as "to put as much distance as possible between the 'serene' search for truth and the violence that cannot be entirely effaced from punishment,"[175] the authorities to whom judges make appeal translate the juridical elements of a given case into essentially nonjuridical terms. Therefore, Foucault argues, the judicial appeal to social scientific and medical experts should not be viewed foremost as a way for judges to draw on the wisdom of others outside their insulated field in order to rejuvenate a criminal justice system in need of reform. Rather, in their own self-interest they have turned to the social scientists and doctors "in order to stop this operation being simply a legal punishment; in order to exculpate the judge from being purely and simply he who punishes."[176] Instead of incorporating the social sciences into an earlier logic of legal codes and procedures, modern judges have aligned themselves with external and detached experts in an effort to wash their hands of the morally abhorrent yet politically essential obligation of judging other human beings. The expert redescription of the criminal's past, present, and possible future in language borrowed from a putatively scientific enterprise leads one to suppose that the determination of guilt or innocence is a dispassionate product of what Foucault calls "a strange scientifico-juridical complex."[177] "As a result," he writes, "justice no longer takes public responsibility for the violence that is bound up with its practice. If it too strikes, if it too kills, it is not as a glorification of its strength, but as an element of itself that it is obliged to tolerate."[178] The danger, of course, is that once essentially political interactions are recast as a function of scientific or medical processes, they can be justified in nonpolitical terms as necessary interventions that simply ensure therapeutic progress. By slowly replacing the disjunction of licit/illicit with that of normal/abnormal, the modern jurisprudential system can make its operations seem less coercive and therefore less political. What might otherwise appear as morally questionable exercises of political muscle can assume the naturalistic guise of scientific medicine.

This gradual alignment in the modern era of the penal system generally and judges in particular with the "life-administering power" of science and medicine has had two related effects on the way North Atlantic societies view and (in the United States, at least) administer the death penalty. With respect to the former, Foucault offers a few lines near the end of the introductory volume to his history of sexuality, published a year after *Discipline and Punish:*[179]

> How could power exercise its highest prerogatives by putting people to death, when its main role was to ensure, sustain, and multiply life, to put this life in order? . . . Hence capital punishment could not be maintained except by invoking less the enormity of the crime itself than the monstrosity of the criminal, his incorrigibility, and the safeguard of society.[180]

My only quibble with this characterization is the strictness of the distinction drawn between the crime and the criminal. I would argue that rather than being set aside or minimized, the crime becomes, in the hands of the scientific and medical experts, evidence of the depravity of the condemned so that any countervailing evidence of habits, routines, relationships, personal identity, and reputation fall into the penumbra of the crime. Prosecutors use their expert witnesses not simply to connect the crime to the accused but also to persuade jurors and magistrates that the accused is so abnormal as to breach the boundaries of what is considered human. For they know that it is easier to condemn an animal than a person to death.

The difficulty of the decision faced by judges (in Foucault's extended sense of the term) is further attenuated by the use of lethal injection. Such executions provide a particularly vivid example of the phenomenon we have been examining of social relations that were once considered political because of their coerciveness being redefined and concealed through their attachment to the seemingly antiseptic operations of science and medicine. To all appearances, the condemned does not suffer. He does not convulse; there is no bloodshed; no sparks fly. A physician injects the lethal drugs into the arm of the condemned, who quietly slips from life into death. "[T]he execution itself," Foucault concludes, "is like an additional shame that justice is ashamed to impose on the condemned man; so it keeps its distance from the act, tending always to entrust it to others, under the seal of secrecy. It is ugly to be punishable, but there is no glory in punishing."[181] Superficially, at least, the differences between this and the spectacle of early modern torture Foucault described could not be more pronounced. Yet the very lack of drama is deeply troubling. As a witness to a lethal injection in Texas remarked: "It was bizarre to look around and see all these people just doing their job. It was just another day at the office."[182] There is something utterly chilling in the apparent normalcy surrounding the taking of another's life. To borrow Augustine's remarks about those who would rejoice over their victory in a just war, the executioner and entourage seem to have lost all human feeling. Although they may not rejoice, they seem oblivious to the tragedy in which they are involved. Whatever one's position on the death penalty may be, Augustine's insights about just war provide a stern rebuke of our cultural attitude. As in the case of justified aggression, so here too one can distinguish between the justice of the execution and the moral requirement those who participate in it are under to recognize the horror of what they do. From Augustine's perspective, at least, even if the execution is deemed just, that does not in any way militate against the sense of remorse one should feel for having to exercise such power over another. While not disagreeing with Augustine, Foucault would press the point further. The medicalization of the execution serves to anesthetize not just the participants but also and more important, the public at large. By having doctors at the center, if you will, of the carceral network, not only the work of judges, but the whole range of disciplinary techniques operative within it receive an implicit scientifico-medical imprimatur.

For some, no doubt, this fusing of science, medicine, and political power is the answer to the prayer uttered by Augustine's judge that he be released from his obligation to make decisions based on indeterminacies that he knows will cause others to suffer. Arbitrations over "guilt" and "innocence," which were fraught with such danger and anguish for Augustine's judge, are now drawn away from the disturbing political necessities of legal punishment to the seemingly beneficent agenda of medicine. By entering the world of scientific and therapeutic experts, modern authorities strive to free their judgments of the messiness of political force. Although it may appear that adopting such scientifico-juridical methods would naturally protect against the social wounds of exploitation, Foucault points to a festering underside to their objectives. In attempting to identify, control, and ultimately cure "deviants" in society, contemporary mechanisms of power show themselves in their pursuit of certitude as no less coercive; they use their own technologies of violence and force, only now they are administered in such a way that they no longer admit to being violent or forceful. The painful indeterminacy described so eloquently by Augustine is, Foucault would conclude, and a moral burden that modern judges and leaders are no longer willing to bear. In so doing, whatever "progress" grasping after certitude has achieved has been purchased by numbing ourselves to the ambiguities and conflict endemic to the *saeculum,* and by turning our backs on the tragic risks of power.

Augustine, as discussed above, attempts to puncture analogously arrogant pretensions of the rhetoric of glory by carefully scrutinizing Roman republican and imperial history, by blurring distinctions his audience would have taken for granted, and by offering a disquieting and paradoxical alternative story.[183] Foucault adopts a similar counterhistorical strategy when deconstructing the rhetoric of scientific progress and employs similar historical and rhetorical tactics to carry it out. We already addressed in the previous chapter Foucault's penchant for bringing to light seemingly insignificant and thus long-forgotten persons and stories. His illumination of the shadows that had obscured an isolated plague-ridden town is another example of this. Lacing his descriptions with biting turns of phrase and evaluative terms, he uses those who have been silenced and dispossessed to transform this seventeenth-century drama into a window on problems of our own times. Although such strategic readings can lead to historical misrepresentations, they can also sharpen our vision of what might otherwise remain blurry images of troubling contemporary proclivities and trends. Foucault is also famous for detecting dangers tucked in the folds of various discourses, technologies, and practices that others regard as benign or even beneficent. Here one thinks not only of the plague-stricken town and various carceral reforms, but of the concentration on details that forms an essential element in the spread of the panoptic system. From one angle, this modern absorption in minutiae can be linked to the spectacular growth in worker productivity that fueled the past three centuries of economic expansion, with its increase in global wealth. But from another angle, prescinding from the catastrophic environmental costs of such growth, this same focus on details exposes us in new and seemingly innocuous ways to being put to use "productively" and "efficiently" by others. Above all, Foucault's historical investigations are intended to unsettle his audience, juxtaposing features of one era with those of another. By comparing what we normally regard as clashing historical vignettes, he shocks and offends his readers, just as Augustine had done with Alexander the Great, making the familiar seem morally questionable and strange. He wants thereby to jar citizens out of apathy or complacent confidence and to incite them to remain critical of the status quo. To this end, the most common tactic Foucault shares with Augustine as he seeks to undermine the legitimacy of our culture's privileged rhetorics and practices is to blur supposedly self-evident distinctions. Either implicitly or explicitly he likens dreary medieval dungeons to the bright, open cells of the Panopticon; black-hooded executioners to physicians in white lab coats; the grisly spectacle of a prisoner being drawn and quartered to isolated "captive silhouettes";[184] the marshal law in a quarantined town to "the little tactics of the habitat"[185] evident in the carefully arranged spaces of hospitals, factories, barracks, and schools. He does not collapse the distinctions between the phenomena compared; rather he alerts his readers to certain unnoticed and sordid reflections that throw into question the apparent progress we have made in our movement from the one to the other. The changes he charts may well yield improvements in some areas, but their more unseemly sides are papered over when presented in the tidy packages of "advances" and "improvements" and "therapies." We may aim to clean up the streets, restore order, mop up the "mad," make the world safer for our children, but we also and inevitably cause harm as we do so. His work, then, leaves us disturbed, dubious about our culture's achievements. It is not just the blatant forms of coercion and sociopolitical injustice that should trouble us. Even the most noble-seeming endeavors need to be subjected to the severest scrutiny with an acute sensitivity to the costs we all, but especially the marginalized, are forced by them to bear.

Epilogue

Paradoxes of Political Hope and Humility

Augustine's and Foucault's common call to be restlessly critical of political institutions, arrangements, and ideologies raises two perplexing questions. First, do they provide adequate resources to identify, evaluate, and respond to sociopolitical dangers? And second, given their contention that every attempt to ameliorate injustice is inherently ambiguous, forever dogged by the possibility of causing even greater harms than those one might manage to redress, what prompts Augustine and Foucault to remain hopeful? The answers they give to these questions reveal significant congruities and differences. We can examine both more readily if we begin with Foucault.

We have already observed several times that Foucault provides neither foundationalist nor metanarrational norms for his cultural criticisms.[1] This has laid him open to varying charges of being immoral, amoral, or incoherent. All relate to Foucault's refusal to do two things: he does not explicitly set out a normative framework to guide his research and criticisms, and he does not sum up his books with evaluative conclusions or propose alternatives. Such objections assume that in order for a cultural analyst to make a credible case for changing something about the current state of affairs, she must have from the outset a clearly defined, systematically structured, consistently employed, and—as at least some critics hold—universally applicable standard of judgment. On this view, Foucault cannot just sling around evaluatively loaded terms like "domination," "submission," and "resistance" without explicitly tying them to a set of beliefs about meaning and value that give his account its gravity and purpose. Absent that connection, it would seem one can only ask, with Nancy Fraser, "Why is struggle preferable to submission? Why ought domination to be resisted? Only with the introduction of normative notions of some kind could Foucault begin to answer such questions."[2]

If one looks for a tightly argued, philosophically sophisticated standard of evaluation in Foucault's writings, one will be disappointed. It is wiser, to recur to an image introduced in chapter 4, to treat his work as akin to literature. After reading several novels by the same author, one can begin to get a feel for his sense of right and wrong, of what he finds praiseworthy and what contemptible. In much the same way, one can elicit from Foucault's stories of the forgotten and the marginalized a relatively low-flown, unadorned set of convictions about how persons ought to relate in order to ensure communal flourishing. I outlined these at the end of chapter 1. He highlights the importance of ensuring that all participants in power relations be able to develop skills that give them mastery over their own lives and protect them from being manipulated to the sole advantage of others. Such instrumental uses of persons can be more easily avoided if relations of power remain fluid, so that hierarchies can be altered or even reversed. It strikes me that none of this is particularly hard to discern in his work. He does not keep these convictions tucked safely in his vest pocket so no one can get at them. True, they are not set forth in finely crafted arguments, but from a nonfoundationalist perspective that does not make them incoherent or of no normative use.

Having teased out of the sprawl some commonsensical guideposts for evaluating human conduct, what can we do with them? Here again, we find ourselves confronting the contention that Foucault must explicitly formulate his own standards and alternatives in order for his work to have any normative traction. Don't we need, so the argument goes, something more systematic to inspire and sustain a critical response to social injustices? I don't think so. I find it more reasonable to say that cultural critics can make criticisms in much the same way anyone else does, by appeal to different elements of a diverse and dynamic set of background beliefs that sustain a given culture's mutual interaction. Because such beliefs are the result of prolonged conversation and conflict, they do not constitute a fully coherent system of ideas. Although one can with reasonable accuracy identify the main threads, other, finer strands can be isolated and used to tug either particular parts or the whole web of belief in new directions. Moreover, one can argue that the very existence of such historically and communally diverse traditions keeps the social fabric supple and open to alteration. Having many perspectives, I believe, enhances our awareness of moral dangers and gives us more possibilities to respond in creative ways. It increases the opportunities for taking action against identified social problems. Foucault can plausibly be read as facilitating such an ad hoc critical enterprise. Margaret Miles defends such a reading, citing an interview in which Foucault responds to those who wonder how he can act without the assurance that his actions rest on indisputable principles: "The ethico-political choice each of us has to make every day," he says, "is to determine what is the main danger and to focus our efforts there."[3] Elaborating on the point, she writes:

> This principle of personal responsibility without categorical pretensions is a promising one for twentieth-century Christians. Everyone does not have to agree on what the "main danger" is if we can agree that this danger is not a single danger. Each person can focus her effort on what she identifies as the main danger, reassured and strengthened by the awareness that others are focusing their efforts on other dangers they take to be the most pressing. To act as a historical subject is to take the risk and responsibility of deciding on the focus of my efforts without requiring that they be supported and reinforced by the efforts of others. It is, finally, to be grateful that I need not consider my efforts normative for everyone, but that others are correcting the one-sidedness of my vision by addressing dangers that my experience has not prepared me to detect.[4]

Foucault's critiques do not rest on a single foundationalist standard, nor do they seek to comport themselves to an overarching narrative of cosmic or even human history, with its vision of the true, the good, and the beautiful. But I would argue that does not prevent him from being put to constructive normative use.[5]

What might Foucault's work provide for those who are unpersuaded that one can mount a sustained criticism of prevailing social institutions and practices without a set of principles grounded in a carefully articulated philosophical anthropology or metanarrative? The answer lies in how one interprets his suspension or bracketing of epistemological and ontological questions about truth.[6] This language signals that he is involved in a different project addressing a different set of social problems with a different methodology. Foucault is not trying to stabilize truth claims so as to reassure us of our capacities to make normative evaluations. Nor is he trying to tell us anything about what truth is or what is true. Epistemic and ontological questions are thus not critically relevant to his purposes and tend, because their focus is elsewhere, not to further his social agenda. However, terms like "suspension" and "bracketing" make it plain that he is not saying that no one can pursue such questions; only that he is not, and that he is not for a reason. This is a creative clearing for his own work rather than a deconstructive attack.[7] He is inquiring into the political and social functions specific historical truths fulfill, that is, what they as rationalizing concepts actually *do* in certain cultural circumstances. Such research, he says, is not "a skeptical or relativistic refusal of all verified truth. What is questioned is the way that knowledge circulates and functions, its relations to power. In short, the *régime du savoir*."[8] Foucault targets in his genealogical works not norms in general but certain normative disciplines in which the functioning of norms as organizing rules and rituals can come to have unintended and frequently deleterious sociopolitical effects.[9] He is especially worried about those normalizing technologies in which "human science . . . constitutes their domain and clinical knowledge their jurisprudence."[10] However one may go about defending the ontological foundations of Truth or our capacity to know it, truths are still employed in a practical context that is relational, and as such open to the ambiguous dynamics of power. Because he suspends both ontological and epistemic questions, his work does not undermine those who want to pursue such issues.[11] It therefore should be viewed as expanding rather than narrowing horizons by widening the range of questions one asks of knowledge. Nevertheless, his research sounds a warning that one should not pursue such projects without acknowledging that truth claims are always historically and communally situated and put to use with concrete social effects.

One last point that bears on both my argument concerning Foucault's reluctance to provide clearly defined moral standards and my argument about his suspension of ontological and epistemological questions regarding truth should be mentioned. He saw his decision not to supply such explicit standards at the outset or at the conclusion of his work as fulfilling a normative function. A recurrent theme in Foucault's work is the need to balance, on the one hand, the desire to provide interpretive means by which people can better comprehend and thus effectively act within specific cultural situations and, on the other, his heartfelt belief that, in carrying out such a task, "[t]he role of an intellectual is not to tell others what they have to do."[12] "There is always something ludicrous in philosophical discourse," complains Foucault, "when it tries, from the outside, to dictate to others, to tell them where their truth is and how to find it."[13] Moral and political strategies, tactics, and goals, Foucault firmly believes, should always be left open to individuals personally struggling in a given context; they are not for others to set up or arbitrate beforehand, but must be assessed in accord with the problems and capacities of those directly involved.[14]

I would argue that Foucault's reticence regarding normative claims and his bracketing are both compatible with Augustine's perspective. First, because Foucault does not engage in a defense of or an attack on ontological truth claims or our ability to make them, he is not competing with Augustine's theological understanding of truth. (Obviously, I am not suggesting that Foucault would agree with Augustine that truth has an ontological grounding—namely, in God—or that such grounding means that there exist absolute standards; I am simply saying that by suspending or bracketing such questions, he does not set up an alternative metanarrative that must be deconstructed before putting its parts to use.) Second, Augustine would resonate with Foucault's view that because of finitude, knowledge is an endlessly striving and dynamic activity that never comes finally to rest. Augustine would go on to say that this is true both of our knowledge of creation and of God. Third, Augustine would likely appreciate Foucault's authorial humility in not insisting on a single, univocal reading of his texts, since he also leaves to others a certain interpretive latitude:

> For my part I declare resolutely and with all my heart that if I were called upon to write a book that was to be vested with the highest authority, I should prefer to write it in such a way that a reader could find re-echoed in my words whatever truths he was able to apprehend. I would rather write in this way than impose a single true meaning so explicitly that it would exclude all others, even though they contained no falsehood that could give me no offense.[15]

And finally, of course, Foucault's sensitivity to the potential abuses of culturally privileged discourses and practices would tap into Augustine's own concerns with vainglorious employments of rhetoric and power.

Given the abiding suspiciousness of established patterns of power relations that animates Foucault's works, does he provide any reason to be hopeful? There are, it seems to me, clear disadvantages to assuming the role of perpetual critic. When allowed to degenerate into cheap cynicism, it can incline one to abandon all confidence in constructive, political action. A recent bumper sticker sums up the attitude well: "I don't know. I don't care. And it doesn't make any difference anyway." Does Foucault offer resources to counter such sentiments? First, it ought to be said that indifference or quietism is a problem for the comfortable, not the afflicted. Those, for instance, who suffer from economic injustice may not resist the sociopolitical structures that contribute to their lot, but that is more likely due to sheer exhaustion from overwork or to despair. What does Foucault have to say to such as these? His message is simple: What has been made can be unmade. Being storied selves means that our stories can change. Although we enter the drama in medias res, the plot lines are sufficiently multilayered to allow us and other actors to alter their course and meaning. Foucault seeks to explode the myth that change can only come about by total revolution. It is in the everyday and the in between that we have power. Although not against revolutions,[16] he encourages activism at the local level: in fields, marketplaces, schoolrooms, workshops, offices, and homes. Wherever people engage each other in the affairs of life, in the "real material, everyday struggles," there one can seek to resist and reshape. His view of power relations as constituting a web or matrix in which all of us find ourselves offers an additional resource. Binary models of power's operation simply sustain the revolutionary myth. They lead one to suppose that the only way to change a given power structure is to bring it down at a stroke. On the contrary, disassembling and recombining its pieces will often prove more effective. In addition, his work can be of service to those so engaged by "following lines of fragility in the present [in order] to grasp why and how that-which-is might no longer be that-which-is."[17] It is not essential, of course, to know how the structures one opposes came to be, to see the tiny fractures or major fault lines that scar their surface. But if Foucault is right, it most certainly helps, since it opens up spaces in otherwise monolithic-seeming structures, spaces in which practices of "concrete freedom, i.e. of possible transformation," can go on.[18]

Naturally, there will be setbacks and reversals in the course of such struggles. But Foucault counsels that those fighting injustice see themselves as engaged in "a patient labour giving form to our impatience for liberty."[19] What might that mean? What basis does he have for hope amidst defeat? The answer lies in his technologies of the self. As I argued in chapter 3, Foucault maintains that the habits entangling us in manipulative, self-destructive relations of power can be unlearned. Stated differently, just as activists can gain a toehold for transforming freedom in the cracks of seemingly monolithic sociopolitical structures, the fissures in our ambiguous self-relations open up possibilities for self-transformation. By applying with painstaking care the very same sorts of disciplinary techniques that currently constrain us, we offer ourselves the possibility of gradual but nevertheless significant change. We ought not suppose that Foucault believes such self-perfecting will ever be complete. We should realize that we are like a potter who cannot manage to center the clay on the wheel and are thus incapable of fully realizing the proportionality, balance, and beauty we imagine. No matter how tirelessly we labor over the clay, pushing it this way and that, trying to trim an edge here, smooth out a bump there, our creation betrays us, always wobbling in the end with imperfections. Nor should we suppose that the "beautiful existence" he urges us to fashion should pattern itself after the image of the isolated, socially disengaged artist. He would have us aim instead for an aesthetically pleasing balance of noncoercive self- and other-relations. His "ethic of care," therefore, involves both concern for oneself and concern for others. Finally, he wants us to recognize that our freedom is not unlimited; it is exercised within the more or less rigid boundaries imposed by our culture, language, race, gender, age, health, education, and so on. But genuine freedom it remains, on his view, because although such factors will narrow the range of aesthetic options before us, they do not wholly determine the choices we actually make.

Augustine would certainly praise Foucault for his concern for the marginalized and forgotten. This obviously comports well with the preferential option for the poor, to use a term of recent coinage, found in both testaments. But he would dismiss Foucault's decision to ground our hope in the capacity to create a beautiful existence as little more than a modern version of paganism's self-reliant humanism. His alternative—a humble, self-sacrificial love nourished by hope in the full consummation of God's just reign—has been subjected to sharp criticisms from two quite different quarters. One set of critiques portrays him as a Christian imperialist, seeking to impose his vision of the faithful life on those who disagree; the other sees him as a complacent contemplative who has given up on a largely depraved world. In either case, so it is held, Augustine's political ethic serves the interests of the status quo.

William Connolly, in *The Augustinian Imperative*, forcefully articulates from a post-modern perspective the imperialist reading of Augustine. Connolly maintains that Augustine naively assumes that he can discover and reliably act on an essential truth about himself through internal reflection, recollection, and confession. This provides the warrant for condemning or praising self-conceptions, personal desires, and forms of life, not only for himself, but also for all persons at all times. Connolly links Augustine's quest to discover his "true self" to the "Augustinian imperative," namely, "the insistence that there is an intrinsic moral order susceptible to authoritative representation."[20] The political implications of this linkage are wholly problematic, for it denies genuine pluralism. "The Augustinian confessional complex is an incredibly powerful mechanism through which to nurture an authoritative identity and foster the experience of intrinsic moral order."[21] Confession thus understood comprises a set of tactics by which both moralization and demoralization (i.e., scapegoating) occur.[22] Connolly acknowledges that as individuals and as communities we form our identities by separating from and taking a stand against certain adversaries.[23] What matters in a political ethic is not whether we determine ourselves over against others but how we do so. In Augustine, Connolly asserts, we find hostile eradications, a depiction of one's opponents not simply in light of intellectual or practical disagreements but as sinners and heretics. Because Augustine understands his rivals' positions to be based on waywardness from and corruption of a divine order, he feels compelled to draw an absolute line against them. "Augustine would have to attenuate the universality, or morality, or certainty, or definiteness of the god [to whom] he confesses to modify significantly the politics by which he seeks to fix, stabilize, and generalize things. Augustinian politics presupposes the confessional imperative and the confessional imperative constitutes the core of Augustinian politics."[24] By thus conjoining confession to a political imperative, Augustine disguises a forceful will to power under the cloak of humility. Although he may seem to be humbling himself before God, Connolly holds that he actually exemplifies a "transcendental narcissism," treating as divinely mandated what are in fact his own private desires and opinions.[25]

On this reading of Augustine, Foucault's ethic of care could not be more different: "[I]t is a political problematic of interrogation, engagement, and negotiation, not a political doctrine of intrinsic identity, consensus and resolution. . . . It locates freedom in the gaps and spaces fostered by collisions and negotiations rather than in a pattern of harmonious unity or private sanctuary it hopes to realize."[26] Because this ethic is accompanied by suspicion and criticism as one of the conditions of its possibility,[27] Connolly argues that it reminds us that political activism operates in highly ambiguous circumstances. Without minimizing the dangers inherent in our relational fragility and the ambiguity of our judgments and actions, this ethic uses them to open up new and creative responses to social injustice. Once we recognize the limitations and historical contingency of the human condition, our inherited attitudes, relations, and practices become questionable and revisable. This strictly limits our confidence in moral knowledge, but it also keeps us from lording over others what insights we lay claim to. For these reasons, Connolly endorses Foucault's ethic of care and the political ethics derivable from it.[28]

In *Self/Power/Other*, Romand Coles adopts a more charitable reading of Augustine's "confessing self."[29] In what he regards as a positive conceptual development, Augustine understands the self as being constituted not on the basis of its own ontological ground but in relation to an "other," namely, God. Such a conception helps to protect us from a perennially dangerous temptation, one to which Augustine's Roman contemporaries fell prey: regarding oneself as self-originating being.[30] Confidence in the "pagan self" or, in more general terms, "the self of ontological conceit" justifies placing other persons and the natural environment under one's self-aggrandizing control.[31] Given the costs of such personal and cultural egoism, Coles believes Augustine is wise to repudiate it. Notwithstanding this strength, Coles argues that Augustine's view of the self is inadequate for much the same reason Connolly does. Although Augustine appears to open the door to the recognition of the dignity and value of difference, both in oneself and in others, the appearance is deceptive. "[T]hat which is not obedient to God is 'nothingness,' and hence we discover that the confessing self confronts its non-Christian other in a manner very different from, but every bit as relentless and extirpating as the way the pagan self confronted its others."[32]

For an alternative ethos, Coles turns, again like Connolly, to Foucault, whom he applauds for recognizing the dangerous underside to the confessional practices Augustine advocates.[33] One's personal identity is not discovered internally through any confessional process but is continually formed in dialogical encounters with persons and things that are different from ourselves.[34] Foucault's work, he maintains, "aims not at the end of all self-recognition, but at a recognition of the distinct and often multiplicitous dimensions of the self which do not fit comfortably within . . . hegemonic categories."[35] In contrast to the ethos of exclusion that he found embedded in Augustine's notion of a perfectly ordered and harmonious self, Foucault's philosophical perspective, he believes, inclines us to adopt an ethos of openness and engagement with otherness, whether it be otherness in our own selves or in different persons. Hence, he concludes, Foucault's insights encourage us on a personal, social, and political level to appreciate and explore rather than obliterate diverse ontological variations.[36]

Connolly and Coles present a sound analysis of the political implications of Foucault's emphasis on the ambiguity of our self- and other-relations. They are right to stress the inherently pluralistic character of Foucault's view of our political life. But I have considerable reservations about their decision to view Augustine's political ideas primarily in light of his remarks about the confessing self. I believe this interpretive strategy blurs two closely related distinctions that are of fundamental importance in understanding what Augustine is up to. First, by contending that Augustine's views of the political sphere rest on a logically prior notion of a unified, morally capable confessing self, both authors confuse Augustine's description of the spiritual life of those in the church with a totalizing expectation of political regeneration. For Augustine, the grammar of believing and the grammar of living peaceably with those who hold contrary beliefs are different. What grounds his political ideas is not a conception of who persons are as believers (as ones who confess to and journey toward God) but who persons are as disbelieving creatures. Politics, on his view, is tied to our *inability* to create unity, harmony, and order and to our *failure* to rule wisely over other persons, alike or dissimilar, on the basis of ultimate beliefs. Grounding Augustine's political ethics on his descriptions of his spiritual pilgrimage, as Connolly and Coles have done, obscures this basic distinction and thus distorts his view of the *saeculum.*

Connolly and Coles also tend to collapse Augustine's doctrine of the fall into his doctrines of creation and redemption. Although both authors mention some of the effects of sin on Augustine's thought, their highlighting the supposedly normative, ordering force of Christian faith on political existence indicates that they overlook the profound difference between our present fallen condition and our promised social regeneration. Augustine believes that politics has to do exclusively with this currently unresolvable tension. From a narrowly political perspective, all humans live wholly under the effects of the fall. As I indicated in chapter 5, the political order, according to Augustine, was not part of prelapsarian community, nor will it be present in the eschaton. Thus our political expectations and desires must not be confused or equated with the social harmony of creation or redemption. Instead, Augustine admonishes his readers to acknowledge that all humans, faithful or not, live in this tension between what is and what is to come. He warns that we must recognize the profound limitations and temptations of governing and accept the political world as a restricted, provisional space where different sorts of persons with contrary ultimate values must get along. Connolly and Coles appear not to realize how deeply, from Augustine's point of view, the fall affects everyone, Christians and non-Christians alike. Political existence is not a matter of "we believers" against "those sinners" or of we "confessing selves" against those "pagan selves." All share in the temptations and perils of the political world, and all must work together, despite fundamentally different personal beliefs, to carve out a peaceful political environment. As we attempt to make sense of Augustine's attitude toward otherness, therefore, we must keep in mind his two central and related distinctions: first, that between the community of faith and the political community, and second, that between fallen political existence and the social harmony of creation and redemption. If we muddle either one, we risk misunderstanding him.

In light of the importance of these two distinctions for Augustine, some liberation and political theologians criticize him for being overly skeptical of our moral capacities and unduly dubious about the prospects for progress in the political sphere. Whether one pictures Augustine as primarily having privatized, interiorized, and individualized the Christian faith to the detriment of community, or as having overemphasized the pilgrimage character of Christian fellowship, the effects seem to be twofold.[37] First and foremost, history becomes devalued as an instrument of redemption. Augustine, on this interpretation, although perceiving some change in history, views it as mere motion devoid of religious significance. It constitutes an essentially fruitless holding pattern in which the faithful have no choice but to wait for God to fulfill God's promise. If the Kingdom of God is a strictly future state, then the human drama ends up being a sideshow or inconsequential warm-up act for the main event coming only at the end of time. Second, as a consequence of this, Christian hope is divorced, on this view, from anticipating and helping to bring about new social and political possibilities. It risks encouraging contemplation without corresponding action. Minimizing in this fashion hope's active dimension, one's ability and indeed responsibility to participate in efforts to thwart injustice are compromised. Moreover, since the Messianic age is seemingly without present even if proleptic impact, it cannot provide a standard by which to criticize both illegitimate ecclesiastical and secular structures of power. Social injustices within the church or the state, it is argued, tend not to be brought to light when one places so much emphasis either on an inaccessible future eschaton or on one's own individual faith-relation to God. Thus both serve, wittingly or not, the interests of those who benefit from current unjust sociopolitical structures. The essential question, writes Rosemary Radford Ruether, "is not whether theology is political or nonpolitical, but whether the political dimension of theology uncritically endorses the *status quo* or whether it places the *status quo* under judgment in the light of the divine mandate of history that 'God's will be done on earth.'"[38]

The criticisms of Augustine's political ethics by Connolly and Coles and by some political and liberation theologians stand in a curious relation: one is the photographic negative of the other. If Connolly and Coles are right, Augustine is a Christian triumphalist, an authoritarian uncompromising in his imposition of Christian truth claims and practices on society at large. From the other side, he is either an individualistic liberal or a sectarian purist, although in either case his politics is functionally quietist. In my judgment, both readings should be faulted for failing to grasp the political import of the wisdom of sorrow I set forth in chapter 4.

Against the triumphalist reading, I would argue that Augustine's ethic of humility is grounded in what he would describe as the paradoxical power of the cross, not a will to power. He believes that God in Christ both enacted a life of self-emptying love and enables others, through his Spirit, to be conformed to it. Ideally, at least, this should lead to a chastened knowledge, which, as I argued earlier, recognizes the limitations of any finite perspectives, standards, and projects. This humility shapes Augustine's view of the certainty of his knowledge of God and of himself. Near the end of his lengthy discourse on the Trinity, for instance, he acknowledges that all the work he has done proves inadequate.[39] And his portrayal of confession reminds readers that the self-identity they long to grasp securely is in perpetual flux, contingent, and relationally dependent. On his view, the wisdom of sorrow one gains in the life of faith does not, ideally at least, lead one to better possess the self, which then becomes a standard for evaluating the selves of others. Rather, it leads one to realize that one finds one's "self" in the process of squandering it for others. A rightly ordered love depends on decentering oneself in relation to God and for the sake of one's neighbors. It is true that some Augustinians, particularly the medieval ones who identified the institutional church as the earthly embodiment of the City of God,[40] used their confidence in their knowledge of God and self as a warrant for an exclusionary political ethic. But that is a complaint about how Augustine has been read, not about his own uses of the norm or what his ethic provides us today. If interpreted according to its own logic, though he did not always use it this way, it should lay everything, both inside and outside the church, open to critique and revision. Far from providing a license for tyrannical assertions of power over others, it should prompt a radical questioning that relativizes every absolutizing ideology. All that individuals aspire to, advocate, create, and defend falls short of the eschatological standard of justice that illumines, if only momentarily, the twilight in which they presently walk.

Nor should one suppose that Augustine presented an image of Heavenly Jerusalem as monolithic or homogenizing and then used that as his touchstone for criticizing ecclesiastical or political diversity. On Augustine's view, the life to come for the redeemed is harmonious not because all differentiation has been obliterated. The citizens of the Heavenly City subordinate themselves to the common good; they do not lose themselves in an undifferentiated mass. The harmony of which Augustine speaks and for which he longs is not a monophonic identity but the euphonious blending of differences. Differentiation, then, is not an obstacle to harmony; it is one of its essential conditions. This has important ecclesiastical and political consequences. Augustine is keen to avoid excluding, without strong reason, any of the richly variegated customs and cultures manifest within the church. "It is completely irrelevant to the Heavenly City what dress is worn or what manner of life adopted by each person who follows the faith that is the way to God, provided that these do not conflict with the divine instructions."[41] And he affirms that people maintaining different fundamental beliefs should coexist and share in the tasks of temporal peace. "While this Heavenly City, therefore, is on pilgrimage in this world, she calls out citizens from all nations and so collects a society of aliens, speaking all languages. She takes no account of any difference in customs, laws, and institutions, by which earthly peace is achieved and preserved."[42]

Even though the confessing self does not form the basis of Augustine's political ethic, it still has an impact on how Christians should act politically. Politics may not be grounded in the life of faith, but that does not mean the life of faith is uninvolved in politics. Indeed, the love of God and self is, on Augustine's view, truncated unless it involves love of neighbor. Being conformed to the cross, with its "ethic of humility" and "wisdom of sorrow," will inevitably have political consequences since it transforms one's virtues. In short, what the faithful learn about faithfulness in the *Confessions* should enrich what they bring to politics. This has an obvious bearing on how one might respond to those who accuse Augustine of quietism.

Against that interpretation, I would argue that Augustine's hope is not otherworldly but at least strives to be self-sacrificing. By participating in the liturgical life of the church, particularly though not exclusively the Eucharist, Augustine believes that one is broken open for others. The cross inspires one, by grace, to reach out in solidarity to those inside and outside of the church. One is thus enabled, he affirms, to reenact Christ's self-sacrifice in concrete acts of mercy toward others. From this perspective, Christian hope drives the faithful to seek some measure of victory over sociopolitical injustices. The standard by which they evaluate their work is, of course, the Kingdom of God revealed and inaugurated in Christ, foretastes of which the elect at present enjoy. One's grasp of and ability to act in accord with the perfect justice of that Kingdom is strengthened in proportion to one's love for God and neighbor. But the justice the faithful seek will always outstrip the justice they attain. Augustine reminds Christians that in view of their disheartening history of performative inadequacies and failures, they can discern with more confidence how far they have fallen short than whether they will be able to solve a social problem successfully. Ambiguity and precariousness always attend every effort to unravel the entangling consequences of sin. However, the fact that our problems have more certainty than our solutions undercuts neither the importance nor the necessity of making both critical judgments and revisions. The chastened knowledge that comes with love and humilty does not—or ought not—eviscerate the desire for earthly justice. Rather, by making one more attentive to the limitations and risks inherent in political activism and by prompting acts of self-forgetting love, it actually can yield greater even if not fully adequate justice.

Of what help might Foucault be to Christians seeking to establish such rough justice? He offers no metanarrative, and he does not speak of transcendence, let alone grace. But he does provide analytical tools and display how one might use them to be more attentive to the voices of the neglected, abused, and "unworthy." He also heightens one's sensitivity to the dangers of both finitude and pride that shadow aspirations for perfecting others and oneself. He alerts even the most accomplished to humanity's limitlessly inventive capacity for self-delusion, for blinding ourselves to our manifest shortcomings. Foucault can thus considerably aid Christians in recognizing the difficulties of and in committing themselves to a life of compassion, of care, and of justice.

His voice is not the only one that Christians ought to hear, of course; it needs to be accompanied and tempered by others. The faithful, according to Augustine, are to be humble, yet hopeful. They should be neither arrogant nor despairing. The way to avoid both extremes, from his perspective, is through a begraced self-sacrificial love. To understand Augustine's political ethics, then, we must see that for him humility and hope are not so paradoxical as they may first appear. They come together in his understanding of the cross, the wisdom of sorrow, and the virtues that these foster. For when these are viewed in light of the resurrection, Augustine believes one can see in their burdens a divine promise that self-emptying, self-forgetful, self-squandering love will ultimately win out over evil. The faithful, he affirms, experience foretastes of that victory in their common ecclesial life and are sustained by them as they shoulder the political risk of unleashing new harms when seeking to ameliorate injustice. Neither resting content with the status quo nor turning their backs on an engaged social life, he urges them to follow his anguished judge and take their seat at the bench, willing to carry out their always ambiguous sociopolitical responsibilities.

Notes

Introduction

1. Michel Foucault, document D250 (7) of the Foucault Archive, Paris, 21 April 1983 discussion between M. Foucault and P. Rabinow, B. Dreyfus, C. Taylor, R. Bellah, M. Jay, and L. Lowenthal, 32 pp., p. 11. I am indebted to James Bernauer for passing on this excerpt to me in personal correspondence. The translation is his. Professor Bernauer later added most of this excerpt, though not what follows, to his foreword to Michel Foucault, *Religion and Culture,* ed. Jeremy R. Carrette (New York: Routledge, 1999), xvi.

2. Michel Foucault, document D250 (7) of the Foucault Archive.

3. For well-argued examples, see John Milbank, *Theology and Social Theory: Beyond Secular Reason* (Oxford: Blackwell, 1990, 1993); and William C. Placher, *Unapologetic Theology: A Christian Voice in a Pluralistic Conversation* (Louisville: Westminster/John Knox Press, 1989).

4. By using the term "prophetic" to describe Foucault's work, I mean to highlight his concern for social outcasts. Foucault cannot be seen as prophetic in terms of making universal truth claims that prescriptively apply to all people and all times. That would be contrary to Foucault's impulses.

5. Jürgen Habermas, "Taking Aim at the Heart of the Present," in *Foucault: A Critical Reader,* ed. David Couzens Hoy (Oxford: Blackwell, 1986), 106. See also Jürgen Habermas, *The Philosophical Discourse of Modernity* (Cambridge, Mass.: MIT Press, 1987), 253.

6. Michael Walzer, "The Politics of Michel Foucault," in Hoy, ed., *Foucault: A Critical Reader,* 51.

7. R. A. Markus, *Saeculum: History and Society in the Theology of St. Augustine* (New York: Cambridge University Press, 1970), 169–70.

8. Michel Foucault, *Power/Knowledge: Selected Interviews & Other Writings, 1972–1977,* ed. Colin Gordon (New York: Pantheon Books, 1980), 65.

CHAPTER 1 Dynamic Fragility:
An Analysis of Power and Love

1. Miika Roukanen presents this contrast between Augustine as a moral pessimist and ontological optimist in his *Theology of the Social Life in Augustine's* De Civitate Dei (Göttingen: Vandenhoeck & Ruprecht, 1993).

2. Augustine, *City of God*, trans. Henry Bettenson (London: Penguin Books, 1972), 14.28; and *The Literal Meaning of Genesis*, trans. John H. Taylor (New York: Newman Press, 1982), 11.15. I use "desire" as a more or less adequate place holder for a variety of terms Augustine employs, including *appetitus, concupiscentia, cupiditas, desiderium,* and *libido,* whose meanings overlap sufficiently to justify, at this level of generality, my designating them with one English word. When more detail is required, I indicate which term I mean or Augustine uses. For "habit", I have in mind *consuetudo,* especially when considering a bad habit (following Augustine), and *habitus,* for a good habit or virtue.

3. Augustine, *City of God*, 10.7, 12.1, 19.13.

4. Ibid., 12.1.

5. Ibid.

6. Ibid., 19.13; see also 12.21, 19.12, 19.15.

7. Gene Outka significantly shaped my understanding of the importance of analyzing Augustine's view of the consequences of the fall chiefly in performative terms. See his "Augustinianism and Common Morality," in *Prospects for a Common Morality,* ed. Gene Outka and John P. Reeder, Jr. (Princeton: Princeton University Press, 1993), 114–48.

8. Augustine, *City of God*, 19.5–8. See also R. A. Markus, *Saeculum: History and Society in the Theology of St. Augustine* (New York: Cambridge University Press, 1970), xiv.

9. "We see then that the two cities were created by two kinds of love: the earthly city was created by self-love reaching the point of contempt for God, the Heavenly City by the love of God carried as far as contempt of self." Augustine, *City of God*, 14.28.

10. Ibid., 14.11, 14.13, 19.12. Compare the following: "For even in their very sins souls are only striving for a certain likeness to God in their proud, perverted, and so to speak, servile liberty. Thus our first parents could not have been persuaded to sin if it had not been said to them: 'You shall be as gods.'" Augustine, *The Trinity, The Fathers of the Church: A New Translation,* vol. 45, trans. Stephen McKenna, C.SS.R. (Washington, D.C.: Catholic University of America Press, 1963), 11.5.8. And compare: "All who desert you and set themselves up against you merely copy you in a perverse way." Augustine, *Confessions,* trans. R. S. Pine-Coffin (New York: Penguin Books, 1961), 2.6. See also Peter Brown, "Political Society," in *Augustine: A Collection of Critical Essays,* ed. R. A. Markus (New York: Doubleday, 1972), 320 f.

11. Augustine, *City of God*, 12.8, 15.7, 19.12, and 19.15.

12. Ibid., 19.12. "For pride hates a fellowship of equality under God, and seeks to impose its own dominion [*dominationem*] on fellow men, in place of God's rule. This means that it hates the just peace of God, and loves its own peace of injustice."

13. Ibid., 14.13.

14. Ibid., 14.12.

15. Augustine, *Confessions,* 11.29.

16. Augustine, *City of God,* 22.22.

17. Ibid., 12.8. See also *The Trinity,* 13.13.17.

18. Augustine, *Confessions,* 12.11.

19. Augustine, *City of God,* 19.7.

20. Ibid., 19.5; see also 15.4.

21. Ibid., 19.5. For an analysis of flattery in the context of ancient Greco-Roman views of friendship, see David Konstan, "Friendship, Frankness, and Flattery," in *Friendship, Flattery, & Frankness of Speech: Studies on Friendship in the New Testament World,* ed. John T. Fitzgerald (Leiden: E. J. Brill, 1996), 7–19.

22. I do not mean to imply that Augustine believed persons are ontologically bifurcated, with a good will and a bad will pulling in opposite directions. Despite some passages in Augustine's work suggesting otherwise, his view of the will is essentially unitary. Indeed, it appears misleading to speak as though Augustine conceived of the will as a discrete faculty. Still, fallen humans experience an inner turmoil that Augustine describes in terms of the will being divided against itself and drawn in different directions by reason and emotion. See Gerald W. Schlabach, "Augustine's Hermeneutic of Humility: An Alternative to Moral Imperialism and Moral Relativism," *Journal of Religious Ethics* 22:2 (fall 1994): 299–330, esp. 308 ff. I discuss this topic in detail in chapter 3.

23. On Augustine's view, the faithful by grace certainly experience foretastes of the harmony of the celestial city in their common life of worship and sacrifice in the church. But the church is not the theological equivalent of a nuclear-free zone, where one can somehow escape sin's impact on the rest of the world. I return to this theme in chapters 4 and 5.

24. Michel Foucault, *Power/Knowledge: Selected Interviews & Other Writings, 1972–1977,* ed. Colin Gordon (New York: Pantheon Books, 1980), 109–23, 139–45; *Discipline and Punish: The Birth of the Prison,* trans. Alan Sheridan (New York: Random House, 1979), 3–69; and *The History of Sexuality, Volume 1: An Introduction* (New York: Vintage Books, 1980), 135 f. I found Kyle A. Pasewark's discussion of orthodox definitions of power particularly illuminating. "Generally, political theories of power have understood power either as domination or as the capacity to dominate. Indeed, despite growing discomfort, most recent reformulations of power dispense neither with these categories nor with the central assumptions that produce their identification with power—among them, that power is a possession, that it is applied only externally, and that it is occasional. Not surprisingly, such reflections about power often are restricted solely to politics, conceiving of power by means of a dichotomy

between the externally politically powerful and dominating and the externally powerless and dominated. . . . [I]f power is domination, it is ultimately destructive of beings. The perfection or fulfillment of power as domination is 'absolute power,' the tyrannical enslavement or eradication of whatever opposes such power. Particular uses of power may have temporary value, but if power becomes total and dominates a being entirely, it necessarily destroys all special value of that being." *A Theology of Power: Being Beyond Domination* (Minneapolis: Fortress Press, 1993), 1, 3; cf. 1–27. See also Joseph Rouse, "Power/Knowledge," in *The Cambridge Companion to Foucault,* ed. Gary Gutting (Cambridge: Cambridge University Press, 1994), 92–108; Jon Simons, *Foucault and the Political* (New York: Routledge, 1995), 51–59; David Couzens Hoy, "Power, Repression, Progress: Foucault, Lukes, and the Frankfurt School," in *Foucault: A Critical Reader,* ed. David Couzens Hoy (Oxford: Blackwell, 1986), 123–37; and Christine Firer Hinze, *Comprehending Power in Christian Social Ethics* (Atlanta: Scholars Press, 1995), 13–60. These focus on Foucault's concerns with traditional conceptions of power during his mid- to late career. Peter Miller examines Foucault's understanding of power and domination in his early works in *Domination and Power* (New York: Routledge & Kegan Paul, 1987), 97–158. Nikolas Rose discusses contemporary versions of orthodox definitions of "the political" in "Governing 'Advanced' Liberal Democracies," in *Foucault and Political Reason: Liberalism, Neo-Liberalism and Rationalities of Government,* ed. Andrew Barry, Thomas Osborne, and Nikolas Rose (Chicago: University of Chicago Press, 1996), 37–62.

25. See the political and philosophical objections of Michael Walzer, Clifford Geertz, and Mark Taylor in their contributions to Hoy, ed., *Foucault: A Critical Reader.*

26. An especially informative discussion of this issue is to be found in Michel Foucault's article entitled "The Subject and Power," the afterword to Hubert L. Dreyfus and Paul Rabinow, *Michel Foucault: Beyond Structuralism and Hermeneutics,* 2d ed. (Chicago: University of Chicago Press, 1983), 208–26. See also Michel Foucault, *Power/Knowledge,* 110 f., 142, 198; Michel Foucault, "The Ethic of Care for the Self as a Practice of Freedom," in *The Final Foucault,* ed. James Bernauer and David Rasmussen (Cambridge, Mass.: MIT Press, 1988), 3, 18; Pasewark, *A Theology of Power,* 51; John Caputo and Mark Yount, "Institutions, Normalization, and Power," in *Foucault and the Critique of Institutions,* ed. John Caputo and Mark Yount (University Park: Pennsylvania State University Press, 1986), 5; Ian Hacking, "The Archaeology of Foucault," in Hoy, ed., *Foucault: A Critical Reader,* 37 f.; and Hoy, "Power, Repression, Progress," 144.

27. Foucault, *The History of Sexuality, Volume 1,* 93.

28. Foucault, *Power/Knowledge,* 141 f.

29. Foucault does not like to use the term "depth" in reference to persons. However, his notion of power being operative in all relations, including intrapersonal ones, points to an interiority whose complexity can be described with this metaphor.

30. See Simons, *Foucault and the Political,* 82; and Pasewark, *A Theology of Power,* 42 ff. Colin Gordon writes in the afterword to *Power/Knowledge,* 255: the micro-dynamics of power "may be sub-individual or trans-individual." These fragmented and frequently competing relations should not be monolithically equated with the individual per se, but they do interactively constitute the individual. I examine these issues in chapter 3.

31. Foucault, *The History of Sexuality, Volume 1,* 199f.

32. Augustine, *City of God,* 19.7.

33. Foucault, *Power/Knowledge,* 96.

34. Ibid., 99.

35. Ibid., 100 f.

36. Ibid., 187.

37. I do not say "political and personal" because for Augustine politics is a postlapsarian development. The broader term "communal" can be applied to both figures because it covers all social relations. I discuss the issue of the postlapsarian nature of politics in more detail in chapter 5.

38. Foucault, *The History of Sexuality, Volume 1,* 96.

39. Augustine, *City of God,* 1.35. See Jean Bethke Elshtain, *Augustine and the Limits of Politics* (Notre Dame: University of Notre Dame Press, 1995), 34–42, for a discussion of the permeable boundaries between the private and public spheres in Augustine's thought. Elshtain compares Augustine to Aristotle and Aquinas on this issue in *Public Man, Private Woman: Women in Social and Political Thought* (Princeton: Princeton University Press, 1981), 68–80. See also, Markus, *Saeculum,* 58–62, 101, 157–68, and 179 f.

40. Brown, "Political Society," 326, 313.

41. One can argue, as Markus does, that the same can be said of Augustine. "The radically revolutionary character of Christian hope makes it, in practice, compatible with almost any political programme which does not set itself up as an ideology with absolute claims upon men's ultimate loyalties." *Saeculum,* 172.

42. Foucault, "The Ethic of Care for the Self as a Practice of Freedom," in *The Final Foucault,* 11 f.

43. Foucault, *The History of Sexuality, Volume 1,* 94.

44. Rouse uses the term "co-constituted" to describe the relational dynamism of power in "Power/Knowledge," 108. Pasewark speaks of its fundamental interactivity as involving "the mutual presence of powers" in *A Theology of Power,* 5. Marc P. Lalonde argues that Foucault's notion always involves some sense of joint participation in his "Power/Knowledge and Liberation," *Journal of the American Academy of Religion* 61:1 (1993): 90.

45. Foucault, *Power/Knowledge,* 89. See also Foucault, "The Subject and Power," 219; and Caputo and Yount, "Institutions, Normalization, and Power," 5.

46. Foucault, *The History of Sexuality, Volume 1,* 92.

47. Ibid., 94.

48. Foucault, *Power/Knowledge*, 98. Foucault would contend that since power is inherently relational, it will assume different forms and use different tactics in various societies and eras, but it cannot be substantially accumulated. John Milbank appears to misunderstand this when he asserts that for Foucault, power is "more present in some epochs than others." *Theology and Social Theory: Beyond Secular Reason* (Oxford: Blackwell, 1990, 1993), 286.

49. Augustine, *Letters* 44, 343. The citation is from Elshtain, *Augustine and the Limits of Politics,* 89. Augustine goes on to say that "money is diminished by expenditure and love is increased." Elshtain observes that Augustine's story is one of "increase through apparent (but only apparent) depletion." Ibid. She notes earlier: "A human being will not be denuded if he or she gives, or makes a gift of the self, to others. One's dependence on others is not a diminution but an enrichment of self. . . . The Christian is not afraid that he or she will lose something by offering him or herself. That is what the ethic of *caritas* is about—not moralistic self-abnegation but an abundant overflowing of the fullness of life" (36).

50. See Augustine, "Christian Instruction," in *The Fathers of the Church: A New Translation,* vol. 2, trans. John J. Gavigan, O.S.A. (Washington, D.C.: Catholic University of America Press, 1947, 1950), 1.1.1. See also *The Literal Meaning of Genesis,* 11.15; and *The Trinity,* 12.10.15. As Gerald Schlabach writes, "In preaching, Augustine once explained [*caritas*] with a memorable portrayal of love as 'the hand of the soul,' which must let go of what it is holding in order to receive what is given (*s.* 125.7). Accordingly, the 'hand' that opens to embrace and cling (*haerere*) to God is a love that also receives all good things from God as gifts. In contrast, all concupiscent loves close the 'hand of the soul' tightly, privately, domineeringly, and at last destructively on its object of desire." "Continence," in *Augustine through the Ages: An Encyclopedia,* ed. Allan D. Fitzgerald, O.S.A. (Grand Rapids: Eerdmans, 1999), 237. R.A. Markus notes that "'[p]rivate' and 'sociable' are two fundamentally opposed forms of loving: the one enclosing the self in its own narrowness, the other setting it free in sharing with others. These are the two opposed 'loves' which define the earthly and heavenly Cities: the heavenly City is structured by mutual love and sharing, the earthly by 'possessive individualism.'" *Saeculum,* xviii. Roukanen also argues that the basic disruption of our dependence on God leads to viewing power as one's own private possession. *The Theology of the Social Life in Augustine's* De Civitate Dei, 63.

51. Augustine, *The Trinity,* 9.2.2. See 8.10.14, 9.1.1, 9.12.17–18, and 15.2.2 for other descriptions of love as inherently active, striving, and dynamic.

52. Augustine, *City of God,* 22.22.

53. Although Foucault is unquestionably anti-Humanist, he has a more complex relation with the Enlightenment, at times rejecting its atomistic notions and at other times embracing its questioning of the conditions that make the present social arrangements possible.

54. Augustine, *The Trinity,* 12.11.16.

55. Peter Brown argues that delusions about self-reliance and ultimate inde-pendence appear far more politically dangerous to Augustine than threats of tyranny. See his "Political Society," 312–15.

56. Augustine, *Confessions*, 4.16.

57. Augustine, *City of God*, 11.1; cf. 15.4: "And if, when victorious, it is exalted in its arrogance, that victory brings death in its train. . . . For it will not be able to lord it permanently over those whom it has been able to subdue victoriously."

58. According to Markus, "the chief symptom of man's estrangement from his own self was the only too palpable experience of ceasing to be under his own control." *Saeculum*, xiv.

59. Augustine, *City of God*, 11.1.

60. Augustine, *Confessions*, 13.17.

61. Brown, "Political Society," 313–17.

62. Foucault, *Power/Knowledge*, 59, 98.

63. Michel Foucault, *Politics, Philosophy, Culture: Interviews and Other Wri-tings, 1977–1984*, ed. Lawrence D. Kritzman (New York: Routledge, Chapman, & Hall, 1988), 118. See also Foucault, *Power/Knowledge*, 92, 139 f.

64. Foucault, *The History of Sexuality, Volume 1*, 85.

65. Foucault, *Power/Knowledge*, 125 and 97.

66. "Love is the great power of life, not transparent or controllable by man. The phenomenon of love molds human reality more than anything else. Humans are what they love." Roukanen, *The Theology of the Social Life in Augustine's* De Civitate Dei, 48f.

67. Augustine, *Confessions*, 8.1: "Let my whole self be steeped in love of you [*dilectione tua*] and all my being cry, Lord, there is none like you."

68. Augustine, *The Trinity*, 9.12.17–18, 11.9.16.

69. Augustine, *Confessions*, 3.4 (*ardebam*), 12.16 (*amor*), and 13.9 (*amor*). Au-gustine also and often expresses the attractive power of love, its ability to draw us out of ourselves, with the word *dilectatio*. See also William S. Babcock, "Augustine and the Spirituality of Desire," *Augustinian Studies* 25 (1994): 179–99.

70. As Peter Brown argues, Augustine understands "flesh" in Pauline terms as being distinct from the "body." It is configured in relation to our dynamic loves. See his *The Body and Society: Men, Women, and Sexual Renunciation in Early Chris-tianity* (New York: Columbia University Press, 1988), 47 ff., 318.

71. Augustine, "Homilies on the First Epistle of John," in *Nicene and Post-Nicene Fathers, First Series*, vol. 7, ed. Philip Schaff (Peabody, Mass.: Hendrickson Publishers, 1994; 1886–89), 2.14, 5.7–8.

72. Pasework persuasively argues that contemporary theology does not ade-quately appreciate the constructive and generative aspects of power, dwelling in-stead only on its destructive ramifications. He then develops a fascinating argument concerning how power should be theologically explored as an all-pervasive dimen-sion of "Being." See his *Theology of Power*, esp. 7–55.

73. This is true at least of those in the fallen world. In Holy Jerusalem, individuals are constituted socially, but that constitution is not stretched over time. They are held in eternity. However, they must remain actively engaged, and this has both a temporal and eternal element to it.

74. Foucault, "The Subject and Power," 220 f.

75. Foucault, *Power/Knowledge*, 119.

76. Augustine, *Confessions*, 8.4. Cf. his description of Christ: "He spoke words of love and inflamed our hearts, and now *we hasten after the fragrance of his perfumes.*" Ibid., 13.15.

77. Ibid., 13.9. Italicized texts in the *Confessions* indicate biblical phrases that Augustine weaves into his own writings. The emphasis is in the translation.

78. Ibid., 10.40.

79. *Delectatio* is the power of attraction that entices us through loving desires without any need for external coercion. See Augustine, "Homilies on the Gospel of John," 26.425. As we have seen, Augustine also uses *amor* to convey the same idea.

80. Foucault, "The Subject and Power," 220 f. As John Caputo observes, "Power is a way [of] inducing, seducing, conducing . . . ; power is conductive. It is stronger (more coercive) than what Husserl calls 'motivation,' which is pure intentional freedom, because it is a way we have of being led (*ducere*) around (*con*), but like motivation it belongs in a quasi-intentional sphere of human behavior and is not to be reduced to physical causality. . . . Power is a way of 'governing,' shaping, forming." "On Not Knowing Who We Are: Madness, Hermeneutics, and the Night of Truth in Foucault," in Caputo and Yount, eds., *Foucault and the Critique of Institutions*, 254.

81. Augustine, *City of God*, 12.4. See also Augustine, *On Free Choice of the Will*, trans. Anna S. Benjamin and L. H. Hackstaff (New York: Macmillan, 1964), 3.18. One needs to remember that this leading is not simply external, but penetrates in depth. It forms the flesh as well as desires, dispositions, and habits. It leads the person as a whole. For a discussion of Augustine's use of "second nature," see Peter Brown, *Augustine of Hippo* (Berkeley: University of California Press, 1967), 173; and Babcock, "Augustine and the Spirituality of Desire," 185.

82. James W. Bernauer, *Michel Foucault's Force of Flight: Toward an Ethics for Thought* (London: Humanities Press, 1990), 147; Pasewark, *A Theology of Power*, 51.

83. Foucault, *Power/Knowledge*, 138.

84. Ibid.

85. Words are a way of controlling that reality of persons, and this deeply disturbs Foucault. It is ironic that this is exactly what he is accused of in making the person susceptible to historical and social currents. James Bernauer describes Foucault's philosophy as an ascetical and almost mystical exercise: "Although it may seem strange to employ the model of mysticism for Foucault's thought, it is not an arbitrary imposition on my part. The severe techniques he developed in his archaeological and genealogical methods of questioning, as ways of breaking

the spell humanism had placed on the modern mind, reintroduced into the contemporary landscape of thought that negative theology that had 'prowled the borderlands of Christianity' for a millennium. . . . Foucault's negative theology is a critique not of the conceptualizations employed for God but of that modern figure of finite man whose identity was put forward as capturing the essence of human beings. Nevertheless, Foucault's critical thinking is best described as a negative theology, rather than a negative anthropology, for its flight from man is an escape from yet another conceptualization of the Absolute." *Michel Foucault's Force of Flight*, 178. John Caputo also argues that this is an important element in Foucault's work. He writes that "no historical constitution is exhaustive or totalizing." A "negative hermeneutics" is used by Foucault, he argues, "not in order to skim along the surface of positivistic descriptions, but in order to open a hermeneutic depth, a depth of negativity: that we do not know who we are." "On Not Knowing Who We Are: Madness, Hermeneutics, and the Night of Truth in Foucault," 253, 257.

86. Foucault, "The Subject and Power," 219–26.

87. Ibid., 225.

88. Michel Foucault, "On the Genealogy of Ethics: An Overview of Work in Progress," first part of the second afterword (1983) to Dreyfus and Rabinow, *Michel Foucault: Beyond Structuralism and Hermeneutics*, 236. Foucault, *Politics, Philosophy, Culture*, 259; Michel Foucault, *Technologies of the Self: A Seminar with Michel Foucault*, ed. Luther H. Martin, Huck Gutman, and Patrick H. Hutton (Amherst: University of Massachusetts Press, 1988), 18.

89. Bernauer, *Michel Foucault's Force of Flight*, 1–6. See also John Rajchman, *Michel Foucault: The Freedom of Philosophy* (New York: Columbia University Press, 1985), 121–25; and Simons, *Foucault and the Political*, 86 f.

90. It is not just humanism that tends to understand freedom within this paradigm. Charles Taylor, a nonfoundationalist, argues that the two must be conceived as in opposition. See his "Foucault on Freedom and Truth," in Hoy, ed., *Foucault: A Critical Reader*, 69–102.

91. Foucault, "The Ethic of Care for the Self as a Practice of Freedom," 4.

92. Foucault, "The Subject and Power," 221 f.

93. Although Foucault speaks of liberty in general, he often argues that the phrase "practices of liberty" leads to less confusion because it guards against essentialism. "Practices of liberty" points to the active and concrete manifestations of freedom and away from metaphysical or ontological explanations. He does not exclude these as possibilities, but he does exclude them from his descriptive categories. Like the elusiveness of the person, he prefers to regard such topics as mysteries eluding our ability to articulate.

94. Foucault, "The Subject and Power," 222 f.

95. Foucault, *Politics, Philosophy, Culture*, 123.

96. Hoy, "Power, Repression, Progress," 135 f.

97. One of the worst misinterpretations of Foucault takes him to view the subject as determined and thereby pinned down by history and society. Ironically, since liberty is fundamental to his work, the accusation of determinism goes squarely against one of his main concerns. See Foucault, "The Ethic of Care for the Self as a Practice of Freedom," 13.

98. Foucault, "The Subject and Power," 220.

99. Foucault, "The Ethic of Care for the Self as a Practice of Freedom," 4, 12, 20; and "The Subject and Power," 221, 226.

100. One possibility for understanding this paradox is to use the battle motif, wherein one can be endlessly active in charging, changing one's position, and redirecting the attack. This constantly keeps freedom under one's personal control. However, one is still tangled up in endless conflicts that do not convey any kind of aesthetic promise. Whatever balance can be had in battle is not an aesthetic balance but a strategic standoff. At the end of his life, Foucault seems to be aiming at a much more profound transformation. One possibility is that he simply changed his mind over time and mellowed later in life. If this is so, then Foucault, as he matured, went in the opposite direction from Augustine. Foucault seems to become increasingly optimistic, whereas Augustine's vision grows darker as the years proceed. Jon Simons argues that interpreters should regard Foucault's thought as moving between two poles, constraining limitations on the one hand and limitless freedom on the other. The most constructive interpretations of Foucault, he contends, are ones that see him as usually maintaining this dynamic and fruitful tension. "On the whole, but not always, Foucault resists the magnetism of the two poles, riding the tension by adopting unstable positions between them." *Foucault and the Political*, 3. Simons concludes: "This is an ethic of permanent resistance, in which constant activism is required in order to prevent enabling limits from congealing into constraining limitations and to generate new limits that constitute selves and polities" (22).

101. Augustine revels in the mystery of human dignity being rooted not in the autonomous self but in an inexplicable relationality: "I should not exist unless I existed in you.... And when you pour yourself out over us, you are not drawn down to us but draw us up to yourself: you are not scattered away, but you gather us together.... You are the most hidden from us and yet the most present amongst us, ... ever-enduring and yet we cannot comprehend you. You are unchangeable and yet you change all things.... You welcome all who come to you although you have never lost them.... We give abundantly to you so that we may deserve a reward; yet which of us has anything that does not come from you?" *Confessions*, 1.2–4.

102. Ibid., 11.29.

103. Ibid., 13.9; see also 11.29.

104. See Babcock, "Augustine and the Spirituality of Desire," 189–95.

105. Augustine speaks of a rightly ordered will (whose object of devotion is God) as bearing, by grace, a true or Christian freedom and of a disordered will

(whose object of devotion is the self) that operates with a false, servile, or empty freedom.

106. In his classic biography of Augustine, Peter Brown notes that Augustine was rarely alone. It is difficult for contemporary readers, at least those raised in North Atlantic societies, to appreciate the complete sociality of the world to which he belonged. Any movement toward interiority takes place in the context of a community that penetrates and is penetrated by individuals. See *Augustine of Hippo*, 32, 61, and 180.

107. Charles P. Carlson, Jr., contends that Augustine produced "a purely psychological account of sin." See "The Natural Order and Historical Explanation in St. Augustine's *City of God*," *Augustiniana* 21 (1971): 442. Brown, *Augustine of Hippo*, 131 f., esp. n. 4, provides examples and citations of other reductive psychological interpretations of Augustine. For a philosophical instance of the tendency to interpret Augustine as beginning a tradition of "radical reflexivity," see Charles Taylor, *Sources of the Self: The Making of the Modern Identity* (Cambridge, Mass.: Harvard University Press, 1989), 127–42 passim. The quotation appears on 131. For a theological response to the modern inclination to psychologize Augustine's understanding of the self, see Elshtain, *Augustine and the Limits of Politics*, 4–11.

108. John Milbank rightly emphasizes the fundamental sociality of Augustine's theology and complains about liberal Protestantism's tendency to individualize Augustine's contributions to spirituality and ethics. See *Theology and Social Theory*, 401 ff.

109. Foucault, "The Ethic of Care for the Self as a Practice of Freedom," 18. This is one of the most widespread misunderstandings among Foucault's critics, namely, that power is all force and domination and therefore bad. See Hoy, "Power, Repression, Progress," 123–47, for a discussion of and response to such criticisms.

110. Augustine, *City of God*, 12.8.

111. Augustine, *The Trinity*, 13.13.17; see also 15.4.6.

112. Foucault, "On the Genealogy of Ethics," 231 f.

113. In my judgment, critics of both Augustine and Foucault do not pay sufficient attention to how power can be used positively as well as negatively. Admittedly, the two devoted perhaps inordinate attention to power's restrictive dimensions. But they also spoke of it as enabling. This interpretive mistake is especially characteristic of Foucault's commentators. One likely reason for the error is that he addressed the more positive dimensions of power later in his life and so had less time to develop it. Still, if one dwells solely on the negative aspects of power rather than on its inherent ambiguity, one will misread the works of both figures.

114. Foucault understands his role to be that of an agitator and a provider of instruments so that people in particular contexts will be both better able to recognize and pressured to address complex social problems. He is uncomfortable with prescribing what specific changes should be made, or supplying a formally enunciated normative framework within which one could make evaluative judgments.

Nevertheless, I am persuaded that one can discern a relatively low-flown set of normative convictions in Foucault's work that I identify in what follows. And as I argue in chapter 5, that Foucault does not systematically elaborate and defend these convictions does not make his work incoherent or of no normative value. Indeed, his tentativeness in this regard makes it significantly easier for others to apply elements of his work within a more comprehensive normative frame. In his essay "Power/Knowledge and Liberation," Lalonde provides an excellent example of how Foucault's analytic tools can be constructively analyzed and applied in a Christian normative context.

115. Foucault expressed concerns about critics overemphasizing his use of organic metaphors to describe power for fear that they would misconstrue it in functionalist terms (*Power/Knowledge*, 206 f.). Indeed, this is one of the primary objections to his work because in the totality of power's symbiotic operation it appears to leave no room for piecemeal resistance. However, as long as this does not become the reigning definition of power relations, but only one among many images for its influences, the functionalist critique loses its force. In chapter 2 we will encounter a formally similar interpretive mistake when examining Foucault's use of martial metaphors to describe power. There again, privileging a single image as the sole or principal means by which Foucault understood power distorts his views, and in its reductive polish, flattens the richer texture of his analysis. I should also note that for Foucault, "circulation" has organic as well as tactical connotations. In a martial context, open and reversible movements are likewise central to power relations, but, of course, such fluidity is understood in more conflictual terms. Organic metaphors allow us to talk about the way that power can socially function in more caring, even if sometimes hierarchical, relationships.

116. Foucault, *Power/Knowledge*, 98. See also Lalonde, "Power/Knowledge and Liberation," 85–89; and Pasewark, *A Theology of Power*, 39–43.

117. Foucault, "The Ethic of Care for the Self as a Practice of Freedom," 18.

118. Ibid., 3. See also Simons, *Foucault and the Political*, 6, 23, 81 ff.; and Pasewark, *A Theology of Power*, 41 ff.

119. In fact, Foucault argues that the former actually displays more power because power needs to move freely to operate. It is dynamically interactive and flowing. Foucault distinguishes between states of domination and relations of power. The former he describes variously as solidifying, congealing, hardening, locking together—all of which reflect his conviction that monitoring the social functioning of power needs to involve an awareness of power's fluidity and reversibility or lack thereof. Slavery is the paradigm for Foucault for a static, ossified state of domination. This contrasts sharply with the aforementioned relations between virtuous lovers, teachers and students, and parents and children. See Foucault, "The Subject and Power," 219–26. Ian Hacking depicts Foucault's conception of power with the metaphor of irrigation (Foucault's own term) where power runs "channels of water from one area to another so the whole can flourish. Without the performance of the

individual acts of irrigation, the power would rot or dry up." "The Archaeology of Foucault," 38.

120. Foucault, "The Ethic of Care for the Self as a Practice of Freedom," 18.

121. Ibid.

122. Foucault, *Discipline and Punish*, 137.

123. Ibid., 137f.

124. Ibid., 138.

125. In *Technologies of the Self*, Foucault criticizes Christian monasticism for having placed the monk in a "fundamental and permanent relation of total obedience to the master" (44; see also 22 ff.). Such remarks, however, need to be balanced against others in which, as we have just seen, he presents monasticism in a more positive light. Indeed, Foucault seems to equate his own philosophical approach to asceticism in the following: "What can the ethics of an intellectual be . . . if not this: to make oneself permanently capable of detaching oneself from oneself . . . ? I would like it to be an elaboration of self by self, a studious transformation, a slow, arduous process of change, guided by a constant concern for truth." *Politics, Philosophy, Culture*, 263f. I return to Foucault's analysis of monasticism in chapter 4.

126. Since the subject involved in that self-relation can be manipulated, it is difficult to know with certainty how to judge what is in one's best interest.

127. Augustine, *City of God*, 5.19, 15.7, and 19.14. See also ibid., 1.preface; 1.30; 3.14; 5.13–15; 12.22; 19.16–17. Miika Roukanen systematically discusses all of Augustine's uses of the phrase *libido dominandi* and its antithesis, benevolent care, in the *City of God*. See his *Theology of the Social Life in Augustine's* De Civitate Dei, 96–106.

128. In the *City of God*, Augustine dwells primarily on family relations; in the *Confessions*, he focuses on friendship as much if not more than the family. For examples, see *City of God*, 12.22, 14.14, 19.6, 13, 14, 16; and *Confessions*, 4.4, 6.7, 14, 8.8. His descriptions of friendship are among the most positive of all social descriptions. Consider this passage from *Confessions*, 4.8: "To talk and laugh. To do each other kindnesses. To read pleasant books together; to pass from lightest joking to talk of deepest things, and back again. To differ without rancor, as one might differ with himself. . . . [T]hese, and such like things, proceeding from our hearts as we gave affection and received it back, and shown by face, by voice, by eyes, and by a thousand pleasing ways, kindled a flame which fused our very souls together, and, of many, made us one." Translation from Peter Brown, *The Body and Society*, 389. Friendship was also developed as an important component of marriage. As Brown writes, "In a fallen humanity, where so much of the original harmony of Paradise had been shattered, the bond of friendship between husband and wife still preceded, justified, and—so Augustine hoped—would long outlast the relatively short interlude of active sex" (403).

129. Augustine, *City of God*, 19.16. See also *The Literal Meaning of Genesis*, 11.15.

130. See Markus, *Saeculum*, xv. Peter Brown argues that the small monastic community that Augustine founded in 386 formed for him one of the most

important paradigms for understanding properly ordered affection. "This monastery, and the single-hearted interpersonal bonds fostered within it by continence and poverty, remained the calm eye of the storm for the remaining forty years of Augustine's life as a Catholic bishop. It provided the ideal against which he would henceforth judge the heartrending dissension of the society around him." *The Body and Society*, 395.

131. Augustine, *Confessions*, 3.2. Augustine goes on to compare our kindness to God's: "This is why the love you bear for our souls and the compassion you show for them are pure and unalloyed, far purer than the love and pity which we feel for ourselves." In so doing, he questions our capacity to imitate God without unwitting distortion. "But *who can prove himself worthy of such a calling?*" And yet, as we will see shortly, the demands to aid the needy are not lessened by this ambiguity. We have to fulfill our religious obligations in the midst of this tension.

132. Augustine, "Homilies on the First Epistle of John," 8.5.

133. Ibid., 10.38.

134. Augustine argues that a "natural" authority would necessarily have existed in the prelapsarian community but would have been based upon the requirements of loving service in relation to God and not upon an intrinsically unequal status or condition. These relations simply offer guidance and care, and never lord power over others through coercive domination. Although such relations may appear in our day to be obviously problematic, it is important to understand what Augustine is attempting to portray about human relationships. Regardless of which individuals or social groups are placed in his categories, we need to note that what Augustine deems important is a caring disposition that holds others' concerns paramount in relation to God and that lacks all coercive impulses. His model for the one in authority, of course, is Christ, who sacrificed himself for the people of God. Similarly, "in the household of the just man . . . those who give orders are the servants of those whom they appear to command. For they do not give orders because of a lust for domination but from a dutiful concern for the interests of others." *City of God*, 19.14. One can therefore argue that Augustine, when we compare him to Aristotle, made a small but significant step toward viewing all persons as equal. For Aristotle, the prelapsarian distinctions Augustine identifies would have been attributed to an intrinsic status or condition, making structures of slavery and social inequality a part of the natural order. For Augustine, because we are equal in the sight of God, both the institution of slavery and political relations, which necessarily involve domination and subjugation, are termed unnatural and are treated as consequences of the fall. See his *Literal Meaning of Genesis*, 8.23. See also *City of God* 19.13, where he offers a list of properly ordered relations. For a discussion of slavery, see *City of God*, 19.15. See also Markus, *Saeculum*, 197–210; and Roukanen, *The Theology of the Social Life in Augustine's De Civitate Dei*, 102–4.

135. Consider the following quotations. "[I]t thinks it has gained something important if it is able to rule over its fellows also, that is, over other human beings. For it is characteristic of a depraved mind to seek after and claim as its due what is owed properly to God alone. . . . But, when it exerts itself to rule even over those who are naturally on a level with it, that is, even its fellow men, its pride is utterly intolerable." "Christian Instruction," 1.23.23. "With proud disdain of a tyrant he chose to rejoice over his subjects rather than to be a subject himself." *City of God*, 14.11. "Thus pride is a perverted imitation of God. For pride hates a fellowship of equality under God, and seeks to impose its own dominion on fellow men, in place of God's rule." *City of God*, 19.12.

136. Augustine, *City of God*, 19.15.

137. Ibid.; cf. 19.23, 11.21.

138. Augustine, *Confessions*, 9.13.

139. Paradoxically, Augustine himself, in justifying his coercion of the Donatists, provides a good example of the failure to be so vigilant. Significantly, the actions against the Donatists took place not in the political but in the religious arena, where Augustine passionately believed ultimate concerns were at stake and could be paternalistically defended. Augustine, then, seems to assume that when our highest religious convictions are at issue, the door is opened to using more extreme measures for accomplishing our end. He repudiates this in the political as distinct from the religious realm. Unfortunately, though, what he failed to realize is, once we take the step of condoning religious pressure, how difficult it is to distinguish this from, and how effortless it is to entangle this with political objectives.

140. As we will see in chapter 2, this is the most obvious but not necessarily the most effective danger. The most effective social danger goes undetected because it invades the flowing process itself and in some sense coagulates without seeming to, and thereby determines an asymmetrically instrumental participation without our noticing its harmful effects.

141. For descriptions of how a rightly ordered self-love relates to love of God, see Augustine, *The Trinity*, 9.4.4, 14.14.18, 20.

142. Augustine, "Christian Instruction," 1.1.1.

143. Ibid., 1.22.21.

144. "For since the whole Law and the Prophets depend on these two commandments, love of God and love of neighbor [*dilectio dei et dilectio proximi*], it is not without reason that Scripture generally places one for both." Augustine, *The Trinity*, 8.7.10. Or again: "In your mercy grant what I desire [*desiderium meum*], for it is not for myself alone that I so ardently desire it [*quoniam non mihi soli aestuat*]: I wish also that it may serve the love I bear to others [*sed usui vult esse fraternae caritati*]." Augustine, *Confessions*, 11.2. See also Sermon 90A:12, in *The Works of Saint Augustine: A Translation for the 21st Century*, Part III—Sermons, vol. 11: *Newly Discovered Sermons*, trans. Edmund Hill, O.P. (Hyde Park, N.Y.: New City Press,

1997). And see Letter 155:13–15, in *Political Writings*, ed. E. M. Atkins and R. J. Dodaro (Cambridge: Cambridge University Press, 2001).

145. In the background of this discussion, of course, is Augustine's famous distinction between *frui* (to enjoy, that is, to love something for its own sake) and *uti* (to use, that is, to love something in reference to God). See "Christian Instruction," 1.4.4, 1.22.20; cf. 3.10.16. On the basis of this distinction, Augustine has been criticized for involving self-love in other love. That he does so is plain. He writes, "Since the love of God has precedence, and since the measure of that love has been so defined that all other loves are to fuse in Him, it seems that no mention has been made about our love of ourselves. But, when it is said: 'Thou shalt love thy neighbor as thyself,' at once it is clear that our love of ourselves has not been overlooked." "Christian Instruction," 1.16.27. For a discussion of the criticisms, see Tarsicius J. van Bavel, "Love," and Raymond Canning, "Uti/frui," in Fitzgerald, ed., *Augustine through the Ages*. The critics are concerned with what they see as Augustine's lumping together the love of neighbor and the love of self so that the neighbor is not loved in his or her own right. The neighbor, on their view, becomes a mere means to get to God, and is thus treated instrumentally. There is some truth to the criticism. But for Augustine, everything will in some sense be instrumental because we are intrinsically relational. He is very clear, however, to distinguish between instrumentalism's good and bad forms. I will take this up momentarily. Interestingly, Foucault also relates love or care of oneself to the capacity to care for others. See "The Ethic of Care for the Self as a Practice of Freedom," 8. He criticizes those in early Christianity who assert that self-love is an ethical problem rather than the basis for building a harmoniously ordered ethical life.

146. "And so, if he is rightly said to be our neighbor to whom we must show the service of mercy, or by whom it must be shown to us, it is clear that the holy angels are also included in this command by which we are ordered to love our neighbor." "Christian Instruction," 1.30.33. In 1.30.32 he says that no neighbor is excepted, not even one's enemies. He emphasizes repeatedly that being neighborly means showing mercy and care; it means rescuing and caring for the beaten, the half-dead.

147. "Homilies on the First Epistle of John," 5.7. Also see "On the Catholic and Manichean Ways of Life," in Schaff, ed., *Nicene and Post-Nicene Fathers, First Series*, vol. 4, 1.52–54, for a description of the compassionate pain one should feel for the suffering of others. Love of neighbor includes concern for the concrete: health of body, food, shelter, living in peace and without oppression.

148. Augustine, *City of God*, 22.24. I discuss the theme of natural beauty considered as a temptation in chapter 3.

149. Ibid.

150. Augustine, *Confessions*, 10.6.

151. New forms of social interaction would create new forms of social dangers, but these would not necessarily represent an increase as compared to those already existing. They would simply be different.

152. Augustine, "Christian Instruction," 1.22.20, 22: "We have been commanded to love one another, but the question is: whether man is to be loved by man for his own sake or for another reason. If he is loved for his own sake, we are enjoying him; if he is loved for another reason, we are using him. But it seems to me that he should be loved for another reason. . . . Thus, whoever loves his neighbor rightly ought to stress this point with him, so that he, too, may love God with his whole heart, his whole soul, and his whole mind." Also consider "Christian Instruction," 1.35.39: "Ours should rather be like the transitory pleasure felt toward the road, or conveyances, or any other means to an end. Or it may be possible to express more fittingly this love we are to have for the things by which we are carried along for the sake of the end toward which we are carried." Augustine gives his reason why instrumental use through God is superior in the following: "He shows mercy to us because of His own Goodness, while we show mercy to one another because of God's goodness; that is, He has compassion on us so that we may enjoy Him completely, while we have compassion on another that we may completely enjoy Him." "Christian Instruction," 1.30.33. Without God, we refer things only to our own benefit. The following could also be cited: "God refers that use which He is said to make of us to our benefit, not to His benefit, but only to His goodness. When we show pity on someone or are mindful of his interests, we do so for, and with an eye to, his benefit. But, somehow or other, our own advantage becomes a consequence, since God does not leave without a reward that mercy which we expend upon one who needs it. Our greatest reward is that we may enjoy Him perfectly and that all of us who enjoy Him may perfectly enjoy one another in Him." "Christian Instruction," 1.32.35.

153. Foucault pursues these issues in *Discipline and Punish*, especially parts 3 and 4 (135–308).

154. Ibid., 202.

155. I have in mind especially *The Archaeology of Knowledge*, trans. A. M. Sheridan Smith (New York: Pantheon Books, 1972), though the same could be said with some justification of *The Order of Things: An Archaeology of the Human Sciences* (New York: Random House, 1970).

156. I have purposely not referred to the natural world as "fallen," following H. Paul Santmire's treatment of this topic in Augustine's thought in *The Travail of Nature: The Ambiguous Ecological Promise of Christian Theology* (Philadelphia: Fortress Press, 1985), 55–73.

157. Foucault, *Discipline and Punish*, 177.

CHAPTER 2   Vertigo and Complicity:
Unraveling the Complexities of Social Evil

1. Michel Foucault, *Power/Knowledge: Selected Interviews & Other Writings, 1972–1977*, ed. Colin Gordon (New York: Pantheon Books, 1980), 156 f.

2. Foucault, *Power/Knowledge*, 156, 158. As I mentioned in chapter 1, Foucault always prefers working in specific contexts and does not like to generalize to more universalizable conclusions. I believe that one can respect his desire to put forward particular examples of social evils while also exploring what they may mean for the human condition. Although he fails to provide a rigorously systematic evaluative framework, he does not put his reservations about drawing larger conclusions into a definite ideology. Indeed, he encourages others to use his critical tools in any way that they find helpful, given their own normative presuppositions and critical objectives. I would argue that one can trace a certain moral coherence or vision in Foucault's examples that he did not explicitly delineate. Many of Foucault's critical terms carry normative weight even though he claims to be engaged in a purely historical, descriptive task. It is therefore both possible and useful to piece together different aspects of evil that Foucault identifies here and there so as to compare them with the work of Augustine, who makes much broader interpretive claims.

3. Foucault uses the language of machinery in strictly negative terms to depict a multitude of power relations. It is frequently used in describing discipline but it is also used to describe confession and bio-power. See *Power/Knowledge*, 156–58 and 211, for examples of how he applies it to both. Since he develops it most extensively with respect to disciplinary forms of power, it occurs frequently in *Discipline and Punish: The Birth of the Prison*, trans. Alan Sheridan (New York: Random House, 1979).

4. Foucault, *Power/Knowledge*, 116.

5. Ibid., 158.

6. Ibid.

7. Foucault, *Discipline and Punish*, 202.

8. Ibid., 206. I address different ways in which these kinds of power relations operate in concrete historical contexts when I examine politics and questions concerning historical progress in chapter 5. My concern here is to explore some of the general outlines of Foucault's views about the darker sides of power rather than to go into the details of how it operates through specific mechanisms and in particular contexts.

9. In contrast to images of machinery, which are always used negatively, these are ambivalent terms, sometimes used in a positive and sometimes in a negative way.

10. Foucault, *Discipline and Punish*, 176.

11. Foucault, *Power/Knowledge*, 98.

12. Foucault, *Discipline and Punish*, 201.

13. In *Discipline and Punish*, 137 f., Foucault speaks of a "mechanics of power" that lays hold of the body, "that explores it, breaks it down and rearranges it."

14. Augustine, *City of God*, trans. Henry Bettenson (London: Penguin Books, 1972), 12.7.

15. Ibid. Notice that Augustine is speaking about evil as ontologically deficient. Although it is not substantive, it is still active. We cannot get hold of it even though we are all familiar with it. As will become clear later, this is not so different from Foucault's nonsubstantive view of power. It lives in its acts and its exercise but not as an inert thing.

16. Augustine has been criticized for not being sufficiently logical in these pursuits. William S. Babcock describes his efforts as too ephemeral, "too thin, too attenuated." "Augustine on Sin and Moral Agency," *Journal of Religious Ethics* 16:1 (1988): 47f.

17. As Malcolm Aflatt writes, "[T]he individual's situation could not be adequately explained solely in terms of the individual's own existence. Augustine's thought came to place the individual always within a nexus of human relationships. . . . The individual is never to be held responsible simply as an individual, but always as a member of the race existing in solidarity with Adam." "The Responsibility for Involuntary Sin in Saint Augustine," *Recherches Augustiniennes* 10 (1975): 180f.

18. To repeat a point made in the previous chapter, I use "desire" to designate a fairly wide range of words Augustine uses (e.g., *appetitus, cupiditas, desiderium, libido,* and *concupiscentia*) whose meanings are sufficiently synonymous, when speaking at this level of generality, to warrant one English word. When more detail is required, I indicate which term I mean or Augustine uses. For "habit," I have in mind either *consuetudo* (for a bad habit) or *habitus* (for a good or virtuous one).

19. I agree with Peter Burnell that although one can distinguish among Augustine's uses of original sin, concupiscence, and inherited guilt, when considered in their deepest sense as a fundamental disruption of the self arising from an arrogant self-absorption and disdain for God, they are essentially synonymous. See his "Concupiscence," in *Augustine through the Ages: An Encyclopedia,* ed. Allan D. Fitzgerald, O.S.A. (Grand Rapids: Eerdmans, 1999), 224.

20. Aflatt, "The Responsibility for Involuntary Sin in Saint Augustine," 174ff.

21. These finer meshes are the subject of the next section and chapter 3; the coarser social matrix is examined in chapter 5.

22. Eugene TeSelle, *Augustine the Theologian* (New York: Herder and Herder, 1970), 291ff., 318.

23. Gilbert Meilander, "The First and the Second Adam: Reflections on James Wetzel's Reformulation of a Doctrine," *Journal of Religious Ethics* 23:1 (1995): 30ff.; Gerald W. Schlabach, "Friendship as Adultery: Social Reality and Sexual Metaphor in Augustine's Doctrine of Original Sin," *Augustinian Studies* 23 (1992): 134ff.

24. Aflatt, "The Responsibility for Involuntary Sin in Saint Augustine," 178–86; and "The Development of the Idea of Involuntary Sin in St. Augustine," *Revue des Études Augustiniennes* 20 (1974): 130ff.

25. Foucault, *Power/Knowledge,* 64.

26. Ibid., 82.

27. Foucault, *Discipline and Punish,* 27.

28. See *City of God,* books 1–9, where Augustine enumerates a long list of cruelties perpetrated throughout the course of human history.

29. R. A. Markus writes in *Saeculum: History and Society in the Theology of St. Augustine* (New York: Cambridge University Press, 1970), 21: "[H]istory . . . cannot be mapped out in terms of a pattern drawn from sacred history. . . . [I]t can no longer contain decisive turning-points endowed with a significance in sacred history. Every moment may have its unique and mysterious significance in the ultimate divine *tableau* of men's doings and sufferings; but it is a significance to which God's revelation does not supply the clues." He also notes: "By 414 . . . Augustine had come to see 'sacred history' as confined to the history to be found within the scriptural canon, and he came to deny this status to any other interpretations of historical events. Beyond this, all history is starkly secular, that is to say, it is incapable of being treated in terms of its place in the history of salvation" (43). I return to this topic of the relativizing of historical progress in chapter 5.

30. Augustine, *City of God,* 15.5.

31. Augustine, *The Trinity, The Fathers of the Church: A New Translation,* vol. 45, trans. Stephen McKenna, C.SS.R. (Washington, D. C.: Catholic University of America Press, 1963), 12.9.14.

32. Augustine, *Confessions,* trans. R. S. Pine-Coffin (New York: Penguin Books, 1961), 1.8.

33. Foucault, *Power/Knowledge,* 114.

34. Ibid., 56.

35. Ibid., 196.

36. Ibid., 97.

37. Ibid.

38. Ibid., 195.

39. Ibid., 203.

40. Ibid., 208.

41. As Foucault writes: "[O]ne should not assume a massive and primal condition of domination, a binary structure with 'dominators' on one side and 'dominated' on the other, but rather a multiform production of relations of domination which are partially susceptible of integration into overall strategies." Ibid., 142.

42. Ibid., 163f. This provides one instance of Foucault mixing martial and mechanistic metaphors in the same sentence.

43. Ibid., 115.

44. One of the most prevalent misconceptions about Foucault's work is that many commentators construe all that he says through the lens of his military language. They see this as the key to understanding his various descriptions of power as "combative force." For an example, see John Milbank, *Theology and Social Theory: Beyond Secular Reason* (Oxford: Blackwell, 1990, 1993), 289. As we will see below and in chapter 3, "influence" is perhaps a more all-embracing definition to help us understand Foucault's very broad conception of power.

45. Foucault, *Power/Knowledge,* 164.

46. Even though Augustine uses binary distinctions—for example, the heavenly and earthly cities, the two kinds of loves, and *frui* and *uti*—we have to keep in mind his belief that we cannot be sure who are the citizens of those cities until the end of time. So he relies on them in theory without being able to separate people definitively into distinct groups with boundaries that are reliably clear here and now. See *Confessions,* 13.14; *City of God,* 1.35, 18.49; and Sermon 299A:8 (in *The Works of Saint Augustine: A Translation for the 21st Century,* Part III—Sermons, vol. 11: *Newly Discovered Sermons,* trans. Edmund Hill, O.P. [Hyde Park, N.Y.: New City Press, 1997]; hereafter cited as *WSA* III/11).

47. Aflatt, "Responsibility for Involuntary Sin in Saint Augustine," 171. Aflatt proceeds to defend Augustine against this attack on the basis of his understanding of habit.

48. Babcock, "Augustine on Sin and Moral Agency," 28.

49. Ibid.

50. Ibid., 28 f.

51. Ibid., 29.

52. Ibid.

53. Ibid., 30.

54. James Wetzel, *Augustine and the Limits of Virtue* (Cambridge: Cambridge University Press, 1992), 64.

55. James Wetzel, "Moral Personality, Perversity, and Original Sin," *Journal of Religious Ethics* 23:1 (spring 1995): 22. Gerald Schlabach writes that of all Augustine's doctrines, original sin is perhaps the most difficult for modern persons to grasp and appreciate. And yet, he argues, "no Augustinian teaching illumines the modern situation more potently." It thus throws light particularly well on modern predispositions that we are unwilling to reexamine or surrender, and modern problems that are rooted in our distinctive individualistic frame of mind. "Friendship as Adultery," 125.

56. Wetzel, "Moral Personality, Perversity, and Original Sin," 5.

57. Ibid., 22.

58. Charles Taylor, "Foucault on Freedom and Truth," in *Foucault: A Critical Reader,* ed. David Couzens Hoy (Oxford: Blackwell, 1986), 86. As Hoy points out, it is interesting that Lukes and Taylor agree on this criticism even though they do not share a similar conception of power. See Hoy's "Introduction," in Hoy, ed., *Foucault: A Critical Reader,* 11.

59. Hoy, "Introduction," 9–12.

60. Taylor, "Foucault on Freedom and Truth," 69.

61. Michael Walzer, "The Politics of Michel Foucault," in Hoy, ed., *Foucault: A Critical Reader,* 63. Taylor agrees with this in his "Foucault on Freedom and Truth," 83–90.

62. Walzer, "The Politics of Michel Foucault," 62. Walzer is confusing what I call Foucault's evaluative reserve—where he allows others to make normative

interpretations about his historical descriptions—with an explicit moral claim that clearly asserts Foucault's own position. Walzer is thus both drawing out of and imposing on Foucault's reticence an unsupportable charge. Foucault's interviews repeatedly undermine such a reading.

63. Taylor, "Foucault on Freedom and Truth," 90f.

64. Walzer, "The Politics of Michel Foucault," 53–55; Taylor, "Foucault on Freedom and Truth," 72–77.

65. Wetzel, "Moral Personality, Perversity, and Original Sin," 3.

66. Ibid., 24.

67. I do not want to undermine the importance of intentions and decisions that help to build and reinforce character or that open new avenues of change for individual agents. What I hope to point out is that for Augustine and Foucault, such choices are always made in an inherited world that is socially constituted. A morally complex sociality, therefore, always precedes and follows our personal decisions. This is part of the mystery of our being socially interdependent creatures. I explore these themes in detail below and in the last three chapters.

68. Peter Brown, *The Body and Society: Men, Women, and Sexual Renunciation in Early Christianity* (New York: Columbia University Press, 1988), 360. The citation is from Schlabach, "Friendship as Adultery," 145f.

69. Although Wetzel relies on modern presuppositions and Rorty relies on post-modern ones, their shared confidence in the evolving moral capacities of persons to ameliorate the most deep-seated social evils leads them in a similar direction, leaving them exposed to individualistic or Pelagian pitfalls.

70. Richard Rorty, *Contingency, Irony, and Solidarity* (Cambridge: Cambridge University Press, 1989), 195.

71. Ibid.

72. Bringing into social discourse diverse narratives and self-descriptions is also important for Foucault. However, the resulting social environment he expects to be created from such an endeavor is one of conflict (I would argue, prophetic conflict) rather than one of harmonious coexistence. Rorty's optimism in controlling the tragic stands in stark contrast to Foucault's suspicious questioning of noble objectives and achievements as well as those that are obviously "cruel and humiliating." This topic is pursued at length in chapters 4 and 5.

73. Meilander, "The First and the Second Adam," 32.

74. Ibid., 30.

75. Ibid.

76. Rorty, *Contingency, Irony, and Solidarity*, xvi. Foucault also speaks positively about self-creation through practices of freedom, as we will see in the next section. However, it is always from within a culturally configured world that such "creative" work operates in honing one's self-identity. "I would say that if now I am interested, in fact, in the way in which the subject constitutes himself in an active fashion, by the practices of the self, these practices are nevertheless not something

that the individual invents by himself. They are patterns that he finds in his culture and which are proposed, suggested and imposed on him by his culture, his society and his social group." Michel Foucault, "The Ethic of Care for the Self as a Practice of Freedom," in *The Final Foucault*, ed. James Bernauer and David Rasmussen (Cambridge, Mass.: The MIT Press, 1988), 11. This does not undermine the subject's freedom; it simply means that transforming practices of liberty operate within certain social boundaries.

77. I agree with James Bernauer when he notes: "Having wondered for several years about the violent reactions Foucault evokes, I have come to conclude that his work . . . exposed an especially sensitive area of contemporary consciousness, not only its reluctance to think differently, but more important, its sacralization of the modern experience of the self." James W. Bernauer, *Michel Foucault's Force of Flight: Toward an Ethics for Thought* (London: Humanities Press, 1990), 160.

78. Meilander, "The First and the Second Adam," 30f.

79. Ibid., 31. The literature on the social constitution of the self is far too vast to cover here. But I would mention one other Augustinian scholar who voices a similar concern. Gerald Schlabach says: "Complex webs of social solidarity shape and permeate our very identities. . . . From the moment of conception on, we are part of this complex, we are members of the human race, we accept human standards as our own, we are intimately bound up in Adam. There is simply no other way to be a human being without implicating ourselves in this social network." "Friendship as Adultery," 134.

80. Meilander, "The First and the Second Adam," 39.

81. Foucault, *Discipline and Punish*, 206.

82. Foucault, *Power/Knowledge*, 151 f.

83. Ibid., 186.

84. Michel Foucault, *The History of Sexuality, Volume 1: An Introduction* (New York: Vintage Books, 1980), 135–45.

85. Colin Gordin argues in the afterword to *Power/Knowledge*, 255, that "the facts of resistance are nevertheless assigned an irreducible role within the analysis. . . . [T]he human material operated on by programmes and technologies is inherently a *resistant* material."

86. Michel Foucault, "The Subject and Power," afterword to *Michel Foucault: Beyond Structuralism and Hermeneutics*, 2d ed., by Hubert L. Dreyfus and Paul Rabinow (Chicago: University of Chicago Press, 1983), 222–26.

87. Michel Foucault, *The Use of Pleasure: The History of Sexuality, Volume 2* (New York: Pantheon Books, 1985), 95. See also Foucault, "The Ethic of Care for the Self as a Practice of Freedom," 19; and "The Subject and Power," 226. In the latter, power is defined as a mode of action on actions of others (221).

88. Foucault, "The Subject and Power," 226.

89. Foucault, *Discipline and Punish*, 28 f., 43, 108.

90. Ibid., 50.

91. Foucault, "The Subject and Power," 220 f.

92. It may be incapable of being in relation to the abused body, but it of course can still remain in relation to others, especially when the disfigured body is used as a political symbol and sign that instrumentally serves the power developed between the sovereign and the population as a whole. See Foucault, *Discipline and Punish*, 33–58. I return to this topic in chapter 5.

93. Foucault, *The History of Sexuality, Volume 1*, 85.

94. Foucault, *Discipline and Punish*, 49 ff., 58–69, 80, 87.

95. James Bernauer writes, "Unlike Nietzsche, Foucault identified with the weak and the vanquished, the mentally ill and the deviant, with the lives of such infamous people as Pierre Riviere and Herculine Barbin, in whose accounts 'one feels under words polished like stone, the relentlessness and the ruin.'" *Michel Foucault's Force of Flight*, 182.

96. Foucault, *Discipline and Punish*, 208.

97. Foucault, *Power/Knowledge*, 186.

98. Ibid., 186–87.

99. Joseph Rouse discusses power relations in terms of competing alignments and counter-alignments and refers his arguments to those of Thomas Wartenburg. See Rouse's "Power/Knowledge," in *The Cambridge Companion to Foucault*, ed. Gary Gutting (Cambridge: Cambridge University Press, 1994), 92–108.

100. Foucault, "The Subject and Power," 224 f.

101. Ibid., 224.

102. Ibid., 222, 224.

103. An interesting comment on the constant danger of manipulative processes is that this very examination also opens us to instrumental misuse. Extensive self-examination is one of the prime targets of Foucault's analysis of modern forms of power where this has been transformed and employed in institutional contexts. Knowing the self is thus a double-edged sword. It can help to develop exercises of freedom, yet it also opens one to different vulnerabilities that can be manipulated by others just like any other capability. Foucault focuses on confession in depth, as we will see in chapter 4, but his primary concern is with how it has been transformed in a modern context. Interpreters are mistaken to draw the conclusion that everything he criticizes is problematic in all contexts. I would urge that we turn that around. Everything that empowers us can also be used to manipulate us. Most things are left ambivalent, open to being used for or against our own well-being, depending on how personal governance takes shape.

104. I am, in effect, pulling together two parts of Foucault's career. Over his life, he moved sequentially from analyzing negative technologies of domination to more constructive technologies of self. His earlier works point in the direction of the latter in that he indicates that resistance is possible at the very smallest levels of power where an individual can make significant changes. But he does not develop this theme extensively in these works. Once Foucault begins to focus more narrowly

on emancipatory technologies, he seems to have grown somewhat tired of all the talk about domination. He does at times correlate this new interest in an ethics of self with a responsible politics that counters social domination, but it is not something he adequately develops. I would argue that drawing these insights more closely together protects Foucault from two different criticisms. One, corresponding to the first stages of his career, is that he does not provide sufficient avenues for resistance and thus is all gloom and doom, leading some to call him "a prophet of entrapment." (See Jon Simons, *Foucault and the Political* [New York: Routledge, 1995], 49 f.) The other, directed at his later works, is that he only develops the "creative" but not the "darker" potentialities of the self. (See Kyle A. Pasewark, *A Theology of Power: Being Beyond Domination* [Minneapolis: Fortress Press, 1993], 48 f.) If these two parts of his writings are brought together, they can address both concerns. One can thereby emphasize the importance of freedom and change in configuring one's sense of personal identity while acknowledging that what is most empowering in the self can always be manipulated by others within the self's own boundaries.

105. Michel Foucault, "On the Genealogy of Ethics: An Overview of Work in Progress," first part of the second afterword (1983) to Dreyfus and Rabinow, *Michel Foucault: Beyond Structuralism and Hermeneutics,* 246, 239. There he defined himself or his own vision as an undefined work of freedom.

106. This training concerns the whole person and all of his or her physical and mental capacities: "technologies . . . implies modes of training and modification of individuals, not only in the obvious sense of acquiring certain skills but also in the sense of acquiring certain attitudes." *Technologies of the Self: A Seminar with Michel Foucault,* ed. Luther H. Martin, Huck Gutman, and Patrick H. Hutton (Amherst: University of Massachusetts Press, 1988), 18.

107. Foucault, "On the Genealogy of Ethics," 243.

108. Ibid., 236.

109. Michel Foucault, *Politics, Philosophy, Culture: Interviews and Other Writings, 1977–1984,* ed. Lawrence D. Kritzman (New York: Routledge, Chapman, & Hall, 1988), 259.

110. Foucault, *Technologies of the Self,* 18.

111. Foucault, "On the Genealogy of Ethics" 240. As we saw in chapter 1, Foucault does not want to define this universally. That, he believes, should be left up to individuals living in the context of particular communities.

112. Referring back to the movement of power discussed in chapter 1, salutary or injurious governance of oneself and of others depends on whether one is attempting to harden and make permanent asymmetrical interactions. Self and other governance are inherently related. When one tends to have a rigidly domineering and thus fossilized relation with oneself, one is inclined to govern others in a like manner. This is when patterns of domination solidify, shutting off the intrinsically reversible fluidity of power relations. Governance, like all power relations, is ambivalent— presenting both beneficial and exploitive opportunities for transfiguring oneself and

others. Foucault, *Technologies of the Self*, 18 ff.; "The Subject and Power," 220ff.; *Politics, Philosophy, Culture*, 257–63. Mitchell Dean concisely reviews Foucault's historical research into the relationship between self and other governance in the ancient world and considers questions it poses for contemporary debate in "Foucault, Government and the Enfolding of Authority," in *Foucault and Political Reason: Liberalism, Neo-Liberalism and Rationalities of Government*, ed. Andrew Barry, Thomas Osborne, and Nikolas Rose (Chicago: University of Chicago Press, 1996), 209–29. In chapter 3, I analyze in detail the performative fragility of governance in relation to desires and habits that constitute acting individuals and the communities to which they belong. Chapters 4 and 5 then examine, from Augustine to Foucault and from Foucault to the present, distinctive cultural transformations of the modes and understandings of self and other governance.

113. Foucault, *The History of Sexuality, Volume 1*, 103.

114. Foucault, *Discipline and Punish*, 294f.

115. Foucault, *The History of Sexuality, Volume 1*, 163.

116. Foucault, *Power/Knowledge*, 199 ff.

117. Ibid., 99.

118. Recall that Peter Brown argues that Augustine, in contrast to many of his contemporaries, follows Paul's conception of the "flesh" as being distinct from the "body." "Flesh" is a fundamentally interactive reality and is constituted by relational desires and acts. The "flesh" therefore dynamically involves the body but cannot be reduced to its physicality. See his *Body and Society*, 47 ff., 318. One could apply such a definition to Foucault as well. As we saw earlier, the "materiality of the body" is most vulnerable to the "materiality of power," not in terms of its sheer biological exposure and plasticity, but in terms of its relational capacities and social functioning.

119. Foucault, *Power/Knowledge*, 199.

120. Foucault, *The History of Sexuality, Volume 1*, 44, 99.

121. Foucault, *Discipline and Punish*, 226.

122. Ibid., 27

123. Foucault, *Power/Knowledge*, 62

124. Ibid., 98.

125. The language here serves Foucault in that he believes this is one of the ways in which such power operates. But he sometimes gets entangled in it and has difficulty analyzing the situation outside of the purview that it offers him.

126. See Bernauer, *Michel Foucault's Force of Flight*, 175–84, for a fuller discussion of these issues.

127. Augustine, *Confessions*, 11.31.

128. Ibid., 10.6.

129. Ibid., 4.7.

130. Ibid., 4.16.

131. Ibid., 3.4.

132. Ibid., 10.29.

133. Ibid., 10.17.

134. Ibid., 10.40, among many others.

135. Ibid., 10.4. See also Sermon 29B:1, in *WSA* III/11.

136. Foucault, *Discipline and Punish,* 27.

137. Ibid., 139.

138. Ibid.

139. Ibid., 139 f. This is about disciplinary power and its exploitative infiltration. He is referring here to institutional power gaining a material hold over individuals, but the way it does that is through the operational functioning of the individual in his or her day-to-day activities. It is here that institutional power must permeate if it is to operate effectively and hiddenly.

140. Ibid., 139.

141. Michel Foucault, "The Subject and Power," 217.

142. The first book, and indeed the first paragraph, of the *Confessions* emphasizes the importance of the themes of rest and restlessness as one of the defining characteristics of religious life: "[O]ur hearts find no peace until they rest in you" (1.1). The last chapter restates this, signaling as he comes to the close of the book how important this theme is. Things are displaced, he writes, and "always on the move until they come to rest where they are meant to be" (13.9). And the book ends with the following words: "[W]e hope that we shall find rest, when you admit us to the great holiness of your presence. But you are Goodness itself and need no good besides yourself. You are forever at rest, because you are your own repose. What man can teach another to understand this truth? What angel can teach it to an angel? What angel can teach it to a man? We must ask it of you, seek it in you; we must knock at your door. Only then shall we receive what we ask and find what we seek; only then will the door be opened to us" (13.38).

143. Augustine, *The Trinity,* 9.12.18.

144. Augustine, *Confessions,* 2.2.

145. Ibid., 11.29. Paul also finds this a burden. "Even Paul . . . *goes sighing and heavy-hearted. His soul thirsts for the living God, as a deer for running water. . . . He longs for the shelter of that home which heaven will give him.*" Ibid., 13.14; biblical citations in text.

146. Augustine, *The Trinity,* 9.1.1.

147. Ibid., 15.2.

148. In the context of this life, Augustine speaks of finding some respite at times like a person who is on a journey: "[T]his, too, is referred to something further, so that it may be regarded not as the rest of the citizen in his native land, but as it were the refreshment, or even the lodging of a traveler." Ibid., 11.6.

149. Augustine, *Confessions,* 10.17.

150. Ibid., 12.11.

151. Ibid., 12.15; see also 12.11.

152. Ibid., 13.14.

153. Michel Foucault, "What Is Enlightenment?" trans. Catherine Porter, in *The Foucault Reader*, ed. Paul Rabinow (New York: Pantheon Books, 1984).

154. Although Augustine's discussions of memory indicate that he is interested in how the past, present, and future can be united in an all-encompassing present, he nevertheless comes to the conclusion that in this fallen life the present is always tragically divided, leaving persons distended, distracted, and torn. Only when individuals reach Holy Jerusalem will they be able to transcend this morally problematic tension. For now, they can only anticipate that future reality and rely on that anticipation to help them endure their present trials. See *Confessions*, 11.20, 21.

155. The fact that Augustine, in the end, will conclude that such personal control can only be enabled by God will be important to his understanding of a "beautiful" existence and what kind of "aesthetic" shape we are able to give our own lives. In this respect, his vision overall is very different from Foucault's. At this level of examination, however, Augustine's conclusions about grace need not disrupt the comparison.

CHAPTER 3   Desires, Habits, and Governance:
A Case Study of Performative Vulnerabilities

1. Augustine, *Confessions*, trans. R. S. Pine-Coffin (New York: Penguin Books, 1961), 10.16.

2. In fact, even when he is caught up in his more philosophical discussions, Augustine is drawn to the moral tragedies of performative problems. His examination of time and eternity is brought to the moral level when he talks about the problems with being distended and scattered. His analysis of knowledge always comes back to the limitations of what we are able to see through a glass darkly. See *Confessions*, books 11 and 10, respectively.

3. Augustine, *Confessions*, 13.20.

4. Ibid., 10.4.

5. Peter Brown writes that this would have stood out when compared not only to ancient but also to medieval biographies, in which we tend to meet only "heroes described in terms of their essential, ideal qualities." *Augustine of Hippo* (Berkeley: University of California Press, 1967), 173. Brown goes on to say that conversions in the ancient world were "often thought of as being as dramatic and as simple as the 'sobering up' of an alcoholic. . . . Seen in such a light, the very act of conversion has cut the convert's life in two; he has been able to shake off his past. Conversion to philosophy or to some religious creed was thought of as being the attainment of some final security, like sailing from a stormy sea into the still waters of a port" (177).

6. Augustine, *Confessions*, 10.28.

7. Ibid., 11.2.

8. Ibid., 2.2. As we will see when examining Augustine's description of how he feels tempted by the objects of his five senses, *concupiscentia* can also mean "having a weakness for something," a sense that these quite violent images fail adequately to convey.

9. Ibid.

10. Notice that the earlier quote on Adam does not focus on sexual desire but on a prideful turning away from God. See also *City of God*, trans. Henry Bettenson (New York: Penguin Books, 1972), 14.3: "It is in fact not by the possession of flesh, which the devil does not possess, that man has become like the devil. It is by living by the rule of self, that is, by the rule of men." Augustine emphasizes the magnitude of the disordering impact of the fall on our sexual experiences in *City of God*, 14.16–18, 20–23. This intensifies as his participation in the Pelagian debate hardens his position. Trying to focus on the organs becomes important for him in finding a way to speak about the inevitable transmission from generation to generation. So we can identify his focus on organs as his way to speak about the spreading of sin, the biological component in the spread, bringing it into nature. But this is the spread, not the root, of the disorder. It is not the germ that starts the illness but the means by which it is spread, like coughing or sneezing.

11. Augustine, *Confessions*, 10.1.

12. Ibid., 1.13.

13. Ibid., 5.12. When praising Paul in a sermon, Augustine has this to say: "How he utterly rejects being worshiped instead of Christ, how jealous he is for the bridegroom, and refuses to parade himself as the bridegroom to any soul bent on fornication!" Sermon 198:15, in *The Works of Saint Augustine: A Translation for the 21st Century*, Part III—Sermons, vol. 11: *Newly Discovered Sermons*, trans. Edmund Hill, O. P. (Hyde Park, N. Y.: New City Press, 1997); hereafter cited as WSA III/11. Cf. Sermon 198:33.

14. Augustine, *Confessions*, 6.5.

15. Ibid., 4.16.

16. Gerald W. Schlabach shows that Augustine also describes friendship both in erotic terms and as occasions for the "adulterous" spirit to be unfaithful. Again, Augustine is clearly employing the language of sexual intimacy and betrayal to communicate nonsexual but intensely personal relational dynamics and loyalties. "Friendship as Adultery: Social Reality and Sexual Metaphor in Augustine's Doctrine of Original Sin," *Augustinian Studies* 23 (1992): 125–47. As Schlabach points out, in *Confessions* 4.8.13, Augustine laments that his all-consuming love for friends has become an "adulterous fondling" dissipating his devotion to God (128). In 2.9.17, Augustine describes friendship as an "unfathomable seducer of the mind" (130). But as Schlabach rightly argues, it should be remembered that Augustine considers friendship a great blessing as well. That is why its misuse or improper orientation in relation to God has such significance for Augustine.

17. See J. van Oort, "Augustine on Sexual Concupiscence and Original Sin," in *Studia Patristica,* vol. 22, ed. E. A. Livingstone (Louvain: Peeters Press, 1989), 382–86.

18. To cite one among virtually innumerable examples: "The whole cause, you see, of our mortality, the whole cause of our feebleness, the whole cause of all the torments, all the difficulties, all the miseries which the human race suffers in this age, is nothing but pride." Sermon 159B:11; cf. Sermon 198:33. Both in *WSA* III/11.

19. Theologians and historians who hold this view include Peter Brown, *The Body and Society: Men, Women, and Sexual Renunciation in Early Christianity* (New York: Columbia University Press, 1988), 418 f.; Eugene TeSelle, *Augustine the Theologian* (New York: Herder and Herder; 1970); J. Patout Burns, "Augustine on the Origin and Progress of Evil," *Journal of Religious Ethics* 16 (spring 1988): 9–27; Reinhold Niebuhr, *The Nature and Destiny of Man: A Christian Interpretation,* vol. 1, *Human Nature* (New York: Charles Scribner's Sons, 1941, 1964), 246–64. One can find plenty of evidence for pride's central importance for Augustine, whether in his descriptions of Adam's pride being the primary motivator of the fall (*City of God,* 14.13, 15) or with the fact that the fall of the angels did not involve sexual concupiscence or bodies at all (*City of God,* 11.11, 33).

20. The commentators I find most persuasive are those who attempt to find a balance between embodiment and the prideful spirit understood both in its personal and in its larger social dimensions. Gerald Schlabach persuasively argues that sexual imagery is used by Augustine as a critical social metaphor without undercutting the fact that Augustine also understood sin as being biologically rooted. Indeed, argues Schlabach, Augustine may not have understood the full significance of his own social metaphors. As he aged and became increasingly consumed with battling Pelagianism, he seemed to become more and more invested in circumscribing a clearly definable target with which to battle, namely, sexual concupiscence. See Schlabach, "Friendship as Adultery," 125–47. Paula Fredrickson argues that Augustine should be understood as standing out from his contemporaries in how he overcame the body/soul dualism in her "Beyond the Body/Soul Dichotomy: Augustine on Paul against the Manichaens and Pelagians," *Recherches Augustiniennes* 23 (1988): 87–114. For an interesting Trinitarian analysis of these themes, see Paul Rigby, *Original Sin in Augustine's* Confessions (Ottawa: University of Ottawa Press, 1987).

21. Augustine clearly does confirm an order of mind over body that parallels the order of heaven over earth, men over women, parents over children, and so on. But like the family in prelapsarian and redeemed communities, one could argue that although the spirit and the body are distinguished in light of their different functions, this need not entail servitude or "dominion." Loving care would be the proper relation between spirit and body and that loving care would work in both directions. Care of the body is a main theme Augustine often returns to when speaking of properly ordered loves. See, in particular, "Christian Instruction," in *The Fathers of the Church: A New Translation,* vol. 2, trans. John J. Gavigan, O. S. A. (Washington,

D.C.: Catholic University of America Press, 1947, 1950), bk. 1. Just as in Holy Jerusalem, where differentiations do not sever the working unity of the community as a whole, so too could one understand the spirit and the mind forming a unity that has no divisions even though it exhibits differentiations in function.

22. The example of Augustine's attachment to his first mistress also shows the convoluted ways in which desires intermix in a sexual relation of love. Although we can surmise from his earlier comments about his life that the relationship was initially based on lustful attraction, when his mistress finally is forced to leave, Augustine does not describe the loss in terms of lust but as a "sharp and searing" wound to his heart: "this was a blow that crushed my heart to bleeding, because I loved her dearly." As the wound festers, he takes a new mistress who does not alleviate his emotional pain but only intensifies it and enslaves him to bodily desires. Augustine's enduring attachment to his first mistress, then, was clearly formed by an intermingling of bodily and emotional desires, and it would be difficult to detach the two if one were trying to determine what was the propelling motivation for his illicit behavior. *Confessions,* 6.15.

23. Augustine, *Confessions,* 10.31–34.

24. Ibid. For example, he laments the snare of concupiscence (*laqueus concupiscentiae*) that awaits him as he satisfies his hunger (10.31). He notes that David "reproached himself for longing for a drink of water [*aquae desiderium*]" and asks rhetorically if there is anyone not enticed (*non rapiatur*) beyond the limits of need (10.31). The pleasures of sound entangled and captivated him (*voluptates aurium tenacius me inplicaverant et subiugaverant*) (10.33). And he confesses that he is tempted by the pleasure (*volupta,* again) of beautiful forms. He states that of these temptations, fragrances posed the least problem for him, and yet it is interesting that fragrance is one of the primary sensual images he uses to speak of spiritual attractions. Together these examples demonstrate that the temptations of bodily desires (*temptationes concupiscentiae carnis*) that worry him and for which he has a weakness extend well beyond mere sexual lust. Tellingly, it is in a discussion of beauty that he states that he has become a problem to himself (10.34).

25. Ibid., 10.33, 34.

26. Ibid., 10.33.

27. Augustine makes this point in a sermon: "I am not saying that you should have no loves; I simply want your loves to be properly ordered. Put heavenly things before earthly, immortal things before mortal, everlasting things before transitory ones. And put the Lord before everything, and not just by praising him, but also by loving him." Sermon 335C:13, in *Political Writings,* ed. E.M. Atkins and R.J. Dodaro (Cambridge: Cambridge University Press, 2001).

28. Speaking of the gift of light, he says: "Yet those who have learnt to praise you for this as well as for your other gifts, O God, Maker of all things, sing you a hymn of praise for it: they are not beguiled by it in their dreams. For myself, I wish to be as they are." *Confessions,* 10.34.

29. Ibid., 5.1. See also 10.6 where Augustine asks creation who God is: "Clear and loud they answered, 'God is He who made us.' I asked these questions simply by gazing at these things, and their beauty was all the answer they gave."

30. Ibid., 10.27.

31. I examine this in more detail in chapter 5.

32. Augustine, "On Continence," 2.5 (written ca. 418), in *Nicene and Post-Nicene Fathers of the Christian Church, First Series,* vol. 3, ed. Philip Schaff (Edinburgh: T. & T. Clark; Grand Rapids: Eerdmans, n.d.).

33. Ibid., 2.3–4.

34. His concern with this is demonstrated by how much time he devotes to examining susceptible children, women, and the mentally ill. I talk about these interests in the next two chapters when I turn to examine authoritative cultural discourses and how they target particular individuals in society. For now, I am more interested in an analysis of desires that can be applied to the general population rather than subpopulations or subgroups with their own vulnerabilities.

35. Michel Foucault, *The History of Sexuality, Volume I: An Introduction* (New York: Vintage Books, 1980), 67.

36. Foucault examines medical and scientific transformations of confessional practices as forming a cultural trend that makes such sensualization possible. I explore these issues in depth in chapter 4. We can get at Foucault's point by looking at more everyday examples, at least for the sake of my present argument.

37. See Susan R. Bordo's excellent use of Foucault in discussing anorexia and the distortions of images of female bodies in "The Body and the Reproduction of Femininity: A Feminist Appropriation of Foucault," in *Gender/Body/Knowledge: Feminist Reconstructions of Being and Knowing,* ed. Alison M. Jaggar and Susan R. Bordo (New Brunswick: Rutgers University Press, 1989), 13–33.

38. Although these are deinstitutionalized, such practices form what Jon Simons calls "technologies of seduction" whereby we are culturally enthralled, shaped, and guided as desiring subjects. *Foucault and the Political* (London: Routledge, 1995), 40. James W. Bernauer notes that Foucault's volumes on the history of sexuality were "concerned less with sexuality than with the 'desiring man' who comes to recognize himself as a subject of desire. While the studies contained detailed analyses of the sexual domain, their interest is in how sexual desire was problematized as an issue for moral conduct." *Michel Foucault's Force of Flight: Toward an Ethics for Thought* (London: Humanities Press, 1990), 158.

39. Foucault, *The History of Sexuality, Volume 1,* 151.

40. Ibid., 44.

41. Ibid., 45.

42. Ibid. See Jeremy R. Carrette's illuminating discussion of sexualization, spirituality, and politics in *Foucault and Religion: Spiritual Corporality and Political Spirituality* (London: Routledge, 2000).

43. Augustine, "On the Spirit and the Letter," 25, in *Nicene and Post-Nicene Fathers, First Series*, vol. 5, ed. Philip Schaff (Edinburgh: T. & T. Clark; Grand Rapids: Eerdmans, n.d.).

44. Ibid., 26.

45. Michel Foucault, *Politics, Philosophy, Culture: Interviews and Other Writings, 1977–1984*, ed. Lawrence D. Kritzman (New York: Routledge, Chapman, & Hall, 1988), 118; *Power/Knowledge: Selected Interviews & Other Writings, 1972–1977*, ed. Colin Gordon (New York: Pantheon Books, 1980), 92, 139 f.; and *The History of Sexuality, Volume 1*, 85.

46. Foucault, *The History of Sexuality, Volume 1*, 17.

47. Christos Yannaras argues from an Eastern Orthodox point of view that western Christianity has become harmfully influenced by its strictly negative and juridical understanding of desire, as that has developed from the time of Augustine. See his *Freedom of Morality*, Contemporary Greek Theologians, vol. 3, trans. Elizabeth Briere (Crestwood, N.Y.: Vladimir's Seminary Press, 1984). Although I agree with the sentiment here, I disagree that Augustine puts forward a juridical notion of individual guilt. His emphasis is repeatedly on solidarity, not individuality. And even though he stresses the necessity of living by certain guiding principles in his teachings—for example, in his prohibitions against lying—he reveals a distinctly unjuridical streak both in his understanding of how the desiring person is transformed so as to fulfill such obligations and, as we will see in chapter 5, in his conception of political society as a community that agrees on a shared desire rather than a universal conception of justice. The effects of grace and sin in relation to juridical prescriptions are increasingly held in tension for Augustine and become especially prominent in his later, more Pauline writings. Prohibitive laws force individuals to realize that they cannot fulfill the commands by themselves and thus are drawn back from an isolating guilt to a recognition of their shared complicity and communal need for grace. See Burns, "Augustine on the Origin and Progress of Evil," 22.

48. Augustine, *The Trinity, The Fathers of the Church: A New Translation*, vol. 45, trans. Stephen McKenna, C.SS.R. (Washington, D.C.: Catholic University of America Press, 1963), 8.10.14.

49. Ibid., 9.12.18.

50. Ibid.

51. Augustine, *Confessions*, 10.35.

52. Ibid. See also Jean Bethke Elshtain, *Augustine and the Limits of Politics* (Notre Dame: University of Notre Dame Press, 1995), 61, where concerning Augustine's view of beauty she writes: "Notice how different this version of knowledge of the world is from knowledge that is the form of mastery and appropriation, where what I come to know I must make my own, exploit, and dominate with no reference to the integrity of the thing's own being."

53. Augustine, *The Trinity*, 12.11.16.

54. Augustine, *Confessions*, 5.1.

55. Augustine, *The Trinity*, 12.10.15.

56. Indeed, Peter Brown contends in *The Body and Society*, 416, 418, that in Augustine's later years, "[t]he terrible cascade of helpless misery, of ignorance, arrogance, malice, and violence set up a deafening roar. Beside these devastating ills, sexual temptation was no more than an irritating trickle. . . . Concupiscence was a dark drive to control, to appropriate, and to turn to one's private ends, all the good things that had been created by God to be accepted with gratitude and shared with others. . . . Sexual desire was no more tainted with this tragic, faceless concupiscence than was any other form of human activity. But the very incongruities associated with sexual feelings used the human body as a tiny mirror, in which men and women could glimpse themselves."

57. Augustine, *The Trinity*, 9.9.14.

58. In *Confessions* 2.6, he writes about friendship: "So the soul commits *fornication* when it is turned away from you and, apart from you, seeks such pure, clean things as it does not find except when it returns to you" (translation from Schlabach, "Friendship as Adultery," 130). Cf. 4.8: "My greatest comfort and relief was in the solace of other friends who shared my love of the huge fable which I loved instead of you, my God, the longdrawn lie which our minds were always *itching to hear*, only to be defiled by its adulteress caress." This makes it clear that endless grasping for the noble and the beautiful are also forms of "fornicating" that participate in an endless cycle of reproducing social disappointments and desires to possess. Even sorrow is implicated in such begetting. Augustine speaks of clinging to sorrow as if it were a way to keep alive the presence of his loved one. "Tears alone were sweet to me, for in my heart's desire they had taken the place of my friend" (4.4). Or: "I wept bitter tears and found my only consolation in their very bitterness" (4.6). Augustine's discussions of love and loss, in this regard, show that "fornication" is not just a base grasping but any kind of grasping, even for what is most lovely and temporally sustaining.

59. See Schlabach, "Friendship as Adultery," for a perceptive discussion of "social procreation." As I have already indicated, I generally agree with his argument, but as will become clear in the next section on habit, I would want to emphasize the body's role in this social procreation a little more strongly than he does. I especially appreciate Schlabach's reading of social procreation in terms of instrumental misuses of power. This is central to a more social and historical understanding of sin. He writes: "So the interest here is not to salve the consciences of a promiscuous age but to prick the consciences of an imperialist race bent on overreaching itself." A misguided obsession with sexuality, he continues, "has all too often distracted Christians from applying its lessons to economics, militarism, and violence against the environment" (135).

60. Foucault, *The History of Sexuality, Volume 1*, 136 f.

61. Of course, for Augustine, this transformative hope rests in the grace of God, whereas for Foucault, it rests in the self's own formative potentiality.

62. Foucault discusses these issues in *History of Sexuality, Volume 1,* 25, 123 ff., 136–50.

63. See Peter Brown, "Political Society," in *Augustine: A Collection of Critical Essays,* ed. R. A. Markus (New York: Doubleday, 1972), 317.

64. Augustine, *Confessions,* 4.6, 4.8, 6.16. See Brown, *Augustine of Hippo,* 180, for a discussion of Augustine's having been "delightfully and tragically exposed to 'that most unfathomable of all involvements of the soul—friendship.'" Compare the following from Brown: "the most characteristic anxiety of Augustine, was the manner in which he still felt deeply involved with other people" (180).

65. Augustine, *Confessions,* 4.4.

66. Ibid., 4.8.

67. Ibid., 4.9.

68. See the following, all from the *Confessions:* Augustine wishes to "savour [God's] sweetness" (2.1). He asks God to "[l]et us scent your fragrance and taste your sweetness" (8.4). He notes that "when the fragrance of [God's] perfume allured" he did not answer (9.7). Although one does not yet see God's Word face-to-face, Augustine believes we still "hasten after the fragrance of his perfumes" (13.15).

69. Ibid., 8.11.

70. Ibid., 8.5. Augustine describes habits as at one and the same time being active in sweeping him along and intransigent in holding him fast to those dynamic patterns.

71. Ibid., 8.8.

72. Ibid., 8.11.

73. Ibid.

74. Ibid., 8.5.

75. Ibid.

76. Ibid., 8.11.

77. Augustine wants to separate himself completely from the Manichees, whom he addresses directly in the following: "So let us hear no more of their assertion, when they observe two wills in conflict in one man, that there are two opposing minds in him, one good and the other bad, and that they are in conflict because they spring from two opposing substances and two opposing principles." Ibid., 8.10.

78. Ibid., 8.8.

79. Ibid., 8.9.

80. Ibid., 8.5.

81. Ibid. Cf. "twisted and turned in my chain" from 8.11.

82. Ibid., 8.5.

83. Ibid., 8.10.

84. Ibid., 1.6.

85. At the end of book 8, it seems that he has broken free from his chains. But as we have already noted, Augustine goes on in the *Confessions* to reveal that a long-lasting liberation was a false hope. He is freed to act on conversion, but habits remain for him a performative struggle for the rest of his life. It is one of the main ingredients in his view that the life of the regenerate remains one of convalescence. As William S. Babcock notes in his "Augustine on Sin and Moral Agency," *Journal of Religious Ethics* 16:1 (spring 1998): 28–55, conversion breaks the compulsive hold but does not end the struggle.

86. Michel Foucault, *Discipline and Punish: The Birth of the Prison*, trans. Alan Sheridan (New York: Random House, 1979), 140.

87. Augustine, *The Trinity*, 12.11.16.

88. Augustine, *Confessions*, 8.5.

89. Foucault, *Discipline and Punish*, 156, 161, 163.

90. As I have noted, Foucault contends that this makes them more efficient. I examine this in chapter 5 when addressing institutional power relations.

91. Foucault, *Discipline and Punish*, 141.

92. Ibid., 136 f.

93. Foucault, *Power/Knowledge*, 80.

94. I return to the topic of hope at the end of chapter 5.

95. Foucault, *Discipline and Punish*, 202 ff. I examine Foucault's concerns about the political uses of habituation in chapter 5.

96. Augustine, *Confessions*, 8.5.

97. Foucault, *Discipline and Punish*, 16 ff. See Jeremy R. Carrette's telling critique and commentary on Foucault's use of the term "soul" in *Discipline and Punish* in his *Foucault and Religion: Spiritual Corporality and Political Spirituality* (London: Routledge, 2000), 122 ff.

98. Foucault, *Discipline and Punish*, 18, 104–15, 131.

99. Ibid.

100. Jon Simons notes in *Foucault and the Political*, 32 f.: "It is then, not only the excluded and abnormal who pay the cost of the humanist regime, but all the rest of us who must suppress that part of ourselves that identifies with these excluded others in order to remain normal. . . . So, although resistance is most likely to come from those who are most put upon and marginalized . . . everyone is a potential opponent to humanism."

CHAPTER 4   Fragile Relations and the Price of Perfection:
The Lust for Certitude

1. Augustine, *City of God*, trans. Henry Bettenson (New York: Penguin Books, 1972), 12.6, 12.8. When "the will leaves the higher and turns to the lower, it

becomes bad not because the thing to which it turns is bad, but because the turning is itself perverse" (12.6).

2. Ibid., 12.1.

3. Ibid., 12.9.

4. Ibid., 12.1.

5. Ibid., 12.13.

6. Ibid., 12.13.

7. Ibid., 12.18.

8. Augustine, *Confessions*, trans. R.S. Pine-Coffin (New York: Penguin Books, 1961), 12.1.

9. Ibid., 1.13.

10. Ibid., 1.16.

11. Ibid., 5.6.

12. Augustine, *The Trinity, The Fathers of the Church: A New Translation*, vol. 45, trans. Stephen McKenna, C.SS.R. (Washington, D.C.: Catholic University of America Press, 1963), 9.1.1.

13. Augustine, *Confessions*, 5.3.

14. Augustine, *City of God*, 9.5.

15. This is a repeated theme of Augustine's. For one example, see the opening chapters of *City of God*, bk. 19.

16. Ibid., 19.27.

17. Ibid.

18. Ibid., 19.4.

19. Ibid., 5.14.

20. Ibid., 5.12.

21. Ibid., 5.15.

22. Ibid.

23. Ibid.

24. Ibid.

25. Ibid., 5.17.

26. Ibid., 10.32.

27. Ibid., 19.7.

28. Ibid., 5.19.

29. Ibid.

30. Ibid., 14.28.

31. Ibid., 8.6.

32. Ibid., 8.9.

33. Ibid., 10.29.

34. Ibid.

35. Ibid.

36. Ibid., 10.28.

37. Ibid. Compare the following: "What good, I mean, does it do them to see the home country from the vast distance of their pride? They can't find the way to it, because the way to those heights of the home country starts from humility. They can see the home country, as it were, from the mountain of pride, from the mountain on the other side of the valley. But nobody can go up to it without first coming down. They refuse to come down so that they can go up; that is, they refuse to be humble so that they can become Christians. When they say to themselves, 'And am I going to be what my janitress is, and not rather what Plato was, or Pythagoras?' . . . they are refusing to come down, so they cannot go up." Sermon 198:59; cf. 198:61, both in *The Works of Saint Augustine: A Translation for the 21st Century,* Part III—Sermons, vol. 11: *Newly Discovered Sermons,* trans. Edmund Hill, O.P. (Hyde Park, N.Y.: New City Press, 1977); hereafter cited as *WSA* III/11. See also *Confessions,* 3.4.

38. Augustine, *City of God,* 19.1.

39. "That's how our Lord Jesus Christ did all these things, and because he could see that pride was the root cause of all our disorders, he cured us with his own humility." Sermon 159B:11, in *WSA* III/11; cf. Sermon 159B:13 and Sermon 360B:17, in *WSA* III/11.

40. Augustine uses a variety of metaphors when speaking of sin and salvation. I will be focusing on that of disease/cure, but one should not forget that he also uses other pairings, including guilt/forgiveness, debt/redemption, captivity/liberation, and death/life.

41. See Sermon 159B:12, in *WSA* III/11.

42. Augustine, *City of God,* 10.29.

43. On baptism, see, for instance, Augustine, "The Enchiridion: Being a Treatise on Faith, Hope, and Love," in *Nicene and Post-Nicene Fathers, First Series,* vol. 3, ed. Philip Schaff (Edinburgh: T. & T. Clark; Grand Rapids: Eerdmans, n.d.), chap. 52: "[B]aptism in Christ is nothing but a similitude of the death of Christ." On the Eucharist, see *City of God,* 10.6: "[T]he whole redeemed community, that is to say, the congregation and fellowship of the saints, is offered to God as a universal sacrifice, through the great Priest who offered himself in his suffering for us—so that we might be the body of so great a head—under 'the form of a servant' [Phil. 2.7]"; see also 10.20, 10.31, 17.20.

44. For Augustine, however, there is a crucial distinction between our experience of weakness and that of Jesus Christ; namely, as fully divine, Jesus Christ freely chooses to endure in his full humanity what the rest of us are simply subject to. See, for instance, "The Enchiridion," 49, where Augustine's discussion is focused on Christ's free decision to be baptised and die.

45. Augustine, *City of God,* 10.24.

46. "And the reason why . . . the one who is equal to the Father wished to be the one mediator and himself become man was so that we through a related substance (because he is man) might attain to the supreme substance (because he is God)." Augustine, Sermon 198:49, in *WSA* III/11.

47. On the offense that Christ's lowliness caused, see Sermons 159B:12, 13; 198:40, 41; and 360B:17, 18, in *WSA* III/11.

48. Augustine, *The Trinity,* 2.17.28.

49. Augustine, *City of God,* 19.17. Also see *The Trinity,* 13.14.18, where through this act, Christ's power is promised to the helpless. And compare the following: "The Son of God became a son of man, in order to make sons of men into sons of God. . . . [T]he maker of man was made man, so that man might be made a receiver of God." Sermon 23B:1, in *WSA* III/11. See also Sermon 198:49, in *WSA* III/11; and *Confessions,* 7.18.

50. Augustine, *City of God,* 19.17.

51. Augustine, *The Trinity,* 4.3.6. See also 8.5.7: "[T]he humility, whereby God was born of a woman and was led through such great insults to His death by mortal men, is the most excellent medicine by which the swelling of our pride may be cured." Or again, from Sermon 302:3: "He was a doctor—even while he was being put to death, he was healing the sick with his own blood, by saying, *Father, forgive them, for they know not what they do'* [Lk 23.34]" (in *Political Writings,* ed. E.M. Atkins and R.J. Dodaro [Cambridge: Cambridge University Press, 2001]).

52. Augustine, *The Trinity,* 4.1.2.

53. Ibid., 4.1.1.

54. Ibid., 10.3.5.

55. Augustine, *City of God,* 10.24.

56. To keep the social elite humble, Augustine reminds his parishioners that the lowly come first. "[Christ] didn't choose kings, or senators, or philosophers, or orators; on the contrary, he chose common people, poor people, uneducated people, fishermen. Peter was a fisherman, Cyprian an orator. Unless the fisherman had faithfully gone ahead, the orator would not have humbly approached." Sermon 198:60, in *WSA* III/11; cf. Sermon 360B:24.

57. Augustine, *The Trinity,* 4.1.2. Compare the following: "people should not in humility despair of themselves, nor presumptuously rely on themselves in pride." Sermon 198:44, in *WSA* III/11.

58. Augustine, *City of God,* 10.6.

59. Augustine, Sermon 299A:8, in *WSA* III/11. Compare the following: "In the uncertainty which still restricts our human knowledge you alone can distinguish between us and those who are still in darkness, for it is you who *scrutinize our hearts* and *call the light day and the darkness night.* Who but you can tell us apart?" (Augustine, *Confessions,* 13.14). One cannot, on Augustine's terms, simply equate the institutional church with the heavenly city, for "many reprobates are mingled in the Church with the good, and both sorts are collected as it were in the dragnet of the gospel; and in this world, as in a sea, both kind swim without separation, enclosed in nets until the shore is reached" (Augustine, *City of God,* 18.49). Nor did Augustine contend that all those outside the church are necessarily lost. The City of God "must bear in mind that among these very enemies are hidden her future citizens; . . .

some predestined friends, as yet unknown even to themselves, are concealed among our most open enemies" (*City of God,* 1.35) For further discussion, see R. A. Markus, *Saeculum: History and Society in the Theology of St. Augustine* (New York: Cambridge University Press, 1970), 61. I return to this topic in the context of addressing myself to John Milbank's criticisms of Markus's work in chapter 5.

60. Augustine, *Confessions,* 13.13. The emphasis (indicating biblical phrases) is the translator's.

61. Peter Brown, *Augustine of Hippo* (Berkeley: University of California Press, 1967), 177, citing A. D. Nock, *Conversion: The Old and the New in Religion from Alexander the Great to Augustine of Hippo* (1933), 179 f.

62. In chapter 5, we examine two of the more influential of these: William Connolly, *The Augustinian Imperative: A Reflection on the Politics of Morality* (Newbury Park, Calif.: Sage, 1993); and Romand Coles, *Self/Power/Other* (Ithaca: Cornell University Press, 1992).

63. Michel Foucault, *The Order of Things: An Archaeology of the Human Sciences* (New York: Random House, 1970), 387.

64. Augustine, *Confessions,* 1.13.

65. Ibid., 7.8; see also the following description of Paul, from 10.31: "But he too was dust and could not do all things by his own power."

66. Ibid., 6.11; cf. 4.14.

67. Ibid., 11.28; cf. 12.15.

68. Ibid., 1.8.

69. Ibid., 1.19.

70. Ibid., 1.18.

71. Ibid., 1.9.

72. Ibid., 1.19.

73. Ibid., 1.9.

74. Ibid., 6.4; cf. 3.3.

75. Michel Foucault, *Politics, Philosophy, Culture: Interviews and Other Writings, 1977–1984,* ed. Lawrence D. Kritzman (New York: Routledge, Chapman, & Hall, 1988), 156.

76. For a fuller discussion of these issues, see James W. Bernauer, *Michel Foucault's Force of Flight: Toward an Ethics of Thought* (London: Humanities Press, 1990), 178–84; and "Cry of Spirit," foreword to Michel Foucault, *Religion and Culture,* ed. Jeremy R. Carrette (New York: Routledge, 1999), xiv–xvi.

77. Augustine, *Confessions,* 1.6.

78. Ibid., 1.20.

79. Ibid., 12.10.

80. Ibid., 10.34.

81. Michel Foucault, *Power/Knowledge: Selected Interviews & Other Writings, 1972–1977,* ed. Colin Gordon (New York: Pantheon Books, 1980), 126. See also Foucault, *Politics, Philosophy, and Culture,* 155.

82. Michel Foucault, *The History of Sexuality, Volume 1: An Introduction* (New York: Vintage Books, 1980), 59.

83. Ibid., 64.

84. Foucault, *Politics, Philosophy, Culture*, 30.

85. Foucault, *History of Sexuality, Volume 1*, 78.

86. Ibid., 79.

87. Foucault, *Politics, Philosophy, Culture*, 111.

88. Foucault, *Power/Knowledge*, 193.

89. Michel Foucault, *Discipline and Punish: The Birth of the Prison*, trans. Alan Sheridan (New York: Random House, 1979), 293.

90. Michel Foucault, "The Life of Infamous Men," in *Michel Foucault: Power, Truth, Strategy*, ed. M. Morris and P. Patton (Sydney: Feral, 1979), 79 f. Cited in Jeremy R. Carrette, *Foucault and Religion: Spiritual Corporality and Political Spirituality* (London: Routledge, 2000), 34.

91. Foucault, "The Life of Infamous Men," 77; cited in Carrette, *Foucault and Religion*, 34.

92. Foucault, "The Life of Infamous Men," 77; cited in Bernauer, *Michel Foucault's Force of Flight*, 182.

93. Some may argue with me on this point because in lectures and interviews he will at times draw a fairly straight line from the Christian focus on sexual discourse to a modern one. For an example of such imprecision in a lecture, see Michel Foucault, *Technologies of the Self: A Seminar with Michel Foucault*, ed. Luther H. Martin, Huck Gutman, and Patrick H. Hutton (Amherst: University of Massachusetts Press, 1988), 48. My point is simply that in his lectures such errors are relatively rare. In *The History of Sexuality, Volume 1*, he argues for the existence of a distinct shift in the modern era that is related to a scientific understanding of truth.

94. Foucault, *Technologies of the Self*, 38–49. See also Michel Foucault, "On the Genealogy of Ethics: An Overview of Work in Progress," second afterword (1983) to *Michel Foucault: Beyond Structuralism and Hermeneutics*, 2d edition, ed. Hubert L. Dreyfus and Paul Rabinow (Chicago: University of Chicago Press, 1983), 244–48; and Foucault, *Religion and Culture*, 157. These are the same dangers later penitential practices responded to in the seventeenth century. See Foucault, *History of Sexuality, Volume 1*, 19 ff.

95. Foucault, *Technologies of the Self*, 38–49. Foucault describes these under the term *exagoreusis*, which he interprets as the ancient precursor to medieval confessional practices. He also discusses early Christian penitential practices, *exomologesis*. However, his analysis completely misses the communal power of the ritual.

96. Foucault, "On the Genealogy of Ethics," 242 ff. Mobility was both an asset and a threat. It made one malleable but also presented difficulties in keeping hold of the ever-moving soul. See also Foucault, *Religion and Culture*, 156, where Foucault talks both about the "mobility of soul" and the constantly vigilant sorting process involved in spiritual decipherment. See also *Religion and Culture*, 195.

97. Foucault, *Technologies of the Self,* 21–22, 35–49.

98. Ibid., 21.

99. Foucault, "On the Genealogy of Ethics," 249 f. See also Foucault, *Religion and Culture,* 157. Foucault clearly prefers Greek philosophy but becomes fascinated by Christian asceticism near the end of his life. He is especially interested in John Cassian and St. Anthony.

100. Foucault, *Religion and Culture,* 195.

101. Foucault, *Technologies of the Self,* 46.

102. Foucault cites along with Augustine, certain ancient Greek writers who use this technology in *Technologies of the Self,* 28.

103. Foucault, *Religion and Culture,* 195. See also 156 f. and 194–97.

104. Ibid., 196.

105. Augustine, *Confessions,* 10.23 (Peter Brown's translation, from *Augustine of Hippo,* 178).

106. Peter Brown, *Augustine of Hippo,* 178–79.

107. Foucault, *Religion and Culture,* 45.

108. Ibid., 142.

109. Ibid., 138.

110. Ibid., 143.

111. Ibid., 143, 157.

112. Ibid., 196. I am relying primarily on one article that develops this theme in depth. Foucault's view is somewhat inconsistent up until the end. This article, however, presents the monastic technologies of the self in an illuminating way and is more helpful than many of his other writings in establishing his view of the differences between early and later Christian practices.

113. Ibid., 193.

114. Ibid.

115. Ibid., 189.

116. Peter Brown, in distinguishing Cassian's understanding of sexual lust from a post-Freudian one, makes a point similar to Foucault's: "Sullen resentments, unacknowledged egotism, and a diffuse anger lay congealed, in the soul, like undispersed residues of noxious humors. Only by remaining alert to his own sexual temptation could the monk measure the continued, debilitating presence within him of more tenacious spiritual ailments. He must approach his sexual fantasies much as a doctor felt the pulse to learn about his patient's true condition. Such medical terminology bears so striking a resemblance to the clinical language of 'depth psychology' that a modern reader is easily misled. Cassian, however, was a loyal follower of the Desert Fathers on this issue. Sexuality, for him, was not what it has become in the lay imagination of a post-Freudian age. It was not the basic instinctual drive, of which all others were secondary refractions. It was the other way around. The colder drives that lured the human person into collusion with the demonic world were more basic to the monk's concern. They lay deeper in his identity than did sexual desire.

Sexuality was a mere epiphenomenon." *The Body and Society: Men, Women, and Sexual Renunciation in Early Christianity* (New York: Columbia University Press, 1988), 421f.

117. Although they must be reformed together through renunciation, fornication is still treated differently since it is the only vice that one can try to extirpate completely. With the others, one reaches virtue through a certain degree of moderation.

118. Foucault, *Religion and Culture*, 196.

119. My aim in the following analysis is not to assess the accuracy of Foucault's description of ancient, medieval, and Tridentine confessional practices. Rather, my focus is on making clear the important cultural changes he sees as evidenced in the historical eras he studies. Having said that, however, let me briefly comment on the narrow scope of his research. Foucault does not pay sufficient attention to the Celtic influences when he develops the idea of confession as "individualizing." Nor does he adequately investigate the popular (in contrast to institutional) development and use of penitential manuals. The institutional pressures to make confessional practices uniform arise from a diverse web of local practices that differed widely depending on what particular manual was being used for self-examination and spiritual direction. His historical portrayal is thus extremely one-dimensional.

120. Foucault, *Religion and Culture*, 191.

121. Ibid., 188.

122. Foucault, *History of Sexuality, Volume 1*, 20.

123. Ibid., 188.

124. Foucault, *Religion and Culture*, 196.

125. Ibid.

126. Foucault, *History of Sexuality, Volume 1*, 19.

127. Ibid.

128. Ibid.

129. Ibid., 20.

130. Ibid., 35.

131. Ibid., 11.

132. Ibid., 35.

133. Ibid., 21.

134. Ibid., 35.

135. Ibid., 32, 66, 58, 64.

136. Ibid., 69.

137. Ibid., 59.

138. Foucault, *Power/Knowledge*, 154.

139. Ibid., 153.

140. Foucault, *The History of Sexuality, Volume 1*, 53.

141. Ibid., 55.

142. Ibid., 55f.

143. Ibid., 29.

144. Ibid., 24.

145. Ibid., 32.

146. Ibid., 117.

147. Ibid., 113.

148. Ibid., 117.

149. Michel Foucault, "The Subject and Power," afterword to Dreyfus and Rabinow, *Michel Foucault: Beyond Structuralism and Hermeneutics*, 215.

150. Michel Foucault, "History, Discourse, and Discontinuity," *Salmagundi* 20 (1972): 244.

151. Dreyfus and Rabinow, *Michel Foucault: Beyond Structuralism and Hermeneutics*, 163.

152. Foucault, *The History of Sexuality, Volume 1*, 67.

153. For Foucault's discussion of the hysterization of women's bodies, see *The History of Sexuality, Volume 1*, 104, 121, 146 f. He also discusses the vulnerability of women in marriage in terms of how they have been classified as the nervous woman, frigid wife, or indifferent mother on 110. See also Foucault, *Politics, Philosophy, Culture*, 115; and *Power/Knowledge*, 191, 220. His analysis of modernity's intense focus on the sexuality of children can be found in *The History of Sexuality, Volume 1*, 38, 41 f., 98 f., 104 f., 120 f. Modern attitudes to homosexuality are discussed on 37–43 and 101. For sexuality and the mentally ill, see 30, 36–38, 111 f.

154. Foucault, *The History of Sexuality, Volume 1*, 39 f.

155. Ibid., 31 ff.

156. Ibid., 89. See also Foucault, *Power/Knowledge*, 106 f.

157. Foucault, *The History of Sexuality, Volume 1*, 39.

158. Foucault, *Discipline and Punish*, 192; *The History of Sexuality, Volume 1*, 47 f.

159. Foucault, *The History of Sexuality, Volume 1*, 44.

160. Foucault, *Discipline and Punish*, 191; *The History of Sexuality, Volume 1*, 58.

161. Foucault, *Discipline and Punish*, 192.

162. Foucault, *The History of Sexuality, Volume 1*, 43 f.

163. Ibid., 44; see also 47 f. and 65.

164. Foucault, *Discipline and Punish*, 193; see also *The History of Sexuality, Volume 1*, 58.

165. Foucault, *Discipline and Punish*, 189 ff.

166. Ibid., 192 f.

167. Foucault, "The Subject and Power," 215.

168. Foucault, *The History of Sexuality, Volume 1*, 71.

169. Ibid., 67 f.

170. Ibid., 44.

171. Foucault, *Discipline and Punish*, 193.

172. Foucault, *The History of Sexuality, Volume 1*, 45. Emphasis in original.

173. Ibid., 7.

174. Foucault, *Politics, Power, Culture*, 114.

175. Foucault, *The History of Sexuality, Volume 1*, 33.
176. Ibid., 159.
177. Ibid.
178. Ibid., 11.
179. Ibid., 29 f.
180. Ibid., 66 f.
181. Ted Peters, ed., *Genetics: Issues of Social Justice* (Cleveland: Pilgrim Press, 1998), 15.
182. Ibid.

CHAPTER 5   Deconstructing Privileged Discourses:
The Ambiguity of Social Achievements

1. There has been considerable debate among Augustinian scholars regarding the sociological status of the political society constituted by these relations (i.e., of what Augustine called the *saeculum*). I find Eugene TeSelle's reading the most consonant with my own, in that he does not regard the *saeculum* as a neutral sphere between the earthly and heavenly cities. The earthly and heavenly cities are simply too intermingled to support such a view. See Eugene TeSelle, *Living in Two Cities: Augustinian Trajectories in Political Thought* (Scranton: University of Scranton Press, 1998), 42 f.

2. Augustine, *City of God*, trans. Henry Bettenson (New York: Penguin Books, 1972), 19.15. My reading of *City of God*, book 19, where Augustine provides his most sustained, mature treatment of the political sphere of human association, owes much to the work of R. A. Markus, *Saeculum: History and Society in the Theology of St. Augustine* (New York: Cambridge University Press, 1970/1988), esp. chap. 4. See also his "Two Conceptions of Political Authority: Augustine, *De Civitate Dei*, XIX.14–15, and Some Thirteenth-Century Interpretations," *Journal of Theological Studies* (NS) 16 (1965): 68–100. I would also mention Miika Roukanen, *The Theology of the Social Life in Augustine's* De Civitate Dei (Göttingen: Vandenhoeck & Ruprecht, 1993). Both Markus and Roukanen believe that because Augustine's description of political power makes *libido dominandi* fundamental, it would be contradictory to try to justify including the political realm in the naturally good, prelapsarian social structures. Peter Brown agrees, noting in "Political Society," in *Augustine: A Collection of Critical Essays*, ed. R. A. Markus (New York: Doubleday, 1972), 31: "The symptoms . . . which tend to predominate in [Augustine's] description of human political activity can only be thought of as symptoms of a disease." Rowan Williams voices a similar view in "Politics and the Soul: A Reading of the *City of God*," *Milltown Studies* 19:20 (1987): 63. For a contrary opinion, see Donald X. Burt, O. S. A., "St. Augustine's Evaluations of Civil Society," *Augustinianum* 3 (1963): 87–94. John Milbank does not hesitate to describe Augustine's view of prelapsarian society as "political," though he is careful

to note that postlapsarian political relations are coercive while prelapsarian ones are not. See his *Theology and Social Theory: Beyond Secular Reason* (Oxford: Blackwell, 1990, 1993), 406, 410. Ernest L. Fortin adopts the same usage as Milbank, although he bases his decision on a relatively early text (*De libera arbitrio* [On the Free Choice of the Will], written between 387 and 395) that Milbank does not cite. See Fortin's *Classical Christianity and the Political Order: Reflections on the Theologico-Political Problem* (New York: Rowman & Littlefield, 1996), 52.

3. Augustine, *City of God*, 19.12. For his definition of a "people" in terms of the object of their love, see 19.24.

4. Ibid., 19.12.

5. Jean Bethke Elshtain, Review of *The Limits of Virtue* by James Wetzel, *Augustinian Studies* 24 (1993): 190. See also her *Augustine and the Limits of Politics* (Notre Dame: University of Notre Dame Press, 1995), 91.

6. Augustine specifically criticizes Rome's longing or desire for glory (*cupiditas gloriae*) in *City of God*, 5.12–14. I borrow the phrase "rhetoric of glory" from the insightful essay by Robert Dodaro, "Eloquent Lies, Just Wars and the Politics of Persuasion: Reading Augustine's *City of God* in a 'Postmodern' World," *Augustinian Studies* 25 (1994): 77–94. Dodaro's discussion led me to reflect on the similarities and differences between Augustine's and Foucault's deconstruction of privileged discourses in their respective societies. Elshtain also helped to shape my analysis of the political and critical significance of similar passages in the *City of God*, especially as they pertain to just war, in *Augustine and the Limits of Politics*, 105–12. She and Dodaro persuasively argue that in passages like these Augustine anticipates modern cultural criticism.

7. On the narrow point of war's "peaceful" purpose, see Augustine, *City of God*, 19.12. More general discussions of war can be found in that book, as well as in books 1, 3, 4, 5, 15, 18.

8. Ibid., 3.26.

9. Ibid., 19.7.

10. Ibid.

11. Ibid., 4.15.

12. One can identify an exception to this generalization. On Augustine's view, combatants in a just war that is authorized by divine command (e.g., the battles recounted in Joshua) fight in obedience to God. Their motive is thus free of the taint of the *libido dominandi*. See Frederick H. Russell, "War," in *Augustine through the Ages: An Encyclopedia*, ed. Allan D. Fitzgerald, O.S.A. (Grand Rapids: Eerdmans, 1999), 875f. The post-incarnational significance of this exception is limited, if not eliminated altogether, by Augustine's refusal in his mature theology to identify any event or period after the coming of Jesus Christ as unambiguously salvific. "Every moment may have its unique and mysterious significance in the ultimate divine *tableau* of men's doings and sufferings; but it is a significance to which God's revelation [in scripture] does not supply the clues." Markus, *Saeculum*, 21. Accordingly,

we must remain alert to the ways our desire to control others infects even our most just wars.

13. Augustine, *City of God*, 3.11, 5.12.

14. Ibid., 3.10.

15. Ibid., 19.7.

16. Ibid.

17. Ibid.; cf. 1.21.

18. Ibid., 4.3. Augustine here describes the joys obtained by Roman wars, some of which, as I have noted, he believed were just. Augustine could also have illustrated the fragility of peace secured by just wars with Alaric's sacking of Rome in 410, for he believed Constantine's conquest of the city, as well as his subsequent expansion and defense of his empire, was just. Indeed, they numbered among the gifts "heaped" on Constantine by God. Ibid., 5.26.

19. Ibid., 3.14.

20. Ibid., 19.7; cf. 3.14.

21. Ibid.

22. Ibid., 3.14.

23. Ibid., 4.4.

24. Ibid.

25. Ibid., 19.13.

26. Ibid., 3.14.

27. Ibid., 4.5.

28. Ibid., 3.14.

29. Ibid., 19.7; cf. 3.14.

30. Ibid., 3.14.

31. Ibid., 5.22.

32. Ibid., 3.14.

33. Ibid.

34. Augustine, Sermon 23B:13, in *The Works of Saint Augustine: A Translation for the 21st Century*, Part III—Sermons, vol. 11: *Newly Discovered Sermons*, trans. Edmund Hill, O.P. (Hyde Park, N.Y.: New City Press, 1997); hereafter cited as *WSA* III/11.

35. Augustine, *City of God*, 4.3.

36. Ibid., 5.18. See also Letter 229:2, in *Political Writings*, ed. E.M. Atkins and R.J. Dodaro (Cambridge: Cambridge University Press, 2001).

37. Augustine, *City of God*, 3.14.

38. Although in the following excerpt from a sermon Augustine is making a point about earthly success in general, rather than in combat, the same principle applies. "Think of all those Christians who are carried off before they grow up; and of the idolaters who survive this life and live to a frail old age. On the other hand, many of them also die young. Christians suffer many losses; the impious often make profits; but then again, Christians often make profits while the impious suffer losses. Many of the impious receive honours, and many Christians get rejections; but then

again, many of the impious get rejections, and many Christians win honours. Success and failure are shared by both groups." Sermon 302:3, in *Political Writings*. On the narrower military point, Rowan Williams notes that for Augustine, "[t]he well-governed state is not automatically the victorious state; God gives or withholds extensiveness and duration of dominion as he pleases." "Politics and the Soul," 65.

39. Augustine, *City of God*, 5.17.

40. Ibid., 4.3.

41. Ibid., 3.14.

42. Ibid.

43. Ibid., 5.14.

44. Ibid., 10.21.

45. Ibid., 10.22. See also 5.14; and "Homilies on the Gospel of John," 116.1, in *Nicene and Post-Nicene Fathers, First Series*, vol. 4, ed. Philip Schaff (Peabody, Mass.: Hendrickson Publishers, 1994; 1886–89).

46. Augustine, *City of God*, 19.14. This is a general directive for all Christians, not just martyrs, although they best exemplify it.

47. Augustine, Sermon 335C:4, in *Political Writings*; and *City of God*, 5.14. See also Letter 138:13 and Letter 173:5, both in *Political Writings*.

48. Augustine, *City of God*, 5.14.

49. Ibid. See also Sermon 335C:1, in *Political Writings*.

50. Augustine, Sermon 335C:11, in *Political Writings*; and *City of God*, 5.14.

51. Augustine, *City of God*, 5.14.

52. Ibid. See also Sermon 283:1, in *WSA* III/11.

53. Augustine, *City of God*, 10.21

54. Augustine, Sermon 306E:2, in *WSA* III/11.

55. Sermon 283:1, in *WSA* III/11.; Sermon 335C:4, in *Political Writings*; "Homilies on the Gospel of John," 6.23.

56. Sermons 335C:12 and 302:9, both in *Political Writings*.

57. Peter Brown observes: "Citizens of the Roman Empire at its height, in the second century A.D., were born into the world with an average life expectancy of less than twenty-five years. Death fell savagely on the young. Those who survived childhood remained at risk. Only four out of every hundred men, and fewer women, lived beyond the age of fifty. It was a population 'grazed thin by death.'" *The Body and Society: Men, Women, and Sexual Renunciation in Early Christianity* (New York: Columbia University Press, 1988), 6, quoting John Chrysostom, *De virginitate* 14.1.

58. Augustine, Sermon 306E:7, in *WSA* III/11.

59. Sermon 306E:8; cf. 306E:7. In *WSA* III/11.

60. Sermon 335C:12, in *Political Writings*.

61. Sermon 306E:6, in *WSA* III/11.

62. Sermon 302:9, in *Political Writings*.

63. Augustine, *City of God*, 10.5.

64. Ibid.

65. Ibid., 4.3.

66. Ibid., 19.2.

67. Ibid., 19.17.

68. See Todd Breyfogle, "Punishment," in Fitzgerald, ed., *Augustine through the Ages*, 689.

69. Recall from the discussion in chapter 1 that Augustine does not believe that hierarchical relations are necessarily abusive. Still, recognizing that all leaders operate to one degree or another under the condition of original sin, he warns us to be alert for ways in which differentials of power can be misused.

70. Augustine, *The Trinity, The Fathers of the Church: A New Translation*, vol. 45, trans. Stephen McKenna, C.SS.R. (Washington, D.C.: Catholic University of America Press, 1963), 8.8.12.

71. Augustine, *City of God*, 5.19. They had to wield that power, however, in the service of cultivating a deeper love for God and neighbor among the people. See Letter 155:10, in *Political Writings*.

72. Markus makes the same point in *Saeculum*, 146 ff. John Milbank agrees; see his *Theology and Social Theory*, 407.

73. Augustine, *City of God*, 17.4; cf. 2.21.

74. Ibid., 5.24.

75. Peter Brown famously dismisses these pages as among the most shoddy in the *City of God*.

76. Augustine, *City of God*, 5.26.

77. Markus details the transformations in Augustine's thought on the question in chapter 2 of *Saeculum*; see especially 29 ff. Markus's argument would seem to depend on Augustine having adopted the optimistic patriotism of Eusebian establishment theology, a point denied by F. G. Maier, *Augustin und das antike Rom* (Stuttgart: W. Kohlhammer, 1995). Ernest Fortin also doubts that Augustine underwent the dramatic transformation from establishment theologian to restless theological critic (*Classical Christianity and the Political Order*, 125). The crucial point, for my argument at least, is not threatened by this dispute, since Markus's critics acknowledge that in the *City of God* Augustine dismisses the Eusebian idea that the conversion of the Roman Empire was, in Fortin's words, "a crucial turning point in the history of the Church," characterizing it instead as "a mere episode in an ongoing process no single moment of which is to be privileged over any other moment" (*Classical Christianity and the Political Order*, 128).

78. Markus, *Saeculum*, 40.

79. Ibid., 21: "Every moment may have its unique and mysterious significance in the ultimate divine *tableau* of men's doings and sufferings; but it is a significance to which God's revelation does not supply the clues." Compare Ernest Fortin's similar comment, quoted above.

80. Augustine, *City of God*, 19.17.

81. Markus discusses Augustine's debate with the Donatists in *Saeculum*, chap. 5. In light of that discussion, John Milbank's criticism of Markus for under-playing Augustine's explicit identification of the visible, institutional church with the City of God on pilgrimage is unpersuasive (Milbank, *Theology and Social Theory*, 400 ff.). Markus repeatedly acknowledges that Augustine makes such an identi-fication. He argues that Augustine simply assumes "as a given . . . the identity of the Church and the 'heavenly city'" (*Saeculum*, 118; cf. 117). Nor is Milbank cor-rect when contending that Markus minimizes the importance of the sacramental life of the church in Augustine's definition (Milbank, *Theology and Social Theory*, 402). Markus contends that for Augustine, "[t]he Church was primarily the so-ciety of the redeemed, the holy, the pious gathered in worship and sacrifice. This was its fundamental reality, unimpaired by the hidden workings within it of an 'underground movement' [i.e., the earthly city]" (Markus, *Saeculum*, 118). It is certainly true that Markus emphasizes Augustine's conviction that the holiness of the *corpus permixtum* of the church as pilgrim attains its fullness eschatologically, but that reflects the dialectical view of Augustine's ecclesiology, the Pauline ten-sion between the already and the not yet. Markus insists that for Augustine the visible church "is subject to the permanent tension between what is here and now and the eschatological reality to be disclosed in and through it" (*Saeculum*, 120). In my view, because Milbank fails explicitly to address this tension, his account of Augustine's ecclesiology is misleading. His highly polemical response to Markus is troubling for the ease with which, in his characterization of Augustine's views, he uses "true Church," "true society," "the City of God," and "the realized heavenly city" interchangeably with "the visible, institutional Church" (Milbank, *Theology and Social Theory*, 402 f.). Such straightforward identifications need to be bal-anced with an open discussion of Augustine's contention that inhabitants of both cities can be found within and without the confines of the visible, institutional church, and that only in the life to come will one be certain to which city he or she belongs.

82. Elshtain, *Augustine and the Limits of Politics*, 91.

83. Paradoxically, Augustine himself, in justifying imperial coercion of the Donatists, provides a good example of this. Admittedly, such coercion took place not in the political but in the religious arena, where Augustine passionately believed ultimate concerns were at stake. Augustine, then, seems to believe that when our highest beliefs are at issue, the door is open to using more extreme means for accomplishing our end. Unfortunately, however, Augustine failed to realize the diffi-culty, once we take the step of condoning religious coercion, of distinguishing this from political coercion to achieve political ends. See Milbank's insightful discus-sion of the incoherence involved in Augustine's endorsement and use of coercion, even in religious matters, in his *Theology and Social Theory*, 417 ff.

84. Augustine, *City of God*, 19.6.

85. Ibid.

86. Ibid.

87. Ibid.

88. Ibid.

89. Ibid.

90. Ibid.

91. Ibid. See also Sermon 302:16, in *Political Writings*.

92. Augustine, Sermon 13:4, in *Political Writings*.

93. Augustine, Letter 95:3, in *Political Writings*. Augustine writes this in the context of judicial judgments, over which he often expressed great concern and perplexity. "[W]hat limit ought to be set to punishment with regard to both the nature and extent of the guilt, and also the strength of spirit the wrongdoers possess? What ought each one to suffer? What ought he to avoid, not just in case he doesn't progress, but even in case he regresses? Again, I don't know whether more people are reformed than slip into worse ways through fear of impending punishment (when they fear it is coming from human beings, that is). What do we do when, as often happens, punishing someone will lead to his destruction, but leaving him unpunished will lead to someone else being destroyed?" Ibid.

94. Augustine, Letter 153:8, in *Political Writings*. See also Letter 133:1 and Letter 134:2, both in *Political Writings*.

95. In a sermon against vigilantism, Augustine urges his parishioners, "[I]t is not enough to refrain from this sort of thing yourselves, and it is not enough to grieve, unless you also do your very best to prevent an action that ordinary people have no authority to carry out. . . . [I]n your own homes you have each got your sons, your slaves, your friends, your neighbours, your dependents, your juniors. Make sure that they don't behave like this! If you can persuade any of them not to, do so." Sermon 302:19, in *Political Writings*.

96. Augustine, *City of God*, 19.6.

97. In the foregoing I have relied heavily on Markus's account in *Saeculum*, 72 ff., of the classical *polis*-centered tradition of Greco-Roman ethics.

98. Milbank, *Theology and Social Theory*, 400f.

99. Augustine, *City of God*, 19.4.

100. Williams, "Politics and the Soul," 61.

101. Ibid., 68.

102. Augustine, *City of God*, 19.15.

103. Augustine, *Confessions*, trans. R. S. Pine-Coffin (New York: Penguin Books, 1961), 1.9.

104. Ibid., 1.13.

105. Ibid., 1.18, 1.12.

106. Augustine served as the orator for the city of Milan from 384 until 386. His responsibilities included delivering panegyrics in honor of Emperor Valentinian II and Flavius Bauto, the *magister militum* to the emperor. See R. A. Dodaro's "Principal Dates," in *Political Writings*, xxxiii.

272 — Notes to Pages 181–90

107. Although one can certainly argue that contemporary military exercises of power continue to use a rhetoric of glory to guard themselves against moral scrutiny, even now they speak of "surgical strikes" and "smart weapons" and "collateral damage" in an effort to minimize the horrors of war.

108. For this and the rest of the description that follows, see Michel Foucault, *Discipline and Punish: The Birth of the Prison*, trans. Alan Sheridan (New York: Random House, 1979), 195–200.

109. Ibid., 196.

110. Ibid.

111. Ibid.

112. Ibid., 195.

113. Ibid., 196 f.

114. Ibid., 198.

115. Ibid.

116. Ibid., 197.

117. Ibid., 198.

118. Ibid., 199. It is imperative that we realize that Foucault is not targeting all uses of discipline. Techniques of discipline can be used positively to constitute and cultivate one's own intellectual and practical capacities. Foucault's concern lies with those practices that have as their aim dominating and subjecting other persons and forming them in such a way as to make them politically or economically useful.

119. Ibid., 199 f.

120. Michel Foucault, *L' Impossible prison* (Paris: Editions du Seuil, 1980), 31; cited in Hubert L. Dreyfus and Paul Rabinow, *Michel Foucault: Beyond Structuralism and Hermeneutics* (Chicago: University of Chicago Press, 1982), 133.

121. Sissela Bok, *Secrets: On the Ethics of Concealment and Revelation* (New York: Vintage Books, 1982, 1989), 115.

122. *Pièces originales et procédures du procès fait à Robert François Damiens*, III, 1757, 372–74. Cited in Foucault, *Discipline and Punish*, 3.

123. Augustine, *City of God*, 19.1–9.

124. Foucault, *Discipline and Punish*, 34.

125. Ibid., 188.

126. Ibid., 49.

127. Ibid., 51.

128. Ibid., 48.

129. Ibid., 49.

130. Ibid., 40.

131. Ibid., 57.

132. Ibid., 10.

133. Ibid., 11.

134. Ibid., 200.

135. Ibid., 201.

136. Ibid., 187 ff.

137. Ibid., 202.

138. Ibid., 202 f. Compare the following: "There is no need for arms, physical violence, material constraints. Just a gaze. An inspecting gaze, a gaze which each individual under its weight will end by interiorising to the point that he is his own overseer, each individual thus exercising this surveillance over, and against himself." Michel Foucault, *Power/Knowledge: Selected Interviews & Other Writings, 1972–1977*, ed. Colin Gordon (New York: Pantheon Books, 1980), 155.

139. Foucault, *Discipline and Punish*, 202.

140. Ibid., 205.

141. Ibid., 93.

142. Ibid., 220.

143. Ibid., 149.

144. Ibid., 137.

145. Ibid., 137 f.

146. Ibid., 138. By investing the body's operations, this form of domination does of course involve in its web of complex effects both self-involvement and self-relation. I discussed Foucault's view of our complicity in social evils in chapter 2. We will note the intricacies of complicity once again when we examine his model of generalized disciplinary power, "panopticism," below, particularly in my treatment of the role of judges.

147. Ibid., 150.

148. Ibid.

149. Ibid., 154.

150. Ibid., 152.

151. Ibid., 151.

152. Ibid., 143.

153. Ibid.

154. Ibid., 144.

155. Ibid., 148.

156. Ibid., 150.

157. Ibid., 235 f.

158. Ibid., 236.

159. Ibid., 170.

160. Ibid., 208.

161. Ibid., 26.

162. Ibid., 137.

163. Ibid.

164. See Foucault, *Power/Knowledge*, 116, 126, 131.

165. Foucault, *Discipline and Punish*, 19.

166. Ibid., 17 f.

167. Ibid., 100.

168. It is the attempt to settle these escalating concerns, on Foucault's analysis, that finally conjoins the theoretical fields of "science" and "medicine" to "jurisprudence."

169. Foucault, *Discipline and Punish*, 19.

170. Ibid.

171. Ibid., 21.

172. Ibid., 18 f. See Jeremy R. Carrette's discussion of the *soul* in *Foucault and Religion: Spiritual Corporality and Political Spirituality* (London: Routledge, 2000), chap. 6.

173. Foucault, *Discipline and Punish*, 10.

174. Ibid., 11.

175. Ibid., 56.

176. Ibid., 22.

177. Ibid., 19.

178. Ibid., 9 f.

179. Michel Foucault, *The History of Sexuality, Volume 1: An Introduction* (New York: Vintage Books, 1980), 135 ff. The quotation ("life-administering power") is from 136.

180. Ibid., 138.

181. Foucault, *Discipline and Punish*, 9 f.

182. Michael C. Brannigan and Judith A. Ross, eds., *Healthcare Ethics in a Diverse Society* (Mountain View, Calif.: Mayfield, 2001), 171.

183. I am not suggesting that these are the only tactics Augustine employs. As Robert Dodaro points out in his "Eloquent Lies, Just Wars and the Politics of Persuasion," Augustine also uses irony to create the same effect. See especially Augustine's send-up of the attitudes of Rome's ruling class in *City of God*, 2.20, which Dodaro discusses at 84 f.

184. Foucault, *Power/Knowledge*, 149.

185. Ibid., 147.

EPILOGUE   Paradoxes of Political Hope and Humility

1. Hubert L. Dreyfus and Paul Rabinow argue that Foucault is not explicitly hostile to metanarratives; he simply is engaged in a different enterprise, which, given its parameters, does not take into account any kind of larger overview. "Foucault is not trying to construct a general theory, nor deconstruct the possibility of any metanarrative; rather, he's offering us an interpretive analytic of our current situation." See "What Is Maturity? Habermas and Foucault on 'What Is Enlightenment?'" in *Foucault: A Critical Reader*, ed. David Couzens Hoy (Oxford: Blackwell, 1986), 114 f.

2. Nancy Fraser, "Foucault on Modern Power: Empirical Insights and Normative Confusions," *Praxis International* 1 (1981): 286.

3. Michel Foucault, "Power and Strategies," in *Power/Knowledge*, 134; cited in Margaret R. Miles, *Practicing Christianity: Critical Perspectives for an Embodied Spirituality* (New York: Crossroad, 1988), 183.

4. Miles, *Practicing Christianity*, 183.

5. I would argue that Jeffrey Stout's interpretation of moral justification is most compatible with Foucault's own efforts and can be used without contradicting Foucault's ad hoc and limited critical objectives. See *Ethics after Babel: The Languages of Morals and Their Discontents* (Boston: Beacon Press, 1988).

6. The term "bracketing" was first used by Dreyfus and Rabinow but has entered into the general philosophical debate about how best to read Foucault. It is referred to by both Foucault's opponents and his supporters.

7. See Foucault, *Politics, Philosophy, Culture*, 107 f.

8. Foucault, "The Subject and Power," afterword to Hubert L. Dreyfus and Paul Rabinow, *Michel Foucault: Beyond Structuralism and Hermeneutics*, 2d ed. (Chicago: University of Chicago Press, 1983), 212; cf. 217.

9. Many of Foucault's critics confuse his wariness about our potential to cause suffering in using normative judgments with a nihilistic deconstruction of all forms of evaluation. Charles Scott argues in *The Question of Ethics* (Bloomington: Indiana University Press, 1990) that Foucault does not want to undermine our abilities to make evaluative judgments. He is simply recommending that, as we involve ourselves in specific exercises of judgment, we remain intensely alert to and humble about our capacities to harm others, even when we intend good. "Our attempts to evaluate and establish a hierarchy of values include forces that run counter to such an effort, forces that put evaluating and hierarchizing in question in the midst of the evaluating process. That does not make evaluation wrong or bad, but it functions as a caution to evaluative processes" (7).

10. Michel Foucault, *Discipline and Punish: The Birth of the Prison*, trans. Alan Sheridan (New York: Random House, 1979), 106 f.

11. Gary Gutting, who has written extensively on misinterpretations of Foucault's philosophical agenda, writes in *Michel Foucault's Archaeology of Scientific Reason* (Cambridge: Cambridge University Press, 1989), 273: "Despite their popularity, such criticisms, based on the charge of global skepticism or relativism, are unfounded. They ignore three aspects of Foucault's work that definitely distinguish it from any universal assault on the notion of truth. First, there is the explicitly local or regional nature of his analysis. His historical critiques of reason are always directed toward very specific applications (psychiatry, clinical medicine, human sciences) with no suggestion that the inadequacies of any one domain can be extrapolated to others. Second, Foucault's focus is always on the domains of 'dubious disciplines.' . . . Third, even for the dubious disciplines that are the objects of his critique, Foucault does

not deny all truth and objectivity." See also David Couzens Hoy, "Power, Repression, Progress: Foucault, Lukes and the Frankfurt School," 129; and Barry Smart, "The Politics of Truth and the Problem of Hegemony," 186 ff. (both in Hoy, ed. *Foucault: A Critical Reader*); and Todd May, *Between Genealogy and Epistemology* (University Park: Pennsylvania State University Press, 1993), 104 f. All of these authors reinforce this reading of Foucault's narrowly targeted purposes.

12. Foucault, *Politics, Philosophy, Culture*, 269.

13. Michel Foucault, *The Use of Pleasure: The History of Sexuality, Volume 2* (New York: Pantheon Books, 1985), 9.

14. "To say to oneself at the outset," writes Foucault, "What reform will I be able to carry out? That is not, I believe, an aim for the intellectual to pursue. His role, since he works specifically in the realm of thought, is to see how far the liberation of thought can make those transformations urgent enough for people to want to carry them out and difficult enough to carry out for them to be profoundly rooted in reality." Foucault, *Politics, Philosophy, Culture*, 155.

15. Augustine, *Confessions*, trans. R. S. Pine-Coffin (New York: Penguin Books, 1961), 12.31.

16. He would, however, ask whether the arrival of their "promised tomorrow" can be so confidently assumed. See Michel Foucault, *Religion and Culture*, ed. Jeremy R. Carrette (New York: Routledge, 1999), 133.

17. Foucault, *Politics, Philosophy, Culture*, 36.

18. Ibid.

19. Michel Foucault, "What Is Enlightenment?" trans. Catherine Porter, in *The Foucault Reader*, ed. Paul Rabinow (New York: Pantheon Books, 1984), 50.

20. William Connolly, *The Augustinian Imperative: A Reflection on the Politics of Morality* (Newbury Park, Calif.: Sage, 1993), xvii.

21. Ibid., 86.

22. Ibid., xviii, 81.

23. Ibid., 74, 81.

24. Ibid., 87.

25. Ibid., 66.

26. Ibid., 157.

27. Ibid., 158.

28. Ibid., 157.

29. Romand Coles, *Self/Power/Other* (Ithaca: Cornell University Press, 1992), 16.

30. Ibid., 10.

31. Ibid., 18, 28.

32. Ibid., 11.

33. Ibid., 10.

34. Ibid., 85.

35. Ibid., 78.

36. Ibid., 76.

37. See David Snyder's article, "Augustine's Concept of Justice and Civil Government," *Christian Scholar's Review* 14:3 (1985): 244–55, for a critique that reads Augustine as individualizing the Christian faith. See Rosemary Radford Ruether's article, "Augustine and Christian Political Theology," *Interpretation* 29:3 (July 1975): 252–65, for a development of the problems surrounding Augustine's sojourning motif. These two criticisms, though distinguishable, can be analyzed as two sides of the same coin.

38. Ruether, "Augustine and Christian Political Theology," 252.

39. Augustine, *The Trinity, The Fathers of the Church: A New Translation,* vol. 45, trans. Stephen McKenna, C.SS.R. (Washington, D.C.: Catholic University of America Press, 1963), 15.25.45.

40. Not that it is restricted to the Middle Ages. Although the modern representatives of this interpretive trajectory tend to be associated more often with Roman Catholic theology, they also include some Protestant scholars. Schilling (1910), Scholz (1911), Troeltsch (1915), Offergelt (1914), Mausbach (1929), Combés (1934), Chroust (1944), Demmer (1961), and Burt (1963) are a few of the scholars who advance different versions of this theme. See Miika Roukanen, *The Theology of the Social Life in Augustine's* De Civitate Dei (Göttingen: Vandenhoeck & Ruprecht, 1993), 9–18, for a summary of the scholarship. Roukanen labels this the "traditional," as distinct from the "modern," school of Augustinian scholarship. John Neville Figgis, in *The Political Aspects of Saint Augustine's "City of God"* (London: Longmans, Green, 1921), identifies the medieval interpretation of Augustine with what he calls the "clericalist doctrine." Rex Martin speaks of it in "The Two Cities in Augustine's Political Philosophy," *Journal of the History of Ideas* 33:2 (April 1972): 195–216, in terms of the "clericalist doctrine" or the "identification model."

41. Augustine, *City of God,* trans. Henry Bettenson (New York: Penguin Books, 1972), 19.19. See also Peter Brown, *Augustine of Hippo* (Berkeley: University of California Press, 1967), 87, n. 3.

42. Augustine, *City of God,* 19.17.

Selected Bibliography

Aflatt, Malcolm. "The Development of the Idea of Involuntary Sin in St. Augustine." *Revue des Études Augustiniennes* 20 (1974): 8, 114–34.

———. "The Responsibility for Involuntary Sin in Saint Augustine." *Recherches Augustiniennes* 10 (1975): 171–86.

Allison, David B., ed. *The New Nietzsche: Contemporary Styles of Interpretation.* Cambridge, Mass.: MIT Press, 1985.

Arac, Jonathan, ed. *After Foucault: Humanistic Knowledge, Postmodern Challenges.* New Brunswick: Rutgers University Press, 1988.

Armstrong, Timothy J., ed. and trans. *Michel Foucault: Philosopher.* New York: Routledge, 1992.

Augustine. *Anti-Pelagian Writings. Nicene and Post-Nicene Fathers of the Christian Church, First Series,* vol. 5, ed. Philip Schaff. Edinburgh: T. & T. Clark; Grand Rapids: Eerdmans, n.d.

———. "On the Catholic and Manichean Ways of Life." In *Nicene and Post-Nicene Fathers, First Series,* vol. 4, ed. Philip Schaff. Peabody, Mass.: Hendrickson Publishers, 1994; 1886–89.

———. "Christian Instruction." In *The Fathers of the Church: A New Translation,* vol. 2. Trans. John J. Gavigan, O.S.A. Washington, D.C.: Catholic University of America Press, 1947, 1950.

———. *City of God.* Trans. Henry Bettenson. New York: Penguin Books, 1972.

———. *Confessions.* Trans. R.S. Pine-Coffin. New York: Penguin Books, 1961.

———. "On Continence." In *Nicene and Post-Nicene Fathers of the Christian Church, First Series,* vol. 3, ed. Philip Schaff. Edinburgh: T. & T. Clark; Grand Rapids: Eerdmans, n.d.

———. "The Enchiridion: Being a Treatise on Faith, Hope, and Love." In *Nicene and Post-Nicene Fathers, First Series,* vol. 3, ed. Philip Schaff. Edinburgh: T. & T. Clark; Grand Rapids: Eerdmans, n.d.

———. *On Free Choice of the Will.* Trans. Anna S. Benjamin and L.H. Hackstaff. New York: Macmillan, 1964.

————. *On the Holy Trinity, Doctrinal Treatises, Moral Treatises. Nicene and Post-Nicene Fathers, First Series,* vol. 3, ed. Philip Schaff. Edinburgh: T. & T. Clark; Grand Rapids: Eerdmans, n.d.

————. "Homilies on the First Epistle of John." In *Nicene and Post-Nicene Fathers, First Series,* vol. 7, ed. Philip Schaff. Peabody, Mass.: Hendrickson Publishers, 1994; 1886–89.

————. "Homilies on the Gospel of John." In *Nicene and Post-Nicene Fathers, First Series,* vol. 4, ed. Philip Schaff. Peabody, Mass.: Hendrickson Publishers, 1994; 1886–89.

————. *The Literal Meaning of Genesis.* Trans. John H. Taylor. New York: Newman Press, 1982.

————. *The Political Writings.* Ed. Henry Paolucci. Washington, D.C.: Regnery Gateway, 1962.

————. *Political Writings.* Ed. E. M. Atkins and R. J. Dodaro. Cambridge: Cambridge University Press, 2001.

————. *Sermons.* In *The Works of Saint Augustine: A Translation for the 21st Century,* Part III—Sermons, vol. 11: *Newly Discovered Sermons.* Trans. Edmund Hill, O. P. Hyde Park, N. Y.: New City Press, 1997.

————. "On the Spirit and the Letter." In *Nicene and Post-Nicene Fathers, First Series,* vol. 5, ed. Philip Schaff. Grand Rapids: Eerdmans, n.d.

————. *The Trinity, The Fathers of the Church: A New Translation,* vol. 45. Trans. Stephen McKenna, C.SS.R. Washington, D.C.: Catholic University of America Press, 1963.

Babcock, William S. "Augustine and the Spirituality of Desire." *Augustinian Studies* 25 (1994): 179–99.

————. "Augustine on Sin and Moral Agency." *Journal of Religious Ethics* 16:1 (spring 1988): 28–55.

————. "Augustine's Interpretation of Romans (A.D. 394–396)." *Augustinian Studies* 10 (1979): 55–74.

————. "Grace, Freedom and Justice: Augustine and the Christian Tradition." *Journal of the Perkins School of Theology* 26:4 (summer 1973): 1–15.

Babcock, William S., ed. *The Ethics of St. Augustine.* JRE Studies in Religious Ethics, vol. 3. Atlanta: Scholars Press, 1991.

Barry, Andrew, Thomas Osborne, and Nikolas Rose, eds. *Foucault and Political Reason: Liberalism, Neo-Liberalism and Rationalities of Government.* Chicago: University of Chicago Press, 1996.

Bavel, Tarsicius J. van. "Love." In *Augustine through the Ages: An Encyclopedia,* ed. Allan D. Fitzgerald, O. S. A., 509–16. Grand Rapids: Eerdmans, 1999.

Berger, Peter. "The Significance of the Avant-Garde for Contemporary Aesthetics: A Reply to Jürgen Habermas." *New German Critique* 22 (1980): 19–22.

Bernauer, James W. *Michel Foucault's Force of Flight: Toward an Ethics for Thought.* London: Humanities Press, 1990.

Bernauer, James, and David Rasmussen, eds. *The Final Foucault.* Cambridge, Mass.: MIT Press, 1988.

Bok, Sissela. *Secrets: On the Ethics of Concealment and Revelation.* New York: Vintage Books, 1982, 1989.

Bonner, Gerald. "Augustine and Pelagianism." *Augustinian Studies* 24 (1993): 27–47.

Bordo, Susan R. "The Body and the Reproduction of Femininity: A Feminist Appropriation of Foucault." In *Gender/Body/Knowledge: Feminist Reconstructions of Being and Knowing,* ed. Alison M. Jaggar and Susan R. Bordo, 13–33. New Brunswick: Rutgers University Press, 1989.

Børrensen, Kari Elisabeth. "Patristic 'Feminism': The Case of Augustine." *Augustinian Studies* 25 (1994): 139–52.

Brannigan, Michael C., and Judith A. Ross, eds. *Healthcare Ethics in a Diverse Society.* Mountain View, Calif.: Mayfield, 2001.

Breyfogle, Todd. "Punishment." In *Augustine through the Ages: An Encyclopedia,* ed. Allan D. Fitzgerald, O.S.A., 688–90. Grand Rapids: Eerdmans, 1999.

Brown, Peter. *Augustine of Hippo.* Berkeley: University of California Press, 1967.

———. *The Body and Society: Men, Women, and Sexual Renunciation in Early Christianity.* New York: Columbia University Press, 1988.

———. "Political Society." In *Augustine: A Collection of Critical Essays,* ed. R. A. Markus, 31–35. New York: Doubleday, 1972.

Burnell, Peter. "Concupiscence." In *Augustine through the Ages: An Encyclopedia,* ed. Allan D. Fitzgerald, O.S.A., 224–27. Grand Rapids: Eerdmans, 1999.

Burns, J. Patout. "Augustine on the Origin and Progress of Evil." *Journal of Religious Ethics* 16 (spring 1988): 9–27.

———. "The Interpretation of Romans in the Pelagian Controversy." *Augustinian Studies* 10 (1979): 43–54.

Burt, Donald X., O.S.A. "Friendship and Subordination in Earthly Societies." *Augustinian Studies* 22 (1991): 83–123.

———. "St. Augustine's Evaluation of Civil Society." *Augustinianum* 3 (1963): 87–94.

Butler, Judith, and Joan W. Scott, eds. *Feminists Theorize the Political.* New York: Routledge, 1992.

Byrne, James W. "Foucault on Continuity: The Postmodern Challenge to Tradition." *Faith and Philosophy* 9:3 (July 1992): 335–52.

Caldwell, Gaylon L. "Augustine's Critique of Human Justice." *Journal of Church and State* 2:1 (May 1960): 7–25.

Canning, Raymond. "Uti/frui." In *Augustine through the Ages: An Encyclopedia,* ed. Allan D. Fitzgerald, O.S.A., 859–61. Grand Rapids: Eerdmans, 1999.

Caputo, John. *Against Ethics: Contributions to a Poetics of Obligation with Constant Reference to Deconstruction.* Bloomington: Indiana University Press, 1993.

———. "On Not Knowing Who We Are: Madness, Hermeneutics, and the Night of Truth in Foucault." In *Foucault and the Critique of Institutions,* ed. John Caputo and Mark Yount, 233–62. University Park: Pennsylvania State University Press, 1993.

Caputo, John, and Mark Yount, eds. *Foucault and the Critique of Institutions.* University Park: Pennsylvania State University Press, 1993.

——. "Institutions, Normalization, and Power." In *Foucault and the Critique of Institutions,* ed. John Caputo and Mark Yount, 3–23. University Park: Pennsylvania State University Press, 1993.

Carlson, Charles P., Jr. "The Natural Order and Historical Explanation in St. Augustine's *City of God.*" *Augustiniana* 21 (1971): 417–47.

Carrette, Jeremy R. *Foucault and Religion: Spiritual Corporality and Political Spirituality.* London: Routledge, 2000.

Chidester, David. "Michel Foucault and the Study of Religion." *Religious Studies Review* 12:1 (January 1986): 1–9.

Clarke, Thompson. "The Legacy of Skepticism." *Journal of Philosophy* (1972): 754–69.

Cochrane, Charles Norris. "The Earthly City versus the Heavenly City—A Conflict of Values." In *Church and State in the Middle Ages,* ed. Bennett D. Hill, 33–41. New York: John Wiley & Sons, 1970.

Coles, Romand. *Rethinking Generosity: Critical Theory and the Politics of Caritas.* Ithaca: Cornell University Press, 1997.

——. *Self/Power/Other.* Ithaca: Cornell University Press, 1992.

Connolly, William. *The Augustinian Imperative: A Reflection on the Politics of Morality.* Newbury Park, Calif.: Sage, 1993.

——. "Taylor, Foucault, and Otherness." *Political Theory* 13 (1985): 365–76.

Crowley, Paul G., S.J. "Rahner's Christian Pessimism: A Response to the Sorrow of AIDS." *Theological Studies* 58:2 (June 1997): 286–307.

Davidson, Arnold I., ed. *Foucault and His Interlocutors.* Chicago: University of Chicago Press, 1997.

Davis, Charles. "Our Modern Identity: The Formation of the Self." *Modern Theology* 6:2 (January 1990): 159–71.

Dean, Mitchel. *Critical and Effective Histories: Foucault's Methods and Historical Sociology.* London: Routledge, 1994.

——. "Foucault, Government and the Enfolding of Authority." In *Foucault and Political Reason: Liberalism, Neo-Liberalism and Rationalities of Government,* ed. Andrew Barry, Thomas Osborne, and Nikolas Rose, 209–29. Chicago: University of Chicago Press, 1996.

Deane, Herbert A. *The Political and Social Ideas of St. Augustine.* New York: Columbia University Press, 1963.

Deleuze, Gilles. *Foucault.* Minneapolis: University of Minnesota Press, 1986.

Diamond, Irene, and Lee Quinby, eds. *Feminism & Foucault: Reflections on Resistance.* Boston: Northeastern University Press, 1988.

DiLorenzo, Raymond D. "Ciceronianism and Augustine's Conception of Philosophy." *Augustinian Studies* 13 (1982): 171–76.

Dodaro, Robert. "Eloquent Lies, Just Wars and the Politics of Persuasion: Reading Augustine's *City of God* in a 'Postmodern' World." *Augustinian Studies* 25 (1994): 77–94.

Dougherty, James. "The Sacred City and the City of God." *Augustinian Studies* 10 (1979): 81–90.

Dougherty, Richard J. "Christian and Citizen: The Tension in St. Augustine's *De ciuitate dei.*" In *Augustine: "Second Founder of the Faith,"* ed. Joseph C. Schnaubelt, O.S.A., and Frederick Van Fleteren, 205–24. New York: Peter Lang, 1990.

Dreyfus, Hubert L., and Paul Rabinow. *Michel Foucault: Beyond Structuralism and Hermeneutics.* Chicago: University of Chicago Press, 1982, 2d ed. 1983.

———. "What Is Maturity? Habermas and Foucault on 'What Is Enlightenment?'" In *Foucault: A Critical Reader,* ed. David Couzens Hoy, 109–21. Oxford: Blackwell, 1986.

During, Simon. *Foucault and Literature: Towards a Genealogy of Writing.* New York: Routledge, 1992.

Elshtain, Jean Bethke. *Augustine and the Limits of Politics.* Notre Dame: University of Notre Dame Press, 1995.

———. *Public Man, Private Woman: Women in Social and Political Thought.* Princeton: Princeton University Press, 1981.

———. Review of *Augustine and the Limits of Virtue* by James Wetzel. *Augustinian Studies* 24 (1993): 187–94.

———. *Who Are We? Critical Reflections and Hopeful Possibilities.* Grand Rapids: Eerdmans, 2000.

Elshtain, Jean Bethke, and J. Timothy Cloyd, eds. *Politics and the Human Body: Assault on Dignity.* Nashville: Vanderbilt University Press, 1995.

Eribon, Didier. *Michel Foucault.* Cambridge, Mass.: Harvard University Press, 1991.

Figgis, John Neville. *The Political Aspects of Saint Augustine's "City of God."* London: Longmans, Green, 1921.

Fitzgerald, Allan D., O.S.A., ed. *Augustine through the Ages: An Encyclopedia.* Grand Rapids: Eerdmans, 1999.

Flynn, Thomas R. "Partially Desacralized Spaces: The Religious Availability of Foucault's Thought." *Faith and Philosophy* 10:4 (October 1993): 471–85.

Fortin, Ernest L. *The Birth of Philosophic Christianity: Studies in Early Christian and Medieval Thought.* New York: Rowman & Littlefield, 1996.

———. *Classical Christianity and the Political Order: Reflections on the Theologico-Political Problem.* New York: Rowman & Littlefield, 1996.

Foucault, Michel. *Aesthetics, Method, and Epistemology.* Ed. James D. Faubion; trans. Robert Hurley et al. In *The Essential Works of Michel Foucault, 1954–1984,* vol. 2. New York: New Press, 1998.

———. *The Archaeology of Knowledge.* Trans. A.M. Sheridan Smith. New York: Pantheon Books, 1972.

———. *The Birth of the Clinic: An Archaeology of Medical Perception.* New York: Pantheon Books, 1973.

———. *The Care of the Self: The History of Sexuality, Volume 3.* New York: Random House, 1988.

———. *Discipline and Punish: The Birth of the Prison.* Trans. Alan Sheridan. New York: Random House, 1979.

———. "The Ethic of Care for the Self as a Practice of Freedom." In *The Final Foucault,* ed. James Bernauer and David Rasmussen, 1–20. Cambridge, Mass.: MIT Press, 1988.

———. *Ethics: Subjectivity and Truth.* Ed. Paul Rabinow; trans. Robert Hurley et al. *The Essential Works of Michel Foucault, 1954–1984,* vol. 1. New York: New Press, 1997.

———. "On the Genealogy of Ethics: An Overview of Work in Progress." Second afterword (1983) to *Michel Foucault: Beyond Structuralism and Hermeneutics,* 2d ed., by Hubert L. Dreyfus and Paul Rabinow, 229–52. Chicago: University of Chicago Press, 1983.

———. "History, Discourse, and Discontinuity." *Salmagundi* 20 (1972): 225–48.

———. *The History of Sexuality, Volume 1: An Introduction.* New York: Vintage Books, 1980.

———. *Language, Counter-Memory, Practice: Selected Essays and Interviews.* Ed. Donald F. Bouchard. Ithaca: Cornell University Press, 1977.

———. *Madness and Civilization: A History of Insanity in the Age of Reason.* New York: Vintage Books, 1965, 1988.

———. *The Order of Things: An Archaeology of the Human Sciences.* New York: Random House, 1970.

———. *Politics, Philosophy, Culture: Interviews and Other Writings, 1977–1984.* Ed. Lawrence D. Kritzman. New York: Routledge, Chapman, & Hall, 1988.

———. *Power/Knowledge: Selected Interviews & Other Writings, 1972–1977.* Ed. Colin Gordon. New York: Pantheon Books, 1980.

———. *Religion and Culture.* Ed. Jeremy R. Carrette. New York: Routledge, 1999.

———. "Structuralism and Post-Structuralism: An Interview with Michel Foucault." *Telos* 55 (1983): 195–211.

———. "The Subject and Power." Afterword to *Michel Foucault: Beyond Structuralism and Hermeneutics,* 2d ed., by Hubert L. Dreyfus and Paul Rabinow, 208–26. Chicago: University of Chicago Press, 1983.

———. *Technologies of the Self: A Seminar with Michel Foucault.* Ed. Luther H. Martin, Huck Gutman, and Patrick H. Hutton. Amherst: University of Massachusetts Press, 1988.

———. *The Use of Pleasure: The History of Sexuality, Volume 2.* New York: Pantheon Books, 1985.

———. "What Is Enlightenment?" Trans. Catherine Porter. In *The Foucault Reader,* ed. Paul Rabinow, 32–50. New York: Pantheon Books, 1984.

Fraser, Nancy. "Foucault on Modern Power: Empirical Insights and Normative Confusions." *Praxis International* 1 (1981): 272–87.

———. "Michel Foucault: A 'Young Conservative'?" *Ethics* 96 (October 1985): 165–84.

Frederickson, Paula. "Beyond the Body/Soul Dichotomy: Augustine on Paul against the Manichaens and Pelagians." *Recherches Augustiniennes* 23 (1988): 87–114.

Frend, William H. C. "Augustine and Orosius: On the End of the Ancient World." *Augustinian Studies* 20 (1989): 1–38.

Geertz, Clifford. "Stir Crazy: A Review of *Discipline and Punish.*" *New York Review of Books* (January 26, 1978): 3–6.

Giddens, Anthony. "Modernism and Post-Modernism." *New German Critique* 22 (1980): 15–18.

Gilson, Étienne. *The Christian Philosophy of Saint Augustine.* New York: Random House, 1960.

Gordon, Colin. "Afterword." In *Power/Knowledge: Selected Interviews & Other Writings, 1972–1977,* ed. Colin Gordon, 229–59. New York: Pantheon Books, 1980.

Gunn, Giles. "The Literary and Cultural Study of Religion: Problems and Prospects." *Journal of the American Academy of Religion* 53:3 (1985): 617–33.

Gutting, Gary. *Michel Foucault's Archaeology of Scientific Reason.* Cambridge: Cambridge University Press, 1989.

Habermas, Jürgen. "Modernity versus Postmodernity." *New German Critique* 22 (1980): 3–14.

———. *The Philosophical Discourse of Modernity.* Cambridge, Mass.: MIT Press, 1987.

———. "Taking Aim at the Heart of the Present." In *Foucault: A Critical Reader,* ed. David Couzens Hoy, 103–8. Oxford: Blackwell, 1986.

Hacking, Ian. "The Archaeology of Foucault." In *Foucault: A Critical Reader,* ed. David Couzens Hoy, 27–40. Oxford: Blackwell, 1986.

Haggerty, William P. "Augustine, the 'Mixed Life,' and Classical Political Philosophy: Reflections on *Compositio* in Book 19 of the *City of God.*" *Augustinian Studies* 23 (1992): 149–63.

Halpern, Cynthia. *Suffering, Politics, Power: A Genealogy in Modern Political Theory.* Albany: State University of New York Press, 2002.

Hauerwas, Stanley. *With the Grain of the Universe: The Church's Witness and Natural Theology.* Grand Rapids: Brazos Press, 2001.

Hauerwas, Stanley, Chris K. Huebrier, Harry J. Huebner, and Marle Thiesson Nation, eds. *The Wisdom of the Cross: Essays in Honor of John Howard Yoder.* Grand Rapids: Eerdmans, 1999.

Heschel, Abraham J. *The Prophets.* New York: Harper & Row, 1962.

Hill, Bennett D., ed. *Church and State in the Middle Ages.* New York: John Wiley & Sons, 1970.

Hinze, Christine Firer. *Comprehending Power in Christian Social Ethics.* Atlanta: Scholars Press, 1995.

Honneth, Axel. *The Critique of Power: Reflective Stages in a Critical Social Theory.* Cambridge, Mass.: MIT Press, 1991.

Hoy, David Couzens. "Introduction." In *Foucault: A Critical Reader,* ed. David Couzens Hoy, 1–26. Oxford: Blackwell, 1986.

———. "Power, Repression, Progress: Foucault, Lukes, and the Frankfurt School." In *Foucault: A Critical Reader,* ed. David Couzens Hoy, 123–48. Oxford: Blackwell, 1986.

———. "Taking History Seriously: Foucault, Gadamer, Habermas." *Union Seminary Quarterly Review* 34:2 (winter 1979): 85–95.

Hoy, David Couzens, ed. *Foucault: A Critical Reader.* Oxford: Blackwell, 1986.

Hunter, David G. "Augustinian Pessimism? A New Look at Augustine's Teaching on Sex, Marriage and Celibacy." *Augustinian Studies* 25 (1994): 153–77.

Hutcheon, Linda. *The Politics of Postmodernism.* London: Routledge, 1989.

Huyssen, Andreas. "The Search for Tradition: Avant-Garde and Postmodernism in the 1970s." *New German Critique* 22 (1980): 23–40.

Jagger, Alison M., and Susan R. Bordo, eds. *Gender/Body/Knowledge: Feminist Reconstructions of Being and Knowing.* New Brunswick: Rutgers University Press, 1989.

Kelly, Michael, ed. *Critique and Power: Recasting the Foucault/Habermas Debate.* Cambridge, Mass.: MIT Press, 1994.

Konstan, David. "Friendship, Frankness, and Flattery." In *Friendship, Flattery, & Frankness of Speech: Studies on Friendship in the New Testament World,* ed. John T. Fitzgerald, 7–19. Leiden: E. J. Brill, 1996.

Kusch, Martin. *Foucault's Strata and Fields: An Investigation into Archaeological and Genealogical Science Studies.* Dordrecht: Kluwer Academic Publishers, 1991.

Lalonde, Marc P. "Power/Knowledge and Liberation." *Journal of the American Academy of Religion* 61:1 (1993): 81–100.

Lavere, George J. "The Influence of Saint Augustine on Early Medieval Political Theory." *Augustinian Studies* 12 (1991): 1–9.

———. "Metaphor and Symbol in St. Augustine's *De ciuitate dei.*" In *Augustine: "Second Founder of the Faith,"* ed. Joseph C. Schnaubelt, O. S. A., and Frederick Van Fleteren, 225–43. New York: Peter Lang, 1990.

———. "The Political Realism of Saint Augustine." *Augustinian Studies* 11 (1980): 135–44.

Leigh, David J., S.J. "Michel Foucault and the Study of Literature and Theology." *Christianity & Literature* 33:2 (winter 1984): 75–85.

Macey, David. *The Lives of Michel Foucault.* New York: Pantheon Books, 1993.

MacIntyre, Alasdair. *After Virtue.* 2d ed. Notre Dame: University of Notre Dame Press, 1984.

———. *Whose Justice? Which Rationality?* Notre Dame: Notre Dame University Press, 1988.

MacQueen, D. J. "The Origin and Dynamics of Society and the State According to St. Augustine." *Augustinian Studies* 4 (1973): 73–101.

Mahon, Michael. *Foucault's Nietzschean Genealogy: Truth, Power, and the Subject.* Albany: State University of New York Press, 1992.

Maier, F. G. *Augustin und das antike Rom.* Stuttgart: W. Kohlhammer, 1995.

Markus, R. A. "Augustine." In *A Critical History of Western Philosophy,* ed. D. J. O'Connor. New York: Free Press, 1964.

———. *Augustine: A Collection of Critical Essays.* New York: Doubleday, 1972.

———. *"De ciuitate dei:* Pride and the Common Good." In *Augustine: "Second Founder of the Faith,"* ed. Joseph C. Schnaubelt, O. S. A., and Frederick Van Fleteren, 245–59. New York: Peter Lang, 1990.

———. *The End of Ancient Christianity.* Cambridge: Cambridge University Press, 1990.

———. "The Sacred and the Secular: From Augustine to Gregory the Great." *Journal of Theological Studies* (NS) 36:1 (April 1985): 84–96.

———. *Saeculum: History and Society in the Theology of St. Augustine.* New York: Cambridge University Press, 1970.

———. "Two Conceptions of Political Authority: Augustine, *De Civitate Dei,* XIX.14–15, and Some Thirteenth-Century Interpretations." *Journal of Theological Studies* (NS) 16 (1965): 68–100.

Martin, F. X., O. S. A. "Augustine Interpreted and Misinterpreted: A Response to Professor Williams." *Milltown Studies* 19:20 (1987): 73–82.

Martin, Rex. "The Two Cities in Augustine's Political Philosophy." *Journal of the History of Ideas* 33:2 (April 1972): 195–216.

May, Todd. *Between Genealogy and Epistemology.* University Park: Pennsylvania State University Press, 1993.

McGrath, Alister E. "Pluralism and the Decade of Evangelism." *Anvil* 9:2 (1992): 101–14.

Meilander, Gilbert. "The First and the Second Adam: Reflections on James Wetzel's Reformulation of a Doctrine." *Journal of Religious Ethics* 23:1 (1995): 27–33.

Mellor, Philip. "The Application of the Theories of Michel Foucault to Problems in the Study of Religion." *Theology* 91 (November 1988): 484–93.

Migel-Alfonso, Ricardo, and Silvia Caporale-Bizzini, eds. *Reconstructing Foucault: Essays in the Wake of the 80s.* Postmodern Studies 10. Amsterdam: Rodopi, 1994.

Milbank, John. *Theology and Social Theory: Beyond Secular Reason.* Oxford: Blackwell, 1990, 1993.

Miles, Margaret R. *Practicing Christianity: Critical Perspectives for an Embodied Spirituality.* New York: Crossroad, 1988.

———. *Desire and Delight: A New Reading of Augustine's Confessions.* New York: Crossroad, 1992.

Miller, James. *The Passion of Michel Foucault.* New York: Simon & Schuster, 1993.

Miller, Peter. *Domination and Power.* New York: Routledge & Kegan Paul, 1987.

Miller, Toby. *The Well-Tempered Self: Citizenship, Culture, and the Postmodern Subject.* Baltimore: Johns Hopkins University Press, 1993.

Mommsen, Theodore E. "St. Augustine and the Christian Idea of Progress." *Journal of the History of Ideas* 12:3 (June 1951): 346–74.

Mourant, John A. "The *Cogitos:* Augustinian and Cartesian." *Augustinian Studies* 10 (1979): 27–42.

Nehamas, Alexander. "Subject and Abject: The Examined Life of Michel Foucault." *The New Republic* (February 15, 1993): 27–36.

Nicholson, Linda J., ed. *Feminism/Postmodernism.* New York: Routledge, 1990.

Niebuhr, Reinhold. *Christian Realism and Political Problems.* New York: Charles Scribner's Sons, 1953.

———. *The Nature and Destiny of Man: A Christian Interpretation,* vol. 1, *Human Nature.* New York: Charles Scribner's Sons, 1941, 1964.

Nietzsche, Friedrich. *The Will to Power.* New York: Vintage Books, 1968.

O'Connell, Robert J., S.J. "Peter Brown on the Soul's Fall." *Augustinian Studies* 24 (1993): 103–31.

O'Connor, Thomas Anthony. "The Challenge of Ontotheology." In *Religion, Ontotheology, and Deconstruction,* ed. Henry Ruf, 141–54. New York: Paragon House, 1989.

O'Donnell, J. J. "The Inspiration for Augustine's *De Civitate Dei.*" *Augustinian Studies* 10 (1979): 75–79.

O'Donoghue, Fergus, S.J. "The Use of St. Augustine's Thought: A Response to Professor Williams." *Milltown Studies* 19:20 (1987): 83–85.

O'Donovan, Oliver. "Augustine's *City of God* XIX and Western Political Thought." *Dionysius* 11 (December 1987): 89–110.

O'Farrell, Clare. *Foucault: Historian or Philosopher?* New York: St. Martin's Press, 1989.

Oort, J. van. "Augustine on Sexual Concupiscence and Original Sin." In *Studia Patristica,* vol. 22, ed. E. A. Livingstone, 382–86. Louvain: Peeters Press, 1989.

Outka, Gene. "Augustinianism and Common Morality." In *Prospects for a Common Morality,* ed. Gene Outka and John P. Reeder, Jr., 114–48. Princeton: Princeton University Press, 1993.

Pasewark, Kyle A. *A Theology of Power: Being Beyond Domination.* Minneapolis: Fortress Press, 1993.

Peters, Ted, ed. *Genetics: Issues of Social Justice.* Cleveland: Pilgrim Press, 1998.

Placher, William C. *Unapologetic Theology: A Christian Voice in a Pluralistic Conversation.* Louisville: Westminster/John Knox Press, 1989.

Popkin, Richard H. *The History of Scepticism from Erasmus to Spinoza.* Berkeley: University of California Press, 1979.

Prado, C. G. *Starting with Foucault: An Introduction to Genealogy.* Boulder: Westview Press, 1995.

Rabinow, Paul. "Humanism as Nihilism: The Bracketing of Truth and Seriousness in American Cultural Anthropology." In *Social Science as Moral Inquiry,* ed. Norma Haan et al., 52–75. New York: Columbia University Press, 1983.

Rabinow, Paul, ed. *The Foucault Reader.* New York: Pantheon Books, 1984.

Rajchman, John. *Michel Foucault: The Freedom of Philosophy.* New York: Columbia University Press, 1985.

Ramazanoglu, Caroline, ed. *Up against Foucault: Explorations of Some Tensions between Foucault and Feminism.* London: Routledge, 1993.

Ramsey, Paul. "Human Sexuality in the History of Redemption." *Journal of Religious Ethics* 16 (1988): 56–86.

Raschke, Carl A. "The Deconstruction of God." In *Deconstruction and Theology*, ed. Thomas J. J. Altizer et al., 1–33. New York: Crossroad, 1982.

Reece, Robert D. "Augustine's Social Ethics: Churchly or Sectarian?" *Foundations* 18 (1975): 75–87.

Renna, Thomas. "The Idea of Peace in the Augustinian Tradition." *Augustinian Studies* 10 (1979): 105–11.

Rigby, Paul. *Original Sin in Augustine's Confessions.* Ottawa: University of Ottawa Press, 1987.

Rorty, Richard. *Contingency, Irony, and Solidarity.* Cambridge: Cambridge University Press, 1989.

———. *Philosophy and the Mirror of Nature.* Princeton: Princeton University Press, 1979.

Rose, Nikolas. "Governing 'Advanced' Liberal Democracies." In *Foucault and Political Reason: Liberalism, Neo-Liberalism and Rationalities of Government*, ed. Andrew Barry, Thomas Osborne, and Nikolas Rose, 37–62. Chicago: University of Chicago Press, 1996.

Roukanen, Miika. *The Theology of the Social Life in Augustine's De Civitate Dei.* Göttingen: Vandenhoeck & Ruprecht, 1993.

Rouse, Joseph. "Power/Knowledge." In *The Cambridge Companion to Foucault*, ed. Gary Gutting, 92–108. Cambridge: Cambridge University Press, 1994.

Ruether, Rosemary Radford. "Augustine and Christian Political Theology." *Interpretation* 29:3 (July 1975): 252–65.

Russell, Frederick H. "War." In *Augustine through the Ages: An Encyclopedia*, ed. Allan D. Fitzgerald, O. S. A., 875–76. Grand Rapids: Eerdmans, 1999.

Said, Edward W. "Foucault and the Imagination of Power." In *Foucault: A Critical Reader*, ed. David Couzens Hoy, 149–56. Oxford: Blackwell, 1986.

Santmire, H. Paul. *The Travail of Nature: The Ambiguous Ecological Promise of Christian Theology.* Philadelphia: Fortress Press, 1985.

Sawicki, Jana. *Disciplining Foucault: Feminism, Power, and the Body.* New York: Routledge, 1991.

Scanlon, Michael J., O. S. A. "Augustine and Theology as Rhetoric." *Augustinian Studies* 25 (1994): 37–50.

Schall, James V. "The Limits of Law." *Communio* 2:2 (summer 1975): 126–47.

Schlabach, Gerald W. "Augustine's Hermeneutic of Humility: An Alternative to Moral Imperialism and Moral Relativism." *Journal of Religious Ethics* 22:2 (fall 1994): 299–327.

———. "Continence." In *Augustine through the Ages: An Encyclopedia*, ed. Allan D. Fitzgerald, O. S. A., 235–37. Grand Rapids: Eerdmans, 1999.

————. "Friendship as Adultery: Social Reality and Sexual Metaphor in Augustine's Doctrine of Original Sin." *Augustinian Studies* 23 (1992): 125–47.

Schweiker, William. *Power, Value, and Conviction: Theological Ethics in the Postmodern Age.* Cleveland: Pilgrim Press, 1998.

Scott, Charles. *A Question of Ethics.* Bloomington: Indiana University Press, 1990.

Sell, Alan P. F. "Augustine versus Pelagius: A Cautionary Tale of Perennial Importance." *Calvin Theological Journal* 12 (1977): 117–43.

Sheridan, Alan. *Michel Foucault: The Will To Truth.* London: Tavistock, 1980.

Shumway, David R. *Michel Foucault.* Boston: G. K. Hall, 1989.

Simons, Jon. *Foucault and the Political.* New York: Routledge, 1995.

Smart, Barry. *Foucault, Marxism and Critique.* London: Routledge, 1983.

————. *Michel Foucault.* New York: Routledge, 1985.

Smith, William A. "The Christian as Resident Alien in Augustine: An Evaluation from the Standpoint of Pastoral Care." *Word & World* 3:2 (1983): 129–39.

Snyder, David. "Augustine's Concept of Justice and Civil Government." *Christian Scholar's Review* 14:3 (1985): 244–55.

Starr, Bradley. "Modernity, Antiquity, and 'Thoughts Which Have Not Yet Been Thought': Ernst Troeltsch's Interpretation of Augustine." *Augustinian Studies* 24 (1993): 77–102.

Stout, Jeffrey. *Ethics after Babel: The Languages of Morals and Their Discontents.* Boston: Beacon Press, 1988.

————. *The Flight from Authority.* Notre Dame: University of Notre Dame Press, 1981.

Tanner, Kathryn. *The Politics of God: Christian Theologies and Social Justice.* Minneapolis: Fortress Press, 1992.

————. *Theories of Culture: A New Agenda for Theology.* Minneapolis: Augsburg Fortress Press, 1997.

Taylor, Charles. "Connolly, Foucault, and Truth." *Political Theory* 13 (1985): 377–85.

————. "Foucault on Freedom and Truth." In *Foucault: A Critical Reader,* ed. David Couzens Hoy, 69–102. Oxford: Blackwell, 1986.

————. *Sources of the Self: The Making of the Modern Identity.* Cambridge, Mass.: Harvard University Press, 1989.

TeSelle, Eugene. *Augustine the Theologian.* New York: Herder and Herder, 1970.

————. "The Civic Vision in Augustine's *City of God*." *Thought* 62:246 (September 1987): 268–80.

————. *Living in Two Cities: Augustinian Trajectories in Political Thought.* Scranton: University of Scranton Press, 1998.

————. "Towards an Augustinian Politics." *Journal of Religious Ethics* 16:1 (spring 1988): 87–108.

Thomas, Owen C. "On Stepping Twice into the Same Church: Essence, Development, and Pluralism." *Anglican Theological Review* 70:4 (1988): 293–306.

Thompson, Ian. "Liberal Values and Power Politics." In *Ethics and Defense: Power and Responsibility in the Nuclear Age,* ed. Howard Davis, 82–102. Oxford: Blackwell, 1986.

Tracy, David. *Plurality and Ambiguity: Hermeneutics, Religion, Hope.* San Francisco: Harper & Row, 1987.

Visker, Rudi. *Michel Foucault: Genealogy as Critique.* London: Verso, 1995.

Walzer, Michael. "The Politics of Michel Foucault." In *Foucault: A Critical Reader,* ed. David Couzens Hoy, 51–68. Oxford: Blackwell, 1986.

Weedon, Chris. *Feminist Practice & Poststructuralist Theory.* London: Blackwell, 1987.

Wetzel, James. *Augustine and the Limits of Virtue.* Cambridge: Cambridge University Press, 1992.

———. "Moral Personality, Perversity, and Original Sin." *Journal of Religious Ethics* 23:1 (spring 1995): 3–25.

———. "The Recovery of Free Agency in the Theology of St. Augustine." *Harvard Theological Review* 80:1 (1987): 101–25.

Williams, Rowan. "'Good for Nothing'?" *Augustinian Studies* 25 (1994): 9–24.

———. "Politics and the Soul: A Reading of the *City of God.*" *Milltown Studies* 19:20 (1987): 55–72.

Wolterstorff, Nicholas. "The Wounds of God: Calvin's Theology of Social Injustice." *Reformed Journal* 37 (1987): 14–22.

Yannaras, Christos. *The Freedom of Morality.* Contemporary Greek Theologians, vol. 3. Trans. Elizabeth Briere. Crestwood, N.Y.: Vladimir's Seminary Press, 1984.

Index

abnormalcy, 95, 110, 149–52, 186, 202

Adam, 51, 84, 88, 105, 122, 127, 239n.17, 243n.79, 250n.19

adultery, 86–89, 249n.16. *See also* fornication; procreation

aesthetic harmony, as goal of self-formation, 29, 73–74, 92, 102, 128, 140, 143, 193, 213

affections, 115

Aflatt, Malcolm, 59

agonism, 27–30. *See also* freedom

Alexander the Great, 165, 172, 179, 205

arrogance, 111–13, 122–23, 128, 132, 153, 157, 168, 172, 179, 204, 220

ascetical detachment, 126–28, 139–40, 143

ascetical practices, 36, 73–74, 107, 126, 139–40, 144, 193

autobiography, 84, 123, 127

autonomy, 21–24, 30–32, 59–65, 84, 113, 115–16, 148, 153, 230n.101

Babcock, William, 59–61

baptism, 120, 151, 258n.43

beautiful existence, 74, 77, 84, 136, 140, 212–13

beauty, 41–42, 89, 94, 99, 101, 103, 251n.24

Bellah, Robert, 1

Bentham, Jeremy, 190–91

Bernauer, James, 221n.1, 228n.85, 243n.77, 252n.38

body
    manipulation of the, 36, 188–90, 193–95
    materiality of the, 65–72, 75–76, 79, 85, 88, 92, 101, 108

Bok, Sissela, 187

Brown, Peter, 62, 138, 227nn.55, 70, 231n.106, 246n.118, 248n.5, 254n.56, 255n.64, 262n.116, 265n.2, 268n.57

captivity, 104–6, 108

Caputo, John, 228n.85

care, 130, 139, 156, 170, 213–14, 220, 250n.21

Carrette, Jeremy R., 252n.42

Cassian, John, 136–38, 140–41, 143–44, 148, 193, 262n.116

certitude, 4, 98, 111–12, 115, 123, 125, 127–29, 143, 146–47, 156, 177–78, 191, 200, 204, 218, 220

character, 116, 151, 242n.67

charity, 38, 115, 121, 168–69. *See also* compassion; mercy

chastity, 93, 140–41, 143–44, 148, 193. *See also* continence; purity

Christ, 119–20, 168, 172, 218–19, 258nn.43–44

J. JOYCE SCHULD received her Ph.D. in religious studies from Yale University and is currently a Visiting Fellow at Cornell University where she is working on two books: *Missions of Power: A Cultural Analysis of Indian-Christian Relations in the American Southwest,* for the University of Notre Dame Press, and *Michel Foucault: An Introduction for Theologians,* for Cambridge University Press.